VICTORY IS ASSURED

VICTORY
IS
ASSURED

Uncollected Writings of
STANLEY
CROUCH

Edited with a Preface by
GLENN MOTT

Introduction by
JELANI COBB

Afterword by
WYNTON MARSALIS

LIVERIGHT PUBLISHING CORPORATION

A Division of W. W. Norton & Company
Independent Publishers Since 1923

For information about permission to reproduce selections from this book,
write to Permissions, Liveright Publishing Corporation, a division of
W. W. Norton & Company, Inc.,
500 Fifth Avenue, New York, NY 10110

For information about special discounts for bulk purchases,
please contact W. W. Norton Special Sales at
specialsales@wwnorton.com or 800-233-4830

Manufacturing by Lake Book Manufacturing
Book design by Ellen Cipriano
Production manager: Lauren Abbate

ISBN 978-1-324-09090-8

Liveright Publishing Corporation
500 Fifth Avenue, New York, N.Y. 10110
www.wwnorton.com

W. W. Norton & Company Ltd.
15 Carlisle Street, London W1D 3BS

1 2 3 4 5 6 7 8 9 0

To our mothers,
EMMA BEA
and
BRENDA JOYCE

CONTENTS

PREFACE:
GREAT BOUTS TO COME

All a human being is, when you pull the drawers off, is a little bit
of time and a caravan of feeling.

—STANLEY CROUCH

AFTER STANLEY CROUCH PASSED, everyone had a story—the
musicians, the waitresses, the cooks, the crooks, the poets, and the
critics. To experience Stanley, indomitable, indefatigable, irrepressible
Crouch, was to know the kinetic energy and bombast of an indelible force
of New York, as large and complex as any character this city has produced.
Run into him around town and you encountered a walking contradiction of diddy-bop and *duende*, dressed in Brioni pinstripes or, later on, a
tracksuit, and your chance meeting could end over a three-hour lunch at
a Village bistro, an evening set in the basement at Smalls, or in the chilly
halls of high places.

He preferred his interactions lean on small talk (his health, for
instance, "Hey, man, you think that's interesting to me?"), larded with
jazz anecdotes, and salted by synaptic interconnections fired from that
prodigious brainpan. Above all, there was Stanley talking at levels audible
to the room, with his special emphasis for taboos punctuated by sterto-

rous guffaws—his absolute love of marathon jawbone sessions over what was, and what wasn't, and what is. Sometimes, his audience would just want to shove a pen into his hand and leave the table, such was his voluble profligacy. But you'd be a fool to grab your hat while witnessing the maelstrom of his riffs and improvisations, his combat with ideas, his joy over the plate before him, and with so much of America missing his performance that night. "Presence is always the point," Crouch would say, and he showed up. This was especially true where doldrums needed banishment most: at a St. Vincent's bedside or an uptown jazz funeral, when a significant measure of the man's tenderness and humanity that few spoke about flourished, rather than the pugilist of lore.

Crouch was a physical intellectual up from the streets of South Central L.A. who never lost the presentation of himself as a slightly dangerous and not-to-be-fucked-with individual. At his finest, Crouch's ethos achieves something Harold Bloom said of another poet and journalist, Walt Whitman, that his celebrations and elegies are scarcely distinguishable. He did not slather his praise with treacle or shackle his lament and drew no lines of decorum around "the inevitable christening" in a damning critique. His feuds are well documented, but often as not, the fight came to him. He would enlist adversaries in their own downfall, the way a fighter will get inside the rhythm of an opponent, change the tempo, then "use him as an unwilling accomplice in his own ass-whipping."

A cant-destroying writer who believed the critic's job was to provoke thought, he could, as Greil Marcus observed, infuse doubt into anybody's certainties. Crouch had no use for intellectual congeniality—he'd rather you brought your prejudice and pap to the table and put your feet under it. He was invested in first principles, original causes, not received ideas that pass for thought. His job was no less than what the large man Samuel Johnson had defined for the critic: "to improve opinion into knowledge." As a columnist, literary artist, and cultural critic, Crouch butchered what he called "all-purpose alienation," delighting and enflaming the passions of his readers in equal measure. You didn't need to agree with the man, but the virtuosity of his prose, the authority of his vision, the velocity of his intellect, and his very human story made his best work connect with a purpose as stark and true as blues lyrics. Always authentic, not one to bother with assembling consensus, Crouch trusted his thoughts and was unafraid of his own mind. He didn't want to persuade you, he wanted to connect—"always connect"—and to shock others into fresh thought who had enjoyed too much their own ignorance. In Stanley's view there was a hierarchy: "Heroic engagement should be defined separately from narcissistic anarchy."

By the time I first met him, late in his career, Crouch was already Rabelaisian in stature, intellect, and appetite, with a dash of Cervantes when he was tilting in the saddle of Rocinante. Purposeful to the last, he required intestinal fortitude, even in his most ardent admirers and friends. His public attacks were not *ad hominem*, they went far beyond anything personal, but if he sometimes held the primacy of his ideas over his personal relationships, he also had no problem changing his mind when he saw a better way forward. He retained the ethos of a jazz drummer, who could absorb the rhythm of a soloist's improvisations and add foundation.

From my vantage as his editor at Hearst, then friend, he was unsentimental about his own positions, which made him unpredictable, formidable, a free and unrepentant intellectual. Stanley had all the usual human vanities but was unpretentious about who had the better mousetrap. Socratic to the core, he did not expect you to agree—he didn't seek acolytes. Those he influenced most could also be those who consistently challenged him. Stanley's change of heart on things (on certain jazz forms, most dramatically) has sometimes confused and baffled his critics. When Stanley exited the ring of our contingent world, the gloves were still on the hands of his stupefied opponents. He would have preferred it that way, in the same way he liked restaurants with surly waiters who nonetheless served him fine meals.

Crouch's commitment to his occupation as a writer was total. He discovered early what he possessed and bet his life on it. He publicly argued with and was at times physically belligerent with those he felt were destructive to the idiom to which he had dedicated his life. *There it is*, he might say, with a shrug. Those who didn't understand Stanley's fight didn't appreciate where he'd come from or what that experience taught him. They had to understand that he couldn't be separated from his circumstances—he hadn't come from a place in life where ideas could remain abstractions.

THERE HAS BEEN universal acknowledgment that we have lost one of the great jazzmen, a near mythical figure, an arranger and conductor of himself, one who put his life and career on the line for the music through his writing and advocacy of the art—an art form that has never had as many celebrants and champions as it needs. A reaper has swept over the world these past couple of years and culled many for all time, but we never actually lose a writer unless "the silverfish of disregard do away with the work." So much about the public Stanley Crouch concerned his contrarian opinions and cutting sessions, the absurd accusation of him as some brand of henchman for establishment causes, but not enough has been said about his actual tracks, the intellectual biography, and the personal triumphs, all of which this collection presents to the reader.

These uncollected writings, none of which appear in his five previous collections, contain enough breadth to contribute to an understanding of Crouch's most "radically pragmatic" positions and to a fuller picture of the man as a humanist, an American, and a defender of that idiom of Black

American accomplishment most often referred to as the jazz and blues tradition. Not precisely a summing up, this collection of critical essays, profiles, articles, liner notes, reviews, and eulogies is meant to be an intellectual autobiography: tracing Crouch's beginnings in Watts as a Black Arts movement playwright and poet, with a more than passing apprenticeship in Black nationalism; to his arrival in Manhattan in 1975 as a drummer and participant in the loft scene while also booking the Bowery jazz club Tin Palace; establishing his reputation at the *Village Voice* and eventually laying the foundations for Jazz at Lincoln Center; becoming a televised, filmed, and sought-after public intellectual; and finally, his work of last farewell in the epistolary piece "Black and Tan Fantasy," a stunning coda that fits into some category unknown, perhaps even to its author, who may have been writing his own eulogy. *Victory Is Assured*, then, is a celebration, a second line parade, the brass affirmation of "Didn't He Ramble."

As the gambler in "St. James Infirmary Blues" says, *he died standing pat.* Another man might have held himself back in school where poets with far less capacity have made tidy reputations in what he called, "serving time in the academic foreign legion of the Claremont Colleges"; where, at the age of twenty-two and without a college degree, he managed to talk his way into a faculty position teaching literature and drama at Pomona College. He might have settled comfortably into his hometown of Los Angeles and made it as a drummer until free jazz went bust innovating itself out of existence, but Crouch chose an aesthetic life that could only emerge in New York, where someone from the streets "with a nickel and a nail in his pocket" will meet someone in the parapets of penthouses, to recall Bird's encounter with the Baroness Pannonica.

From the streets and what critic R. P. Blackmur called "the animating presence of a fresh idiom," Crouch became a public intellectual on a par with Norman Mailer, Christopher Hitchens, and Robert Hughes. He wrote with the transcendent soul of a poet and the fiery style of an orator, one who took readers, and later viewers, on a lyrical and analytical journey of swing and the blues. The results were often tone poems akin to sermons on the invisible art (see "Premature Autopsies") and freewheeling experiments in the form of the essay (as in his "Prologue") with an evangelical zeal for democratic vistas on the far horizon.

In conversation, he once traced his style back to his first reading of William Carlos Williams's classic *In the American Grain*, that "great exploration of the specific that achieves the universal," and to a digressive Melvillian technique he admired in works like Evan S. Connell's *Son of the Morning Star*, books that retell stories of this country we thought we knew. *Home*, a volume of essays by his early touchstone (then sparring partner), Amiri Baraka (né LeRoi Jones), brought a poetic sensibility to the discussion of jazz. It was Crouch's youthful *vade mecum*, carried, he wrote, "like an auxiliary part of my wardrobe." What a reader discovers in the present collection are consistent themes and arguments that can go back decades, not caprices that float on the surface of an opinion piece. Crouch eventually considered Baraka an American literary tragedy. Such things pained him. You will find, at root, this is a corner dispute between poets, who *go back*.

I'VE BEEN ASKED during the course of researching and assembling this volume what Stanley would have made of the recent events since his untimely death. For this question, he had prepared. The working title for most of his public talks was "Blues for Tomorrow." If it's happening today, Crouch wrote about it: conspiracy, conformity, cruelty, all ringing true as ever in the paradigm shift toward what America is becoming, as it once and always is, becoming. Undoubtedly, he would double down on the next cultural revolution. He did it once, with separatism and Black nationalism; he'd do it again with the usual suspects: anti-intellectualism, racial supremacists, pretensions in the academy, and you-name-it peacocking mediocrity. Any sclerotic position wouldn't be his; rather, with those who tilted toward mannerism and sentimentality. Crouch was a persistent intellectual threat, not just to the Black nationalist community and the Nation of Islam. He would not stoop to side with what he thought were unsophisticated views of things. This position took strength and cost him lucrative gigs when television producers expected him to be a representative of circumscribed views. He might have had even greater fame but would never be on the side of promoting hate in America, even if he hated aspects of American history. He didn't deny the existence of our darkest past but saw the American project with "tragic optimism"—an incredible journey and an experiment unique in history. On this, he could preach.

Crouch's outright exuberance for the greater prospect of American life is on full display in these writings, many discovered in his papers at the Schomburg Center in Harlem, several never before published. He had a utopian vision of a culture that was still in the full brawl of intellectual engagement and united with possibility. Stanley's beat was an archaeological dig of scenes populated with names as rich as American places: Big Sid Catlett, Tricky Sam Nanton, Goldie Goldmark, Cozy Cole, Shadow Wilson, Snooky Young. In this collection he writes of the fertile spawning grounds of drummer Mel Lewis in his native Buffalo, New York, and of the post-war Hill District of Pittsburgh, Pennsylvania, a kind of lost noir-toned landscape Stanley drew from when writing about the "miscegenated culture" of Americans:

> Looking at these people as they work and as they play, as they primp
> and as they pray, as they compete and as they cooperate, as they eat
> and as they exist in that kind of open-eyed sleep we so perfectly
> describe as daydreaming, we begin to better understand the contours
> of the national culture and how strongly it transcended superficial

differences. Some of the mystery of our past is pushed aside by these pictures in favor of a range of specifics.

For Crouch, the American story is always, unapologetically, *e pluribus unum*, with all the contributions of prior generations, "that we are connected by the history of a nation (one that has chosen to pursue its multiethnic destiny) rather than a state, and by the things that we have either invented or borrowed or refined" to become American.

Crouch himself drew heritage from some major American bloodlines: African (Madagascar), Choctaw, and Irish (a Georgia plantation on his father's side), and he knew the folkways of each. But as he wrote: "Blood accounts for nothing. It doesn't guarantee brilliance or courage or sacrifice or anything of substance. It doesn't guarantee that you won't have any of those qualities either. Exceptional people are mysterious. They come from any place and every place, which is what our democratic conception fundamentally recognizes." He'd dismiss the hint of hagiography with his famous side-eye, but for all his obvious cosmopolitanism, so much remained homegrown and rough-hewn about Crouch, at core a great American character. In this, he shared much with Charlie Parker, James Agee, Richard Wright, Alan Lomax, and Ralph Ellison, among other great American independents.

This is the premise from which Crouch begins: In its most profound and positive aspects, American culture is one of *miscegenation*—an antique word admittedly of another era. Jazz especially reflects this, like crazy quilts, blues, comics, and basketball as arts originating in the United States. On the subject of what he called "the grace, grime, and gore" of American democracy, there are few more impassioned or encyclopedic commentators than Crouch. He made apparent what Alexis de Tocqueville saw in America as the art of combination, essential to a democracy. If you try to impose your purity and perfection on that, you're done for. Stanley's output was vast and unsettled, a reflection of the nation; often messy and hard to categorize, negotiated and legislated, as he said of his friend Larry Neal, in "the bittersweet complexity of his identity as an American."

Crouch could not countenance separatists or re-segregationists either on the right or the left, especially when protected by a moral exhibitionism and politicking he saw as an outright hustle. He arrived at this conviction in youth and through independent study, as he tells it in "Jazz Me Blues," the prologue to *Considering Genius*:

> The tribal appeal is always great and there is nothing more tempting to the most gullible members of a minority group than suddenly hearing that, merely by being born, one is not innately inferior to the majority but part of an unacknowledged elite. I was not so sophisticated that I could avoid the pull of those ideas and found myself reading all kinds of books about Africa, and African customs and religion. . . . I would have been pulled all the way into the maw of subthought, from which it might have taken longer to emerge if Jayne Cortez hadn't introduced me to Ralph Ellison's *Shadow and Act*. . . . Unlike those younger Black people who were busy jettisoning their heritage as Americans and Western people—both of which brought the built-in option of criticism—Ellison took the place of his ethnic group and himself as firm parts of American life and a fresh development in Western culture.

Stanley signed all his correspondence VIA, S.C., an acronym for *Victory Is Assured*, which is assuredly addressed to us as readers in the great bouts to come. We are a nation in need of our "radical pragmatists," contrarian intellectuals, shit-stirrers with brains, now, as never. American culture is not ergonomically suited for individual comfort. But as

Crouch said, "Tribalism is the father of racism." There has never been a Pax Americana within these borders.

In reminiscing about this beloved man and sovereign writer, I don't want to pull your coat too much. Talking excessively about Stanley Crouch would be missing some very good writing. If you're like me, you skip past the barker and slip under the tent for the main attraction. It's all here, as they used to say in the liner notes. The song, the sorrow, the anger and the pity, the saplings and sequoias. This great improvisation on "Stardust" that was a great American life. Now, let us praise Stanley Crouch in his own words.

(NEEDLE DROP)

V

Glenn Mott
November 18, 2021
Sharon Springs, New York

INTRODUCTION:
THE CHAMPIONSHIP ROUNDS

THE VITALITY OF AMERICAN CULTURE was notably diminished when Stanley Lawrence Crouch—American, critic, novelist, and prose pugilist—hung up his gloves for the last time and took the long, lonely walk down the dark corridor of eternity. Among fighters there exists a rough taxonomy dividing the ranks into sluggers and boxers, the former being rough-hewn, artless men who throw ballistic punches, like a factory worker trying to make his quota. The latter contain the ranks of artists—balletic fighters whose gifts beguile bystanders into forgetting that punching a man in the face is an act of violence. Rarely is the pugilist steeped in both traditions, but there was Stanley on the page, concussive and rhythmic, brutal and beautiful, hands as heavy as his feet were light. Uneasy with received wisdom and hostile toward consensus, Crouch's real opponent was pablum. He fought what he deemed lazy thought that had gained the ballast of public support. Which is not to say he was always ahead on the scorecards—he swung and missed, threw shots after the bell, got caught flat-footed and lost rounds, even whole bouts. But like the great practitioners of both crafts, prose and pugilism, an element of unpredictability ran through his work. The punch that hurts the most, the great George Foreman observed, is the one you did not see coming.

Those who knew Stanley personally or simply appreciated his work will recognize *Victory Is Assured* as a motif in his writing, not simply an adage or postscript, though it is that too, but most significantly as a distillation of what Stanley believed. It's a strange principle. If life, circumstance, and the constant reincarnation of the past as current events have taught us anything, it is that success can never be assured, that evil has triumphed in the past and may well again in the future. It is not surprising then that the oddsmakers, never prone to sentimentality, put even money on our chances of keeping darkness at bay. Stanley knew all this, but he was speaking to a more subtle ideal. Back in earlier times, the gladiatorial title bouts were distinguished from the standard fare by three additional rounds—the *championship rounds*. Students of the craft will recall that the gloved warfare that transpired between Muhammad Ali and Joe Frazier in Manila in 1975 dragged on for fourteen rounds before the latter's corner called for a ceasefire. In 1981 the infernal combat between Sugar Ray Leonard and Tommy Hearns stretched into the fourteenth round before Leonard unleashed the series of brutal left hands that made referee Davey Pearl call a halt to the contest. Those last three rounds operated like a proving ground, settling questions that in lesser conflicts would be resolved far earlier. Stanley in the fashion of men like Ali and Leonard possessed the optimism of a fighter in the late rounds, wading into the thirteenth, fourteenth, fifteenth secure in the knowledge that there is more of the fight behind him than before him, aware that pain is a certainty but also that the skills that sustained him thus far can carry him over the final bell. There's victory to be had in this singular pursuit of victory.

This volume falls within that Crouchian tradition, like seldom seen footage of one of the greats being put through his paces. The familiar themes are here, the blues vernacular and the analytic poetry, the suffer-no-fools disposition—if Stanley practiced any religion it was devout skepticism—and the wide-ranging curiosity that would bring together Charles Johnson, Duke Ellington, Joyce Carol Oates, Quentin Tarantino, and Miles Davis, upon whom Crouch bestowed both his most lavish praise and his most savage jabs. But understanding the virtues of this collection warrants mention of its context and the journey of the man who produced it.

Across five previous collections of essays, one novel, one installment of an intended two-volume biography of Charlie Parker, and an unknown number of surreptitious poems, Crouch authored a grand statement on American identity. He composed it from his vantage point as a Black American—a *Negro* in his antique parlance—and set it to his preferred idiom of jazz. The most discernible theme in his work was the centrality of the Negro to this unwieldy undertaking known as America. His intimate, profound understanding of jazz, his unsentimental, unsparing assessments of politics, film, and literature, all of them were tributaries fed by that first wellspring of understanding. He came to this vantage point honestly, which is to say he'd fought his way through the ranks. Born in Los Angeles in 1945 to James and Emma Bea Crouch, he came of age amid the tumult and discord of the civil rights and Black Power movements.

Crouch's musical education began early, a measure of the influence of his parents, who were both devotees of jazz. Like his eventual north star Ralph Ellison, Crouch started out as a musician—a drummer in his case—only to find his true purpose in crafting sentences. In August 1965, Los Angeles police stopped a young Black motorist in Watts, California, and the ensuing conflict in which nearby residents witnessed the police beating the teenager sparked five days of rioting, cremating the facile hope that civil rights legislation alone could resolve the American quagmire of race. The Watts conflagrations, the "bloody carnival" in his words, affected Crouch in two crucial ways. It heralded the arrival of an incendiary new zeitgeist that came to be known as Black Power and which, for a time, influenced Crouch's own thinking, particularly in matters of race. (This preceded a decades-long recanting of those positions.) Then, on a more direct and practical level, the destruction inspired the screenwriter Budd Schulberg to found the Watts Writers' Workshop, out of which came a number of prominent Black writers, Crouch being among the most notable. The Black poetry of that era, every bit as incendiary as the zeitgeist in which it was produced, unabashedly wed art to a specific view of politics. The epitaph for a particular brand of Negro optimism came to be written in fire—legible in the flames that incinerated swaths of Watts, Harlem, Detroit, Newark—and a dozen other locales in the mid-1960s, all of it prefacing the grand national incineration that followed the assassination of Martin Luther King Jr.

A number of writers from the Watts workshop, including Quincy Troupe and Jayne Cortez, rose to prominence in this moment. Crouch's primary contribution to this climate came in the form of *Ain't No Ambulances for No Nigguhs Tonight*, his concussive 1972 collection of poems (not to be confused with his 1969 recorded lecture of the same name). The title poem is a verse narration of the Watts uprising, its sentiments captured near the end of the piece:

> *The Devil Ages were the days now that we were in*
> *never too cool to kill a brother*
> *but always*
> *dropping the gun*
> *when the beasts with the badges arrived*

(and they shot little Fats all of nine times
after having made him get down on his knees
and raise his arms in prayer)

Shot through with anger and nationalist themes, the poems highlight the influence of the burgeoning Black Arts movement, most notably the influence of Crouch's fellow jazz critic Amiri Baraka, with whom Crouch shared a fond and then bitterly contentious relationship that mirrored both men's evolution away from Black nationalism, albeit in opposite directions. The album cover for the lecture features young Stanley poised among the ruins of a building, a visual reference to the fiery bedlam that Watts had endured. A cigarette dangles insouciantly from the corner of his mouth, a perfectly Crouchian expression of mild disdain playing across his face—the portrait of a man as one with his times.

Culturally, Crouch's position was scarcely distinguishable from those of the most committed Black nationalists of the period. As he noted of the popular white musicians of the day:

Janis Joplin, who is like an imitation nigga, is more well known by Black people than the Black blues musicians she's trying to copy. She and the Beatles and the Rolling Stones and all the rest of those people are imitation niggas and that's why they're successful. We have, I believe, spiritually, emotionally, and aesthetically subsidized white America as long as we have been here.

This situation was compounded by what later generations would term *cultural appropriation*: "We have not only had our greatest artists hidden from us," Crouch argued, "but the white man has thrown imitators of those Black artists at us and we know them even better than we know the ones who really did the first thing." This was both indisputably true and starkly different from his later perspective on the transcendent, collaborative nature of creative production.

Crouch's contrarian streak and his irrepressible (and substantial) artistic ambition made him restless. His abortive career as a drummer brought him east to New York City in 1975. An inveterate and voracious reader, Crouch encountered the works of Albert Murray in this era and quickly began to question his own presumptions about race, identity, and the United States. Murray, a critic and novelist who'd attended Tuskegee University with Ralph Ellison in the 1930s, had come to the fore in 1970 with his essay collection *The Omni-Americans*. The title alone suggested Murray was swimming against the popular tides of Black literature at the time.

Devoutly anti-ideological, Albert Murray rejected what he thought was the shibboleth that Black American history and culture neatly conformed to the strictures of any one movement. Moreover, at a point when a not-insubstantial number of Black Americans felt that Black people constituted an internal colony within the United States, a colony whose populace could not honestly be referred to as citizens, Murray contended that Black people were the *essential* Americans. His critics howled in derision, but at a moment when the rage prophets of Black art rejected the idea of integration as culturally suicidal, Murray argued—just as the Black novelist and commentator George Schuyler had maintained during the Harlem Renaissance—that Black life was already inextricably and fundamentally American. In terms of this logic, Murray overlapped with his lifelong friend Ralph Ellison, who'd evocatively conveyed similar sentiments in his masterwork, *Invisible Man*. If the prevailing nationalist aesthetic provided an index of white depredations, Murray (and subsequently Crouch) fixated upon the triumphalist genius of Black survival to such an extent that whole acres of historic wrongs receded into the backdrop. Ellison notably summed up this perspective in his review of *American Dilemma*, when he rhetorically asked if it were possible for any people to survive for more than three hundred years *simply by reacting* to the world around them. If not, he argued, Black life could not be fully understood through the lens of racism. In Crouch's own work, this idea is most succinctly distilled in the essay "Blues to Be Constitutional," which appeared in his collection *The All-American Skin Game*. The Constitution, Crouch averred, is anchored in an understanding of the human potential for tragedy, a reckoning with fallibility and pain; its most accessible analog in American culture is found in the blues. The willingness, even the desire, to wring optimism from this awareness of the potential for failure became Crouch's perspective and the very essence of his definition of American identity.

Decades after his rejection of Black nationalism and his embrace of omni-Americanism, Crouch, in a conversation we had in his book-laden West Village apartment, compared his evolution to a man who has long been involved with one woman but then meets someone else whom he knows he ultimately belongs with. And as with many divorces, the situation turned bitter. Crouch had first arrived at the *Village Voice* in 1975 and began trading (mostly metaphorical) shots at an array of opponents. His early work—collected in his impeccably titled 1990 book *Notes of a Hanging Judge*—is effectively a slaughterhouse of sacred cows. Crouch skewered Malcolm X, heretofore unimpeachable within his former ranks; parted ways with James Baldwin (he "sold out to rage, despair, self-righteousness"); assailed Toni Morrison's *Beloved* ("*Beloved* is, above all else, a Black holocaust novel"); and generally ridiculed the centrality of suffering as a theme in Black art. It was easy to assume the worst motives—bashing Black critics of racism has always been a potentially lucrative gig. But for all his resolute assertions of his American identity, Crouch was not enamored of whiteness, or, more precisely, he placed no special premium on white people's admiration—something that was not necessarily true of his bomb-throwing counterparts.

His provocations fueled a career that was in rapid ascendance, but more and more often when Crouch appeared before Black crowds, he got the kind of reception an out-of-town challenger receives when he shows up to fight a hometown favorite. But Stanley knew even then that fistic provocation is a finite hustle. I once had a conversation with him about the enigma of Ben Webster, the mercurial saxophonist whose sometimey-ness led to clashes with his peers and friends as well as to his dismissal from Duke Ellington's band. Yet the hell-raising coexisted with a vulner-ability that produced moments of nearly tangible tenderness within his music. "He could get wild, cussing people out, fighting in bars," Crouch said to me. "Then he'd pick up the horn and you'd hear this de-boo-be-booo-woo-woo-weee. And you'd say, wait a minute, is the wild guy from the bar the same as this guy with the tenor saxophone?" On some level Stanley was also describing himself.

Crouch's pugnacity tended to obscure his immanent capacity for sub-tlety and empathy, especially early on. In this regard, his remembrance of the novelist Lionel Mitchell, written in 1984, is instructive. Writing at the nadir of the AIDS crisis, Crouch conjured a beautiful, nuanced ren-dering of Mitchell's life. He wrote of his grace in the face of antagonism directed at gay men by much of the Black community and what had been lost when Mitchell succumbed to the dreaded virus, known then as "the gay cancer," at the age of forty-two. It warrants recollecting that in the mid-1980s there was an empathy deficit, and for gay men suffering from a scourge often cast as divine retribution, there was precious little empathy to be found. That grace and compassion should fall from the saber-pen of Stanley Crouch suggested that there was more to him than his antago-nists wanted to concede. This was something that those who knew him came to understand implicitly. Knowing Stanley invariably meant spar-ring with Stanley, which itself was a reminder that pugilism, at its heart, is a mode of communication.

I first met Stanley in the mid-1990s at the National Black Writers Conference at Medgar Evers College in Brooklyn and grew fond of him despite my commitment to dislike him. He'd made a point during the panel discussion about Black participation in every war that the United States had ever fought—including the Alamo—which inspired me, a twenty-six-year-old history grad student, to confront him afterward and launch into a disquisition about racial minorities being drafted into imperialist forays in the Philippines, Korea, and Vietnam. At the end of our exchange, Crouch did something I didn't anticipate: He handed me his card and told me to keep in touch. I kept it almost as a curio for months before I cold-called him one day. We thus began a long series of contentious, although eventually amiable, exchanges about history, music, film, literature, politics, and human nature that stretched across the next twenty-five years. We clashed most predictably and consistently over his steadfast rejection of hip-hop, a genre of music that he saw as indicative of spiritual decay and bereft of any profound consideration of life and its meaning. I found it bewildering that Stanley couldn't see the familial resemblances between hip-hop and his beloved blues. (I continue to argue this point with him, at least in my head, even now after his death.) We also differed on the significance of Malcolm X, the relative importance of Africa in African American life, the NYPD, Barack Obama's claim to Black identity, and any number of other topics that would have typically been unbridgeable gulfs to polite socializing. It would take years for me to recognize my debt to Stanley, his subtle impact on my thinking, the way that his ceaseless challenges forced me to hone my own argumentative reflexes. Those conversations left me less certain about what I knew or believed and thereby, in corresponding measure, more curious about the world. It took equally long for me to recognize that he had cultivated a whole network of relationships like this with younger writers, people whom he called to provoke and pick fights with, but also to encourage, support, and advise. Much of this Crouch cenacle would not then (or really even now) be caught dead in the same room with each other, but Stanley—bellicose, shit-starting Stanley—was the unlikely tendril connecting us all.

Stanley's death in September 2020 came amid a season of woe. We failed then, amid the welter of hardships and the titanic scale of our losses, to give his departure the attention it warranted. One potential definition of a pandemic is a season in which death outpaces your ability to properly reckon with it. This collection, on some level, is a fitting remedy, an attempt to do for Stanley what he had done for Lionel Mitchell, his encomium written in the miasmic fog of a different pandemic, almost forty years before. So here is Stanley Crouch, archival like an old Joe Louis newsreel, a showcase of what made him truly great. Look at him now: back in the ring, klieg lights beaming, he feints and he weaves. He works his combinations and lands shots you never expected him to throw—the ones you never saw coming. He finds victory in the very pursuit of victory—precisely the way he always did. Champions, he seems to be telling us, are not made at the end of the fifteen rounds. They're created the moment that, despite titanic odds, they climb into the ring in the first place.

Jelani Cobb
September 2021
New York City

VICTORY IS ASSURED

PROLOGUE OF BLUES AND SWING
TO BE THERE, WAY DOWN YONDER
IN NEW ORLEANS

Originally published in the Oxford American, *Winter 2012, under the title "Way Down Yonder in New Orleans," S.C. later retitled, intending this piece to serve as the prologue to a future collection of writings that would frame his historical approach to the jazz tradition and democracy. Despite the fact that it appears first here, the work is one of Crouch's last great omnibus essays on the "art of the invisible," making it the appropriate prologue to this posthumous collection.*

ALL AESTHETICS ARISE from life and end up going home to the world of art, no matter how or where one started, in the church or the counterfeit palace of pleasure known as the cathouse. What was understood by jazzmen the likes of Jelly Roll Morton, King Oliver, Sidney Bechet, and Louis Armstrong was of such profound importance to jazz performance that it has continued to influence every solid approach to the music, regardless of style.

In the playing and thinking of Lester Young, Count Basie, Walter Page, and Jo Jones we hear a sense of group playing, a balancing of the band's sound, that leads right back to what the supreme New Orleans jazzmen discovered. In the music of Duke Ellington, we can hear the indelible influence of New Orleans on his conception of counterpoint, brass timbre, and the overriding importance of the blues. In the best or most representative work of players and leaders such as Charlie Parker, Dizzy Gillespie, Thelonious Monk, The Modern Jazz Quartet, Charles Mingus, George Russell, and Ornette Coleman we hear the basic conceptions of New Orleans reinterpreted for very different styles or multiple styles. Aesthetic motion through time is a long and intricate story that refutes adolescent visions of rebellion that have nothing to do with art, which is always about ordering the material used in specific ways that we usually call styles. However many styles come about, they are united by conceptions that are so fundamental, so basic that they somehow transcend the schools, as they always have, while making their joyful or sorrowful or bittersweet noises in the world.

IT IS ALWAYS good to realize that any linear interpretation of the art of jazz is completely wrong. Aesthetic reality is always omnidirectional, making nothing old and nothing new. This is often misunderstood in jazz writing because its practitioners are overly impressed by the intellectual powers that have underlaid so much European music since Debussy. But some of the finest thinking about jazz and its aesthetic elements comes from people who have thought about art enough to see clearly what makes jazz unique and valuable in itself, not as an imitation of anything else. Superior aesthetic thinking has been done by writers such as Ralph Ellison and Albert Murray, as well as musicians like Jelly Roll Morton and Wynton Marsalis—who, by the way, is unlike anyone else. Marsalis is the least impressed by European manners of making order—perhaps because, by his middle twenties, unlike any jazz musician that preceded him, he was already one of our finest concert trumpet players. Knowing concert music at the highest level, Marsalis came to understand its grandeur, which underlined the contrasting aesthetic facts of jazz.

Aesthetic facts, in jazz as in all the arts, are proof of an old saying from the 1960s: "Feelings are facts." This is quite true of the meaning of New Orleans music. That factual feeling arrives in notes as invisible as the notes of any music; all music being an art of the invisible, equal to forces as deeply palpable as thought and emotion, the elements of existence we attempt to recognize from symbolic references we know as styles. The feeling of jazz is often about what is brought to the music by giving emotional shapes to the invisible. Those shapes arrived not out of nowhere but were a response to the world of music by writers and players who brought a new logic, a collective sense of interpretation that has individuated itself.

Some are so misled today, impressed by European avant-garde rebellion, that they think jazz is simply improvisation—absolutely free of any limitations and existing only with reference to itself, or to everything else. At its worst and most pretentious, this turns into an instantly hollow "openness" to the music of the planet at large called "world music." That might sound good to academics who seek to make names for themselves, or pseudo-academics who have poorly read a few books, or people filled with tawdry ideas and rhetoric about oppressed minorities or colonized cultures, who find their voices in modern clichés justifying an avant-garde as a revolt against the powerful. Those clichés might defend certain schools that claim to be jazz but are connected to it only through improvisation, which demands high talent.

The height of that talent is often left out of the discussion because it is so strongly connected to a sense of how one brings order on the moment. Leaving behind the idea of talent and a sense of form that has a loose body of playing rules makes it much better for those cliché mongers. They use this supposed thinking to bully their way into the very academy to which they claim to have no commitment—but once there, well, it can get very sticky. Too often, they utilize easy ways to make students think that contrivance replaces skill and, most important, talent. Just learn your patterns or make up some yourself. But jazz playing is not merely reciting patterns while at the same time improvising. New Orleans musicians knew that almost from the jump. They talked about playing together and getting a balance in the sound of the band. All of that was about learning how to listen, so that you could play better. They knew that improvising well had something to do innately with hearing.

Hearing is a supreme talent in the world of music and often completely trumps academic knowledge. Supremely sophisticated musicians like Coleman Hawkins could make music with those best described as technically uninformed or intuitive, such as Billie Holiday. There was always artistic room in Western music for a Hawkins, but there was no place in sophisticated art for someone like Holiday, who would fail all academic tests but pass all artistic ones. She had a small sound, a very narrow range, and would have been helpless or largely inaudible without a microphone; but she could sing in tune, had a perfect sense of time through her gifted interpretation of Louis Armstrong, and a very artful ability to reshape songs and change notes wherever she could find her aesthetic way. In short, for all of her limitations, Holiday could hear and she could execute what she heard.

That is what separates the titans of New Orleans from so-called primitives, which was always a lucrative mask for Black musicians to wear, just as it was for whites like the cinematic genius John Ford, who pretended to be simple-minded and barely aware of what made a masterpiece in his idiom. Eubie Blake once gave an interview in which he said that when a hit song made the rounds, he would write an intricate arrangement of it, pretend that he and his musicians did not know it, and ask a listener to hum a few bars before breaking into a complex version of the song; this convinced the assembled audience that all the talent they were hearing was proof that these people were simply natural musicians. If that story of Blake's is true, we know what happened next, and how a party joke and clever ploy to get jobs helped deepen a stereotype. The struggle against that stereotype led to excessively pretentious stances from the 1920s until just yesterday.

The New Orleans titans heard a brand new way to play collectively, all the while improvising within an order that had plenty of room for individuality. They heard and conceived, for instance, an original version of counterpoint in which a melody is played by a trumpet or cornet while two other horns create thematic variations that expand the nuanced dimensions of the melody. We can hear this in the playing of Lester Young, who was born in Mississippi but grew up very near New Orleans and used to follow the wagons on which musicians played. Young was influenced by Louis Armstrong, but the tailgate trombone players also touched him thoroughly—though they touched him in a conceptual way, which is how the great individuals always handle influences: Once they know why something is done, they reshape that thing to fit themselves. Tailgate trombonists often began their features with a startling low note, which was a favorite device of Young the tenor saxophonist. But Young was also able to improvise alongside another horn or two in small groups. That is a high skill that has had diminishing presence in jazz ensembles over the years, but it is always possible.

This extremely sophisticated hearing ability can also be found in the work of Charlie Parker, as when he reinterpreted New Orleans counterpoint in compositions such as "Ah-Leu-Cha" or "Chasin' the Bird." Contrapuntal group improvising was central to the sound of The Modern Jazz Quartet and was also important to Charles Mingus in the way his so-called front lines improvised in New Orleans form, but in his own style, or a number of styles. George Russell did remarkable things with his sextet on *Stratusphunk* and made one of his best recordings with the same instrumentation but new personnel on *The Outer View*. It featured Don Ellis, who invented his lines within Russell's Lydian Chromatic Concept but used the horn as Lester Bowie would have if he had had Ellis's talent for playing across styles in a perfect way. That came forward for Ellis through his work with Charles Mingus, who once led his band at the Village Vanguard for two weeks, playing what was called Dixieland.

The ultimate "free jazz" appropriation of New Orleans music was heard on Ornette Coleman's *Free Jazz* recording, about which Coleman complimented Eric Dolphy, also a veteran of playing with Mingus, for sometimes sounding as if Dolphy were playing all the horns behind him. That is the greatest achievement of jazz and jazz playing: to empathetically hear the surrounding context while improvising, creating order from second to second, in a speed that rivals the Internet velocity we now have the technology to measure. We no longer have to wonder if we were dreaming. The dreamscape can now be proven.

We can now understand in objective terms the fallacies transcriptions create in jazz education, which is too often the greatest enemy of jazz understanding. The single-line transcription tells us nothing about how those notes came about, or what they were a response to, on the spot and immediately. The incomplete "understanding" made by single-line transcription now seems rather dumb after all of these years of supposed jazz education. That version of the dumb and perhaps the deaf would be as backward and incorrect as using one line of a Haydn, Beethoven, Debussy, or Bartók string quartet to tell you something profound other than how certain notes related to each other. This is far outside of the phenomenon of jazz, which is the result of what tones, literal pitches or timbres, appear in a mobile context when the ensemble work is improvised.

That is what jazz actually is, and we will not understand it very well, at least in an academic sense, until we have complete transcriptions. At Lincoln Center we are presently developing an online magazine of entire transcriptions that will be discussed by musicians across generations: performers such as Jimmy Heath, Tim Hagans, Christian McBride, Ben Wolfe, and Aaron Diehl. With complete transcriptions including the horn-line improvisation and the improvised context provided by the rhythm section, students will begin reading a performance like a string quartet score, which will vastly change things and sweep some of the ignorance out the door. Then students will actually see what makes a performance great. It is about how musicians interact, almost instantaneously, with a sense of form within a context. That is what came most importantly out of New Orleans and was firmly based in blues and swing.

BECAUSE THE BLUES is so often the feeling that gives what must be given to the melodies to make them into jazz, we should understand the influence of New Orleans music on Duke Ellington, the greatest and most varied creator of blues in the history of the music. New Orleans music resulted in two indelible legacies. King Oliver's way of handling his horn influenced Bubber Miley to the core in his own use of plunger mutes. Miley sought to make his horn talk, shout, mutter, and swing. That defined the sound of Ellington brass from the late 1920s to the end of the composer and bandleader's life. Ellington also hired Crescent City titan Sidney Bechet, which may have had something to do with Will Marion Cook—one of Ellington's mentors—who took Bechet with him on a tour of Europe, which resulted in the very first serious recognition of jazz playing by concert conductor and writer Ernest Alexandre Ansermet.

Ansermet knew that he was hearing something new and appreciated its distance from European convention, because jazz had the same things in mind that any music has if played by serious musicians, whose job is to evoke the mournful mood of a funeral, the roller coaster passions of a love affair, the ongoing drama and comedy of life, and the inevitable christening—no matter the religion—which could include the introduction of new life to the world by full-fledged atheists. That range of feeling matured the music and the musicians; they were as accustomed to meeting the demands of a funeral as they were in setting the pace for frivolity. Not acknowledging that plurality often explains why the weight of the music was frequently described as limited only to the glands, instead of realizing it was as ready for human sensuality as it was for the spiritual sense of life that was present in the blues.

BY THE TIME they toured Europe in 1918, the members of the Southern Syncopated Orchestra knew how to play their instruments with a virtuosity that is powerfully captured by Rick Benjamin and the Paragon Ragtime Orchestra in *Black Manhattan*, a recording issued with the subtitle "Theater and Dance Music of James Reese Europe, Will Marion Cook, and Members of the Legendary Clef Club." In its variety of moods and grooves and the high-minded jubilance that underscores so many of the themes and techniques demanded of the players, it is easy to hear what the audiences of the day well knew. This music was not written for amateurs to play and has a tone far from dour or solemn. It sets well and firmly in place the opportunity for the emergence of jazz, which was always a music made from many parts, parts that were all so well comprehended that a new art form could break through the smooth shell of ragtime—an art that allowed for improvisation, which ragtime did not. Many of the composers or conductors were writing out folk or plantation melodies for their orchestras, and they were already including moments when the music moved beyond the page and entered an adventurous and exciting world that was largely unknown. The great Bechet was among the players Ansermet heard in the Southern Syncopated Orchestra. He was already slipping past straight ragtime, improvising when he could and when allowed the space.

Ansermet was such an intelligent musician himself that he realized these were musicians who had a professional level of technique. They were playing what they wanted to, not because they were hiding their incompetence with exotic coon songs or plantation songs. What Ansermet wrote demonstrates how well he could hear, and that the European audience for Negro American music was already in place. The young Swiss heard so much better than Americans did who were not themselves musicians. He accurately described what he heard and instantly intuited the motives of the players and singers:

> The first thing that strikes one about the Southern Syncopated Orchestra is the astonishing perfection, the superb taste and the fervor of its playing. . . . They play generally without notes, and even when they have some, it only serves to indicate the general line, for there are very few numbers I have heard them execute twice with exactly the same effects. I imagine that, knowing the voice attributed to them in the harmonic ensemble, and conscious of the role their instrument is to play, they can let themselves go, in a certain direction and within certain limits, as their heart desires. They are so entirely possessed by the music they play, that they can't stop themselves from dancing inwardly to it in such a way that their playing is a real show, and when they indulge in one of their favorite effects which is to take up the refrain of a dance in a tempo suddenly twice as slow and with redoubled intensity and figuration, a truly gripping thing takes place, it seems as if a great wind is passing over a forest or as if a door is suddenly opened on a wild orgy.

He then considers the leader, obviously a special artist and talent. "The musician who directs them and to whom the constitution of the ensemble is due, Mr. Will Marion Cook, is moreover a master in every respect, and there is no orchestra leader I delight as much in seeing conduct." Ansermet writes well of Cook and of his compositions, but his deepest observation is what he hears in the blues and in Bechet.

Ansermet hears the music as an art and does not descend to the demeaning talk of primates in clothes:

> The blues occurs when the Negro is sad, when he is far from his home, his mammy, or his sweetheart. Then, he thinks of a motif or a preferred rhythm, and takes his trombone, or his violin, or his banjo, or his clarinet, or his drum, or else he sings, or simply dances. And on the chosen motif, he plumbs the depths of his imagination. This makes his sadness pass away,—it is the Blues.

This is no different from the many blues musicians who instead of giving a sociological explanation for the art say that *one does not play the blues in order to get the blues, one plays it in order to do away with those blues.* It is a sophisticated sense of fighting with the troubles of life itself, not only a social position, though there was always a sense of unfairness in the world, symbolized by the story of Moses and the Israelites looking for the Promised Land, as well as the story of the Crucifixion, a cosmic blues tale if there ever was one. Ansermet was better off than many of those "race men," Black or white, who think they love Black people but only as receptacles for theories that use data to remove the mystery from life.

There is an old saying I once heard in Texas that fits this subject: A pig-foot-eating Negro, a chicken-steak-eating white man, and a hot-sauce-guzzling Mexican are all mysterious in the same way, usually because mystery comes along with nightfall. That's when the love, the hate, the violence, and the good times come down. But don't count on that, else it will get you in trouble when you're not looking, right about high noon. One can say the same about the blues.

HERE IS WHAT Ansermet had to say about Sidney Bechet:

> There is in the Southern Syncopated Orchestra an extraordinary clarinet virtuoso who is, so it seems, the first of his race to have composed perfectly formed blues on the clarinet. I've heard two of them which he had elaborated at great length . . . they are equally admirable for their richness of invention, force of accent, and daring novelty and unexpected turns. These solos already show the germ of a new style. Their form is gripping, abrupt, harsh, with a brusque and pitiless ending like that of Bach's second *Brandenburg Concerto*. I wish to set down the name of this artist of genius; as for myself, I shall never forget it—it is Sidney Bechet. When one has tried so often to find in the past one of those figures to whom we owe the advent of our art—those men of the seventeenth and eighteenth centuries, for example, who wrote the expressive works of dance airs, cleared the way for Haydn and Mozart—what a moving thing it is to meet this Black, fat boy with white teeth and that narrow forehead, who is very glad one likes what he does, but who can say nothing of his art, save that he follows his "own way" and when one thinks that his "own way" is perhaps the highway the whole world will swing along tomorrow.

While we know that Bechet was not at all Black, but brownish yellow at best, he was big and he did have a narrow forehead, but most of all he could improvise thrilling and seriously contemplative blues delivered with virtuosity, daring, and surprise in a well-ordered way. That may be why Duke Ellington called him "the great originator," recalling how he sounded when the nascent composer heard him swinging "I'm Coming, Virginia" in 1921 in Washington, D.C.

What Ellington saw was a man of mixed heritage from New Orleans, where white racism had brought about or *played a large part* in the making of a timelessly beautiful aesthetic achievement.

When the light-skinned Creole musicians were banned from playing for white audiences, that brought together the sophistication of the penthouse and the vitality of the sidewalk. Those Creole musicians were esteemed for decades because they were such good technicians and readers and interpreters of written music. When they were pushed from the competition in order to provide jobs for white musicians, they were flushed down an impoverishing toilet. If they were going to work, they had to sell their musical wares to the same people who listened and danced to Buddy Bolden; they had to learn the "dirty" vocalizing techniques that the people loved to hear, during which time they *taught* many of those raw unschooled blues players how to better perform with their instruments.

Here was an integration of the high and the low, the sophisticated and the common, the European sensibility brought together with deep blues knowledge. This was New Orleans at its best, ironically, because it constituted, by accident, the greatest moment of integration in the history of the music. From this moment on it was an artistic phenomenon, it went beyond race in favor of aesthetics. The "real" white people, from musicians such as Bix Beiderbecke through Joe Lovano, understood the bringing together of supposedly opposed technical information in the interest of a distinctly American music while they made their individual ways as jazzmen.

ALL OF THIS comes through in Alan Lomax's greatest work, *Mister Jelly Roll*, a biography of Jelly Roll Morton that perfectly fits with Lomax's

Library of Congress recordings, the interviews of Morton that consti-
tute something unlike anything else in jazz. Morton's tall tales, jokes,
funny stories, tales of obnoxiousness and terrible murder that arrive in an
overview of precise musical memories are as important to jazz history as
Homer is to Western literature. The sheer range of what Morton not only
knew, but was able to articulate, has never been challenged. He forms
a path that takes a reader from beneath the gutter to the tiptop of the
penthouse. His answers and monologues form an epic of musical information, frequently illustrating how certain styles relate to the variety of
the lives lived, but Morton's jazz epic always goes beyond all that because
an aesthetic achievement immediately ceases to be a time period's or a
people's music and becomes the world's. People such as Leontyne Price,
who grew up in segregated Mississippi but went on to become one of the
world's finest opera singers, showed us what Stan Getz showed us in jazz.
Beginning as a follower of Lester Young, Getz evolved into a truly great
individual player who could sing through his horn, play the blues, and also
swing almost as hard as anyone else, unless they were in the magic circle
of the grandest of grand masters. Those like Price and Getz, given their
objectively superior talent, may have a destiny beyond color and sociology.
Art never fails to show us that.

When we listen to the nineteen pieces in *Black Manhattan*, it is easy
to see what was available in that music for Morton's aesthetic imagination. Morton heard well enough to understand what would work in jazz.
That was because ragtime was perhaps the first professional American
music that was both virtuosic and popular. Morton recognized that forms
needed to shift and to have unexpected parts to keep the listener surprised
and intrigued. Morton was much more informed than Ansermet because
he was more than a witness, he was a leader and a participant.

Morton knew how to use riffs, changes of tempo or rhythm, a three-
part horn line, dynamic changes, breaks, and what he called the "Spanish

tinge." This meant beats that actually came from the Caribbean or from the Iberian Peninsula, coating flamenco, or Spanish melodies with a particular intensity. These elements were just as important to Kansas City swing, blues, and big- or small-band music. In Morton's "Black Bottom Stomp" and "Dead Man Blues," we can hear the sweep of his authoritative imagination.

ALL THESE ELEMENTS come together in King Oliver's sense of a band, which we can hear perfectly in 1923's "Snake Rag," in which he and Louis Armstrong execute some breaks that foreshadow all that was to come. While a sideman of Oliver's in Chicago, Armstrong made one of his finest recordings as a young man, teaming up in January 1925 with Bechet for "Cake Walkin' Babies from Home," which must be one of the hottest and most soulful performances ever caught electronically. Bechet's breaks are so heartbreakingly heated and graceful that they let you see why Ellington so esteemed him. Armstrong, who had been smoked by the reed player on the same tune a few months earlier, dominates the opening space with the size of his sound, almost pushing the formidable first jazz master of the saxophone into the background. Armstrong is softer on the part following the vocal and the snake charmer in the other man comes forward, far from rough but ready to throw anyone for a tumble. Dippermouth was ready for him. His tone is afire from the first notes, all of his breaks are full of unexpected accents, and the building logic of the performance shows that a brand new version of a master was inside the music. There was one who had been there already.

The first one, apparently, to accomplish that combination of dual techniques and musical emotions was Sidney Bechet. This aesthetic combining is why he so impressed Ansermet in 1918—just as Louis Armstrong did in another European place almost fifteen years later. The one

with the satchel mouth astounded the trumpet players of the Royal Philharmonic Orchestra, who asked to see if he was playing a special horn,
one constructed to make possible all that stuff filling the air, like the very
blue of the sky.

Both Bechet and Armstrong were known early on as special talents,
way down yonder in New Orleans. Bechet remembered going to Armstrong's house because he had heard there was a boy around who could
play on his brass horn the clarinet part from "High Society." Having never
heard such agility from a trumpet player, Bechet was shocked to hear
the young man do just what the clarinet and soprano saxophone giant
had been told. This was one of the grand moments of revelation, as when
the young Charlie Parker broke out in a cold sweat when he heard what
Lester Young was playing one night at a Kansas City jam session in the
mid-1930s.

Young benefited from the innovations of Armstrong—multidirec-
tional freedom in the time—as much as from what Beiderbecke and
Frankie Trumbauer played. Taking a piece of that firmament from the
Armstrong sky allowed Young the saxophonist to float above or move
behind the beat while still swinging, even at a strange rhythm angle.
During the formative years of his highly original style, Young's repeating
of single notes through different fingerings made the single pitch into a
melody of mobile timbre, which was one of Armstrong's specialties.

In the 1930s, when Young and Eddie Barefield traveled together as a
two-man band that played entire dances by themselves—one improvising
while the other kept time by stomping out the beat—Barefield remembered Young often pleasurably listening to Armstrong records. Far from
surprising is the fact that Young went along with jazzmen such as Beiderbecke, because Buster Smith made it clear that so few people could even
play jazz at that point that the musician didn't care where anyone came
from or looked like. If he could learn something about playing his horn,

a musician got as close to that person as possible and used the knowledge to make something for himself.

Even so it is befuddling that some jazz writers appear to believe Beiderbecke brought introspection to jazz. They must have never heard the contemplation essential to the slow blues or known that W. C. Handy had written of the lyrical desires of a woman who liked her blues soft and slow. Perhaps they could not figure out the tempo shifting of the Armstrong title "I'm Not Rough" or realize, as Martin Williams did, how clearly available was the impact of the New Orleans man on Billie Holiday. Writers only had to get to that by comparing his-and-her versions of "I Gotta Right to Sing the Blues," hers second and dripping stardust beamed from the first. Armstrong and Bechet are all over Lester Young, as was Beiderbecke, who is, like the tenor player, one whom we still talk about because he went his own way, all while listening to the New Orleans titans in order to learn how and what to do.

Young became famous for leaving Kansas City, doubtless a wide-open gangster town where musicians played, as they had in New Orleans, for all kinds of people and all kinds of ceremonies or entertainment. The most important thing that happened there was bassist Walter Page getting the rhythm section even, as he heard it. Page relaxed the phrasing of the meter into two bars of eight beats, setting up a smoother cycle of rhythm. No longer 1—2—3—4, but 1—2—3—4—5—6—7—8.

"The clouds began to rise," as Kansas City bassist Gene Ramey said of the way things changed when that flowing time came to the bandstand, where it still remains, every musician having submitted to its swing. All jazz bands began to realize that such a beat raised all the music up and made it easier for a rhythm section to measure itself. That and major improvisers in Young, Buck Clayton, Sweets Edison, and Basie himself made the ease, lilt, and the power of Count Basie's band very impressive, because it imposed the swinging blues on the land and reinterpreted the victories of New Orleans in the ability of so many of its musicians to harmonize, finding the best place in the time for a riff, and even, as the small-group recordings show, effectively improvising while more than one horn was up front.

Ellington continued to develop his take on New Orleans music, even though he claimed to have hated Jelly Roll Morton and said the older bandleader could not play the piano. The man got on many nerves for being such a braggart and claiming to have invented more than he could have single-handedly. Morton's music still stands up and, in its essence, perfectly opens the way for Ellington's 1931 "Creole Rhapsody" and his *Black, Brown, and Beige* from the early 1940s. Those works continued the jazz identity that Lomax called the "hybrid of hybrids," pulling together concert sophistication and the omnidirectional singing, dancing, and street vitality given special aesthetic power by the blues. It unmistakably influenced Mingus, who worked out a way of playing multiple styles in one piece, as his band does in such a timeless and penetrating manner in *Tijuana Moods*. It is not only one of the best recordings of that era but also called his best recording by Mingus himself when the work was released, after five years, in 1962. Mingus uses the sound of bebop, riffs, and modal harmonic brevity that can be heard in two chords used by Armstrong and Earl Hines in 1928 on "Tight Like This."

Mingus was becoming known for his powerful and unprecedented virtuoso bass playing, but he added the raw power of the Black sanctified church to his mix, bringing that mix as close to the "Holy Ghost" as he could by mimicking the shrieks and cries and moans of those wanting to be anointed by celestial energy. Rarely did it sound fake or contrived when Mingus chose to use his voice as another instrument in his work or to demand of his players that they have more than one musical personality, which he also learned from Ellington, seeing how musicians could seem to have alternately lyrical or turbulent moods when instructed to play beautifully or get down there in a hole with a mute.

On *Tijuana Moods*, this can often be heard in the playing of trombonist Jimmy Knepper or trumpeter Clarence Shaw and saxophonist Shafi Hadi. The creation of a three-horn front line allowed them and their leader to reiterate another version of three-part melody invention and collective playing.

The rhythm section is mobile and superb, playing a variety of rhythms and knowing how to give the blues an anchor and a stomping beat-down when needed. This was Mingus's response to the two-horn unison playing—same note, same register—that pushed out collective playing, or the interpretations made by musicians who had the sophistication to play together and at the same time not step on one another's feet. This was one of his wishes that grew large, becoming an aesthetic star that still shines brightly from mood to mood, making jazz itself bigger.

George Russell also wanted to open a way for himself and restate the combining of European intellectual depth with blues and the power of swing, asserting the timbre and the originality of New Orleans color to what had happened when Charlie Parker and Dizzy Gillespie made their marks in the art. A former drummer, Russell made a handful of good albums with small groups and some big bands.

The best of the small groups is heard on *The Outer View*, an album that uses a three-horn front line like Mingus did, but the difference could not have been greater, outside of the rethinking of traditional concepts. The moods shift and so do the tempos. The reed and trumpet timbres reach as far back as far back goes, and the direction goes as far out as far out goes. But, unlike much of the pure noise that came out during Ornette Coleman's first years in New York, Russell's band sounds like professionals, not amateurs. Nor is this music full of practiced technique but devoid of beauty, which was the problem with a few of his small-group recordings.

Tenor man Paul Plummer had given up on the ugly sound that dominated most of the playing done seven months earlier on *The Stratus Seekers*. His sound is smooth and pretty but not sticky, far beyond wet cotton candy. He is inspired by the two other horns when they join in with him. Trumpeter Don Ellis took to the open brass world of fresh melodies, bold colors, and shocking register changes inspired by Coleman's sideman, Don Cherry. At this time, Cherry influenced men as different as Miles Davis, Bill Dixon, and Ted Curson. It was exciting to hear someone who could really play his instrument and who understood why New Orleans trumpeter Henry "Red" Allen was so great.

This is what makes *The Outer View* such a good set of performances. Every track is much more firmly grounded in the music itself than in the academy, or the so-called vanguard pretension that justified all ineptitude if there was enough talk about rebellion or spirituality attached. For a large contingent of the rebels, there seemed to be a fundamental adage keeping them together: If you can't play, pray.

MADE IN 1960, *Free Jazz* summed it all up. Ornette Coleman had many sad personal stories to tell about his life and how often he had been rejected by musicians who felt that he did not have enough jazz data mastered. Then something truly miraculous happened. In whatever order, Billy Higgins, Charlie Haden, and Don Cherry came to him, so moved by what he made them feel that they were ready to learn his music.

Pianist Dick Katz had not heard an alto and a trumpet play this closely since Charlie Parker and Dizzy Gillespie in the late 1940s. Cherry accepted the fact that Coleman could remember his tunes but did not write them in a way that a musician could read. Cherry was so touched that he took the time to learn what Coleman's scores should sound like. Higgins and Haden would practice tempos and beats alone, sometimes not stopping for an hour. They got as close as they could. So when Coleman's quartet opened at New York's Five Spot, it turned Manhattan's jazz community around, and some who were there remember loud arguments going on at the bar while the four men played. But drummer Roy Brooks remembered it this way:

> I heard the guys complaining about Coleman and his group not play-ing any changes. I heard that loud and clear, but I also heard some-thing else. And I *saw* something. Ornette and Don never looked at each other, no tempo was counted off, fast or slow, and nothing was said. Then wham! and they all came in together. Ornette played and I couldn't count any bars or hear the form they were playing. Then Ornette would end and Don would start immediately as if he knew what was going on. Still, nothing that could be counted, no bars, no form. When Don finished, they all came in together!
>
> It went on like that and it swung. It had the sound of the blues in it and they were all swinging their cakes off. I didn't know if I liked it, but I knew they had something going. It was mysterious but it had a groove.

Coleman made a series of recordings with that quartet and wrote music for many different ensembles, from string quartets to symphony orchestras, but what I consider his strongest success and boldest jazz inno-vation was homemade. He took nothing from the European disavowal of song. In the case of jazz that meant composed or improvised melody, melody dipped lightly or deeply in the indigo mood that has always given a certain human tinge to the moment. It was all about empathy and trust.

In December of 1960, Coleman took two quartets into a studio, set them in different tempos, wrote some dissonant battle cries, and produced *Free Jazz*, his strongest paean to New Orleans music. Bobby Bradford, who had recorded with Coleman and followed Cherry into the new 1961 quartet, says:

> For people to play with Ornette, they have to be sympathetic to the kind of music he loves to make. He is always willing to try to cross a cliff on a tightrope, but it is not a trick. He doesn't have any insincere notes in his music. All of it is real and you have to be real to play it. There are no road maps beside the melody. That was why so many people didn't understand what he was trying to do, which was figure out another way to play together, another way to listen. There were less rules to protect you, and Ornette had decided you did not need those rules to sound good. You could be inspired by your ear and your feeling. When you were up there with Ornette, you learned night after night how well he could hear and how much emotion went with his hearing.

That is not how Coleman's music was judged, however. What he was doing in order to retool jazz playing—without conventional chords, keys, or tempos—was thought to be another highway to chaotic disorder. As usual, jazz was caught between the shortcomings of show business and the insubstantial impudence of the academy. That is why exceptional musicians such as John Lewis of The Modern Jazz Quartet, Charles Mingus, and George Russell all supported what Coleman did.

Coleman's music is glorious and affirmative but remains a special taste fated for a smaller audience. In those transitional times, the popularity of Miles Davis, John Coltrane, Horace Silver, The Modern Jazz Quartet, and Art Blakey and the Jazz Messengers was far larger than Coleman's, but none of them were able to make it past the commer-

cialized funky soul movement of the time, the crucifix—once called
fusion—on the back of the art.

MUSICIANS ESTEEMED FOR their integrity began to submit to pop
music, regressing to adolescence rather than rising to the level of art.
Louis Armstrong showed us what could be done with popular material,
as did John Coltrane, who was set up in the catbird seat by "My Favorite Things," an accidental jazz hit. But that is not what was wanted this
time around.

The art began to waiver under the tasteless costumes and antics of
hip-hop, a doomed misunderstanding of the vitality that can come from
the street, from the point at which humanity manages to transcend disad-
vantage and hard times through community.

That community is always found in the blues, which is never limited to
the sordid subjects of pornography, the stripping away of a resonant inner
life from what can be romantic intimacy. A large but enhancing intimacy
is one of the gifts of art to its audiences. Like all art, blues contends with
the ironies that arise from being an individual and apart from everyone
else while being inextricably part of what living means. Jazz improvising,
always interwoven with the blues, stood for things like romantic love,
friendship, and trust.

But America returned to the dark ages when materialism and criminality became attractive and fashionable. Those in fusion music used
respectable track records in the jazz art to justify selling out. They had
already played plenty of music, was the argument, now was the time for
profit. Things were getting critical because this period of selling out was
celebrated as a new direction, an upsurge of power that would draw a
young audience who confused volume for fire.

At about that time Wynton Marsalis arrived in Manhattan. Marsalis has always irritated the jazz press because he refuses to buy into what Rimbaud termed "the love of sacrilege." He called the clichés as he saw them and stood up to all of those famous players willing to genuflect before fusion, before rock, and lastly before hip-hop. He did not accept ignorance and incompetence as a form of "authenticity."

Marsalis took the position that one did not have to be provincial; he set out to be an explorer of the depths of jazz in order to keep in touch with the purity of the art. He agreed with Albert Murray that timelessness was the best way to keep up to date.

Near the end of his career, Ellington said something similar whenever he introduced Money Johnson to let the audience hear what music would sound like in a hundred years: Johnson sang "Hello, Dolly" and gave an Armstrong impression. That made clear what Ellington thought about music: New stuff would always happen, but what Armstrong once called "the good old good ones" will perpetually remain in place. Picasso said it this way: "To me, there is no past or future in art. If a work of art cannot live always in the present, it must not be considered at all."

What the great painter said definitely applied to the surprising rise of Wynton Marsalis—who came out of nowhere, it seemed. He appeared at first as a woolly-headed country boy, from way down yonder in New Orleans, with his leather cap on backward. The newcomer to Manhattan went to Juilliard and was already one of the best concert trumpet players in the world, and his potential was recognized by master jazzmen such as Buster Williams, Ron Carter, and Woody Shaw.

He soon joined Art Blakey and began to quick-step away from what was expected. Having played both classical and tradition-rattling concert music, as well as popular funk stuff in New Orleans, he was overly impressed by neither. He was shocked when a purported innovator sat in on a blues session with Blakey's band and got lost; the man showed no mastery of a fundamental form and its feeling.

Working with one band led by another supposed innovator, Marsalis was disturbed when neither the leader nor any of his musicians could spontaneously harmonize themselves on "Just a Closer Walk with Thee." But whenever he got together with players such as John Lewis, Dizzy Gillespie, Elvin Jones, Ron Carter, Max Roach, Stan Getz, or Betty Carter, he found they were surprised that he had vehemently declined to buck dance with pop music.

The trumpeter made up his mind to play jazz, but not any particular style. Here his Crescent City background paid off. His playing displayed a freedom to access any style in the pursuit of his vision.

These were years of commercial mess and muddle, but Dexter Gordon returned from Europe in midlife vitality and reminded listeners how elegance, beautiful ballad playing, and hard-swinging blues should sound. His was a new kind of rebellion in jazz that should have been known as a *renaissance*, a renaissance that refused to be melted down into a lucrative but trivial product sold as a new version of a fine art that had made its reputation by rebelling against convention.

Gordon had a reputation from the days when bebop stood up and moved from pretentious eccentricity to form a legitimate style. During the 1970s, the trumpet was in big trouble, and there was only one large and famous talent left in Manhattan; a man who was unwilling to sell out. At every performance, he played as if it were his last night to live. That was Woody Shaw, who helped make the Dexter Gordon Quintet an almost peerless force. Though he wasn't a bebopper, Shaw held high the standards of the music and was something of an innovator. Like Gordon, who refused to be confined below the plateaus of his art by 2—5—1 bebop harmony, Shaw was also far above the Coltrane influence that too many musicians took seriously, thinking it placed them beyond the conventions of standard songs—which was possible but it could also make them sound like rats in a maze, chained to the wall of minor keys and modes. Coltrane did well inside his new conventions, but most of his imitators were hyperventilating, muscular bores. Woody Shaw was not one of them. He was a real swinger, a real inventor. Shaw even told his wife that Wynton Marsalis, though far from there yet, would play an important part in the future of jazz.

DECEMBER 1994 WAS a great month for jazz because Marsalis brought his band to the Village Vanguard to make a live recording of *Citi Movement*, a forty-minute composition that is one of the finest achievements in the history of the art. Jazz musicians love to dismiss displays of technique that have no soul, and they should. This was not one of those occasions. The finest leaders and composers in jazz have always shown through in the quality of players who create the context in which all of them work as featured and supporting players.

In *Citi Movement*, Marsalis and his band executed some very difficult material, with plenty of swerve, irony, humor, and swagger. We hear a comprehensive set of allusions to ragtime, New Orleans, Kansas City, bebop, and the developments made by talents as different as The Modern Jazz Quartet and Ornette Coleman, the dialogue between horns and ensembles, or the use of all four of the lead instruments to set material up against two or three parts simultaneously performed at the top, middle, or bottom of a voicing. These are fragments or motives from forthcoming melodies or those that had already been played.

Unity is all-important. Every note is an idea and is always moving forward, not static or undeveloped. At certain places, there are exchanges between Marsalis and Wessell Anderson, short responses from Gordon to a swift passage, setting up two ways to hear the space and the thematic development. Victor Goines introduces Eric Reed with some breaks that are delivered with swift but bracing effect. Just as George Russell's

"D.C. Divertimento" had to do with Black people taking the trains north from Dixieland, living soulfully inside the southern exposure, this is a portrait of New York City, from the streets to the high buildings to vistas filled with spark and romance.

The two brass features of Marsalis and Gordon seem to say all that there is to run down about country boys in the big city. Marsalis invents one of the premier statements of the era, improvising a single line that takes both the spare parts of a dialogue and its fast note return, both sides thematically laid out with red-hot technique and rhythmic nuance. It is virtuosic, as would be expected from perhaps the greatest trumpet player in jazz since Dizzy Gillespie—and surely one of the best bandleaders, a fact revealed by the context he creates with his players, whose abilities always reflect the leader.

Marsalis had confidence that the blues and swing could stand up to the culture of decadence. He was right. We still have many lessons to learn from what the grand masters of New Orleans had to say about the ability to listen to others and to react with creativity and with grace, and in that reaction *create a context for everyone*. E pluribus unum.

That is the democracy of jazz, and those who doubt it either haven't been listening or don't know how.

PART ONE

Outlaws and
Gladiators

This collection opens with a fusillade of S.C.'s core concerns: of hustlers, zealots, and tricksters; of rebellion as an American commodity; the romance of extended youth among adult men and women; jazz improvisation as democratic expression; the resilience of America's cultural vitality against scorn, adolescence, and sentimentality; opportunistic defeatists, peddlers of cant, and the "prematurely cynical." Against this backdrop, there is the dignity of a domestic worker who stands in the smoke and ruin of Watts. Crouch is at pains to connect specific incidents and localized atrocities to individual psychologies of victims and predators and to a neglect of the entire country's highest ideals.

Crouch's early work reflects his development from a poet and playwright in the Black Arts movement, one who had a more than passing acquaintance with Black nationalism and the academy, into a formidable reporter, cultural critic, and prose stylist. The earliest pieces in this part provide a window into future positions on figures as diverse as Amiri Baraka (né LeRoi Jones), Miles Davis, and James Baldwin; these early works contribute to an understanding of Crouch's development of "radical pragmatism" in his later career. They also reveal his thoughts on and participation in the avant-garde before his transition away from free jazz aesthetics, one of the very few from the scene who made such a journey. "Laughin' Louis Armstrong" was a personal triumph for Crouch, an essay that, along with "Papa Dip: Crescent City Conquistador and Sacrificial Hero" a few years later (1985), would almost single-handedly revise Armstrong's reputation, which was at an all-time low with arbiters of Black genius at the time of its publication. His arguments with Malcolm X and the root of his feud with Baraka are inside the tent.

Befitting the poet, the opening salvo is in the form of a poem and declares what would be a lifelong pursuit to rebuild "wingéd creatures."

AFTER THE RAIN

John's words were the words
Bird and the other wingéd creatures
sang:
    How the darkness could
    and would someday
    sink behind the sun,
    how we, when we grew
    to ourselves, past what we were,
    how we would dance outside
    bucking the eyes of all stars and all light
    how we would be as gentle
    as the rebuilt wings of a broken sparrow,
    how we would lick back the rain
    and wash ourselves with light
    and our eyes would meet His
    our God, our Om, our Allah, our Brahman.
    And we, like all oceans,
    would know
    and love each other.
    Salaam.

June 1968

LOOK OUT MOAN
WE STANDING ROUND

Previously unpublished, S.C. described this as a "flash essay," sending it along with a note to Larry Neal, scholar, poet, and a major catalyst for the Black Arts movement; it was discovered in Neal's papers at the Schomburg Center for Research in Black Culture.

WHAT IS NEEDED NOW is a National Black Arts Consciousness, a consciousness that would utilize the *substance* of Black culture as opposed to the *surfaces*, the merely slick, the only hipty-dip. This consciousness, with the artist as vessel, would at once create works that would function not only as expression but also as direction and destination. That is, a profound artwork is a story, a signpost, a place; a profound work telescopes whole epochs of meaning through its form, stretches substances to new places. Sun Ra and Duke Ellington are perfect examples of this. Both men carry with them the music of many men, many women, many forms of Black music, project the qualities that, as Ralph Ellison says, "endure through change." But these men are at once change themselves; for, to make change, to want change, one must *be* change. Dreams, memory, and disciplined invention for the pyramid of innovation and, as we must know, the innovator is always telling us how much of the future exists this very moment and how much the past has to do with this instant, this vision. . . . Consequently, we must absorb all that is of significance (significance, of course, being up to the individual) and telescope it into the world. Merely mentioning the names of former kingdoms and/or changing one's religion and name does not make for new art, new consciousness, new anything: becomes only name-dropping and pseudonyms for understanding. There are more important connections that are here to be made; I just looked at a quilt my grandmother made that cleans out most of the so-called cubist painting, Black or white, that I've seen. What does that tell us? Does it indicate that we should at most crossroads of artistic decision embrace the perpetual innovative qualities inherent in Black culture? I think it does. There are many things already there to be used. Romare Bearden knows this and so do Jacob Lawrence and K. Curtis Lyle and Quincy Troupe and Jayne Cortez and James Alan McPherson ("Solo Song for Doc") and others. In this hemisphere, not to mention this country, we have a million things to understand and explore and utilize before we even can begin to wonder about Africa as a direction giver. It is primal that bourgeois Negroes have always wanted to be some sort of elite other than straight-in Black American Nigguh Black. First it was white, then light, now, often, African. Always an elite, always something other than domestic nigguh self. Not that we don't have to clean up many things, change many things, remove shackles and the madness that they often create, but we do not have to pretend that we are not what we are. We do not have to imitate Africans with the same selfless sickness with which ofays imitate us. I believe Africans love Duke Ellington and Louis Armstrong because they are distinct, are unique, and are themselves come out beautifully another way. And that is what we are: another way. We are African stories told in another tongue, another tone, are as distinctly different but as much a unit as the styles of Duke Ellington and Sun Ra—to use a term of LeRoi Jones's, "the changing same." Hambone, in many ways, is more important to us than

Damballah. Hambone, the wandering mythic hero ("round the world and back again"). But, if a blend can be accurate, can be substantial and at the same time be another thing, such as the nasal African sound the Jihad Singers laid on R&B, then, on the real side, we're going somewhere because we are *domesticizing* influences, not just sucking in on something else. We have ring games, dozens, tales, macks, way out forms of worship, cuisine, new art in the radical way we reappropriate car designs and colors and so many other things. The point now is the same point that has always been the point: Can you play the Blues? And when I says the Blues I mean the national music consciousness, the nature of a people more than just sound, the "dance beat improvisional" approach to living that Albert Murray has pointed out, the continuity of self-knowledge Sun Ra's music indicates. Can you play the Blues. If you can, you can collect the knowledge and make the art happen.

August 1970

WHEN WATTS BURNED

It burst like a Mexican piñata stuffed full of statistics about economics, racism, and frustration. Some said that it was a setup, that the men who exhorted crowds on the streets in those first days and nights were not from Watts but were strangers working for some violent cause— Marxists or the ubiquitous CIA. I think it had more to do with younger Blacks who were exchanging the southern patience and diligence of Martin Luther King for the braggadocio of Malcolm X, made attractive by the Muslims' self-reliance program.

It also said something about the concepts of manhood, self-defense, and "justifiable revenge" that dominated much more television time than did the real suffering of the civil rights workers. Every tactic of King's was contradicted by weekly war films, swashbucklers, Westerns, and detective shows. Men did not allow women and children to be beaten, hosed, cattle-prodded, or blown up in Sunday school. Nonviolence, both as tactic and philosophy, was outvoted.

For all that, even though I was a member of the community and had seen many a confrontation between community people and police, I was not prepared for what I saw in these days. Sure, I had seen my street filled before with gang members beating each other over the head with tire irons, chains, bottles. But it was almost always possible for two police cars to break the thing up. And a year before the big riot, I had seen a smaller one take place at Jefferson High School when a pillhead had been arrested, and his sister, who had been trying to intervene, was pushed away. Bricks and bottles knocked down many police officers that day— but three drawn guns brought an end to it.

I had also read LeRoi Jones and James Baldwin, had felt enraged, but considered most of their threats no more than romantic literature or, at best, impotent fist-waving. Then, too, barbershops were always full of "would've, could've, and should've" conversations about violent reactions to the racial tensions of the period. I was bearing all of this, at nineteen, while writing speeches for an important person in Los Angeles's very nearly worthless poverty program. Because this person was an *expert* on the community, I was sent out there to find out what the disturbance was about in case the official ever had to speak authoritatively from a wellspring of hired information. Another street disturbance, I thought. Of course, I was wrong.

I never saw the very important woman who finally sparked it all. She was actually seen by very few, but for a moment she was every Black woman victim of white racism. She was part of a crowd that gathered to watch the arrest of a Black man. As the scene got heated, the story goes, she was singled out by the police and physically abused. But momentum swept away symbols, and she was soon forgotten as windows shattered under the weight of hurled bricks, tire irons, and feet.

People were in the street that night, Wednesday, August 11, talking rebellious talk, throwing bottles, milling around the projects on Imperial

Highway, a six-lane artery that ran east toward the white suburbs and west toward the Harbor Freeway, passing the borders of Watts.

They were still there the next day, and by that night they had started tearing things up. The next day, Friday the 13th, the crowds were bigger, covering the sidewalks of 103rd Street, a strip of stores that sold overpriced second-rate merchandise.

The police were obviously frightened—these Black people did not avert their eyes, did not tremble and stutter, but stared into their white faces with a confident cynicism, a stoic rebelliousness, even a dangerous mischief. This was unusual for Los Angeles Blacks, who long before had literally been whipped into shape by Chief Parker's thin blue line, a police force known in the community for shooting or clubbing first and asking questions later. No one was afraid of them now, and no one would follow the bullhorn orders to disperse. The police did not understand.

The store owners did. They left for home. Windows were smashed and goods snatched. A few arrests were made, and bottles bounced off the windows of police cars. The police made a show of force, a slow-moving line of fifteen or twenty police cars, provoking more bottles and more bricks. The police pulled out and the surge began in full force, taking 103rd Street before leaping like the proverbial wildfire over the whole Black community.

I had never seen anything like it before. It was a bloody carnival, a great celebration. Warring street gangs that had been shooting each other for the past two years were drunk in the park, laughing at overturned cars, stoning or stabbing random whites who mistakenly drove through the area, jubilantly shouting how "all the brothers are *together*." Men stood in front of stores with their arms full of dreams—new suits, appliances, hats. The sky was full of smoke and there was occasional gunfire. Well-known local winos reached for Johnnie Walker Black and Harvey's Bristol Cream, leaving the cheaper stuff to feed the flames. The atmosphere at first was festive. Then on Saturday, the National Guard went into action. With their arrival, the blood really began to flow. Within two days they had cordoned off the whole community.

Rumors sparked like random lightning about women and children being shot, and about subsequent cover-ups. Most of all, there was a feeling of occupation as the Jeeps rolled down the streets and the machine guns glinted in the sun, bayonets offering ugly invitations. Romantics thought the riot would take the state. But through the smoke I saw an older Black woman emerge from a display window from which she had just stolen a new domestic worker's uniform. To me, she seemed to say what it was really all about.

1977

DIMINUENDO AND CRESCENDO IN DUES

DUKE ELLINGTON AT DISNEYLAND

In outlines and correspondence, S.C. spoke of his intention to include this extraordinary piece of reporting and cultural geography, along with "Ellington The Player," in a future collection; inexplicably, neither was republished, until now. Ellington at Disneyland catches Crouch at a time when he was working out his style as a critic for Players *magazine (initially edited by Wanda Coleman) while developing his ideas on democracy, the fakery of corporate appropriation, minstrelsy, and the profound fear and pain of death that is so difficult for an American psyche. It's worth remarking that Crouch doesn't use the word kitsch in regard to Disneyland. Instead of keeping hi, low, and mid cult apart, à la Dwight Macdonald and Clement Greenberg, Crouch, the omnivorous humanist of empirical methods, gives us the wonderful world of Disney trying to ingest Ellington (and in the end, they speak to one another), marvelously. Crouch's power with details is shown here in Technicolor, as Paul Gonsalves strolls through the audience, "putting the bell of the saxophone close to a child in a stroller whose leg becomes a baton."*

In Southern California, in a very conservative area known as Orange County, Disneyland, an outpost of American power that parallels Hollywood, exists. It swells fake mountains into the air and hires middle-aged women to slide along wires and pretend to be fairies. In 1973, Duke Ellington played some of his final West Coast performances there. Considering his greatness and international renown, many would probably consider it a supreme irony. It was and it wasn't. For all the praise and glamour of his career, his craft was developed not in places of royalty and great concert halls but in theater shows, dances, and nightclub engagements. They demanded what he needed: the constant creation of new material to stave off boredom, probably the most democratic of American diseases. Like Shakespeare, as Albert Murray points out, Ellington toiled in the arenas of popular entertainment and created exceptional contexts for individual talents. And Disneyland, with all its abundant fakery and pretension, provided a perfect place for him to work his magic.

1. THE MAGIC KINGDOM

In Orange County, the land not only looks from the air like cancer cells, as Norman Mailer has pointed out, but also favors, when you get a grand view of the freeways, a very bizarre pinball game, the metal balls now shaped more like bugs looping and looping in the day or manic stars at night. Here, there is an abundance of amusement parks that are the descendants of the work of P. T. Barnum and Buffalo Bill and which exist, supposedly, for the amusement of children who were brought there in the first place by their parents, who cannot think of too many places that are not about constantly prefabricated minstrel shows orchestrated into a stampede away from the two things men are most sure of and most frightened of: pain and death.

Reactions to pain and death develop into what we call cultures. All men, all women, regardless of where they are in the world, live in societies that have shaped themselves on the basis of those two root realities. And it is the existence of those two constants and people's improvisations in the face of them that create either grand or bland societies, the recognized successes becoming what we call tradition: a continued sense of life. The tradition takes on grandeur if we—whether as mystics or politicians or artists or domestic workers or scientists or skycaps—can show that for all the inevitability of death's winning this fight, feinting constantly and predicting its knockout round with previews of jabs and hooks, that for all that, there are possible victories. Muhammad Ali's fighting Ken Norton for eleven rounds with a broken jaw in their first fight was such a victory. Ali was then fighting against a metaphorical death, becoming a has-been, and his victory over the elevated limitations of extraordinary talent, that place where courage itself becomes a refined form of genius, is a fresh area for consideration: the gladiator artist. It is only from here that we can *begin* to understand the wonders of Mr. Edward Kennedy Ellington and the lack of wonder, in a pall of smog, that strangles Southern California.

Wonder is an odd word for an American to use. It is particularly out-of-place in Southern California because it is too often confused with a benumbing befuddlement, or a collage of technological sleights-of-hand that are exposed as possible by somebody, so that the individual can confront emptiness with entertainment, or that great symbol of our time and our troubles: the arrangement of plastic flowers that seems almost real, yet absolutely free of the spreading browns and wiltings of time. And it is America's refusal to *openly* confront the terrors of pain and death that has led us to the bored, suicidal, "narcotic tobacco haze of capitalism" that swallows all in pursuit of the eternal that can be manufactured and absolutely manipulated. It is about traffic and streetlights ordering the death of night so consistently that when we must move beyond the prepared illuminations of urban life into the back countries of actual darkness, we feel that nature hasn't the right to treat us this badly, to gulp us down in its black coffee and chill us beneath its stars and that a full moon is not a blessing but a put-on. Given all this, Disneyland is a tastelessly and highly ornamented streetlight, while Duke Ellington is a soaring and elegant full-moon, vaulted and vaulting fire song that shakes hands with night and coldness to come out affectionately punching and dancing.

No, there is no magic at all to Disneyland, and that is the essence of its ugliness. It is a lacquered cigar band passed off as a diamond ring and is one of the capitals of our sadness; it is a corpse made of neon lights, plastic, concrete, and funny hats raised up just far enough to be passed off on the fool as a living thing. But there is no fool. Even the children do not believe there is any magic there: just rides and plastic elephants on metal poles spun at a comfortable speed that are supposed to be Dumbo flying if you have the right ticket to ride. There is, by all means, a wide cross section of miraculous technology at work there, but its uses—like the holograms in the Haunted House—are basically trivial. This very fault is what makes Disneyland so hideous—better, frightening: Some of the greatest reaches of human intelligence and intuition that quarter our memories of magic tales and push new information at us do momentarily astound but only as cleverness, never does the means fulfill itself. It is all for jokes and silly laughs. This is the greatest misuse of genius, and it is at the center of America's biggest problem: the squandering of resources—human, natural, or technical—and the trivialization of the profound. From here, all the sadness comes because we are witnessing stuffed angels polished and never changing, are offered no revelations other than surface discovery (no matter how profound), and find that after we gorge ourselves on all of this imitation and synthetic food, we are tired from going through the trip only, never from being full, are, in fact, bone-tired and starving.

Given all of that, when one begins to think about Walt Disney and all that he and his people put together, one begins to realize certain things about mixed blessings. The overall output of Disney Productions is as significant to the American identity of our space in time as mass production, for it is not at all difficult to recall that many children growing up during the Eisenhower era watched *The Mickey Mouse Club* and *The Walt Disney Show* with the deepest reverence because they provided, along with entertainment, all kinds of information about the workings of the natural world. Time-lapse photography, microscopic lenses, and extended film projects produced material that made the growth of plants or the developments of insect life take on a drama and a power that wiped out most of the public school offerings and gave a sense of legitimate wonder to the world, to African lions, desert life, birds, the universes within drops of water and very obviously helped pave the way for things such as Sesame Street—an unarguably important contribution.

However, when we start picking through the output of Mr. Disney's work, we find that after the contributions to scientific documentaries and the entertaining way in which something like the opposable thumb could be explained through a cartoon showing an ape try to use a hammer, most of the other stuff is trite, sentimentalized nonsense and results in a greater understanding of the complexities of the nonhuman world than of our own. Those of us who went past the cartoon versions of the fairy tales and really read *Peter Pan*, *The Wind in the Willows*, *Alice in Wonderland*, or Davy Crockett's autobiography—not to mention Joel Chandler Harris—found that something was shaky: Disney and his people had removed almost all of the sub-meanings in favor of quick understandings and cloyed drawings; the result of which was, and is, that many, many people now probably think they *did* read Lewis Carroll as they sit turning in a gargantuan tea cup in Fantasyland or that they *did* study American history as they take the riverboat into Frontierland. And that is the horror, the razor blade in the bag of books: So much of America and Western culture has been turned into *unresonant* myth that we find insects and lions more interesting than other people and more easy to identify with. Witness the love of dogs and pets, those uncritical faithfuls Americans have, and how much more quickly they'll call the police on you for beating a dog than a wife or abusing a child. Walt Disney and his imitators have a lot to do with this. In short, their bucket has a hole in it.

2. THE MAESTRO IN THE MAGIC KINGDOM

All the way there everything is the same. It is probably easier to get lost in Southern California than just about any place other than a desert of sand dunes because they have made very sure that all is one and one is all—the tract homes (which are nothing more than horizontal apartment houses with fences and sterilized alleys rather than hallways), the gas stations, and the unreasonable facsimiles of restaurants repeat themselves with such regularity, motion seems an illusion. Then you notice that *Last Tango in Paris* is playing at a theater, here in Orange County, where the superintendent of schools had John Hersey's *Hiroshima* and Joan Baez's autobiography removed from the libraries for being subversive. How did it get there? Will the movie house be closed, the film confiscated? Apparently not. Strange. Very much so, this film being a frontal attack on American myth and probably the greatest and most adventurous performance ever given by a white American, Brando almost reaching the magnificence of the Black music, using a violent and frail lyricism that broods and bursts into a victorious expression of our American terror, our American sadness. But traveling farther into Orange County, we realize that the constancy of mediocrity can prevail in even the most emotional of storms, whether they are focused by a growing giant such as Bertolucci or a durable magician such as Mr. Ellington. Again, with the rarity of unique landmarks in this county, we wonder whether, as we pass *Last Tango*, we are moving into the past or the present. Neither. We are always moving into the same thing. Therefore, we are very unhappy, very bored, and very dangerous. If we pretend there is happiness here, that these constant reflections of a few prefabricated decisions bring about happiness, there is more than a hint of the kind of tragic surrender and masochism that fuse and flare into the madness of the housewife piling the bodies of her murdered children in her suburban bathtub and awaiting the return of her husband, or, the husband quietly going on the job and shooting everybody in the office or factory where he's been showing that "selfless and cooperative" smile for the last twenty years.

We are almost there, the brilliant red flare-ups of brake lights telling us we are getting close to something many people are interested in for one thing or another. We see then:

DISNEYLAND
THE KING FAMILY
DUKE ELLINGTON—DAWN

What *dawn* has to do with it, we never find out. Stop at the tollgate of the parking lot and give up fifty cents. Into it. A gigantic parking lot and thousands of cars. The monorail passes overhead. On to the gate where general admission is $4 and you feel as though you're running a game on Disneyland because you can hear Mr. Ellington for so small a price. The girl is asked as she sells you your ticket where one goes to hear Duke Ellington.

"Duke Ellington? Oh, he's at the end of Main Street."

She's not lying, at the end of Main Street, as he has always been—

rather, beyond Main Street. Into Disneyland through a turnstile and it is
then every man or woman for self. One is suddenly swallowed or caught
in a pincer movement of fraudulence and sentimentalized American anti-
quarianism. This is Main Street. Keystone Cops, balloons shaped like the
cartoon head of an internationally famous rodent. Polished cobblestones.
One walks quickly past the plaza that offers a barbershop quartet replete
with striped shirts, straw hats, suspenders, and handlebar mustaches in
the afternoon. Not now, though. It is night. Bells are heard ringing and
you are rushing because the squeeze horns with the rubber bulbs on the
simulated running-boarded cars and the ringing of the horse-drawn trolley's bell seem to tell you the first performance is almost about to jump
off. Moving though the smells, the sweaters, the questions, the cotton
candy, the cloyed explanations, and the flat, harsh refusals, over the gray
rising helmet of a Keystone Cop who swings his night stick with the
innocence of uninformed rehearsal, one can see the concrete Matterhorn,
which contains a hole near the top so that one of the rides, something of
a ski lift, can pass through, and one can also observe Americans screaming in plastic bobsleds attached to rails that cut through and around this
concrete mountain.

We are now at the end of Main Street. Here is where the Ellington
Orchestra resides for six nights. The Plaza Gardens. It is a carousel minus
the horses. The roof is red and white and is held in the air by red and white
poles that match the red and white floor. There are security guards here
wearing Marine spats and flashlights in place of service forty-fives. They
are here to control the crowd, which is queued up four and five deep at the
ropes that keep the intrepid from stumbling out on the floor and block-
ing someone's view. One has the right here to block the view of others
only if one is dancing. There is no standing around. Even though one is
irritated, it is good to see the participants getting first choice as opposed
to the spectators. Almost all of the orchestra is on the bandstand. They

are in white tuxedo jackets and black pants. Shoes, ties, and neck straps for saxophones are obviously about individual color choice and result in a subtle rainbow speaking under its breath. The bass and drums are played by Black men. The trumpets are all Black. The trombones and a French horn are white (though one of the trombone players has the dark hair and handsome features so often misnomered as "Latin" when Afro-Hispanic might be more accurate). All of the reeds are Black except for our Portuguese ally, Mr. Paul Gonsalves, who is called by Maestro Ellington "the hero of the Newport Festival" for his legendary riot-quelling extension of blue tenor saxophone cookery in a long solo at the 1956 Newport Jazz Festival. Someone will tell you, though, very quickly, in a whisper or a shout, "Aw, man, Paul Gonsalves ain't white. He one of them Por-te-gee Newport New nigguhs." (One never knows. DO ONE?)

They are sitting or joking or warming up horns, checking reeds and mouthpieces, tuning strings, making sure drumsticks have personal balance and that cymbals are in place, adjusting chairs so that one can find the most comfortable position from which to play. Cigarettes dangle from some mouths, and they stare or ascend the bandstand as does Cootie Williams, with a baleful elegance, all the way up to the last row and the last trumpet chair to the left. He holds his silver trumpet in one hand and sits forward, his back free of the chair and his body at an angle of rueful perception. But he is looking at no one. Perhaps. Perhaps he is looking at Bubber Miley or Sam Nanton, possibly Johnny Hodges. Whatever, his eyes are focused in the direction of the Matterhorn. It is doubtful that he sees that, though he might be imagining sailing through the hole in the mountain behind his horn like a hip, Botticelli angel announcing the arrival of a major event. It is here, the major event, beginning out of nowhere: C JAM BLUES. Mr. Williams does not feel like coming down to the microphone, so he just rears back in his seat and turns his Black face into a balloon and that balloon intimidates his horn into stepping its music right in front of the band. Mr. Cootie Williams's power out front, slicing and smearing holes in the air, squeezing a sullen yet lyric mucus from the now-beginning light, light breeze, a combination, this music, of honey and acid, pathos, put-on, and jubilance. He is the great trombonist Sam Nanton's brother on a smaller horn, capable of turning a guffaw into a cough, a gurgle, a death rattle, a litany, or a funeral march before grabbing one last note that is sucked on like a mocking standard that is borne above it all. The horn is snatched away from the mouth suddenly as though someone has just poured boiling hot sauce into the mouthpiece, and Williams's face takes on the cast of a cultivatedly dignified snarl, his right shoulder comes up, the horn is now held by one of the curves in the tubing and he is gone, boring another hole in the concrete Matterhorn.

The next piece played is a selection from Ellington's *Togo Brava Suite* that is dedicated to an African beach. During this selection, alto saxophonist Geezil Minerve humorously strikes one index finger on the other in imitation of a percussionist. Following the applause, there is a silence and the Maestro, the *Chief,* comes on stage *in* that walk, that stride that is itself as much a garment or a place as a form of travel. It is a succession of moves that contain the wit, the sensuality, the timidity, precision, and good-natured arrogance that are at the center of the Blues. It is shrouded in myth and a familiarity with wicked and aristocratic places and befits the Lord of the Worlds of Sound, who is also a folk hero, a warrior, a historian, a dignity, and a homemade Black American aristocrat. The Chief is here.

Always a sartorial wizard, the Chief is wearing a very mellow blue suit that is neither dark nor light, collared blue shirt with horizontal "Broadway pleats," as he calls them, a bow tie that is almost a cowboy tie, is almost knotted too large, the bow stopping, like the lapels of his coat, just short of hideous taste, right in the center of disciplined audacious. Elegant, but with that whip and twist of the unfamiliar that seems to telescope his musical victories through his attire. On his feet he wears dark socks and some blue leather that is a personal cross between moccasins and ballet slippers. Ready for the dance.

He goes to the piano after greeting the audience and starts prowling and swooping through the introduction to "Rockin' in Rhythm." This time he has decided to stretch the dancing rhythms that are a combination of stride and ragtime gestures with the symbolic jerks and twists of the whole Afro-American torso in action, at work on the dance. But tonight he is stretching all the motives over the time with a sardonic angularity that is held together by one of the most subtle rhythmic imaginations in twentieth century music. It is strut-march-dance fragmented, splayed, dangled, furled, expanded and contracted; calling, reminiscing, predicting. It is an introduction, this section also known as "Kinda Dukish," to use the words of Julio Cortázar's fictionalized Charlie Parker character, Johnny Carter, which is a kind of playing that seems ". . . like a birthday party or a decent action." And, of course, when a live performance is as vital as the Chief's, it is a birthday party for life itself, a celebration of presence and memory, a gesture of affectionate decency.

The orchestra enters. The swing is affirmative, joyful, informed and at once contemplative, raw, frail, and powerful. It asks questions and answers them with brazen mockery. The complexity of the calls and the responses, the range of colors and the shifting rhythms point up some facts about the dynamics of musical styles. Every stylistic offshoot of a general dynamic develops its own laws, its own standards and insights so completely that whole schools of playing can result from a few men concentratedly developing a few bars of a master's solo or composition (or a couple of bars from a few of each) into a musical worldview or system that will affect every musician dealing with the general dynamic from that moment forward. (I said that to say that) much of what we take for granted in large ensemble playing is the result of the Chief's expanding innovational brass techniques,

such as the use of the bathroom plunger, into a whole functional theory of
sound that was worked out record after record in the 1920s and the 1930s.
He expanded, amplified, and subtly refined the adventurous aspects of
Louis Armstrong's innovations in melody, phrasing, and swing for a large
and bustling ensemble in which the conventional front line of the New
Orleans bands of trumpet, clarinet, and trombone were projected into a
musical house of mirrors in which each instrument was itself and more
than itself. Trumpets could be blasting instruments full of burning coals
or they could carry melody or become drums or squawk, whisper, sing, or
grumble in voices codified by plungers or totally fresh fingering. Trombones had the same flexibility and could be heard as *bigger* drums, louder
voices that could fuse the pathos and mockery of the trumpets. The reed
section not only had the responsibility of sounding like drums and voices,
creating polyrhythms, accentual punctuations, and carrying the melodies and counter melodies, but also it was to become Ellington's home-
wrought string section—and one that gave the string sections of Europe
their walking papers.

All of it, too, with the extraordinary palette of colors that are a keystone
of Ellington's genius, created a range of complex emotional dispositions
over a jubilant rhythmic base of prancing drums. It is a brilliant extension of the polyrhythmic underpinnings of all African-derived music that
brings about, for instance, a double consciousness in which the melancholia
of a melodic line can be counterstated by great celebration in the rhythmic
foundation. That is to say that sorrow and celebration can be fused into a
structure that creates, with a vibrant dialectic, a third entity that more perfectly mirrors the paradoxical emotions of modern life, with all its simultaneous contradictions, than any other single art form. It is the essence of
jazz, African American music, Great Black Music, or whatever you want
to call it, and Edward Kennedy Ellington, up there turning those plungers
into magic masks, has been rattling the frontiers for half a century.

"Rockin' in Rhythm" finishes its tour, which includes Africa, the West Indies, and Harlem (which is both of them in an American translation), and the Chief, his body now brown steam, is at the microphone. After telling the audience that they, with their response, are very warm and very gracious, he says, "I would now like to introduce our newest arrival and the youngest member of the band, our piano player." He gestures toward the piano and, as the late Ralph Gleason pointed out, for a moment, we think we see someone sitting there. Ellington seats himself, removes the handkerchief that covers a glass of his customary soft drink, which is always placed on the piano before he makes his appearance, takes a sip, pulls up each pants leg about two inches or so, spreads his feet, hunches his shoulders, and begins to play.

A waltz is where the music opens, the Maestro tracing melody lines across the air with a control of time and pulsation that is almost shocking in its range. It seems as though each beat is five feet wide. He twists, pinches, and savors each note with the art of a past master constantly broadening the range of his victories. Time is at the center of what he does because so much of the rhythmic force of his playing depends on *inflection*: The *sound* of the rhythm is part of the rhythm. Ornette Coleman has said, as if it were Ellington talking, that the very same notes played in a happy song should not *sound* the same if they are played in a song that is sad. Meaning should color sound. This is one of the reasons why the Chief never really plays the same thing twice: He never means the same thing. He is going, always, farther home, into more lyric and pulsive ambiguities, opening new doors for himself. And this is Billy Strayhorn's "Take the A Train."

The meter changes to four/four, and Ellington the Bear is charging the piano with massive swing, climbing trees and chewing berries. His ankles seem to be roaring, his shoulders pushing the sound up into the air. Head forward, each line in his hands seems to color the music. The ordered violence of his swinging phrases summons the image of a great swimmer thrashing through butterfly strokes, the spray bouncing off the cymbals and the way being made for the full ensemble and soloist.

Enter: One of the favorite sons of 1940. And who is to come down from the highest-level brass seats of the band but Mr. Cootie Williams himself, at the solo ready. People laugh, applaud, or sigh with recognition when the familiar theme, which is something of an urban cultural anthem, is struck up by the band. Williams is a Black, vibrating growl waiting to leap into the party, polish off the drinks, argue about the bill, become cavalier about the whole thing, and hiss or mutter complaints with a jagged nobility. The musical curtain is raised, and the horn or Williams is rendering the famous solos of Ray Nance and Rex Stewart with the same rebellious singularity he gave Bubber Miley's improvisation on the re-created "Creole Love Call" of the 1930s. At this point, his role is the same as that of a musician working in the European concert tradition, with the exception that the composition he is interpreting was retained by electronics rather than notation. Avant-garde as ever, he is using all those strange rhythmic combinations: the staccato dotted notes that come off as sardonic hesitations, as threats, as malicious mischief; the growls that are anguish or joy raised way, way up. Never nostalgia, never sentimentality, just snarling power: decapitated chickens flying the air and becoming swans, like Henry Pace's Black Swans of the old "race" records. Then, too, Williams is up there going through a parody of the arm-waving, eye-rolling minstrel as the band puts a bridge between his solos before he reassumes the elevated stance and facial expression of a bear who has cultivated a sore head for over forty years. Few people ever pick up on this, but it is one of the most scalding put-downs of what is expected of Black musicians you ever will see. He always does it, and it always has the same edge. Babo shaving Benito Cereno. It is magnificent satire and is pushed forward by the twitches of Williams's muscles, the same muscles he uses to kick his notes out of his horn, playing, as Miles Davis says he does, from his legs: each spurt given precision by a well-understood bump or a very, very thin grind. An overdone bow that is another put-on and he moves, with the conclusion of the piece, back up the stairs to the brass seats.

We have just heard an aesthetic scientist at work, for Mr. Cootie Williams is one of those men who, with Ellington's insistence and encouragement, explored the trumpet and its relationship to the plunger and came up with a new and extraordinarily subtle arsenal of possibilities for the brass player. It is as Buckminster Fuller says, "Every great artist is a scientist, and every great scientist is an artist. They are both inventors." And an inventor is what Mr. Williams is all about. Following the lead and tradition established in the Ellington Orchestra by Bubber Miley, he has given things to the horn that Miles Davis is now using on an electrified wah-wah hook-up. However, the range of cracks, whispers, shouts, growls, slurs, and bums that Mr. Williams is master of makes most so-called modern trumpet players seem very conventional (Albert Goldman's calling his techniques "illiterate stammerings" is a complete misreading of the case). Cootie Williams is a great artist, a great scientist, and a great inventor.

The Chief is again at the piano, and we notice that the tempo has gone up just a little and "How High the Moon" is being plucked out of the piano in a manner that prefigures the sound and phrasing of Thelonious Monk. Down from the brass seats comes Johnny Coles, light-skinned, glass-wearing, on his head a beaded African cap, his neck and hands showing pink blotches that look like the result of having been badly burned at one time. Change is here. Coles is coming out of the aesthetic developed by Charlie Parker, Miles Davis, and Thelonious Monk. It's like an earthquake, like hearing what bop must've sounded like when it first hit the scene, and the Chief is right on it. Whatever Coles sets up is turned around so fast it raises the eyebrows of the piano notes in a way that creates a trialogue: trumpet to piano, piano to bass and drums, bass and drums back to trumpet. Ellington is, as Dizzy Gillespie has said, "the greatest comper (accompanist) in the world." We now hear "Ornithology," Parker's melody, blasted by the band over the chords of "How High the Moon." It is Ellington again maintaining things he feels are important to the tradition, just as he has written riffs of the legendary Savoy Sultans into his pieces and carried the message of Louis Armstrong, Sidney Bechet, Sam Nanton, and many others around the world (as the legacy of Johnny Hodges's phrasing is now consciously part of the band's sound).

As Coles's feature ends with a blast, the audience is noticeably getting bigger and dancing more or getting ready to dance. Those of us at the ropes keep feeling somebody pushing at us, feel the crowd opening up and whispers floating through the air. All kinds of people are there, and you wonder if any other performing artist in America pulls such a varied audience. You see Black people who, like the band, are every shade from twelve noon to midnight and shift in attitude from Black nationalists to conservative middle-income doctors and lawyers. You see rednecks, Jews, Chicanos, Africans, and just about everything you would imagine. All in some similar way reverent before Mr. Ellington's music. Little kids in sweatshirts are allowed space in the front so they can see Duke Ellington. There he is. The one at the microphone.

"And now, ladies and gentlemen, I would like to introduce the hero of the Newport Festival, Mr. Paul Gonsalves, who will overindulge himself as a strolling violin. Paul Gonsalves."

Gonsalves, the sidewinder, the will-o'-the-wisp, steps from the bandstand and begins limping through the audience as he plays "In a Sentimental Mood." He plays to the people at the few tables allowed on the corners of the dance floor and puts the bell of the saxophone in the faces of children who are mutually awed and embarrassed, thrilled and made special. This is by no means a gimmick, as Gonsalves is playing beautifully, an aural smoke working its way out of the horn. His sound is plaintive, bitter with the taste of sorrow, but carried by a mysterious and durable romanticism inherited from Ben Webster that is a trademark of the collective Ellingtonian vision. It perpetuates a sense of romance more consistent and more real than just about anything we hear in America or have had the opportunity to hear for so long. All the scars are fingered and detailed along with the fond recollections. Every version of actual romance beyond the bandstand, draped around the notes, is focused by this orchestra as Gonsalves strolls, stopping near us and putting the bell of the saxophone close to a child in a stroller whose leg becomes a baton as the Hero seems, as he always does, to be wrestling the music up out of the tenor.

Gonsalves is back on the bandstand now and the dancers are coming out in full force, covering the striped floor with a range of American dance that is astonishing. For one thing, the most contemporary Black American variations are shot out, not by Black dancers, but by two Asians. Quick finger-poppin' and slick steps just a shade off the time, but cool. There is a white couple right out of the middle working class. She is blond and wearing a mini-skirt (you have to get to Orange County for that to still be going on); her husband is dark-haired and wearing a white shirt and unzipped windbreaker, his dark pants and shoes a contrast to his wife's long legs and bright red shoes. They dance just about every tune for all four sets, older ballroom dances, but joyfully vital, not square at all. A huge Jewish guy is out there dancing like a bear. There are taught dancers and intuitive dancers who try to equal the creativity of the band; shy dancers and young Black and white couples who take it all as a joke from the past that they suddenly find themselves enjoying on another level when they get into it. The younger whites on the dance floor study the moves of the few Black teenagers who arrive, trying out what the next thing will be. But the older white dancers pay no attention to anything other than the band. They have reached their kingdoms of actual magic.

It gets colder.

The Maestro rises from the piano and comes to the microphone as a little Black boy in a hooded sweatshirt starts moving past the bandstand, which is only a foot or two above the dance floor. As the boy gets in front of the Chief, he turns his head, looking up at Ellington, who brightly smiles, "Hold it, young man. Come here, would you? Step right up here. It's not far. Good. Now come over here and sit at the piano. Fine. Play something. It's all right, everyone's listening. Good. Mmmm. C. All right, blues in C."

The bass and drums begin playing and members of the band start puttering around with some riffs. The little boy begins tentatively, but very quickly begins sounding like a surreal Count Basie.

"Stop," Ellington, "you sound too good." Everything halts and the Chief helps the little boy off the bandstand. "Thank you. You know you can't let them play too long. The way things happen to be, quite a few people might start mistaking him for the real thing. And now, ladies and gentlemen, we are going to show you what music will sound like one hundred years from today. Little Money Johnson is going to show you what music is going to sound like exactly one hundred years from today in this asphalt, air-conditioned, *plastic*, prefabricated *jungle*. Little Money Johnson, ladies and gentlemen, Little Money Johnson!"

People are staring and smiling as Money Johnson comes down from the trumpet section, his arms free, subtle dancers, laughing along with his stride, an almost hectic step marshalled by dance time. The Master is at the piano, and the band starts stretching out into dissonances and splintered phrases that are, at bottom, full of mockery. Money Johnson is at the door of a music we're completely surprised by as he counts off two bars for the band and they begin "Hello, Dolly," red beans and ricefully

Louis Armstrong style. The audience breaks up as he wipes the white wing of the handkerchief across his face, and all those images of the man trumpeter Bobby Bradford calls "His Majesty, Louis the First" swell like a huge heart before us. And, yes, people, it is much more than a joke Ellington is telling us: He is saying with a prayerful, irreverent confidence that Louis Armstrong's music is going to BE here. Is going to BE here.

It gets colder.

The remainder of the set includes beautiful renditions of "Sophisticated Lady" and the interminable last note the peerless baritone of Harry Carney achieves by circular breathing (a technique that involves blowing out and breathing in at the same time), "Creole Love Call," a few broad and charming vocals by a lovely brown singer from Texas named Anita Moore, and a get-up-with-it Ellington version of rhythm and blues entitled "One More Time" that is sung by the band's "jackleg preacher," Tony Watkins. On this last piece the whole band moves from a rocking groove into complete ensemble improvisation, and a white girl comes from backstage with a tenor saxophone to join in as the Maestro stands in front of the proceedings dancing with the grace of all his seventy-four years and the moves and attunement of the Black teenagers on the floor who are obviously shocked. He finishes with a hip-shaking flourish and strides off the bandstand, leaving the orchestra to finish up with what has become a king-sized New Orleans blues bash with contemporary underpinnings. The audience is ecstatic.

Almost as soon as he gets off the bandstand, drummer Rufus Jones puts on an overcoat and fur-lined gloves. Many members of the orchestra follow suit or scurry for coffee, hot chocolate, or private firewaters. Cootie Williams is having himself a large helping of chili and beans while passing band members look on with what appears to be animosity and dismay. Many other band members are listening to fans talk about how long they have been listening to Ellington's music. Harry Carney, who is in his late sixties but looks forty, graciously smiles as listeners who go way back ask him when he's going to start getting older, come up with some gray hair and some wrinkles. The Maestro is busy charming the various ladies who come up to him, always ready with a compliment that is delivered with the choicest diction. What is most memorable, though, is his standing on the dance floor, surrounded by teenagers and signing autographs.

With each succeeding set, it grows colder and band members are heard to complain more and more. "Four sets in this goddam cold-assed weather. Shit. What they want to do—work us to death?" Another band member will shrug, agree, or wrap up more tightly in his overcoat, rushing for more coffee. But, when they return to the stand, they play well, going on with the show, glittering in the arena.

Midway through the next to last show, I strike up a conversation with someone who has worked with the band for quite some time and is very close to Ellington. Actually, it wasn't so much a conversation as it was a listening and learning experience.

"As you can see, the weather is really dragging the band. And then you know that Duke and Paul both have terrible arthritis, and this weather isn't helping either case. The contract said four shows a night for six nights, so, four shows it is. Funny, you know, the people out here love the music so much they probably don't realize what those guys are going through up there with those open tuxedo coats. But, then, it isn't always this bad, and Duke's used to it. Over the years they've played worse places. They've played better ones, too. In fact Duke told me about the best treatment he's ever gotten. It was when he went to Russia. Can you believe that? He said that when he went over there he wanted to be a good American and maintain a jaundiced eye and secretly, but graciously, maintain his feelings about things over here. The opportunities and things of that sort. But he said that as soon as they got there they were greeted warmly at the airport, immediately taken to a very fine hotel with excellent service to freshen up and from there to see the Bolshoi. Following the performance, they were introduced to the troupe who received them as artists and taken from there to a reception where Khachaturian and other Russian composers were with records, asking questions about the music and requesting autographs. Duke said he was overwhelmed. It was the first time in his entire career that he was given the *complete* feeling of being an artist. Oh let me get back to my seat, the last set is about to start."

The members of the band are milling around, the younger ones grumbling, the veterans like Carney and fellow reed master, Russell Procope, stoic. Ellington goes to the piano as though he is at home or in a hotel room and starts playing around with a few lines at the keyboard. The lines coalesce into "Jump for Joy," a song from a musical of his written in the early 1940s that mocked and satirized the idea of Black social progress in the urban North, as well as the minstrel stereotypes in films such as *The Green Pastures*. Rather than the exuberant bounce of the original, he chooses a ballad tempo, and what results is a reflective hymn of the intricacy of struggle—the victories, the losses, the momentary truces, and the durability needed if one is to step into the gladiator arena of popular art. Or, life for that matter. There is not the most minuscule tinge of self-pity, maudlin polemics, or sociological sorrow songs. It is more like a great warrior sharpening his sword or cleaning the barrel of his rifle. Or a call to arms, for when the members of the Duke Ellington Orchestra come back to the bandstand, they play with a feisty triumphance that beams through the air as the lights of the various entertainment sectors begin to go off and Disneyland, the pinnacle of American amusement parks, prepares to close.

June 1976

JAZZ LOFTS

A WALK THROUGH THE WILD SOUNDS

I T WAS A LONG WAY FROM BERLIN, but there was George Gruntz, director of the prestigious Berlin Jazz Festival, lounging in the hall-way of a loft at 24 Bond Street. He was on the track of the newest artists on the jazz scene—the innovators of loft jazz—and he tilted his head as music suddenly erupted inside the loft. A rehearsal was under way in Studio Rivbea. Reed master Sam Rivers, who founded the studio with his wife, Bea, was leading the woodwind section of his big band. It sounded like the blues reinvented. Gruntz was exuberant. "The music Sam is making—it is so beautiful! There is nothing like it in the old clubs or in Europe. Only here in the lofts is there such exciting music—so many new ideas, such enthusiasm, such control of the instruments. It's the most exciting jazz in town."

Gruntz is one of a growing number of smart talent brokers who have learned to veer off the beaten path in search of the new jazz. The boundaries of the loft scene stretch south from SoHo to the Lower East Side, up to the East and West Villages and into the mid-20's. The emergence of these jazz lofts, like that of various "little" magazines and SoHo art galleries, was a reaction to the closed doors of the professional marketplace. Though the music they are creating has broken the bounds of familiar jazz, both in form and instrumentation, the burgeoning loft movement is reminiscent of the historic gatherings of jazz musicians that took place in New Orleans and Chicago in the 1920s, Kansas City in the 1930s, and New York in the 1940s. On a given afternoon or evening, one might hear a solo saxophone performance, a trio of violin, bass and drums, a woodwind quartet, or witness a sudden dancing party, as with Hamiet Bluiett's big band. There is a great feeling of elation about most of the performances, in stark contrast to the grayness and despair that pervade much of contemporary avant-garde music.

The radical new-jazz era came into being with the arrival of alto saxophonist Ornette Coleman, who made his debut in 1959 at the legendary—and now defunct—Five Spot. His method of playing caused a "Rite of Spring"–like hysteria among musicians. The sounds from the bandstand seemed more like a barnyard riot than a musical debut. The drummer didn't swing to a foot-tapping beat; the trumpet gurgled; instead of wailing, the saxophone yelped, screamed, and grunted; the bass emitted random thumps. Many considered it anarchy, at best.

Perhaps the most startling result of Coleman's innovations was seemingly to boil away the glue that had always bound improvisatory groups together. He created a quasi revolution that fractured the jazz community. The controversy quickly made Coleman a "hot property," capable of filling any club in New York. But he made no money. Eventually, the saxophonist went into what was called "retirement" by the jazz press but is more commonly known as unemployment. Between 1962 and 1965, he tried to open a club of his own but lost money again. In the process, however, he had become a symbol for musicians of new possibilities not only in music but in business as well.

While Coleman was battling to find a place to play, the movement that had sprung up around him began to grow. Musicians were discovering new rules to break. The music became wilder and wilder and the money thinner and thinner.

Club owners had little interest, and the core serious players found themselves always looking for work. In the late 1960s, LeRoi Jones's articles in *DownBeat* about the Black avant-garde initially drew a lot of attention to the new jazz, but as Jones's ideas became increasingly dominated by Black nationalism, club owners, listeners, and white jazz writers began to associate the new sounds with Black hostility. To whites hearing these fiery ensembles, the music seemed to be a baton passed on from the Nation of Islam to the Watts rioters. At the same time, many of the younger players came to resent the term *jazz* altogether, feeling that it was just another term for *nigger*. They referred to what they were playing as "Black music" and verbally attacked the jazz press for what they thought was favoritism to white musicians. As a consequence, their music was perceived as nothing more than an expression of hatred toward whites. The upshot, of course, was that the proponents of the music were more cut off from the marketplace than ever before. They began to look for alternatives.

Rashied Ali, a drummer who played in the historic John Coltrane quartet and now owns one of the most important loft clubs, Ali's Alley, explained the genesis of the jazz lofts. "They started as places to rehearse and jam. Then like in the 1920s, they turned into 'rent parties.' Back in the 1960s, you could get a loft for next to nothing—just to watch the building for a cat who didn't want to brush the bums off his doorstep. At first, you had to know a musician to get into the loft; then, little by little, the musicians started charging a dollar, dollar fifty, entrance fee."

In 1972, a crucial event occurred. When the director of the Newport Jazz Festival, George Wein, shifted the festival to New York, he hired mostly traditional players to perform. Angered by this exclusivity, trumpeter James DuBoise, bassist Juma Sultan, and saxophonist Sam Rivers joined a crowd of new-jazz musicians who squeezed into Studio We to complain, argue, and—finally—to organize a counterfestival that took place in eighteen locations around the city. The following year, Wein responded by incorporating many of the new musicians into his festival. They have been gaining steadily in popularity ever since.

STUDIO WE, RUN by DuBoise and Sultan, is one of the earliest jazz lofts. It is located in the squalor of a slum at 193 Eldridge Street, not far west of the famous Katz's Delicatessen. The studio stands apart from the gutted buildings, broken sidewalks, and manic sadness of the neighborhood. Its building is brightly painted. The first floor, which used to be a small cabaret, is now being converted into a jazz club. There is a large bandstand to the right of the entrance; the rest of the space is filled with tables, benches, and a bar.

As a result of grants the loft has received since the counterfestival, DuBoise and Sultan can afford to introduce unknown artists, even though they may attract only a small audience. As I talked with DuBoise and Sultan in their upstairs office adjacent to a makeshift recording studio, I watched musicians listening to tapes, giving music lessons, or just hanging out. I asked the two about the loft phenomenon. "The main point," said Sultan, "is that the lofts offer exposure for musicians. Exposure is what it is all about. You can get that only by slowly working your way into the marketplace or by creating your own showcase, which is what we did."

There is an industrial bleakness to the Bond Street block where Studio Rivbea is hidden at no. 24. At a table at the entrance sits one of Sam

Rivers's daughters, toying with leaflets, joking with a boyfriend, humming snippets of some secret song. She collects the $4 contribution and plays straw boss. Beyond the table is a room much larger than most lofts, holding more than 150 people, many of whom know each other by name or sight. They are critics and musicians from the United States, Europe, South America, Africa, and Asia. Some are taking notes, studying, or secretly taping.

A large rug stretches backward from the bandstand but is hardly visible for all the torsos, legs, and bottoms sprawled on top. Above the playing area is a band room covered by gauzy curtains that cannot conceal the movement behind flickering candles—tops of heads barely clearing the pipes, which run the length of the ceiling.

Arthur Blythe is playing. He is one of the three or four most important alto saxophonists in New York. His accompanying group is composed of trumpet, cello, tuba, conga drums, and set drums. The audience is mostly white.

I talk with a woman on my right, a twenty-nine-year-old freelance writer named Mary Bailey. "I outgrew rock-and-roll. What I like about this music is that I never know what is going to happen. The important thing is the feeling that I am watching something suddenly come into being. When the music gets powerful, some white people I know take it as an assault on them, but I feel that it is an assault for me."

As Blythe plays, I ruminate on her comments and why there are so few Blacks in the audience. Like most working-class communities, the Black community is predominantly influenced by the mass media—which cultivate a taste for the sentimental, the overdrawn, and the uncomplicated. The lofts lack the "slickness" of the maudlin disco scene, which has attracted many of the young Black professionals.

———

A TWO-MINUTE WALK on Bond Street to no. 2 brings you to the Ladies' Fort, also known as the Live Loft Jazz (admission, $4). The walls inside are covered with a surrealistic jumble of gadgets, posters of musicians, leaflets, and announcements. The place is crowded mostly with women, all caught in the baritone sway of vocalist Joe Lee Wilson, a relatively unknown talent who possesses a powerful and romantic voice, reminiscent of Billy Eckstine in his prime. Wilson has with him a small rhythm section of guitar, bass, and drums. But the most outstanding musician on the bandstand is an alto saxophonist named Monty Waters, who doubles on the soprano saxophone and flute. The audience is riveted. This band of Wilson's is winning a following, partly because of an often expressed desire among jazz fans to hear a great singer—in a time when disco music reigns, and the mature voice seems to have fallen into popular decline.

Between sets, Wilson tells me how the place operates. "Since we were turned down for a grant, we pay the musicians by giving them two-thirds of the receipts we take in at the door. The other third goes for the rent." He laughs. "Which is two months behind." Soon Wilson returns to the bandstand and begins to sing. His voice is a combination of unsentimental joy and knowledge of low places—the essence of great jazz singing.

IN SoHo, AT 77 Greene Street, is the most remarkable jazz loft thus far: Ali's Alley, owned and managed by Rashied Ali. Now in its fourth year, the loft has been transformed from a place to play—a classic rent party—to a club with food and beverage licenses and cover charge of $3. Rashied Ali and the musicians in his band built the bar, the bandstand, the control room, and the kitchen, installed the carpet, painted the room, and hung the lights. When the Muhal Richard Abrams Quintet played there recently, there were lines in the street at 1:00 a.m. for the last set. The club ran out of the paper plates on which are served the ample and quite delicious portions of fish or chicken, along with black-eyed peas, yams, greens, and bread pudding.

Unlike the rowdy singles bars, Ali's Alley gives off a buoyant feeling that seems a combination of communal joy and serious respect—only occasionally marred by the emcee, who ruffles customers with his commercial announcements. Still, the décor, the excellent acoustics, and the fine food outdistance in ambiance every jazz club I have attended in New York, other than Boomer's, the home of mainstream bebop.

"All this club proves," says Ali, "is that musicians can get up off their behinds, stop complaining to the air, and do something about their conditions. Nobody's getting rich, but it's a start. I just hope the younger cats take it much further than I have. It can be done."

More than a few lofts have appeared since Studio We, Studio Rivbea, the Ladies' Fort, and Ali's Alley began to thrive. Environ, at 476 Broadway, became important through Hamiet Bluiett's baritone saxophone performances there last year; others include the Brook on West 17th Street, managed by saxophonist Charles Tyler, and Jazzmania on West 23rd Street. But the musicians want more than just to play the lofts. Pianist Muhal Richard Abrams puts it most succinctly: "You must watch the term 'loft jazz' because it's too limiting. We didn't come to New York to play in lofts; we came to make a living. But an audience can start, and grow until it gets too big for lofts and the music moves to another level. That's what we're interested in. That's what we're building towards. We *will* make it. There is no doubt about that."

April 1977

LAUGHIN' LOUIS ARMSTRONG

IT WAS QUITE A LONG TIME before I discovered that Louis Armstrong was a genius. In fact, it was quite a while before I knew what to make of him at all. Born in 1945, I grew up with television. That meant growing up on Louis Armstrong, who was a favored guest on talk and variety shows and could be seen as everything from star to supporting actor or cameo performer in films from the 1930s and 1940s. All I knew was that he was the most unusual of all the celebrated personalities who guested on television. He was a man whose size changed from sleek to proverbial butterball in the many films I saw, celebrated or imitated by every comedian at loss for an impersonation. I found him very mysterious.

Armstrong's sound, his manner, his facial expressions, all added up, for me, to some kind of secret language with which he consumed, reshaped, and reiterated songs, words, and music. Music I had become familiar with through radio, or television time, would dissolve in gravel, mugging, and a forward-leaning slight or broad trembling of the body, which was physicalization of a vibrato. As he reared back while singing, say, "St. James Infirmary," the width of his smile was heroic, yet it was more closely related to a grimace or the shadow world of irony and ambiguity than was suggested by the clapping of the audience or by the laughing of my mother as he would make an aside that held sentimentality or self-pity up for mockery, underlining it all with a handkerchief descending across his face, an open-armed gesture, or the motion of his head from side to side.

Unlike my mother, my father didn't find Armstrong charming or amusing; he found him despicable. My old man had been baptized in Lunceford, Ellington, and bebop. He considered Armstrong an embarrassment, a return to an unpleasant identity, or a man who had allowed white people to impose a ridiculous mask on him. In short, an Uncle Tom. But for all my old man's fervor, I wasn't going for it. Though I had no idea what was actually going on, I found Armstrong still mysterious.

But it wasn't until I saw Armstrong in a film with Danny Kaye about the white cornetist Red Nichols that I got a glimpse of the master behind the mask. Nichols goes uptown to hear "the new bugler" play in Harlem. Drunk and laughing, Nichols interrupts Armstrong (who is playing himself) as he gloriously trumpets the blues, to tell him that Louis is not as great as Red's father, who plays in the Midwest. With a gravity and confidence, a contempt and actuality that is rarely heard from Armstrong in any film when he is not performing musically, he replies, "If he ain't Gabriel, he's in trouble."

Nothing else Armstrong says or does in the film other than play is that authoritative, but that was enough. It prepared me for the photographs of Armstrong from the 1920s with King Oliver or Fletcher Henderson. There we see an arrogant, surly young man who seemed to think himself handsome and was not to be fucked with. In *Jazz Masters of the 30s*, trumpeter Rex Stewart remembers Armstrong as a man who arrived in the North wearing a box-back suit, a cap cocked to the side, and some high-topped shoes, all of which were emblematic of a street tough. Armstrong himself has written of knife fights he witnessed, of women who sold their bodies for his benefit, and women who threatened him with knives—one eventually stabbed him in the shoulder. He also spoke of the many gangsters for whom he worked and the shootings he witnessed. At times, he carried two pistols himself.

In many ways, the genial persona Armstrong cultivated in the 1930s was the result of advice from his manager, Joe Glaser. Glaser encouraged Armstrong to mug and sing, and many thought of the great brassman as no more than his lapdog. But one musician claims to have opened Armstrong's dressing room door one evening to find him holding a knife to Glaser's throat, saying, "I can't prove it, but if I find out you've stolen one *dime* from me, I'll cut your goddam throat." Another says Armstrong knocked trombonist Jack Teagarden out cold one evening backstage for getting too familiar. He then calmly went onstage to grin broadly and speak through his teeth, saying, "Thank you very much, ladies, gen'mens. Our first number this evening is dedicated to our trombonist brother Jack Teagarden, who won't be playing this show with us, and it's called — 'When It's Sleepy Time Down South.'" And of course, very little is ever said about how strongly Armstrong spoke out about President Eisenhower's indecisiveness at Little Rock, and the fact that the next string of gigs he played was so bereft of audiences, artillery shells could've sailed through the rooms and harmed no one. Then there was the irony of his yucking it up on screen with white stars who never invited him to their houses. All of those things made Armstrong more than a little tough. No man of his background born in 1900 who was a professional musician for fifty years could even aspire to being a square, a lame, or a chump. The pressure flushed all punks.

A recent RCA reissue on Bluebird, *Young Louis Armstrong 1932–1933*

(AXM2-5519), is invaluable to this discussion, just as it is musically invaluable. The double album contains material from a period most critics find lacking in artistic greatness, which is absurd. Not only does this recording contain some of the finest trumpet playing ever documented, it very clearly shows how influential Armstrong was on singers as different as Bing Crosby, Fats Waller, Billie Holiday, Cab Calloway, and Dean Martin. The emotional range of the work is exemplary, and the variety of things Armstrong does with the horn often startles. Without a doubt, Armstrong was the greatest trumpet player of the century—the most powerful, the most touching, the most varied.

One performance, "Laughin' Louie," perfectly expresses the enigma of the great musician. It opens with a trite theme that collapses into a burlesque of sad jokes and buffoonery from both Armstrong and his band members. The music starts back up and, again, breaks into laughter, Armstrong and the band bantering back and forth. Then, out of nowhere, the trumpeter decides to play something from his New Orleans past. First, he sputters some individual notes; then there is a lovely passage, then more laughter before he quiets the band down for "the beautiful part." Armstrong then plays in unaccompanied melody. Its rich tone conveys a chilling pathos and achieves a transcendence in the upper register that summons the cleansing agony of the greatest spirituals. The band drops a chord under him and it is over. The feeling one is left with is of great mystery.

August 1978

COMRADE, COMRADE,
WHERE YOU BEEN?

SINCE A TRIP TO CUBA IN 1960, LeRoi Jones, now known as Amiri Baraka, has been struggling with political wiring. It has been a difficult evolution, rife with contradiction, and has resulted in a great deal of simplistic and embarrassing work. Easily one of the most talented of the lower Manhattan avant-garde writers of his generation, he dropped a penetrating gift for lyric, compassionate, and complicated statement in favor of objectifications of good and evil. Jones pivoted from Charles Olson, William Burroughs, and Allen Ginsberg to Fidel Castro, Malcolm X, and Elijah Muhammad, from a disavowal of politics to organizing political campaigns and conferences. Yet though it is possible for an artist continually to vary his techniques, it is very difficult to change the core of one's sensibility; it is equally difficult to shift point of view constantly—almost desperately—and avoid creating work that is hollow, superficial, and contrived. LeRoi Jones's world, then, is that of a man periodically terrified of being devoured by incorrect or decadent decisions.

At its best, the work provides brilliant reassessments of history, personality, and culture; at its worst, it descends to ping-pong snobbery, hysteria, inverted stereotypes, and straining attempts to shock.

Though his ideology changes, Jones's preoccupations remain the same. A Marxist-Leninist Maoist writer since about 1975, his newest one-act play, *What Was the Relationship of the Lone Ranger to the Means of Production?*, is currently being performed in a setless production on the bandstand of the Ladies' Fort under the direction of the author, with uninspired music by Charles Tyler. The play reveals him still trying to evaluate the world in aesthetic terms and to show that bad taste has something to do either with bad politics or evil itself. Diet, taste in art, musical and sexual preferences define politics, or underline them. He continues using the archetypes that he, for the most part, exchanged for the realistic characters of *The Toilet* nearly fifteen years ago. The themes and tensions, rhetorically colored somewhat differently by communism, are essentially the same as they were in *Experimental Death Unit #1*, *The Baptism*, *Madheart*, *Dutchman*, and *Slave Ship*. Evil is perverse, tempting, deceptive, and manipulative. Collaboration and corruption are synonymous. Religion, popular imagery, and traditional education are riddled with lies and used to brainwash. The only solution to the continuing ritual of destruction and untruth at the hands of oppressive forces is violent revolution. For purposes of agit-prop, cinematic effects and linguistic contrasts still replace the layered and stream-of-consciousness techniques he was drawn to in the early part of his career.

The work attempts to reinterpret the Lone Ranger as a political metaphor. Taylor Mead, as MM, Masked Man, or Money's Master, is a reiteration of the homosexual villain or symbol of decadence that first appeared on Jones's stage in an early one-act *The Baptism* (called *A Recent Killing* in its full-length variation). Here he represents corporate rule, imperialism, and colonialism; his image is connected to robbers, suggesting robber barons, and his fate is inevitable destruction by the rebellious Tontos of the world. Tuffy, the labor bureaucrat played by Ngoma,* is a collaborator with MM against the heroes of the play, workers in Colonel Motors who are threatening to strike for better job conditions and wages. And though Rocha, Godard, Makavejev, Sembène,† and Peter Schumann have proven that broad symbols can be successfully used, Jones flounders, at least partly because MM and Tuffy are attacked throughout the play in terms of Hollywood horror movies (Dracula, Frankenstein, ghouls, and so forth), images he wore out long before 1970. And mixing sometimes fascinating rhythms and street vernacular with political slogans for his heroes makes them pontifical and automatic, unlike MM and Tuffy, both of whom are surprising, even if only absurdly so. Both Mead and Ngoma do very good jobs, especially Mead. As MM, he takes the sinister gaiety and aloofness of his character and manipulates it to a masterfully comic and snooty performance. Like the Devil Lady's in *Madheart*, MM's language is elliptical, full of pretense, cajolery, vernacular, and political slogans. Mead struts and twirls on stage, puncturing the very caricature itself; he realizes the broken field style Jones's work demands and capitalizes on the cartoon aspects to come up with his own Oil Can Harry, Mighty Mouse's melodramatic foe. Ngoma's breakaway style strongly suggests slapstick and is executed in an energetic fashion that constantly bends back upon itself.

Finally, upon reading his most recent longer play, *The Motion of History*, it became clear to me that Jones is again struggling with a broad and epic vision and is returning to the problem of character. In conversation he admitted that he is scuffling to combine aesthetic and political ideas and admires the penetration of *Godfather I* and *II*. If he is to succeed,

---

* Ngoma Hill, also known as Cordell Hill and Ngoma Osayemi Ifatunmise.
† Glauber Rocha, Jean-Luc Godard, Dušan Makavejev, Ousmane Sembène.

he will have to call back into action a tough and comic worldliness that usually saved his lyricism from sentimentality. He will also have to make greater use of the powers of an ear that perfectly rendered the speech of the lower-class white worker Clarke in the *Lone Ranger* and raise from a didactic grave his gift for creating volatile dramatic situations where surprise and revelation define the nature of tragedy and struggle. If he is able to bring those things together with his politics—whatever they might be—a long brutalized potential may finally emerge.

June 1979

BIG STAR CALLING

DURING THE NATIONALIST PROMENADE and the charade of ineptitude, the very shoddiness of which was supposed to breach a "revolutionary" standard, only one female poet was consistently interesting to me, and that one was Jayne Cortez. Beginning strangely, that is, untutored, combining an emotional adventurousness handed to her by the blues tradition, her work began as an artifact polished with blood and tears, standing up nude and shining, even inept and occasionally maudlin and plagued or deviled by a message stronger than her methods and for which her homemade English was insufficient. Still, there was a passion and an ear for melody and the manipulation of sounds and rhythm units that smoked away the other contenders for the crown, revealing their entrapment in a militant self-pity and adolescent rage more akin to tantrums than the chilling fire and evil of someone like Bessie Smith, the super bitchiness and dignity of a Billie Holiday or a Dinah Washington, and, finally, the swaying sidewalk dance and the country hickish charm and warmth of the South measured by train whistles and big dreams clacking north.

Jayne Cortez is, then, the *real* thing. She is from the streets and free of their platform-shoed slavery; she is a country girl sophisticated by the ravages of urban complexes; she does know Black music and had a crush on Duke Ellington in the 1960s when the myopic nationalist frost was too busy sneering at his glittering and radiant process; and, freed of the pieties of blackface Cotton Mather "morality," she talked the sweet and hot pussy pungence of love and the softly boiling tenderness of touch all laced up with rarely sentimental dreams. Consequently, Jayne Cortez's appearance on the scene was an emergent womanhood, trotting through the changes with thoroughbred arrogance, a lyric Secretariat at the wire while the other ladies were just getting to the starting post. No doubt about it.

1976

THE KING OF CONSTANT REPUDIATION

Published in the Village Voice *opposite a piece by Amiri Baraka (né LeRoi Jones), "What Kind of Crouch Is That?" Baraka's lead paragraph commenced: "Stanley Crouch, The Village Voice's most visible Negro-In-Residence, is becoming a well known Comprador."*

RECENTLY, ON CECIL TAYLOR'S opening night at Fat Tuesday's, LeRoi Jones and I almost got into a fistfight because I was so outraged at his having descended to name-calling. (I had read his response to my criticism of his current work.)* Discipline did out, however, and we sullenly marched to our separate corners, vowing to come out fighting on paper. Handshakes and apologies were included from my side.

Initially, I had no intention of answering him, but I have decided that I should, if only because of the continued dishonesty of most of the smiling faces who greet him now that he has come down from the Black nationalist mud hills of the 1960s. Jones has been the butt of jokes, disgust, and shock within the more serious wings of the Black literary community for at least ten years now, but if he shows up at a party, the

---

* S.C. is referring to Baraka's one-act play *What Was the Relationship of the Lone Ranger to the Means of Production?* S.C.'s review of the play was published in the *Village Voice*, June 11, 1979 (see p. 69).

very people who attack him most virulently in private will not only act as though he never rejected them because he could not dictate to them, but they will perform at benefits in his behalf. I have no doubt that he knows this, for he has always made use of the fact that too many Manhattan people love to be liked by those whom they consider the powerful or the prestigious or those potentially either.

In retrospect, LeRoi Jones is one of the greatest disappointments of this era and one of the most intellectually irresponsible men to have ever addressed a people tragically in need of well-researched and articulated information. He has almost completely traded-in a brilliant and complex talent for the most obvious hand-me-down ideas, which he projects in second-rate pool hall braggadocio.

Early on, Jones's gifts inspired, influenced, and continually surprised the writers of my generation. Then, he was not only grappling with unusual forms but also addressing the ironies and dilemmas of Black intellectuals confronted with an impoverished and oppressed community that nevertheless continually influenced our awesome and intriguing modern age. Yet, in Jones's work, it can easily be seen that his guilt over what he considered his inordinate privilege, his "uselessly literary" work, and what he felt were his decadent life choices resulted in a politics that attempted to purge Jones's own past while megalomaniacally giving the impression that it had something to do with national African American experience.

If one reads *The System of Dante's Hell*, *Tales*, *The Toilet*, and much of his early work, one can easily see why Jones's writing has taken on a consistently homophobic edge. To understand his continual call for bloodletting, one need only take a look at Jones's fascination with action, the Genet-like love of thugs, and his self-hatred for being "skinny, prim, and middle-class"—themes that recur with a tortured persistence. From James Joyce we get the unfortunate idea that the artist is a Christ figure and from Ezra Pound the conception that artists are the antennae of the race. These ideas are not so bad in themselves if, as did the early Jones, one takes care to avoid egocentric self-congratulation. But, if one takes those ideas seriously and pursues guruhood to the exclusion of reason and feels the role of the people is that of yes-folks always performing analingus, then we will have what LeRoi Jones has so pathetically and arrogantly produced over the past fourteen years. (A downtown friend reports that the day of Malcolm X's assassination, February 21, 1965, Jones rushed home from the opening of Eli Wilentz's then-brand-new bookstore on 8th Street and held a meeting in which he told those assembled he would move uptown and take over where Malcolm X had left off.)

The horror and the sorrow of the whole affair is that we all learned some terrible lessons about what gave form to Nazism by watching Jones and buba-clad boobs such as Ron Karenga (founder of the cultural nationalist organization US) strut, condescend, intimidate, and develop race theories of history and culture. That I and many others initially found those ideas attractive is best explained by the observation the wife of a philosophy teacher of mine once made: "There are two ways one can become taller than others—either by growth or cutting off their legs." But as the work of Jones and those he then championed became progressively dictatorial and simplistic, I began to use the term "Dick and Jane Black nationalism" to describe it—"See white man be devil, devil, devil; see Black man be beautiful, beautiful, beautiful."

In those years, allegiance and aesthetic quality were taken as one, and if anyone disagreed with anything the Jones-Karenga axis said, they were described contemptuously as a NE-gro, a catch-term for Uncle Tom, reactionary, or sellout to the Marxist "walking, talking zombie jew," to quote one of Jones's put-downs of the Black Panther Party. He and Karenga surrounded themselves with goons, gofers, and homemade but militant extensions of the most self-deprecating roles imposed on the Black actors of forty years ago. Because I and a few other writers perceived that Jones, like the equally irresponsible Eldridge Cleaver, wrote and spoke with great precision and eloquence when the audience was white, liberal, leftist, or bohemian, then addressed the Black community with condescension and substituted name-calling and hysterical threats for politics, we never became involved with their brand of radicalism. When "Papa Doc Baraka" went on television in 1968 with the very pillars of white power in Newark (whose slaughter he had so shrilly called for but a year before) to blame the Newark riot on white leftists who had "used" his Black brothers and sisters, we began to wonder if he indeed had any integrity or was simply an opportunist out to save his own neck from the weapons charges then held over his head after his arrest during that bloody riot. Point of fact: The Black nationalist movement of the 1960s was as rife with corruption as anybody's Watergate, and its threat to the powers was shown in the fact that—unlike King, Malcolm X, no telling how many Panthers, and other radicals—there were hardly any assassinations or attempts on their lives. It would seem that even the "running dogs of capitalism" know paper tigers from real ones.

I am sure that LeRoi Jones understands *Birth of a Nation* and *Triumph of the Will* because, until his recent conversion to Marxism, he wrote his own versions of both. That he and others could frequently make references in writings and speeches to meticulous Black artists and virtuosos such as Charlie Parker and John Coltrane and then spew the sloppiest work in the faces of Black people suggests a disrespect for that audience that I was then and am now at war with. That he and Karenga could distort the writings of Amílcar Cabral and Julius Nyerere for their own purposes is echoed in Jones's selective distortion of recent reviews of mine. It is not my fault that he has yet to produce a political work as strong as *Burn!* or Márquez's incredible variation on *Citizen Kane*, *The Autumn of the Patriarch*.

Nor am I content to accept the militant self-pity white theater producers prefer to challenging Black art, that which would perforate stereotypes and make clear the fact that what happens to the society's most consistent victims is but a blueprint of what is in store for the rest. For instance, it wasn't until the notoriously violent and abrasive Los Angeles Police Department got so loose with its guns that it started shooting whites that nonbelievers in the Caucasian community began to realize that Black people had been complaining about a serious problem all along. The accusations of the most perceptive Black and white radicals of the past decade were proven by Watergate and the revelations about J. Edgar Hoover, both of which showed that the *entire country* was being victimized. Far too many Black writers—or at least those who are produced—have chosen to simplify the nature of American reality in favor of slogans and work that will allow white audiences to, again, use the Black character as broom closet or attic where they can store their pity and maintain feelings of superiority or, as one white producer did in my presence, dismiss satirically both the politics and craft of a writer he had successfully produced. Possibly, further definitions of compradors are necessary!

Since Jones now repudiates poets Don L. Lee and Nikki Giovanni, both of whom he once championed (just as he did any incompetent writers of the past decade if they recited the litany of racial supremacy), once called for the murder of all whites, and talked of a coming version of heaven no more real than that of Charles Manson or Jim Jones (a fullblown version of our Newark LeRoi), exactly what literary renaissance is he referring to, and why does he no longer embrace their most nationalistic work? Well, he has switched reels again.

I am by no means saying that LeRoi Jones or anybody with an aesthetic sensibility should stay in one place, but if a man is incapable of anything more than completely reversing his position every few years, why should anybody take him seriously in *political* sense? The classic relationship of the artist to politics parallels that of the coordination between diagnostician and surgeon. It can be very dangerous when a diagnostician untrained in surgery is so arrogant as to attempt an operation for which he is unprepared. Ten years ago, I watched Jones browbeating Black students into rejecting books in favor of "our oral tradition" on the assumption that ancestor worship was superior to hard-earned analysis. Jones seems somehow to believe that a perpetual confusion of identity is revolutionary when actually all it denotes is a differently colored treadmill. This is especially true when one considers the fact that *Dutchman* and *Zoo Story** are uncomfortably similar; that his essay "The Revolutionary Theater" is merely lifted Artaud; that his "Black" and "revolutionary" plays quite often seem the backwaters of Genet's *Les Nègres*, and that his anti-Semitic hysteria not only reflected his attempts to purge his first marriage but seemed to be his grabbing of the baton from an earlier influence—the Ezra Pound of the Mussolini broadcasts.

Some years ago there was a very fine essay written about T. S. Eliot in *Evergreen Review* in which the writer concluded that Eliot could not handle the complexities and painful ironies of his earlier work, especially his poetry, and, therefore, ran full force both into the theater and the Anglican Church, where all could be easily measured and explained.

Since becoming an activist, LeRoi Jones has never been very comfortable with the complexity of the African American identity or political dilemma, nor has he been capable of getting beyond what Albert Murray calls "stock political arrangements"—the whole-hog buying of political theories in a fashion totally unlike the extensions Lenin, Mao, and Cabral brought to Marx. He prefers gagging and throttling all opposition. An ex-bodyguard told me once that he had to get away from Jones when he discovered that, for all his talk of *the people*, inside the citadel of leadership the blessed one lived and ate better than his followers. "But the capper came," he continued, "when we were at the National Black Assembly and

---

* Edward Albee.

he ordered some of us to go into one of the opposing delegations and make sure they didn't get to the microphone." Obviously, they hadn't the most politically advanced ideology. But, then, one never knows. Do one?

Finally, it has been clear for many years to most perceptive Black Americans that one of the first things every èmigrè to this country discovers, regardless of culture or color, is that the African American is to be shown no respect all. And as far as Stokely Carmichael is concerned, after Stokely ceased important work with SNCC [Student Nonviolent Coordinating Committee] in favor of rabble-rousing, his code name among movement people became "star-michael," and he was told by more than one group of radicals outside the United States that thank you, but no thank you, they knew how to conduct their own revolutions.

September 1979

AN EPIC AMERICAN HERO

BUDDY BOLDEN

THE VELOCITY AT WHICH Afro-American innovations spread across America is now so swift that it is surprising to discover that the man who seems to have been the first jazzman and the first great urban blues player was hardly known outside the Black community of turn-of-the-century New Orleans. Such a man was cornetist "King" Buddy Bolden. He was the most celebrated musician in his hometown, known for playing with great passion and volume, living the fast life of the sporting and hustling worlds, performing at everything from funky butt dances to formal waterfront farewells for soldiers. Bolden went mad in 1907 at the age of twenty-nine and lived out the rest of his years in a mental institution, floating further and further from communication until he died in 1931 at the age of fifty-four, survived by only two members of his original band and one blood relative of his immediate family.

That Bolden's career was meteoric and tragic initiates something of a pattern for the first "kings" of the jazz cornet and for too many of the music's innovators, regardless of instrument. It appears to say something about the burdens of improvisation and the problems an intuitive genius might have with technical evolution, given the appetite for the new possessed by almost any American audience and the demands that appetite can make on players such as Bolden, who came to prominence through the medium of fresh ideas. Bolden began the liberation of secular American music from the written page. He achieved that in a musical world legendary for its extreme competition. Bolden's style apparently incorporated the vocal techniques of Negro American song and speech while veering away from the straight texts of popular tunes through embellishments, homemade interjections, or substitutions of new ideas for familiar sections. He became "King" Bolden by playing louder and more inventively than those with whom he competed in the many outdoor performances at which the band drawing the most listeners was sure to get the dance hall job. His crown came from the people, not from the world of advertising.

We can surmise from reading the many tall tales told about him, which began to accumulate in the 1930s and continued through an interview with New Orleans musician Danny Barker in a 1965 issue of *Evergreen Review*, that Bolden had become an epic hero among Black people in much the same way Davy Crockett and Brother Jonathan had in the popular American writing and theater that was developed to fit the tastes of the country whites who had begun to move to the cities following the War of 1812. Where those two characters repudiated European criteria with either rowdy humor and arrogant braggadocio or debunking wit that turned the tables on pompous virtue, Bolden's music seemed to express the individual and collective fates and contrary thoughts of his listeners. That music became a heroic metaphor, as had the Uncle John folktales of slavery, the exploits of the "conductors" of the Underground Railroad, or the sermons of Black preachers. It moved audiences as though the powers of incantation, stubbornly improvised embellishments, and syncopated eloquence were secular versions of the church sermon. The emotion of the listeners moved from great sorrow to great celebration because the music could overflow with the ills of romantic failure, become satiric or successively rough, crude, rude, and lewd as it moved toward affirmation. It was apparently given to a frisky elegance that existed in contradistinction not only to the music of the whites but also to that of the light-skinned Creole musicians who played notes exactly as written and dismissed Bolden's revolutionary embellishments as "faking." But, in keeping with the nature of the popular American hero, whether frontiersman or westerner, detective or romanticized gangster, Bolden's exploits were loved as much for the wit, the resilience, and the daredevil attitude of their improvisatory nature as for the great physical prowess with which they were achieved.

Throughout one of the finest books ever written about a jazzman, *In Search of Buddy Bolden* (Louisiana State University Press), Donald M. Marquis tones down exaggeration and separates lies from facts. But what a mythology he had to address! Jelly Roll Morton called Bolden "the blowingest man since Gabriel," and one could, he continued, hear him for ten or twelve miles. For fun or for exhibition or for both, he was said to have gone up in a balloon to blow his horn or to have parachuted out and blasted it on the way down. He was capable of blowing so powerfully into his cornet that a part of it once flew twenty feet. The multiple passions of his music could, by turns, excite the dancers, invoke mournful recollection, or become so erotically evocative that women were seen to jump out of their drawers or their windows or out of both. As sidelines, he was said to have run a barbershop and had three or four "trained" women who lived intimately with him and made up his street entourage, carrying his hat, his coat, his flask. As though playing the low-down dirty blues wasn't enough, Bolden is said to have published a scandal sheet known as "The Cricket," which "put everybody's business in the street." Finally, one musician claimed Bolden went mad because a jealous woman invoked a curse by removing the bow from the sweatband of his hat.

Most of that mythology was created by jazzmen themselves, some of whom, such as resurrected cornetist Bunk Johnson, were trying to ride Bolden's coattails by claiming to have played with him; some of whom were given to fanciful exaggeration brought on by the fact that Bolden had been out of the music business for thirty years and dead for two when the first jazz article was written about him; and some of whom were probably having a good time putting on their white interviewers. But the fascinating thing about *In Search of Buddy Bolden* is that the author's seriousness makes the book essential reading for anyone interested in American vernacular expression. By thoroughly raising from research a bas-relief of post–Civil War and turn-of-the-century New Orleans as well as removing a substantial amount of the mysteries concealing Bolden, Marquis makes him as much an epic hero in reality as he was in myth, legend, put-on, and flat out lie.

Marquis begins by placing Bolden in the legendary context of pirate Jean Lafitte and Voudoun priestess Marie Laveau, explaining that Bolden's story always existed in a shadow world of intertwined myth and reality. He then proceeds to show why and at the same time gives a stiff criticism of the shoddy history of jazz scholarship by refuting a self-serving and fallacious interview and letter given by Bunk Johnson to the editors of *Jazzmen*, the first American collection of critical essays on jazz. Marquis shows how, through birth certificates and other documents, one can only conclude that Johnson had changed other men's ages and probably his own in order to make convincing his claim to have played in the first jazz band. Though Marquis is very kind to Johnson and the editors, his smooth, easeful presentation of thoughtful research deepens the criticism and shows how far jazz scholarship has come since the publication of *Jazzmen*.

With extreme care, Marquis follows the Bolden family from 1806, when the cornetist's grandfather was born, to the present day. Through a baptism ledger, he discovers Bolden's birthday was actually September 6, 1877, almost ten years later than jazz writers had previously believed. The cornetist lost his older sister just short of her sixth birthday in 1881 and his father two years later. From 1887 until just shortly before he was committed in 1907, Bolden lived on the same street in New Orleans with his mother, Alice, and his younger sister, Cora. Little is known about how much education Bolden received, but it is known that he started playing the cornet around the age of seventeen and was leading his own band by the age of twenty—a controversial band at that! Bolden had revolutionary ideas in more than one department. He created the first small jazz ensemble by giving the lead melodies to the cornet and the trombone while putting the strings of guitar and bass in the background, next to the clarinets and drums. In a sense, that begins American music's giving wind instruments the dominant voices in small and large ensembles. Bolden was also changing the music itself. He seems to have combined the practices he participated in at his Baptist church with those of popular songs and dance music. Bolden rearranged the material, played popular songs and hymns up-tempo, with the feeling of "jubilee singing" derived from the church; he "tagged" those marches and whatever other music he performed and shocked the more conservative musicians by blowing improvised passages in place of known ones. Though initially considered bizarre, Bolden and his band were on the way to becoming the most popular New Orleans unit by the early 1900s. The result was that the more legitimate Creole musicians who were banished from the white community by the Black Codes of 1894 had to start taking note of what he did, however much they scornfully thought of what Bolden played as no more than "honky tonk music."

The Creoles, with their light skins, their thin lips, their near-

Caucasoid hair, and their educated backgrounds, had attitudes toward the dark, lower class that parallel those certain upper-class, blond and blue-eyed Jews have been known to have for their dark-eyed, dark-haired, lower-class fellow and sister Jews who look and act "too Yiddish." But the communicative standard set by Bolden's band forced the Creoles to begin filtering European elements from their music in order to work. After Bolden, fewer and fewer of them played as straight as before. Yet there was more to it than that, for the forced prodigal return of the Creoles to the Negro community also meant that the skills they had developed would be brought together with the gutbucket audacity championed by Bolden and his converts. It was the beginning of the fusion of the sophisticated and the primitive that is central to the identity of jazz.

Lionized in the Red Light District and crowned king, Bolden was soon caught up in the fast life of big spending and heaving dissipation. He started playing "like he didn't care," making great demands on himself and on his instrument, which may have been the source of the headaches he began to have shortly before he started to go mad, suffering from advanced paranoia and, later, alcoholism. Almost as though rendering the problems of Charlie Parker, Marquis writes of the first jazzman, "He took an unrouted, sometimes hedonistic path, and unfortunately he did not have the benefit of learning from others how to handle this situation; no one of his circumstances had been there before."

Marquis's suppositions about the reasons behind Bolden's collapse focus on his not being able to go beyond a certain point in his music and the pressure he might have felt as others started developing his ideas in ways that were beyond the cornetist's own abilities. It is not an unusual situation for a musician to find himself in, and the history of jazz has shown the effects of becoming either outdated or imitated into invisibility and the eccentric ways artists have sometimes reacted, to cite circumstances that more often than not have more to do with trends than artistic substance. The last years of Lester Young are one example; the last ten years of Miles Davis are another. But through all the birth certificates, city directories, arrest records, social clubs, and reconstructions of the parks and dance halls in which Bolden performed, maybe one idea stands out most and shows the tradition in popular music that the cornetist was first to exemplify: "He was born twelve years after the Civil War, and if his mother remembered the days of slavery and the aftermath of Reconstruction, being a little uncertain of just what emancipation meant, Buddy was of a generation that didn't know or particularly care what the rules had been and saw life as an open challenge instead of a restricted corridor." Few, in any society, have ever had the opportunity to do what Buddy Bolden did, and few writers about jazz have ever realized what the accomplishments of the music's innovators have meant in the broadest terms. Donald M. Marquis does, and his book is not only a milestone, it is also a challenge to all future biographers of major jazz figures. Let us hope that *In Search of Buddy Bolden* has as large an impact on the field of jazz scholarship as its subject had on the music that has made New Orleans such an important city in the culture of this century.

Previously unpublished, 1979

THINKING BIG

MAX ROACH AND CECIL TAYLOR

Before this concert I thought Max Roach was the king of bebop
drummers. Now I know he's the king of the drummers.

—JEROME COOPER

I T SEEMS, SOMETIMES, that the only clear actions of value, as Quincy
Troupe has pointed out, take place in athletic competition, where academic argument will not lift a knocked-out opponent from the canvas,
and pretension will not carry one across a finish line first. Such were the
dimensions of the duets between Max Roach and Cecil Taylor the evening of December 15, 1979, at Columbia University's McMillin Theatre.

Athletics formed an appropriate analogy from the very beginning of
the evening, for there was an air of expectation, of tension, even of suspense, outside McMillin Theatre on Broadway, in the lobby, and in the
concert hall itself. I was reminded of the kind of excitement I'd felt during the waiting periods before certain Ali bouts—the Foreman fight, the
"Thrilla in Manila," and the second battle with Spinks. The air seemed to
move with the flutter of intestinal butterflies, and the familiar waftings of
marijuana smoke seemed stand-ins for tranquilizers.

There were many musicians in the audience, familiar faces of the followers of new jazz, visitors from out of town and out of the country, then some who seemed more curious than anything else. Yet for all the people one was to see at both shows, notables from the bebop generation were conspicuously absent, which suggests they were working gigs, didn't want to pay the eight or ten dollars, or had no interest in hearing Max Roach perform with Cecil Taylor. I would suspect it was all three, especially because any student of the music knows that Coleman Hawkins got a lot of flack from his generation for hiring Thelonious Monk and for aligning himself with the bebop avant-garde of the 1940s. But like all those who missed it, the loss was theirs, particularly at the second show, which defined the heights of conception, execution, and coherence that avant-garde jazz has achieved.

Playwright Bill Gunn made a nervous introduction to the first show, and grandmaster drummer Max Roach came out alone to perform a solo composition-improvisation for his extended trap set, which included snare drum, two ride toms, bass drum, and three floor toms, one with a pedal that allowed for talking drum–like pitch and timbral shifts. On a table behind the drum set were some percussion instruments, and next to them was a great big gong. Because he was to play with a master orchestrator, the great drummer had brought an orchestra.

Using the bass drum and sock cymbal as a metric pendulum, Roach began one of his solo masterworks, which showed off, again, that his supremacy as a drummer is due to the poetic logic of his phrases and the crystalline precision of his color control. Handsome, immaculately dressed, and looking fifteen to twenty years younger than his age of fifty-five, he improvised with the tension and release of the finest composers, opting for everything from whisper-frail rolls to clattering explosions that left the drums and went to the rims and even the sides of the drums, amazing certain drummers with his ability precisely to state figures such as paradiddles on metal parts of the instrument, which usually push one's rhythms into the area of chance. He would play phrases and rolls on the rims that changed color with each phrase, perfect illustrations of a statement made once in a notation class by a French classical percussionist: "It is not that the drums do not have pitch, it is that the differences in pitch and timbre are much more subtle and complex than most ears perceive." When he finished, the audience clapped loudly, anticipating an incredible duet.

They were to be momentarily surprised, for Cecil Taylor then came on stage, seated himself at the Bösendorfer Rolls Royce of a piano, and performed an extremely lyrical solo piano piece, reminiscent of Ellington's redefinition of impressionism and the singing idealism of Thelonious Monk—especially the way Taylor undercut a concluding and ascendant line of delicately defined melody notes with a jabbed dark chord, seeming to say, "No, regardless of how pretty it is, that shit doesn't go on forever."

Then the duet began. It was brilliant and showed that Roach, probably alone of his generation, was able intellectually to embrace the conception that Cecil Taylor's style demands. He craftily found holes where other drummers hadn't, was able to rearrange a Taylor statement or contrast it with a traditional figure or rhythm, and manipulate dynamics like a master who can make a yo-yo sleep, rock, swing, twirl, or what have you. When Roach went to the percussion instruments, he didn't get hot and bothered; instead he used each instrument as a complement or contrast to Taylor in a minimal, Monk-like fashion. His use of brushes when he returned to the set illustrated, again, how primal many electronic textures are and how far behind the brushes white noise is.

Taylor's playing was as happy as I've heard it, if not the happiest. His technique has gone to another level now, and he is not only able to play with more power and speed than I have heard from any pianist of any discipline but also able to say more because his precision of touch is greater. Usually given to sweeping everything up into his line, like Bud Powell did, he began, in the first show, to echo Roach's ideas and scramble for the colors the drum orchestra was providing, sometimes grabbing the bass drum with both elbows in the lower register. Taylor's reappropriation of runs coming from Ellington, Monk, Powell, and Waller were interlaced with colors from Garner, Silver, and Garland. The conservatory background was cracked open and run through the perfect sifter. The crowd easily got their money's worth and more.

Those who attended the second show, however, witnessed what was probably one of the major musical events of the age. I haven't seen musicians so excited since the mid-1960s, when the John Coltrane quartet had players catching an aesthetic holy ghost. That second show made it clear the only actual equal to the orchestral possibilities of the piano is the trap-drum set. And as great as Cecil Taylor played, the center of attention was Max Roach, who dropped something akin to a whole new world of possibility for the avant-garde. As Steve McCall said afterward, "You have to think big to play the traps, and Max is the master thinker."

It was here that the most crucially human meaning of the evening became obvious, for Roach performed with a heroic nobility and comprehensive manhood that mutated rhythms and colors in a linear and reiterative musical design, capable of controlling a listener's breathing. The limitless range of emotional dispositions trap drummers have brought to twentieth century music—finding expression for everything from the most romantically delicate to the most overwhelming rushes of passion—was made absolutely clear. We heard the man who had been the ideal drummer for Charlie Parker, Bud Powell, Clifford Brown, and Sonny Rollins become the ideal drummer for Cecil Taylor. In face of the innovations of Sunny Murray, Milford Graves, Rashied Ali, Andrew Cyrille, and Steve McCall, Max Roach became that evening the greatest of the so-called avant-garde drummers, for he brought to that style the result of thirty-five years of sharing bandstands with some of the finest musicians of every style of jazz, from the Benny Carter big band to the big synthesis of Archie Shepp. Yet in many ways what he did constituted a complete realization of pulse and tempo playing as opposed to constant statements of meter, which go back, as Martin Williams once pointed out, to Parker's famous "Ko Ko" of 1945. On many occasions since then, Max Roach has shown a concern for aesthetic adventure far broader than any other drummer—as performer, composer, and bandleader. Not only did he up the ante for vanguard drumming in the jazz idiom, but also he made it obvious that what his skill and experience allow him to improvise makes the percussion works of contemporary "classical" composers sound extremely naive, regardless of the superficial complexity.

The second show began as had the first, Roach improvising superbly on the same piece, Taylor performing a wonderful bluesish, gospelish work. Then it took off and, for the first forty minutes or so, Roach solved so many problems about lifting and carrying "unmetered" ideas or making them take on another continuity when processed through the drums and given a variation that many musicians' mouths literally dropped open. There were excited shouts from the audience as the two made more and more intricate music, Roach stepping on the gas in a way I have never heard a drummer do with the grand pianist. During one section, Roach went to the snare drum and played Taylor's things back at him with variations faster than they arrived. The pianist capitulated and cut the tempo, then he comped as Roach soloed. In the middle of the work, Taylor played a translucent ballad that was unaccompanied for the most part, and Roach played an African, rim shot–laden improvisation on the song that was extraordinary. Knowing by now some of Taylor's favorite rhythmic patterns, the drummer began to use them as refrain-like formal elements. By the finale, which was composed of some unison rhythmic figures, the audience went wild, standing up and cheering for an encore. None was to come, but the faces of the two players showed that they were both aware of the depth of the performance.

Now that Max Roach has stepped into the arena of "free" music, it must be clear that the music is valid and that the work of the aforementioned innovators cannot be dismissed any longer. It bespeaks a great achievement for all concerned, for not only did Roach develop something that no avant-garde composer of percussion scores has ever achieved for the single player, but also Cecil Taylor's music was given a strength and a beauty I have rarely heard it have—an absolute relaxation, joy, and authority that can only be described as inspirational. Yes, it was recorded.*

January 1980

---

* S.C.'s concert review was subsequently used for the liner notes to *Cecil Taylor/Max Roach, Historic Concerts*, released on Soul Note, 1984.

CECIL TAYLOR'S
PIANISTIC FIREWORKS

Cᴇᴄɪʟ Tᴀʏʟᴏʀ ɪs ᴛʜᴇ ᴍᴏsᴛ ᴄᴏɴᴛʀᴏᴠᴇʀsɪᴀʟ jazz pianist of the past twenty years. Long a vanguard artist, he was, with Ornette Coleman and John Coltrane, one of the three major figures who gave impetus to the jazz avant-garde of the 1960s. A graduate of the New England Conservatory as a composition major, Taylor has always approached the jazz tradition with high sophistication, as did some of his major influences—Duke Ellington, Thelonious Monk, Bud Powell, and Sonny Rollins. His development since his first recordings in 1955 shows a body of compositions, ideas, and techniques that has had more effect on musicians who don't play the piano than on those who do.

His influence has been similar to that of Monk, who has contributed influential compositions to the jazz repertory, but who left most jazz pianists nonplused. Yet Monk's minor second intervals, clusters, and disruptive rhythms greatly inspired the early work of Taylor, as much for the assault on sentimentality as for the playfulness that parodied conventional harmonies. But Taylor's actual sensibility is more akin to pianist Bud Powell, whose urgent, contradictory passions undercut one another to suggest the complexity of human personality in much the same way as the best country blues. A statement rife with pathos will be satirized immediately; lyricism will give way to jaunty giggles in trills; a songful passage will suddenly become a nearly vicious protest against the limitations of life, delivered with an energy just short of hysteria.

Taylor can project such emotions because of the extraordinary virtuosity of his technique. That technique has impressed classical musicians as well as jazzmen and is part of a tradition wherein jazz has revitalized classical instrumental technique throughout this century. Many followers of concert music would probably be startled by the observations about Taylor made by Ursula Oppens, the noted classical pianist:

> I have been listening to him for about 10 years, and the only person I can think of who might have been able to execute what he does now would have to have been the Horowitz of thirty years ago. Like Horowitz, he has a very individual touch, which you don't have much of in classical music, and he plays with a speed, a size of sound, and an accuracy all his own. In fact, no one in classical music writes anything that demands that degree of speed and power. It's a shame that thousands of classical pianists aren't going out to hear him, especially since he's developed very exciting new techniques.

But for all his energy and technique, the way he blended the styles of Waller, Ellington, Garner, Silver, Powell, and Monk with techniques learned from Bartók, Schoenberg, Stravinsky, and the Impressionists initially proved a bit much for jazz listeners and concert people alike. When performing popular songs, jazz standards, or originals, Taylor frequently played and developed ideas in the rhythm section that appeared to ignore the featured improviser, while his own improvisations contained layers of voicings that tended to obscure conventional harmonies. On albums recorded in 1958 and 1960, he extended the idea of percussive attack by simulating drum phrases and rolls as well as the varied textures a drummer achieves as he moves from his snare drum to his tom-tom or his bass drum. Expressing his love for vocal music, in this period he used trills that began to emulate a singer's vibrato.

Although he composed from the outset of his career, it was his renditions of popular songs that commanded attention up to about 1960—the high point being his recording of "This Nearly Was Mine" in that year. But with his three compositions recorded on the *Into the Hot* album in 1961, featuring saxophonists Archie Shepp and Jimmy Lyons, he first fully revealed his gifts as a composer. Call-and-response, tension and release, metric shifts and the orchestration of both bluesy and unconventional effects come off marvelously. Unfortunately that ensemble, probably his finest, broke up shortly after the recording, and Taylor formed a trio with Jimmy Lyons and drummer Sunny Murray.

Beginning in 1962, at the behest of Murray, this trio began to forego clearly stated meters in favor of thematic and contrapuntal rhythms that built upon Taylor's interest in African and Oriental percussion. The music of this period featured muscular improvisations of such challenging techniques and structure, they bewildered listeners and most fellow musicians alike.

His unprecedented velocities and increasingly epic performances (sometimes as long as two-and-one-half hours uninterrupted) led to the accusation that he and his musicians could express no emotions other than fury and hysteria. Two out-of-print recordings made during the middle 1960s, *Unit Structures* and *Conquistador!*, belie that complaint and demonstrate a further development and diversification of his compositional talent. Yet three volumes of *The Great Concert of Cecil Taylor* from 1969 are indeed apocalyptic enough to substantiate the criticism.

During the past decade, however, his work has evolved steadily and deliberately in its diversity. It now includes exceptionally ordered solo performances as well as ensemble realizations of shifting moods and multiple themes. Those themes make use of sweltering and intricate interplay and lyric melodies notable for their simplicity and tenderness. Equally fascinating is his use of materials from Marvin Gaye's rhythm and blues, showing that he still maintains a strong relationship to the sensibility of the streets, however much sophistication he brings to that sensibility.

Indent (1973) and *Silent Tongues* (1974), two solo recordings done in public performances, are outstanding examples of Cecil Taylor's heroic synthesis and his ability to control long performances. Reminiscent in their colors and rhythms of such Ellington selections as "Caravan," "Wig Wise," "Solitude," and the title track from the *Money Jungle* album, the performances also bring to mind Sonny Rollins's *Freedom Suite*, especially in the manipulation of the thematic material. The works use simple and complex melody, contrapuntal and counterrhythmic ideas, simultaneous development of motives, recurrent blues, and gospel snippets. The layers of harmonic development sometimes sound as if the voicings of Ellington, Monk, and Powell were being played all at once, providing densities that are developed in broad and intersecting linear fashion. By now, Taylor's pianistic fireworks are used to express pathos and joy more often than anger, plus a recurrent mystical and meditative grandeur.

IN APRIL 1978, Taylor recorded two albums for New World Records— *The Cecil Taylor Unit* and *3 Phasis*—with a group that included violin, trumpet, alto saxophone, bass, and drums. Each disk contains exceptional summations of his work over the past twenty years, although each is marred by the improvisational decisions of some of the players. On the first record, there are two suite-like works in which ensemble statements are separated by solo piano interludes, partially composed, partially improvised, which take up side one. Each is superbly controlled. The third work, however, is a sidelong piece that fails because of the inadequacies of the trumpet and drum improvisations (ironically, drummer Shannon Jackson is largely—and brilliantly—responsible for the success of the two former pieces).

The song "3 Phasis" is a 57-minute work that uses the same form of full ensemble separated by solo piano or piano accompanied by a few instruments. It is an essential recording because, like all great jazzmen, Taylor reiterates his blues roots on the second side with a rent-party vamp that inspires Jimmy Lyons and the ensemble to a powerhouse celebration of New Orleans in a new context. The piano interlude, which develops both the vamp and a previous lyric melody simultaneously, is a perfect exposition of the composer's talent. Trumpeter Raphe Malik's repetitiousness and cold tone mottle the work whenever he is featured, but the overall quality of the playing makes up for this lapse.

Right now, Cecil Taylor is continuing his musical development in fruitful ways, as shown by his monumental duets with grand master drummer Max Roach in concert on December 15, 1979, and by his new group featuring two drummers. Fortunately, the duets and the new group were both recorded in public performance, so we may look forward to the continued expansion of the Cecil Taylor discography.

June 1980

GREAT ESCAPES

I N THAT YARD, you could have been on another planet, one made of gravel, ties, and rails that took on the image of some prehistoric skeleton, half implanted in the ground, half raised in bas-relief and creating an area between the sky and the earth, the area on which the trains moved. You knew that the trains and those white men who ran them were all powerful, existing in a land of their own, which may have been why those going home for the evening, however tired, seemed sad as their boots crunched across the yard to the silent steps of the sidewalk as they disappeared.

You felt sad, too, because you didn't know where you were or what would happen to the car in which you were hiding, that you had run alongside and caught, loving the danger and the power of your arms pulling you up from the ground, tucking your legs up as the train took over and you raised one foot to the initial rung of the metal ladder and were there, like a tramp, a bank robber, or someone running away from home. But you weren't running away from home, you were running away from the block, where you saw the backsides of familiar houses and the different fences or noticed older people shaking their heads at those boys risking losing their legs and arms—not to mention their lives—hopping trains.

Everybody's mother was against it, and everybody's father agreed with her, and neither of them were there when you swung up on that train, or, if one was, you pretended not to hear the shouted command to get away from that train, dreaded coming home, and loved the ride that much more. It was, then, the enjoyment preceding the last anxious minutes before the execution of an ass-whipping or some other inevitable penance. Most of all, it was the motion and the percussive sound of the circular wheel metal against the horizontal rail metal, the ground moving past you, the houses, and the air seeming to change density, and everything in your previous moments and everything in your future disappearing before the force of that motion, like on horseback when very small or on a roller coaster any time.

In those yards, with the sun on the way down, as you sat hidden in an unlocked boxcar, you wondered what had been loaded in there—cattle, fruit, toilet paper, lumber—and were caught up in imaginative contemplation as you took great care not to get your clothes torn or dirty. At the same time, you were much younger again, as if coming out of infancy, for the railroad men were not only larger than you but spoke of things you didn't understand at all and made use of powers you knew you didn't have, with their lanterns, their tools, and their on-the-job lingo as they shunted trains into sidings, pulled out boxcars, attached cabooses, held the railings of engines, and swung their lanterns as though they were hypnotizing the stars.

The railroad men were like the truck drivers across the street from where you lived, except the truck drivers were near-black, dark brown,

brown, light brown, yellow and freckled, or yellow and unfreckled, or so high yellow they were nearly bone-colored. Their accents and rhythms were more familiar, but they, too, lived in another world. Theirs was one of braggadocio, checkers, whist, and coon can; sardines or Viennese sausage eaten out of cans with pocket knives and swigged down with Coca-Cola then followed shortly by paper-cupped whiskey; Stetsons, leather, wool, or cotton caps; cigars thrusting from their mouths like single, burning tusks; engineer boots and olive drab work shirts and pants to be replaced by fine dandified outfits that were often pearl gray, and shoes that shone like Klondike gold but were soft and comfortable.

They drove diesel trucks that dwarfed cars and humans, priding themselves on things like being able to back one of those giant rigs up into Mr. Kelly's huge yard through his small driveway, touching nothing but gravel and air, with less than a foot's room on either side. Sometimes they shouted insults at each other or dislocated thumbs in fistfights, had bottles broken in their faces, or laughed with compassion, irreverence, pathos, or the most elevated joy sound could capture.

Sometimes they told terrible stories of men who "took them goddam-assed pills to stay awake on that long sumbitchin drive to Barstow" and what happened when the pills stopped working and they instantly fell asleep on the winding course of the San Joaquin Valley, going through a rail and over a cliff or into a ditch, maybe crossing the lane, rig fishtail-ing, causing an accident of bitter slaughter or surviving a collision with the landscape that made them insurance risks too big to stay in business. Most of all, they told tales you later learned were very beautiful lies, were their improvised theater and imaginative manhood, like Kansas City ten-ors on a jam session bandstand.

For the greatest escape from the familiar, you hopped the trains west, to Exposition Park, where the Los Angeles Coliseum was and where you were disappointed to find out no Christians had ever been eaten there at the speed of inhalation by lions. But even more important than the coliseum was the Museum of Science and Industry because there was always something new to look at—an explanation of the motion of gases, the story of the career of oil as it was drilled for, captured, imprisoned in barrels, and finally reduced to the slave pens of jars of petroleum jelly or gas tanks or what have you. It was always wonderful because the architecture seemed so modern, there was no writing on the walls, and the guards reminded you of deacons or church ushers as they ceremoniously walked their sections or collected tickets for the displays that cost money. There, in the cool and darkened hallways that were highlighted by the illuminated displays, was another world, and one that had very little to do with anything or anyone you knew, which was part of its glory. The laws were clear and you could learn them as they traveled, like those trains and those big trucks, on their own, night and day.

August 1980

MARVIN GAYE'S INTERCONNECTIONS

I don't like to follow my footsteps and my shadow. Singers are
afraid to branch out and try new and exciting things. I did.

—MARVIN GAYE

S INCE *WHAT'S GOING ON* IN 1971, Marvin Gaye has proven himself
the most brilliant and complex thinker in contemporary Black popular music. He's succeeded at bringing ideas beyond the novel to a form
from which we expect wonderfully sung but simple passions, and the successes have expanded the music itself. The result has been the development
of a personal language at ease with gospel quartet crooning, despairing
guttural moans that slide back into the delta, the purple-hearted street-
corner falsetto, and the silken sound of elegant erotic ambition.

His is a talent for which the studio must have been invented. Through
overdubbing, Gaye imparted lyric, rhythmic, and emotional counterpoint
to his material. The result was a swirling stream-of-consciousness that
enabled him to protest, show allegiance, love, hate, dismiss, and desire in
one proverbial fell swoop. In his way, what Gaye did was reiterate electronically the polyrhythmic African underpinnings of Black American
music and reassess the domestic polyphony that is its linear extension.

Much of this probably has to do with his early experience as a Motown drummer, for the arrangements he wrote or supervised staggered off percussion voices and instruments with almost peerless precision. The upshot of his genius was the ease and power with which he could pivot from a superficially simple but virtuosic use of rests and accents to a multilinear layered density. In fact, if one were to say that James Brown could be the Fletcher Henderson and Count Basie of rhythm and blues, then Marvin Gaye is obviously its Duke Ellington and Miles Davis. He seeks an urbanity and sophistication, an intricacy and subtlety that challenge the adolescent sentimentality at the core of the idiom without abandoning the dancing and seductive inclinations of the tradition. Perhaps, as with Davis, his strength developed from his knowledge of his own limitations. Gaye himself has said, "I don't think I do anything according to Hoyle. Voice I do not possess, so I developed a style. I figured out how to make my performance as pleasing as possible."

Not all of his records after *What's Going On* have been pleasing, partly because one doesn't produce a masterwork every time out but also because his primary concerns changed from social comment to sorting out his own experience. Sometimes to the consternation of his listeners, he produced recordings for a few years that seemed to reach for a more narrow satisfaction, an erotic and romantic one in flight from the notorious burden of consciousness. Even so, there was often a spiritual anguish at the back of the dance hall, a mosquito net of sorrow the sleeping Don Juan would have to meet upon awakening.

The boil of bile was lanced by *Here, My Dear*, the controversial double album, inspired by his divorce, which made many feel they were listening to pus running from their speakers. Its emotional range was too great, its bitterness too close to the surface, its despair and self-revelation perhaps too heavy and intricate for both his audience and the form. I also felt that many white reviewers panned it because they didn't like the idea of a Negro complaining about a *million-dollar divorce* (they have long preferred Negroes who need missionaries of some sort). Many women hated it because they thought Gaye was dropping the responsibility on the woman and letting himself off easy (they didn't hear the revelations about his own unfaithfulness and shortsightedness, his own irrational stubbornness and self-inflation). Most important, however, the musical ambition was extraordinary. It was a *Black, Brown, and Beige* of rhythm and blues, with arrangements that mapped a territory stretching from street-corner doo-wop simplicity to the final selection, "Falling in Love Again," which began with Fela-like harmonies and phrasing, then developed its statement with a bold use of overdubbed backup voices and styles. A flawed popular masterpiece, *Here, My Dear*, is his most ambitious album since *What's Going On*.

Now Marvin Gaye has turned it around again with *In Our Lifetime*, a recording on which lust and mysticism are braided like some plait of secular and religious passion strung across a contemporary dance band. One reviewer has voiced dismay at the discontinuity of the album, what with dance exhortations unaccountably flowing into sermons that then change to sexual propositions. But a quote included in Gaye's Motown *Anthology* explains his sense of interconnections:

> Mother kept me singing. She would say, "Get up and sing 'Journey to the Sky.'" The ladies in church, they would hug me and bring me to them. Psychologically, sensually, I liked this.

Few Black musicians who grow up in the church ever forget the image of power and sensuality projected by the best preachers or the amount of lingerie and thighs observed as the church women got the holy ghost and fell on the floor, writhing in ecstasy that had but one parallel.

Though one of his best dance records, this album is simpler in certain ways than what he does at his most adventurous. But the mastery of the idiom and the continued development of his arranging skills give it strength. Though the emotion sloshes back and forth between desire for both salvation and flesh, it is made clear that the latter, while easier to obtain, is never enough. At one point he sings, "Lots of ladies love me but it's still a lonesome time."

Gaye has a superb sense of how to develop his songs chorus by chorus. He usually starts a song singly over the rhythm, adding other instruments, vocals, and occasional improvised instrumental solos or saxophone obbligatos. When he's not developing counterpoint, he will sing a line in unison with one of the rhythm instruments or add a sung note to a chord played by the horns to extend the harmony. Gaye's accents are rarely less than brilliant; he likes to float over the tempos and the rhythms as he italicizes beats that find unexpected spaces in the arrangements. "Far Cry" is a perfect example of his rhythmic invention, while "Love Me Now or Love Me Later" is the high point of his powers of synthesis. In that song, Gaye tells the tale of Creation, speaking of God and the Devil as the composition perfectly combines gospel, blues, and jazz elements. The lyrics, alas, are not very strong, but none of the others are either. Yet Gaye transcends his own lyrics just as jazz singers have transcended those of Tin Pan Alley. That, it seems to me, is the problem at the center of Gaye's work, one that we will probably hear him do battle with for the rest of his career. After all, a man's greatness is often measured by the personal limitations he must overcome. And when Marvin Gaye triumphs, as he does through most of the second side especially, it is pleasing indeed.

March 1981

SAINT MONK

T HOUGH NO ONE KNEW THAT Thelonious Monk would soon have that inevitable meal my grandmother called "breakfast with the moles," there had been a Monk fever in the jazz world for at least two years before he died. On other occasions, I had noticed a spontaneous interest in a master's work break out six months or so before he left us, but nothing like this. It was as if Monk loomed in the air, a symbol and conductor, inspiring virile tributes that would outstrip the soppy praise so predictable in the wake of his demise. Everywhere musicians were buying Monk records, transcribing them, learning the chords and the rhythms, talking about him and his contribution, almost unconsciously making him into a patron saint while he lived.

This was more than nostalgia; it was homage to an illuminative universe, for every aspect of Monk's music comprised what literary critic Hugh Kenner meant by "a homemade world." And, as poet Bert Meyers pointed out to me, world-making is the province of genius, far removed from the merely brilliant creations of a gifted and unique artist. Monk's self-made earth, sky, water, and wind pivoted on its own axis, spinning all the elements of musical craft in the singular rhythms of tension and release that made for his own physics, his own sense of weight and motion. Yet for all its singularity, his art personified what jazz had given to Western music and the world—ways of ordering melody, harmony, color, and rhythm that had eluded the European masters and the virtuosi of folk and ceremonial ethnic music.

Monk's successes embodied the bole and the branches of African American music, but they also put him in two other American contexts. His victories over uninspired convention were aesthetic extensions of the long line of revolutionary American tinkerers like Edison and the Wright Brothers—Monk brought light and aided flight while maintaining the smoke, the bloodstone, the boldness, the humor, and the romance of the jazz tradition. And, like Sherman and Grant, he helped develop a modern strategy for his discipline: Monk's influence made him a decorated officer in the avant-garde campaign of African American assault troops who raised their flags on the Iwo Jimas of the academy and of Tin Pan Alley.

The military metaphor is far from fanciful, for there is a vast difference between the tactician and the strategist—one thinks in short terms, the other in overall shapes achieved by specific effects. The tactician, like the boxer who fights round by round, has no grand design, while design is the talent of the strategist. Monk was a strategist. Every detail of his music had a special place and a desired effect, and every detail was readily distinctive. I once asked the master drummer Roy Haynes why, if you turned on the radio and a horn was improvising with bass and drums while Monk's piano remained silent, you still knew it was his band. "It's the tempos," Haynes answered. "They're always a little slower or a little faster than everybody else's. Once you know Monk's tempos, you recognize it's his music. He doesn't have to be playing."

Even so, he *was* playing, because silence was part of his design, and he was fully aware of how much it could color or shape a performance. More than any of his predecessors—for all his debts to Wilson,* Ellington, and Basie, his use of silence made the pause between musical statements a statement in itself. In Monk's music, silence could be meditative or suspenseful, propulsive or a witty sleight-of-hand in which ideas dissolved into musical air, then hesitantly or boldly reappeared from that same air. When his tinkering inclinations took flight, the upshot was a delicious tension. But even as he sat tinkering, his music often danced with the swelling excitement of someone who is being taught new steps. He'd get a few turns, then stop, trying again, learning another few moves, then repeat them with a bit of an edge, expanding those steps into an increasingly confident rendition that then took on a personal bent and grew into a stomping joy before reversing the process and fading away with an ironic parody of his own beginning steps—a satire so deft it was suddenly obvious that he knew the dance all along and was playing with the form from the outset.

Throughout, Monk did what he did with a domestic virtuosity that developed from the kinds of discoveries Ellington made about jazz piano. It could be a spare set of tuned drums; its registers could lift or lower, darken or lighten the sound of a band; it could orchestrate the ideas within a song, giving them breadth and depth even when only a rhythm section and one horn were the ensemble. At the command of Monk's hands, the piano could also—as had Jimmy Yancey's—imitate a blues singer, or ping one note and drone the next, or give forth swift runs that were subtly but precisely colored with startling inflections and gradations of accent. But whatever the piano was doing, it was always swinging, swinging with the beat or against it, above it or through it.

---

* Teddy Wilson.

To the same quality of playful deception, Monk's compositions added the American ballroom's grand sense of romance. He seemed fundamentally impressed by its cheek-to-cheek fantasy and the disciplined audacity of its wild yet fluid turns, twists, and leaps. The body of his work recasts the ritual elements of existence—everything from comic stories about children to descriptions of the thankless but essential work of tugboats, portraits of spouse, relatives, friends, neighborhood, colors, and the weather. His mementos of sentiment were crafted in the essential moods of jazz—4/4 swing fast, medium, or slow; the blues; the ballad; and the Latin rhythm. What made Monk the third face on the Mount Rushmore of jazz composition (after Morton and Ellington) was that his songs made a world, one that swung or sang with the time, against it, above it, or through it.

It was his ability to go with, against, above, and through that gave Monk such a special place in the hearts of his listeners, lay and professional. Thelonious Monk contributed all that he had—his courage, his cunning, his diligence. He made it quite clear in human terms how much there is to dream—the joy of community and family, the realization of the solitude that underlies all experience, and both the pleasure and the terrible sorrow that can come with that solitude, all tinkered and sung forward with the sometimes hilarious humor of the gods. He made it clear how much there is to have, just as death has made it clear how much we have lost.

March 1982

FIGHTERS

THERE ARE THOSE FOR WHOM SACRIFICE means no more than
a new diet or exercise plan; the glory of the boxer is lost on them.
Through the bitter gruel of discipline, boxers have learned—or soon
will—that they must pay with their bodies for what they want. In the
salty air of the arena or the locker room, on the concrete blocks or the
paths of parks where they run, in the dimly lit rooms where one counts the
fingers of his trainer after he has been knocked out, the fighter prepares
for his work and learns the consequences. From these elemental struggles
we see in microcosm the aches and the blood, the fury and the will, the
pride and the optimism that provide all entries to civilized culture—the
grace that holds barbarism at bay. In their finest light, when their pupils
are masked by melancholy and their muscles are toned, boxers radiate
the quiet perception of risk and morale, reflex and the results of decisions
executed—or fumbled—in an instant. Those with the necessary gifts will
become contenders if not champions, and some might even enter what

is probably the smallest visible minority in America—the shining circle of millionaire athletes. But all know that failure is inevitable for most of them. In this sense, they are like the conquistadors who took what was known of navigation and sailed on their small wooden ships into worlds made nearly impenetrable by danger, willing to see if they could prevail over whatever conditions they met.

Unfortunately, the condescension passed off as social sympathy makes it easy to dismiss the comparison of some Black and Hispanic fighters to conquistadors. It is much easier to define them as people striving for no more than a glorified form of hard labor that italicizes the limitations imposed by race and class—victims of a brutal and senseless sport in which men pulverize each other for pay. This is off the mark; life is no more unfair because the supposedly downtrodden don't have it easy. It's like describing a master chef and the apprentices with their pans of sauce in terms of slaving over hot stoves. A greater percentage of brokers on the stock market floor lose their stomachs than boxers do their eyes or brains; more American youths lose their lives looking for good times as they drunkenly drive our roads; more success stories in other careers end up muttering their disillusionment on the couches of endless analysts than do boxers. And regardless of how much we might deny it in sweet light over good wine on a relaxed day, all of us are in the ring. From our struggle, whatever it might be, we all learn a lot about our capacity to be either winners or losers. Perhaps that is the most essential lesson we will ever learn.

The fighter is a sacrificial hero whose struggles, victories, draws, and defeats physicalize the vitality of the human soul. Like that of the dancer, his art is essentially silent, expressing every aspect of personality bodily. Ideas, strategies, passions, and codes take on the stark form of actions orchestrated for attack and defense. Because the arms get no longer and the height is set when the boxer becomes a man, style develops in accordance with the strengths and limitations of the individual body. If a fighter becomes great it is because he possesses the dimension of heart that exceeds extraordinary physical gifts and makes for the dignity in both victory and defeat that defines true sportsmanship.

It is because the fighter works alone in the most exposed of contact sports that his finest moments take him to a level beyond that of other athletes, where grace is most profoundly elevated to reflex. Though his risk is most individual, his victories are most universal. Visiting the gym, we can contemplate the dreamy face of a boy in a turned-up baseball cap as he studies at ringside, a muscled kid's concentration as he learns to throw a jab into his trainer's hands, another reaching from a bench to pummel the fast bag, two brothers staring with determination and irony as they hold up their dukes side by side, another seated and meditative as his body shines with oil and effort, all aspirants in a preparatory cooker that molds all students for the conflicts they will meet in whatever directions they intend to take their lives. And when they succeed, they are as wondrous as the string virtuosi produced by the Suzuki method.

But finally, fighters provide information about the human soul that transcends victory and defeat. I observed this most recently when I saw a South American superbly defend himself, perpetually frustrating a younger opponent with his cunning, his pacing, his courage. It was obvious soon after the first bell that he had no chance of winning, but the man wrote the terms of his defeat with a physical eloquence and an inner will that hollowed out the younger man's victory. His heroic effort allowed us to discover again how all glory is achieved through the depths of the human heart. This is something all boxers know, and it is a lesson we all learn whenever fine fighters step into the ring.

July 1984

ELLINGTON THE PLAYER

Old men should be explorers.

Retirement is the filthiest word in the language.

Retire to what?

I T OFTEN SEEMS THAT MEN of genius produce their best work after forty. They have outlived all the temptations of celebration that can lead to early and romanticized deaths; if they take care of themselves, they look better than they ever have; the aura emitted from them is both appropriately strong and tender, curious and confident, they are relaxed in face of the expanding details of the bittersweet and tragicomic variables of human experience; and a wit has usually developed that will walk hand-in-hand with them into the showdowns with ambivalence, a wit that endears them equally to the destitute and the affluent.

Duke Ellington's work bears out those observations in many ways. From 1939, when his fortieth birthday was celebrated in song by many

officially assigned Swedish girls as he toured their country, Ellington produced music of such range and variety one feels he would have gone on
forever had he been so unfairly blessed.

Much of what Ellington was able to do was related to his perhaps
unparalleled range of American experience. Probably no other composer in our pantheon, whether working from the blues-derived idiom
of jazz or domestic attempts to redefine European concert music, could
claim the easeful and intimate knowledge of the ways in which Americans live. Ellington, for all his glamour and his aristocratic ambience,
knew the sidewalk, the gutter, the backwoods, the ballroom, the gangsters, the whores, the johns, the dancers, the athletes, the debutantes,
the grand ladies, the superrich, the bookers, the con men, the doctors,
the mathematicians, the mad, and so on. His was a world rich with
infinite variations on human conduct, and the nobility at the center of
his work, a response to what he considered the substance of our existence, was sweeping enough to meet the stretch described in his *A Drum
Is a Woman* (CSP) when he said, "tooth, claw, and petal, feather, fin,
every limb."

This range wasn't achieved only by imagining what happens in those
back rooms where hustlers gamble, those penthouses where high society groans and sighs like everybody else, in the little towns where Negro
musicians were greeted as though they possessed the golden fleece of all
possibility, or the many cities in the world where jazz was embraced as the
embodiment of a sustained primitive vitality intertwined with sophistication. Ellington learned what he knew in person, on an endless amount
of rickety or mediocre or elegant bandstands, on nights where the visual
rhythms of the dancers supplied him with a bottomless variety of ideas
about patterns and accents, in those situations where the band members
played with enough inspiration to goad his composing imagination for
many days, in the late evening or early morning lying sessions where the

lore of Negro America crackled with exaggeration and wit, on the trains
and buses that allowed a man who had once thought of being a painter
to see different qualities of sky color and landscape that this enormous
country provides, not to mention the numberless lessons about tenderness
and passion the man learned from the legions of ladies he came to know
in a biblical sense.

Yet it was Ellington the *player*—accompanist and improviser—who
developed as deeply and broadly as the band's apparently infinite repertoire and who was continually unnoticed or dismissed except by our
greatest musicians, who are usually our greatest listeners (for example,
Dizzy Gillespie: "He was the greatest accompanist in the world"). It is
probably because the dictum about his real instrument being his orchestra
was repeated for so many years that his greatness as a pianist in African American music eluded many. Even so, he was easily one of the best
the idiom has produced, and the same emotional range he brought to
his compositions and orchestrations can be found in his keyboard work.
But Ellington apparently looked upon himself primarily as a pinch-hitter,
calling upon his extraordinary gifts when he found the band in need of
fire, inspiration, or compensation for the fact that, near the end, it was
stripped of almost all major soloists—those gone to time, retirement, or
fatigue in face of the road.

Regardless of what Ellington thought of his own work and regardless of the conventional idea that he played "arranger's piano," it is quite
evident that he had learned well the lessons picked up from the keyboard
masters of New York whom he first encountered in the 1920s, men such
as Willie "The Lion" Smith, Sticky Mack, Fats Waller, and James P.
Johnson. From those players and the endless list of musicians who appear
out of nowhere at a jam session, stun everyone, and disappear into legend,
the young Ellington got his basic training. Part of that instruction was
ear-training—learning what all of those combinations of sounds were;

how one note could change the texture and the meaning of a chord if it was played an octave above or an octave below; how to harmonize lines as they were created either by one's right hand or the urgent imagination of a featured horn player or singer. He also learned how to constantly change the timbre of his instrument through gradations of attack, allowing for a style that would eventually exhibit a range of colors quite stunning in emotional and dramatic effects. Perhaps his most valuable achievement was recognition of the remarkable variety of rhythms available from the reservoir of African American phrasing and accent. In his mature style, Ellington made use of so many rhythmic ideas, so many ways of displacing the beat or creating illusory meters, that it was only his subtlety which kept them from obviousness.

It is also quite possible that Ellington learned as much about piano sound from his band as he had from the Harlem masters, if only because the penchant for rhymes and contrasts led him to demand that the keyboard do many of the things expected of his brass and reeds, his bass and drums. This sensibility made Ellington's accompaniment superb in its relationship to theme, improvisation, and tonal color. That he was a composer became obvious very quickly, because he almost never played merely chords, preferring to shape spontaneous arrangements. The piano will become a reed section suddenly or he will muffle the sound of the notes and the keyboard will appear in the disguise of emulated mutes and plungers. At other moments, the tinkles in the upper register will resemble the sound of either a literal bell or the raised and circular center of a cymbal, also known as a bell.

To illustrate my point, I would like to refer to instances where we hear Ellington working in rhythm sections for vastly different players. On *Echoes of an Era: The Duke Ellington–Louis Armstrong Years* (Roulette), the Maestro crafts some of the best improvised piano arrangements for a singer ever recorded. On "Duke's Place," after playing an introduction in which he "ghosts" a note with easy precision, Ellington invents an antiph-onal arrangement for Armstrong's vocal, barking, grunting, and thump-ing out motifs and chords. (It should also be noticed how, during his extended exit choruses, the piano player sustains notes and imitates slurs, creating an unusual piano attack on the time.) His "I'm Just a Lucky So and So" introduction is as unpretentiously down home as possible, and the responses to Armstrong's vocal sound like everything from trombones to crackling trumpets to bass drums. At every outing, the pianist in Elling-ton invents, never satisfied with a predictable idea, always capable of tak-ing something basic to the vocabulary and twisting it or distorting or disguising it into freshness. Perhaps the emotional high point is the way the keyboard works under both the trumpet and the vocal on "I Got It Bad," which is probably a masterpiece.

His work with John Coltrane, recorded in 1962, is quite different. Ellington chooses to lay out on certain pieces and let Coltrane challenge convention in tandem with Elvin Jones, but there are moments when mag-ical things happen. Listen to the way Ellington sets up things that seem to play on the overtone series during the blues "Take the Coltrane," mak-ing for a very unusual timbre between piano and tenor. Now and again he lets the saxophone state the line, only inserting phrases or a couple of notes, saving his surprise for the out-choruses especially, where it almost seems as though an electronic instrument has been added to the track. Or there is the spare comping on Coltrane's original, "Big Nick," which gives way to a superb piano improvisation after the soprano saxophone. Just as Coltrane finishes, he mutters a few notes through the horn while moving away from the mike. Ellington, hearing them, uses those notes as an organizing motivic block that he expands with wonderful control through his two choruses, inventing a new composition in the process. Then there is the perfect alignment of piano and drum timbres heard on "Angelica" or the way the crafty lion leads Coltrane through "My Little

Brown Book," not to mention the glistening environment he creates for "In a Sentimental Mood."

With his own orchestra, the album *And His Mother Called Him Bill* (RCA) is one of the best examples of what Ellington could do. Listen, for instance, to what he plays under shiny Hodges on "Day Dream." Does he act up! His constantly surprising ideas are damped for darkness, sustained here and there, sparkled out in pearly two- and three-note chords, even combining trills inside oblique runs that imitate the alto's vibrato! A piece such as "Rain Check" shows off his singular and unpredictable phrasing. After the written orchestral introduction, the piece becomes a brief concerto for piano in which Ellington states the theme as he abstracts its rhythm, pushing accents in and out of line, shortening and lengthening the notes as he changes their textures. On the way out, he toys with the opening motif, then the entire melody, compressing and expanding riffs.

Ellington's time is well displayed in a few signal examples from hundreds of moments in the studio or public performance. His introduction to "Take the A Train" on *The Popular Duke Ellington* (RCA) seems as though it is in waltz time but is actually a canny way to phrase over two-beat measures. The 12-bars on "Black and Tan Fantasy" aren't improvised, but the phrasing broaches the question, as the pianist invents an interpretation that begins simply, then seems to totally obscure the time, the pace, and the tone, appearing to take a diving bell down through the tempo as the bass and drums go free; then Ellington resurrects the meter just in the nick of time and stomps his way out. Or there is the way the piano weaves through "Grace Valse" on *Anatomy of a Murder* (Columbia), anticipating the time and the arrangement, delaying the beat at perfect moments, playing runs when unexpected or propping up a melodic kernel that is reharmonized a few times in subtle but rapid succession.

I would also suggest, for those who might still doubt his powers, that they take a listen to the extended piano improvisation on "Ad Lib on

Nippon" from *The Far East Suite* (RCA), the rich beat and rhythms of "Wig Wise" from *Money Jungle* (United Artists), "Fragmented Suite for Piano and Bass" from *This One's for Blanton* (Pablo), and the 1970 Decca version of "New World A-Coming" with the Cincinnati Orchestra. In each instance, his control of tone, time, emotional projection, and the unexpected are exemplary. There are, as I have mentioned, many, many instances of this great musician's stature as a jazz pianist, but I am convinced that once the listener begins to pay attention, the amount of stellar work available is guaranteed to astonish.

August 1984

THE "SCENE" OF LARRY NEAL

NEW YORK IS NOTORIOUS among new arrivals for its cold shoulders, its blasé responses, its thin skins, and its pace. When you get to know it, however, the dispirited image is often a loser to a sentimentality that can roar forth like subway trains climbing miles of track in the open air, leaving the very highest skyscrapers behind. Perhaps it is the combination of legendary purple hearts reared within the Jewish, Italian, Irish, Negro, and Latin populations that makes it so and in the face of which makes it difficult to approach the public mourning of the disappearance of a particular spirit, a spirit such as that of Larry Neal, who died about an hour before midnight in Hamilton, New York, on January 6, 1981, at the age of forty-three.

I had known Larry Neal for almost fifteen years, having met him over the phone in the middle of the furious 1960s, when we were all in pursuit of a new aesthetic and what we thought should be a new image and direction for African Americans. As I was then living in California, we had many transcontinental telephone conversations, for Larry, as critic and writer, was one of the luminaries of the Manhattan Black art scene, and we took something of a liking to each other. We were always discussing politics and art, art and politics. He was one of the most adventurous and intelligent men we had, and his sense of intellectual responsibility often called upon him to disagree with the conventions of Black nationalism as the romance began to fade in face of the megalomania, the lies, the avarice, and the interwoven monstrosities of totalitarian and opportunistic impulses. In fact, over the past few years, Larry had begun to be seen as a conservative.

I saw him pretty much as a radical, for Larry quickly realized that the elevation of a new Black aesthetic shouldn't be a disguised excuse for mediocrity or poor quality (which it too often was). He saw his ethnic particulars as a set of fresh challenges and options that could, if successfully evoked, enrich contemporary criticism, poetry, fiction, and theater, the arenas in which he worked. The goal was to bring those new materials to aesthetic fruition with the breadth of sensibility Ellington had brought to music.

And what makes Larry Neal's early death such a tragedy is that he was constantly preparing himself for such an undertaking. Not only was he a scholar always ready to research a topic, but also he knew quite well the social and cultural intricacies of Harlem and much of the rest of Manhattan. If you were a new arrival, whether visiting or moving here, he opened his brownstone on Jumel Terrace to you and could give the most incredible whirlwind tours, for Larry was one of those guys who had such an epic social awareness and so many friends and contacts that he seemed to quite literally know everybody, or nearly everybody who was important. In his company, you would meet the highs, the lows, and the middles as you moved from penthouses to after-hours hustling joints, leaving early in the evening and returning early the next morning. Each of those places was given a brief but thorough history as you approached them, and the way the habits, character, and dress of the people who lived in or frequented them were noted in his conversation made it quite clear that you were being shown a terrain a certain writer intended to make even deeper through his literary creations.

He once wrote, "I, too, was birthed in conundrum," and the intricate riddle of African American culture and history, its overwhelming influence on domestic folkways, entertainment, art, athletics, language, and dance were always important to him. Early on, Larry began to look at folktales, slang, and street chants as sources for a vernacular surrealism and was in search of a language that would allow for elasticity of reference, diction, and rhythm. His most recently performed play, *The Glorious Monster in the Bell of the Horn*, and even his early work, the poems of *Black Boogaloo* and *Hoodoo Hollerin' Bebop Ghosts*, illustrate his direction and the complexity of his development. As his ideas and his sense of craft and responsibility grew, he encouraged as many different kinds of voices as he found valuable and emphasized the importance of Negro American intellectuals taking on the writing and critical establishments of Manhattan with more than scowls and blood-smeared harangues. Within the Black art community, he first showed this sense of seriousness by exposing a controversial New Lafayette Theatre production of *We Righteous Bombers* as a plagiarized reworking of a Camus play. Recently, he was preparing to work with Max Roach on the great drummer's autobiography, planning panels, working on screenplays, theater, fiction, and essays.

Of course, he will never make the contributions that he was planning as his death approached, that massive congenital heart attack that had taken his father and his grandfather before him. His wit and the sweep of his intelligence are now stilled as is the exemplary courage that, for all his friends, made him something of an isolated man, an intellectual whose sense of struggle and tradition alienated him from the simple-minded as he prepared for the next level of battle with expression and form. There were so many stories that he had yet to tell and so many insights he would undoubtedly have made part of the creative consciousness. But most of all, Larry Neal embodied the depth of soul and sense we ask of our most responsible people, and, with his passing, Manhattan is much less soulful and makes much less sense.

1985

THE INCOMPLETE TURN
OF LARRY NEAL

A N EARLY DEATH is most tragic when someone fully capable of executing a personal plan is snuffed out before bringing it off. Now that Larry Neal has been dead almost ten years, I understand that fact much better, especially after reading his essays collected in this volume.* Beyond the congenital misfortune of Larry Neal's heart attack, there is another grim fact: Death can deem the weight of a man's work a failure. This is not the same as one's success as a person—the sensitivity, affection, wit, passion, intellectual curiosity, and challenge someone can so consistently bring to social and intimate friendships that the loss of a particular presence is deeply mourned. Though Larry Neal had those qualities and exhibits them in the best of the work included here, he never really achieved what he was after *in literary terms*. He was just shaking off the conventions of Black nationalist thought that had driven his intellect to

---

* *Visions of a Liberated Future, Black Arts Movement Writings*, by Larry Neal.

the canvas, was in the process of taking a few rounds, and had a grand strategy for what he was going to do all the way through the fifteenth when he left the ring feet first.

In a sense, Larry was not only a product but also a victim of the anger, despair, and frustration that began to dominate the thought of many younger Black artists and writers in the mid-1960s as the tactics and achievements of the civil rights movement were spurned in favor of ideas coming from Malcolm X and Frantz Fanon. When those ideas were not racist, they were couched in an ethnic version of Marxist revolution that embraced Third World liberation movements and applauded what was then considered the inevitable fall of Western capitalist democracies. Borrowing from Mao Zedong's "Yan'an Talks" on literature and art, those who thought themselves at the forefront of a Black cultural revolution perceived creation as an assault weapon and an affirmation of the virtues of the common people.

In a number of these essays, one encounters the philosophical attacks on the systems of the Western world, romantic celebrations of African purity, denunciations of the purported Uncle Toms who didn't embrace separatist and violent "solutions" to the American race problem, and the demand that all serious younger Black artists commit themselves to a particular vision of political change. Such writing is now more important in terms of its relationship to the thought processes that underlay the work of a generation that produced nothing close to a masterpiece, that failed, as all propaganda—however well intentioned—inevitably fails. We learn little about the human soul from most of that writing: It exists more as evidence of a peculiar aspect of social history than as any kind of aesthetic achievement.

But Larry Neal is important because he was one of the first who had been taken in by the self-segregation of Black nationalist thinking to realize how little it had to offer and how easily it prepared the way for demagogues. During the past decade of his life, Larry became more and more concerned with writing a body of work that could take its place on the shelf with the intellectual champions of this and any previous time wherever they might come from, regardless of their color or class or religion. He was focusing on what Ornette Coleman calls "the human reason," which is the mysterious area all truly ambitious writers must address.

To address that inevitable body of mystery, Larry had to slowly, even painfully, tear himself free of the presumptions that were once thought bold and insightful but were actually manifestations of intellectual sleeping sickness. Even though still caught in the nationalist vision of the world, Larry is moving away from it in "My Lord He Calls Me by the Thunder," where he questions the outright rejection of the Black Christian church, which was under attack from Negro Muslims on one hand and Marxists on the other. In "The Ethos of the Blues," he rejects the limited vision of Ron Karenga, whose cultural nationalism never allowed for the appreciation of art that couldn't be utilized as part of a mishmash of racism and saber rattling. "Uncle Rufus Raps on the Squared Circle" tips its hat to Langston Hughes's Simple stories but contains a startling moment when the listener within the essay suddenly appears inside an example of the subject being explained by Uncle Rufus. Larry's ability to see through Baldwin's self-pitying Niagara of tears and recognize the need for a more comprehensive use of Afro-American culture in fiction is another example of the hairpin turn he was making.

The best essay included here, "Ralph Ellison's Zoot Suit," shows where he was going and finds him rejecting the impositions of propagandist rhetoric on serious literary work. Larry did such a good job of assessing the issues raised by *Invisible Man* and the responses to it that one can quite clearly see where he intended to go and how much he admired Ellison's refusal to be used by placard carriers. It was a statement of intellectual rebirth and a declaration of war against simplistic thinking.

That Larry Neal was never able to write another essay as good has less to do with his talent than the time he was allowed by the riddling whirlpool of human fate. Personal problems and a job in Washington, D.C., had taken up a lot of his time, but he was working to prepare himself for the next stage of his development when he died. Even though I knew him well and talked with him often, I have no idea what he would have done once he got down to the business he intended to take care of, part of which was shaping a more comprehensive aesthetic vision in light of all that had failed, in literary terms, by adhering to the doctrines of ethnic propaganda. But because he was coming to better understand the importance of the Afro-American culture that so many Black nationalists and would-be revolutionaries had such contempt for, I have no trouble imagining that he would have become much more the writer his own ambitions demanded. That he was never able to become that writer is a tragedy of no small proportion, given the astonishing amount of trash that has been written on the subject of Negro American life since his death. Even so, there is much inspiration to be drawn from the fact that Larry Neal, when it was far from popular in his circle, was proudly starting to celebrate the bittersweet complexity of his identity as an American.

February 1989

UPTOWN AGAIN

BETTY CARTER SAT A FEW ROWS in front of me wearing a red hat and a fur-trimmed cape, her head tilted back in the position that says she's listening. I was up in Harlem, seated in an Apollo that was now overheated in places but had been bone-crackingly cold five or six years ago when I had last been there. As I stood in the lobby talking with one of Percy Sutton's sons, James Moody was finishing his set, the roar of his tenor rising over the rhythm. There I was in Harlem once again—a place I rarely visit, though I'm passed up by many cab drivers who assume I'm going there.

Harlem had always been soaked in mythology for me. Oh, from that great distance of three thousand miles, Harlem was another world. It was the place Duke Ellington referred to in "Harlem Air Shaft," a recording I often listened to as a teenager, fascinated by Tricky Sam Nanton's plunger technique. It was where Adam Clayton Powell Jr., who reminded me then of Cesar Romero Jr., ruled the roost and floated down sayings like "Keep the Faith." It was there that hidden cameras recorded the doings of the dope trade, then on 116th and Lenox. Or Harlem was where Negroes with features different from those I was accustomed to used to appear on the evening news and use terms like "the power structure." They looked odd to me and sounded odd, many in possession of the heavy-lidded eyes, the curled lips, and the avian profiles I then associated with illustrations from the *Arabian Nights*. Their talk had cross-pollinated inflections, part Irish, part Jewish, part Italian, and part Negroid—vocal cords soaked in the melting pot.

I was still reading about the Harlem riot of 1964 in *Negro Digest* when Watts blew up a year later, making all Black Los Angeles residents symbols of the refusal to swallow the bile of white mistreatment outside the South. When I visited New York a few years later, I was surprised to be treated like a war hero. Yet in Los Angeles I had begun to notice how all kinds of people who weren't from Watts proper were suddenly locals squawking like baby birds, calling for the fresh worms of poverty-program funds. One guy had even told me how he took his vacation and drove east with a trunk full of bricks, selling each one as the first brick thrown in the Watts riot. He had done well. In Harlem he would have done well, too. People bought you drinks and asked what you had seen. They admired the freedom of Negroes in Los Angeles because in New York, they lived above so many of the businesses that overcharged them, that to set them afire would mean burning down one's home.

But that wasn't what made the first visit so impressive. It was the vitality and the feeling of endless celebration. I had left on a sweltering Los Angeles day and arrived at Newark Airport, where the temperature was 15 degrees. Prepared, I came into Manhattan warmly dressed, heading to meet a friend in the West Village. Soon we were in the New York evening, going to all the jazz clubs downtown—the Village Gate, the Vanguard, Slug's, the Five Spot, Boomer's. Nothing had the sheen and the size that I expected, but the power of the performers knocked me over. I don't remember anybody I heard downtown then except Roy Haynes, who was leading a band with Joe Henderson playing tenor. I can still see Haynes, a grimace on his face and stunning rhythms flying out of his trap set.

Whipped up in the heady swing of the Village, I had no idea that there was still more. We headed uptown, traveling to the vital strip that was Seventh Avenue above 125th Street. Were they swinging! There was nothing like that in Los Angeles, Black people streaming in and out of jazz clubs, the atmosphere rich with the wisdom of rhythm, and the people sauntering or strutting with gauche syncopations. There were waffles and chicken at one room, music at another, cars double-parked everywhere, and a feeling of aliveness I had rarely experienced.

In the after-hours joints, beyond the hustlers who were the same dullards you meet all over the country, many kinds of conversations were going on, and I got a sense of the New York vision. In those accents that were still strange to me, I heard the wounded humor, the opaque aloofness, the riddles of experience, and the humane expansiveness I associated with the South I'd visited as a child. I knew at that point that I wanted to move to New York.

A few years later, I visited New York again and remember quite well an evening spent with Larry Neal, who took me to the Club Baron on 132nd Street and Lenox Avenue, where I was introduced to Teddy Hill, who had once set Kenny Clarke up in Minton's, providing him with the job that made the way for the bebop revolution. In his metal-rimmed glasses and blue suit, Hill was sharp and removed, his handshake the light clutching that is still in Manhattan fashion, except for those feminists who squeeze hands tighter than lumberjacks do.

Up on the stand was Betty Carter, singing to a packed house, stalking her audience, a dress fitting closely over the bulbous glory of her backside, those arms like exclamation points, her turns and bends extensions of her notes. The audience was right with her at every note, urging her on and shouting what amounted to assenting fills every time she paused. If there was such a thing as paradise, I was there. Then Art Blakey came on the bandstand, using three saxophone players, one of whom was small and stood away from the others, nearly alone at the left side of the bandstand, filling the house with no microphone. Who the hell was that? Played strange things, too. Art Blakey introduced him as Don Byas. So that was Byas. I spoke with Byas during the break, even more startled by his elfin size up close. So this was Harlem.

It *was* Harlem. When I arrived in New York in the fall of 1975, most of that was on the way out. There were hardly any clubs left where you could hear first-class players, and the name Harlem had become synonymous with filth, ignorance, and crime. I recall one evening how a musician described the tears that rolled down Kenny Clarke's cheeks when he visited from Paris and saw what had once been a wonderland turned into a full-fledged slum, though pockets of homespun finesse still did and still do prevail. "Klook couldn't believe it. Minton's closed and sealed up, dope everywhere, more ignorance per square inch than in a hotel for morons. It was sad to see him, and he was sad to see Harlem like that."

I thought about all of that a few weeks ago as I sat listening to Etta Jones rock the Apollo, Houston Person's tenor a vibrant rejoinder to her willfully cracked notes and intentional rasps. Around me were the same kinds of people I had seen and met in Harlem twenty years before, people I thought had been spirited away or had lost interest in jazz. I no longer saw them when I was at Smalls Paradise or any of the other clubs struggling to get a jazz footing in Harlem again. But there they were, listening, bobbing, singing along, snapping their fingers. They were well dressed, and they brought that special feeling to the groove that Negroes can never have only through genetics. They were the result of a culture, not a bloodline, and it was good to know that they, in face of all the mediocrity given shiny Black surfaces, are still there. Neither Harlem nor any place in America has better news.

March 1986

AN OPERA BASED
ON MALCOLM X

WHEN COMPARED TO MEN such as Frederick Douglass and Martin Luther King Jr., Malcolm X seems no more than a thorned bud standing in the shadow of sequoias. Given national recognition by television in 1959, Malcolm X was just beginning to realize how empty his platform had been when he was silenced in 1965, shot down in the very same Harlem that he had victimized either materially as a street hustler or intellectually as the loudest mouthpiece for the Nation of Islam. That so few are willing to admit how much more he made of the thorns than the bud that never truly opened is yet another example of the intellectual dishonesty that has dogged Negro America since too many in positions of influence and responsibility started sipping at the well of a Black nationalism.

But misbegotten political programs coming from Negroes haven't been fostered or upheld in isolation; irresponsible whites who think themselves "sympathetic" have also helped fog the horizon. Beverly Sills is the latest culprit. In her position as general director of the New York City Opera, Sills is serving up some buzzard meat incinerated to charcoal, covered with a glistening glop of honey, and calling it pheasant under glass. The name of it is *X (The Life and Times of Malcolm X)*, and it had its world premiere on September 28, 1986. Written by Anthony, Christopher, and Thulani Davis, *X* manages to be neither musically creative nor mythically resonant, tragically piercing nor provocatively memorable. What we are given is one of the most ruthlessly dishonest renditions of a historical figure I have ever seen.

It is ironic that we should get from three Afro-Americans the same thing that almost every wing of the Black community so often complains of when white historical figures are sentimentalized beyond recognition; when, for instance, ice-hearted killers are remade into gleaming folk heroes or defenders of slavery are presented as sublimely humane and intrepidly democratic. Though they avoid the human and political facts of the matter at every turn, the three unwise Davises apparently think themselves the authors of a heroic tragedy. Composer Anthony Davis says in the program notes:

> I always viewed Malcolm X as a truly heroic figure, and thought that he would make a great subject for an opera. His life was a dramatic odyssey—he went from a destitute childhood to street life to prison. He then educated himself, became a minister, and evolved into a powerful political figure. Malcolm's transformation was such a model. He had been a peer to the man on the street, so he could come back and tell them, "You have to change your life." He taught Blacks to help themselves, stirred their racial pride, and gave them hope that they could achieve political and economic power. Although I greatly admired Martin Luther King—I met him when I was a boy—Malcolm's life was just so *dramatic*.

But the opera itself is woefully lacking in drama and is given to the kind of intellectual cowardice that some Negroes justify with terms like "positive Black images" and "the need for Black heroes." *X* treats its audience as much like children as any slave master ever did; it fails to address adult problems and avoids the terrible murkiness of the human soul at every occasion.

Thulani Davis, who wrote the rhymed couplets that in their ineptitude seem embarrassing by comparison with the human illuminations of the blues, suggests a desire for tragedy in her program quote: "We wanted the audience to see the events in Malcolm's life clearly. We want them to be horrified, not crying or upset." Tragedy, however, demands that the doomed hero face his involvement in his fate, that he recognize the merciless consequences resulting from the interplay between his personality and his circumstances. As *The Autobiography of Malcolm X* shows, the man who died at the Audubon Ballroom eleven months after breaking away from the Nation of Islam never really examined the personality flaws that made him so gullible or so dangerous. As he was disentangling himself from one snarl of misconceptions, Malcolm X was strapping himself into another intellectual and political high chair and was gratefully accepting spoon-feed political baby food from another jar—the simplified, self-serving, and sometimes fascistic notions and platforms of Arab and African politicians and students.

During his celebrated trip to Mecca and to West Africa, Malcolm X was again taken in. He accepted the excuse that any Arab racism toward Black Africans was the result of "Western influence," yet another version of the white man as the snake in Eden. This supposedly brilliant man and student of Black history never questioned the Arab slave trade or the Islamic conquest of African countries and the destruction of indigenous African culture, which Ousmane Sembène took to task in *Ceddo*, nor did Malcolm X ask whether the numerous racist Black images in *Tales from a*

Thousand and One Nights that clearly parallel the ones he railed against in Hollywood films were perhaps accurately translated by Sir Richard Burton. When African students were contemptuous of democratic debate and willing to assault anyone who disagreed with Malcolm X's speeches, he was incapable of recognizing what he was witnessing—the ruthlessness that has long bedeviled post-colonial African politics. Malcolm X was so overjoyed to be greeted as a celebrity that his purported abilities for hard analysis were put on hold.

EVEN SO, THE Davises had the opportunity to reach tragedy, to create pathos, to pull the covers off a figure whose psychological and emotional birthday suit was as much that of an elephant man as anything else. He was a man who was constantly misled, both by his ego and by the distortions of one sort or another that he so willingly accepted from others. Malcolm X was given to the cynicism of the parasitic street hustler, of the convict so embittered and atheistic he was nicknamed "Satan" in prison, and of the homemade and racist parody of a theology offered by Elijah Muhammad. He was a man whose bad judgment meant that he eventually had to repudiate his every stage of development and whose vision, however clever at times, never reached the poetic grandeur he so begrudgingly recognized—as did the vast majority of Negro Americans—in the work and thought of Martin Luther King Jr. So what must be faced about the ambitious man who was Malcolm X, who hoped to go down in history as a significant martyr, is that the bulk of his career was spent passing out intellectual and political blanks. His ideology gave off a loud report but had no chance of hitting a target; for the most part, Malcolm X's notions—save in the confused last eleven months of his life—were defeatist, were a racist program of surrender and smug hopelessness grounded in separatism and the belief that white people were devils incarnate.

Though such observations can easily be gleaned from the *Autobiography*, the Davises, cowardly and cotton-candy militant all, never touch any of the man's human qualities with aesthetic and emotional daring. Instead of a tragedy centered in the parasitic world of the hustler and the nihilism of racist Black nationalism (as opposed to reasonable ethnic pride), they settle for a series of cartoon posturings.

By removing the emotional intestines from Malcolm X's life and by avoiding the facts of his career as a hustler and an evangelist for racism, the Davises don't give baritone lead Ben Holt much to really do. His problems with projection are increased by orchestration that too frequently puts a field of instruments in his register as obstacles—perhaps breaking convention, but rather stupidly. Silent in the hustling world of *X*, Holt isn't allowed to change from a country boy into a piranha rising from the mud to show his teeth. He merely puts on different clothes and listens to some chanting celebrants who seem more hipsterish than those who have made wrecks of so many Black communities—and whom Malcolm X described with such depth, detail, and disgust. Instead of the prisoner so swollen with hatred and spiritual pollution that he was dubbed "Satan" by his fellow convicts, the Davises give us a caged prophet who pompously says his "truth" is "too rough." (Actually, Malcolm X gloried in the status he achieved as a sharp and clever debater who never missed an opportunity to inject race into any discussion.) The man who converted to an Islam that was based on race hatred and a homemade version of a chosen people doesn't appear either. The insistence that the white man was the devil and the born enemy of Black people, that Christianity was no more than a tool used to subvert Black consciousness, that the civil rights movement was generaled by boot-licking dupes and cowards, and that separation from an America doomed to fiery destruction by God was the only solution to the race problem never comes from the mouth of this Malcolm X. Nor do the Davises give us any idea of what Malcolm X meant when he told Gordon

Parks, "I did many things as a Muslim that I'm sorry for now. I was a zombie then—like all Muslims—I was hypnotized, pointed in a certain direction and told to march. Well, I guess a man's entitled to make a fool of himself if he's ready to pay the cost. It cost me twelve years."

Malcolm X's first descent into despair came when he found out how successfully Elijah Muhammad had converted him into a chump. "I felt like a fool," he told Alex Haley, "out there every day preaching and apparently not knowing what was going on right under my nose, in my own organization, involving the very man I was praising so." Malcolm X was referring to his discovery that the Messenger of Islam was guilty of the paternity charges brought against him by former secretaries. According to Malcolm X, the secretaries not only confirmed all the rumors but informed him that Elijah Muhammad saw his most charismatic minister as a potential threat. Ever the hustler, however, Malcolm X admitted searching for passages in the Bible that would justify the Messenger's high-handed morality if—and when—everything publicly exploded. When he saw the old man and told him, Muhammad supposedly said that he was only fulfilling prophecy as he impregnated his secretaries, implying that it was his duty to experience sin in order to truly combat it. Are we given this remarkable scene? Is Malcolm X shown as a man desperately trying to maintain his faith in a fraud when the facts point in another direction? Hardly. The libretto only has the sorrowing follower sing to his leader, "I hear things I cannot believe; they say the Messenger has his own law." Such is the flight from dramatic confrontation, from characterization, from the Mississippi nights of the soul.

This is especially unfortunate because the singer Thomas Young was clearly capable of giving much more range and color to the role of Elijah Muhammad. In fact, he is so much more powerful a singer than Holt that he should have had the lead. As a singer and stage presence, Priscilla Baskerville is such a sweltering wonder that one cannot understand why the romance between Malcolm X and Betty Shabazz was reduced to no more than symbolic passing. The way she magnetized him is one of the most charming parts of the *Autobiography*. In *X*, his wife and children merely appear, magically, before the trip to Mecca.

The music matches the libretto in superficiality. In the first act, the score poorly approximates some blues grooves, now and then nearly reaching inspiration but settling for second-rate excitement no more authentic than the Motown imitations of *Dreamgirls*. Nothing in Afro-American music is digested well enough to express the emotional forces available at least since the spirituals. The second act is an abysmally anonymous encyclopedia of twentieth century concert-music clichés. Again, melody never really rears its lyrical head, except in three- or four-note snippets and an occasional ascending arpeggio. The music for the Mecca segment is dull and totally lacking in religious intensity. In the last few minutes, when the tension bubbles as the assassination approaches, drama actually arrives—only to be iced by the curtain as the killers stand and take aim.

X is neither about the life and times of Malcolm X nor anything else deserving so much press attention. It is a fumbled opportunity, no more, no less. But then little of tragic merit can be expected from those who took the saber-rattling politics of Malcolm X seriously. Surface bluster and occasional insight is what he had to offer. Still, we should get more from those who pose as artists.

1987

PREMATURE AUTOPSIES

"A sermon on jazz," written by S.C. for Wynton Marsalis's album The Majesty of the Blues.

THOUGH WE ARE TOLD TO MOURN IT, we must know that it was a noble sound. It had majesty. Yes, it was majestic. Deep down in the soul of it all, where the notes themselves provide the levels of revelation we can only expect of great art, it formed a bridge. That's right, a bridge. A bridge that stretched from the realm of dreams to the highways and byways and thoroughfares and back roads of action. To be even more precise, let me say that this sound was itself an action. Like a knight wrapped in the glistening armor of invention, of creativity of integrity of grace, of sophistication, of *soul*, this sound took the field. It arrived when the heart was like a percussively throbbing community suffering the despair imposed by dragons. Now if a dragon thinks it is grand enough, that dragon will try to make you believe that what you need to carry you through the inevitable turmoil that visits human life is beyond your grasp. If that dragon thinks it is grand enough, it will try to convince you that there is no escape, no release, no salvation from its wicked dominion. It will tell you that you are destined to live your life in the dark. But when a majestic sound takes the field, when it parts the waters of silence and noise with the power of song, when this majestic concatenation of rhythm, harmony, and melody assembles itself in the invisible world of music, ears begin to change and lives begin to change and those who were musically lame begin to walk with a charismatic sophistication to their steps. You see, when something is pure, when it has the noblest reasons as its fundamental purpose, then it will become a candle of sound in the dark cave of silence. Yes, it was a noble sound.

I say it *was* a noble sound because we are told today that this great sound is dead. We are told that because it did not cosign the ignoble proclivities of the marketplace, because it did not lie back and relax in the dungeon with riffraff, because it had an attitude of gutbucket grandeur, and because it sought to elevate through elegance, for all of these things, it has died, for some a most welcome death. But we must understand that the money lenders of the marketplace have never *ever* known the difference between an office or an auction block and a temple, they have never known that there was any identity to anything other than that of a hustle, a shuck, a scam, a game. If you listen to them, they'll tell you that everything is always up for sale. They recognize no difference or distance between the sacred and the profane. For them, everything is fair game to be used in *their* game. Oh, they chuckle when they hear that the coffin for this noble sound has been built; they offer to donate more nails. They send bouquets instead of wreaths. They feel this sound began to outlive its usefulness the moment it could no longer be abused in the world of prostitution, that world where the beautiful, wondrous act of intimate romance and procreation is reduced to one fact: a sham ritual in which the customer's appetite for lies is equaled by the prostitute's willingness to tell those lies in whatever detail he is ready to pay for. The tones of lies are vulgar facts but they are not noble sounds.

But there is another truth, and that truth passes through time in the very same way an irresistible force passes through an immovable object. That's what I said: This truth is so irresistible that it passes through immovable objects. It is the truth of a desire for a refined and impassioned portrait of the presence and the power and the possibilities of the human spirit. Can you imagine that? I said: a desire for the refined and impassioned depiction in music of the presence and the power and the possibilities of the human spirit. That is the desire that lights the candle in the darkness. That is the desire that confounds dragons who think themselves so grand. We have heard the striking of the match and have felt ourselves made whole in the glow of the candle for a long time.

It is possible that we who listened heard something timeless from those who are the descendants of the many who were literally up for sale, those whose presence on the auction blocks and in the slave quarters formed the cross upon which the Constitution of this nation was crucified. Yet, even after that crucifixion, there were those who rose in the third century of American slavery with a vision of freedom; there were those who lit the mighty wick that extended from the candle and carried it; there were those who spoke through music of the meaning of light; those who were not content to accept the darkness in the heart that comes of surrender to dragons who think themselves grand; those who said— *listen closely now*—who said, "If you give me a fair chance I will help you better understand the meaning of democracy." Yes, that is precisely what they said: "If you give me a fair chance I will help you better understand the meaning of democracy." These are they who were truly the makers of a noble sound.

But as we mourn the passing of this noble sound, we are told to accept the idea that no longer are those blessed who are endowed with majestic inclinations; we are told that no longer are those blessed who have the intention of refining those majestic inclinations into rhythm and tune.

If we accept that, however, we might find ourselves ignoring the democratic imperatives of our birthright. We might fail to understand what was meant way back in the day when the sun of liberty had been cloaked by the ignoble practice of slavery. We might fail to understand that those living in the dragon's shadow of bondage fashioned a luminous and mighty chariot that could swing low and carry us back to the home of human hope, which is heroism. I say heroism because it is ever the quality of bravery, of devotion, of the will to nobility that underscores the marvelous phrases of this music. It swung low and it swung upward and it wore wings. It knew that its shining armor would fit it well because it tried that armor on at the gate of slavery's hell. It was the ethereal aerodynamics of musical art in America. It was democratic because it proved over and over that the sound of human glory knows no social limitations, that the sound of human glory has no concern with pigmentation, that the sound of human glory transcends all definitions except those of the human soul itself. Without a doubt, it was a noble sound.

Some people might ask, "What is this man doing talking about nobility? Doesn't he know that this is a dragon-spawned and blood-encrusted century? Doesn't he know that the dragon breath of our time is breathing down the neck of the year 2000? Doesn't he know that this is the era of flash and cash?" I will say to them that the interwoven labyrinths of greed and manipulation are as old as the *first* lie. When you lie you are trying to manipulate; and when you try to manipulate for false profit you reveal your greed; and when you swallow that dragon dust cooperatively you reveal yourself as a chump, a sucker, one of those folks Barnum said was born every minute. But I will answer them also by saying that nobility is always born somewhere out there in the world, and when you live in a democratic nation you have to face the mysterious fact that nobility has no permanent address, you have to face the fact that nobody has nobility's private phone number. Nobility is not listed in the phone book. Nobility is not listed in the society column, nobility shows up where it feels like showing up, and where it feels like showing up might be just about anywhere. If it could rise like a mighty light from among the human livestock of the plantation, you know it can come from anywhere it wants to. You see, nobility is listed though. Yes, it is listed. Nobility lists itself in the human spirit, and its purpose is to enlist the ears of the listeners in the bittersweet song of spiritual concerns.

As we gather here to mourn the passing of this noble sound, we should take the pains to remember something. There are some of us who don't accept the dreams of dragons as their own, no matter how grand those dragons might say they are. Yes, there are some who will refuse to drop the candle even when pushed into a dark cave and locked there behind a stone. Don't forget the people like Duke Ellington, who will not leave the field once it becomes obvious that the sound of a cymbal swinging in celebration is more beautiful than the ringing of a cash register. Remember that there are those who, like Duke Ellington, are willing to face the majesty of their heritage and endure the slow, painful development demanded of serious study. There is, you must recall, a kind of serious study that will give you the confidence to strike your match to the mighty wick that will illuminate yet another portion of the darkness. Out there somewhere are the kind of people who do not accept the premature autopsy of a noble art form. These are the ones who follow in the footsteps of the gifted and the disciplined who have been deeply hurt but not discouraged, who have been frightened but have not forgotten how to be brave, who revel in the company of their friends and sweethearts but are willing to face the loneliness that is demanded of mastery.

In order to carry the candle, you have to accept the fact that when the wax on that candle begins to melt, it will slide down and burn your hand. You must be willing to accept the fact that pain is a part of the process of revelation. You have to be willing to take the field and stay on the field the way Duke stayed on the road, traveling in raggedy cars, traveling in private Pullman cars, traveling by bus, traveling by boat, traveling against his will sometimes in airplanes. Duke Ellington accepted all the pain and the agony and the self-doubt and the disappointment he was faced with because he had been inspired! Duke Ellington was inspired by the majesty he heard coming from the musicians of all hues and from all levels of training. Duke heard the Constitutional orchestra of American life and transformed it into musical form. Whenever they said this music was dead, Duke was out there, writing music and performing the meaning of his democratic birthright in an artistic language that uttered its first words way back on that first day that a slave sang a new song in a new land.

I am here to tell you that there are some who do not accept the premature autopsy of a noble art form. There are some of us out here who are on a quest and, in the process of that quest, who find themselves having to perform conquests. There are some of us out here who believe that the majesty of human life demands an accurate rendition in rhythm and tune. Duke Ellington performed with Sidney Bechet, with Louis Armstrong, with Coleman Hawkins, with Charlie Parker, with John Coltrane, and wrote music for almost all of them. His own orchestra was described by Mahalia Jackson as a sacred institution. The Duke Ellington Orchestra was the manifestation of the elaborately fabricated drum he called this music. He was dedicated without reservation. He knew that you have to listen to a noble sound. You see, you have to watch out for a tradition built on the intention of putting noble inclinations into rhythm and tune. You have to beware of premature autopsies. A noble sound might not lie still in the dark cave where the dragons have taken it. A noble sound might just rise up and push away the stones that were placed in its path. A noble sound might just rise up on the high side of the sky, it might just ring the silver bells of musical light that tear through the cloak of the dragon's shadow that blocks the sun. You got to watch those early autopsies.

A noble sound is a mighty thing. It can mess around and end up swinging low and swinging high and flapping its wings in a rhythm that might
swoop up over the limitations imposed by the dreams of dragons. I said:
You better check those autopsies. A noble sound, the birthright understood
so clearly by Duke Ellington, it might swing low and it might tell you to
get aboard. It might move with so much grace and so much confidence that
you will have to remember what I have been telling you: You had better not
pay much attention to those premature autopsies. This noble sound, this
thing of majesty, this art, so battered but so ready for battle, it just might
lift you high enough in the understanding of human life to let you know in
no uncertain terms why that marvelous Washingtonian, Edward Kennedy
Ellington, *never* came off the road.

1989

PART TWO

Swing Time

Though no one other than a masochist seeks unhappiness, our aesthetic orientation seems to favor the tragic and mistakenly places joy in a position of secondary inferiority, rather than where it stands in the true life of the world. That hard and bittersweet jazz joy is actually a combative philosophical position taking aesthetic war to the inevitable disappointments and indifferent disruptions that life brings to each of us.

—STANLEY CROUCH, *MONK'S DREAM*

The swing groove, for Crouch, was the great defining tempo in jazz, a uniquely American contribution to the history of music, one that separated it from European concert music and the polyrhythmic traditions of the African continent. Crouch often defined the American tradition as miscegenated, grounded in the fundamentals that all true jazz innovators reinvent: the blues, 4/4 swing, the romantic ballad, and Afro-Hispanic rhythms—elements that provide bridges between schools and styles, but which all jazz contains, "the feeling of dance that underlies all swing." Whether it's Fred Astaire in motion or Bird on the bandstand, the swing aesthetic "is one of the most wholly successful expressions of American grace, power, and frailty." All of this, combined with Charlie Parker, could explain Crouch's special affection for the wide-open swing capital that was Depression-era Kansas City, Missouri, under political boss Tom Pendergast, rendered supremely in this part of the book.

Crouch is sometimes given more credit for his opinion than is rightly due his storytelling and narrative journalism, but he was an exceptionally good reporter, with an eye for trenchant detail, and able to draw from his subjects an intimacy others couldn't access. In his profiles of individual musicians the subject shines, even while never neglecting the sidemen and rendering his own exuberance for what is unique about American cultural geography. If you want to know the essence of what Crouch loved about American people and places, the kind of America he thought possible through jazz, his profile of Mel Lewis up from the streets of Buffalo will take you there—and, of course, in the description of Lewis as "a loquacious spirit confident to the point of abrasiveness," Stanley could have been writing about himself.

Of singular interest in this part, especially to those who have read the crowning achievement that is *Kansas City Lightning: The Life and Times of Charlie Parker*, is an unpublished chapter discovered in Stanley's papers of the rumored second volume of his Parker biography. One of the previously unseen jewels of this collection, the piece is also one of the finest descriptions of what it was like to be on 52nd Street in the atmosphere that gathered around Bird in New York. Those who have longed for Crouch's never-to-materialize second volume of Parker's biography and wondered how it would stack up, read on. "Let us face life and live on as long as we can, swinging until there is no time left."

LOS ANGELES

JAZZ

A s I WRITE THIS, it is the spring of 1991, and I am thinking of the fact that my interest in music began more than thirty years ago, when I was a boy who had been born in 1945 and was often asked to put on the 78 rpm recordings that my mother had saved from the swing era. She had been a big fan of jazz and something of a party girl, one who recalled when there were many clubs on Central Avenue and performances by the big bands at the Elks Club, how the arrival of Duke Ellington had the atmosphere of a visiting dignitary, when people got sharp enough to slice a molecule in half. Her record collection included Armstrong, Waller, and others.

But the world I grew up in was very different. Across the street from Jefferson High School was Mrs. Harris's hamburger joint and on the juke box was a Lou Donaldson recording of "The Masquerade Is Over," which the hip high school guys would always play. There were also little groups of listeners and musicians who were listening to jazz, some bemoaning the fact that they couldn't pass for twenty-one in 1961 when Coltrane was playing at the Renaissance in Hollywood with Eric Dolphy. Miles Davis was the deity to many, and there were many hours spent listening to *Sketches of Spain* together, though I do recall that you could hear *Kind of Blue* in a household headed by a mailman who made the observation that, "This music will never sound different. It won't ever get old. That's how good things are." Monk stood behind Miles and so did Mingus, with Coltrane the rising symbol of a fresh direction. Once when I was hitchhiking, the guy driving said to me as we came down Central Avenue, "There's a new sax man out here you better watch out for if you like that jazz. His name is Johnny Coltrane. Watch out for him. He's going to shake 'em up."

Previously unpublished

INVENTION OF THE SELF

JOHN COLTRANE

THE GREATEST ACHIEVEMENT of John Coltrane was perhaps neither musical nor spiritual. Though he was a supreme musical intellectual whose appetite for fresh material and willingness to work for it has never been surpassed in jazz or any other art, what stands out most clearly after one has gone through his various evolutions is the proof that a man can invent himself. That is what John Coltrane did: Like an aesthetic weight lifter of dauntless resolve, he transformed himself from a 97-pound weakling into one of the great strong men of our age.

When one listens to his early work, it is clear that he could have stayed in the middle of the road and been a fine journeyman player with a personal bite to his sound. There is no indication that this man would become an innovator, a tip-top virtuoso, a shepherd whose call would summon both the masses and the asses, a symbol of the serious desire to extend the emotional power of the art into the realm of the spirit. No, even in his very good playing with Tadd Dameron on *Mating Call* in 1955, you hear no intimations of what would stun the saxophone hierarchy within three years, shocking one fellow tenor saxophonist so that he has yet to recover from the lack of self-confidence injected into his consciousness by the jet streams of ambition heard in Coltrane's fury for a finer position of personal expression.

Undated, previously unpublished

KANSAS CITY SWING AND SHOUT

Notes on the program for "Kansas City Swing and Shout" presented at Lincoln Center on Thursday, August 8, 1991. The full lineup that night was Jay McShann, Claude Williams, Charles McPherson, Wynton Marsalis, Jimmy Slyde, and the Jazz at Lincoln Center Orchestra, David Berger, conductor.

A GOOD NUMBER OF OUR MYTHS are as porous as Swiss cheese, but there is no more deservedly mythic city in the jazz story than Kansas City, Missouri. After the smoke and dust storms of exaggeration and outright lies blow away or settle down, the facts of Kansas City rise so high in the pantheon of our national aesthetic, answers to the mysteries of experience, that we understand quite clearly what Hermann Broch meant when he wrote, "The civilization of an epoch is its myth in action." And it was in Kansas City, Missouri, that the collective possibilities of American rhythm were so extraordinarily defined that it was the swing capital of the land for a good number of the Depression years. In Kansas City, an unsuspecting band with an eastern reputation could find itself, either as a unit or as individuals in a jam session, impaled on the horns of a brown-skinned rhythmic dilemma. It was in Kansas City that the blues was shouted, purred, whispered, and cried in such inventive style that the city became a spawning ground for jazz in the way that New Orleans and Chicago had been, the southern city from the turn of the century up through World War I and the midwestern magnate of the big winds throughout the 1920s. Kansas City took its position in the development of jazz for the same reason those other two had—there was a community crazy for the music and a regime that let the good times roll.

In most places, the good times rolled in the evening when the sun went down, when the sobriety and the inhibitions of daylight rarely seemed to hold their ground. But under Tom Pendergast,* there was wall-to-wall sin and wall-to-wall swing, wall-to-wall exotic entertainment and wall-to-wall gambling. People came to guzzle the blues away, to dance the night long, to take the risk of leaving in a barrel as they laid bet after bet; and, as ever, there were those who came to involve themselves in the mercantile eroticism of the chartered courtesans. Some curious type might take in a show of female impersonators in one place or be shocked no end in another while witnessing money lifted off a table by an unexpected part of the female anatomy. Yes, yes, yes: Kansas City roared its way through the 1920s and came crashing as a juggernaut of the fast life when Pendergast was sent to prison in 1939.

But when Kansas City was hot and when it was wild, it allowed for the amount of work that musicians needed who wanted something sure in the Midwest, who could learn and develop on the many jobs the city offered, playing everything from refined high-society situations that demanded "sweet" music to the cauldrons of liquor and dancing where the patrons came to boil the blues out of their flesh, to begin the ritual of courtship on the dance floor, to reduce every chaotic element in life to a series of elegant gestures, steps, turns, and embraces. The pulsing, rusty-

---

* Tom Pendergast was the Democratic Party boss of Jackson County, politically more powerful than the mayor of Kansas City, Missouri—an office Pendergast is often mis-credited as having held—which is why the metropolis was often referred to as "Tom's Town."

dusty groove could always snare, grounded and elevated by the sensually
civilizing lyricism of Negro rhythm, which was an accumulation and an
extension, an abstraction and a form of precision, a pulling together of all
American sources, some from as far away as Europe and Africa, others as
close as the American Indian chant.

That Negro rhythm was the result of a long march that had begun
at the end of slavery, when larger and larger numbers of Afro-Americans
began to make their careers in the world of show business. As soon as the
Civil War ended with the Confederate weeping and the Union rejoic-
ing at Appomattox, the country started to earnestly win the West, and
the Negro began to take an innovative place in American show business,
developing a rich body of original music, dance, and humor that had its
professional initiation through the crucible of minstrelsy. Those with a
flair for performance and a will to invention as well as adventure took
advantage of the mobility that freedom allowed. Before the South fell,
there had been a few Black minstrel shows, none lasting very long. And
only two Negroes had performed in the burnt cork reviews, one a dwarf
and the other William Henry Lane, known as Master Juba. Juba was
the greatest American dancer of his age, proving himself king when he
defeated John Diamond in an 1845 competition that presaged the battles
of the imagination that took place in such rooms as Kansas City's Subway Club. Just as the Kansas City musicians would later add the jabbing,
propulsive short phrases known as riffs to the dictionary of swing, Juba
introduced percussive patterns to the rhythm of the jig that might have
been the first professional example of Negro innovations in American
dance. When Juba traveled to London in 1848, a dance critic wrote that
he had never seen such:

> . . . mobility of muscles, such flexibility of joints, such boundings,
> such slidings, such gyrations, such toes and heelings, such backward-

ings and forwardings, such posturings, such firmness of foot, such elasticity of tendon, such mutation of movement, such vigor, such variety, such natural grace, such powers of endurance, such potency of pattern.

Juba set precedents for Black show business and for the attitudes that would later make jazz what it was, a music ever in pursuit of vigor, variety, elasticity, mutation of movement, and potency of pattern.

Like Juba, the new Black show-business people who emerged in the wake of Appomattox had moved beyond the slave condition of prized livestock that provided entertainment; they were *paid*. Audiences could see and hear *them* sing and dance. Though these entertainers used the convention of burnt cork, it was clear to all that this energy was coming from the source so consistently alluded to by the white minstrels. Because the material was almost always their own, because of the concern with individual touches, and because their roles were used to create personal reputations, the Negro minstrels took great pride in what they did. They wanted to be the best singers, dancers, musicians, jugglers, and comedians in show business.

In the process of developing their identities, the Black show-business people who traveled the South felt much like their counterparts in the Indian West. The atmosphere that prevailed after the Civil War and right up to the moment when Kansas City began to get its musical wings in order—and on beyond that moment—is well described by Tom Fletcher in *100 Years of the Negro in Show Business*. Fletcher was born in 1873 and was on the road with Negro minstrel shows by his adolescence. He remembered when "A colored man with a banjo would draw almost as big a crowd as an elephant in a circus." Most important to our understanding of how these people actually felt and what they saw the power of their work to be is rendered in Fletcher's recollection of the way things slowly changed:

> Opera houses and towns which had large meeting places or town halls would write or contact in some other way the managers of minstrel shows to beg them to play their town. This was not so hard to take after we had found the secret. The old saying that music hath charms to soothe the savage beast worked fine for us. In our minds most of these people did everything savages did except eat humans. We also found that they had the same weaknesses as savages.
>
> In the course of time the minstrel shows, the dances, songs, and jokes proved so popular that the parade had to be cut short so the shows could be longer. I have never quite figured out whether it was the music or the shows which made the people gradually get a little more civilized.

It is easy therefore to understand why, among themselves, the jazz musicians who evolved their art in an endless set of variations on those circumstances had the romantic auras of Native American scouts, Pony Express riders, and Native American traders—they who had stuck their heads in the mouths of lions and, daring fate, periodically bedded down there. Among the things they learned, as had those who crossed the badland territories of the nineteenth century, was that the law changed according to geography, that fierce and unpredictable men who made their own rules still existed and could tragically affect the lives of musical entertainers who might also be artists. The small bands of desperados, the rowdy cowboys, and the Native American Nations with their own codes that you could ignore at your own risk had been replaced by gangsters, ornery police, enraged revelers who might pull knives or pistols at any moment, and the invariably fluctuating racial laws that could change not only from state to state but from county to county. Vocal tone or body posture or look in the eyes or gesture—how a voice rose, lowered, or broke, the way a powerful gangster entered a room, how a policeman adjusted his hat or cap, pulled up his gun belt, or put one foot up on the car's running board, the way a rowdy Negro surveyed the dance hall from one end to the other—all were signals and were adjusted to immediately. As professionals, the jazz players who would become known as "territory musicians" for their periodic barnstorming tours of the Midwest had come to know that the friendly and the hostile might live next door to each other, be standing shoulder-to-shoulder, even dancing together. But swing was the rhythm and the texture of morale, and that was its attraction; that was why the feeling was rhythmically influential, and that was why they played it.

As Pendergast came to power in the 1920s, Kansas City became the hub of those territories. The territories were Texas, Oklahoma, Kansas, Missouri, Iowa, Indiana, Michigan, Arkansas, and Louisiana. Not only did musicians travel to them, they also arrived in Kansas City from those states, fully aware of how much work was available. But when Garvin Bushell arrived in Kansas City in 1921 as part of a touring package headlined by Mamie Smith, he was impressed by the young Coleman Hawkins, who would later be dubbed "the father of jazz saxophone" but who was, then, no more than a mightily imposing seventeen-year-old from St. Joseph, Missouri, who came to read parts with Bushell and the others in the pit band. Recalled clarinetist Bushell:

> We heard music at several cabarets in Kansas City. I wasn't impressed. We felt we had the top thing in the country, so the bands didn't impress me. It may be, now that I look back, that I underestimated them. The bands in the Midwest then had a more flexible style than the eastern ones. They were built on blues bands. They had also done

more with saxophones in Kansas City. They just played the blues, one after another, in different tempos. It was good, but after we'd heard Oliver and Dodds,* they were our criterion. I also heard blues singers in Kansas City, just like Joe Turner sings, and they did impress me.

In Hawkins, Bushell heard a man who would become an innovator in the wake of his working with Louis Armstrong in Fletcher Henderson's band a few years later, but in that feeling for the blues those bands had, he was witnessing the element that was to characterize Kansas City jazz. In no way could Bushell have foreseen that the penchant for saxophones would someday not only result in powerful reed sections that could swing, shout, and croon the blues but also lead the way to Lester Young and Charlie Parker, the two most influential saxophonists between Coleman Hawkins and John Coltrane. Beyond those innovators there were also giants of the instrument who would either blow themselves into the pantheon or arrive there on the whirlwinds of legend—Ben Webster, Budd Johnson, Buster Smith, Tommy Douglas, Dick Wilson, Jack Washington, Herschel Evans, and Eddie Barefield.

The manipulators of that increasingly important wind instrument with its cane reed, pearl buttons, and curved body, what Jackie McLean calls "the golden hook," either worked in or greatly benefited from the developments of Bennie Moten's Kansas City Orchestra and the Oklahoma City pride of swing and fire known as Walter Page's Blue Devils. Initially competitors, the two musical organizations eventually melded, as circumstances of one sort or another led to musicians who had worked with the Blue Devils ending up either in Moten's Kansas City Orchestra or what it evolved into in the wake of Moten's sudden death in 1935— Count Basie's Barons of Rhythm. From the late 1920s through the early

---

* Joe Oliver and Johnny Dodds.

1930s, Moten and Page had dominated the midwestern scene, each having a particular sort of swing that was fused as Moten began to get former Blue Devils—Basie, trombonist-arranger-guitarist Eddie Durham, trumpeter Oran "Hot Lips" Page, singer Jimmy Rushing, and, at the peak of conquest, bassist Walter Page. Basie told Albert Murray in *Good Morning Blues* about the attitude that he, Rushing, and Durham had about what they wanted as a result of their experiences with the Blue Devils:

> . . . Jimmy and Eddie and I started working to gets Lips Page in that trumpet section. We wanted somebody in there to play the kind of get-off stuff we felt we needed for the new things we were adding to the book. Of course, before Eddie and I began bringing in our arrangements, that band had its original Kansas City stomp style. It had a special beat, and it really had something going. I don't know how you would define stomp in strict musical terms. But it was a real thing. If you were on the first floor and the dance hall was upstairs, that was what you would hear, that steady *rump, rump, rump, rump* in that medium tempo. It was never fast. And you could also feel it.
>
> But it was not the kind of jump band or swing band that the Blue Devils band was. The Blue Devils' style was snappier. They were two different things, and we wanted some of that bluesy hot stuff in there, too. So we needed Lips, and Bennie brought him in for us . . .

It was the combination of that four/four beat Basie described hearing through the dance floor above and the blues power that made the Kansas City sound. Another aspect of it was the riff, the short, percussive or vocalized phrase one player might initiate that would be picked up by the entire trumpet, trombone, or reed section, only to be countered by riffs from the other two sections. That gave the music a polyrhythmic quality much like a big, tuned drum; sort of a large ensemble version of the New Orleans front line of trumpet, clarinet, and trombone with the phrasing stripped down for another kind of thrust and propulsion. Then there was the innovative style of bass that Walter Page pioneered, building upon what he had heard Wellman Braud do with Duke Ellington. Page replaced the tuba so often heard in bands and worked out a two-bar, eight-beat rhythm cycle in four/four (12345678) that gave the time a flow bass players use to this very day. It removed any feeling of choppiness and made the pulse of the rhythm section breathe every two bars, switching gears on the ninth beat to begin the cycle again. In tandem with Basie, drummer Jo Jones, and eventually guitarist Freddie Green, Page forged the most influential attitude toward the self-orchestrating ensemble-within-an-ensemble that is the jazz rhythm section.

As original as the Kansas City and Oklahoma City musicians were, they still used the basic influence of New Orleans. In Page, one heard King Oliver, Bubber Miley, and Armstrong quite clearly; in Lester Young the Armstrong of "Mahogany Hall Stomp," floating beat and all, was personalized and passed, first, to Eddie Barefield, whose alto saxophone improvisation on the 1932 "Moten Swing" must surely have touched Charlie Parker; then secondly to Parker himself, who was also taken by Buster Smith, the alto saxophonist, clarinetist, and arranger prominent in the Blue Devils when Young was there and who eventually found himself in blues-based cahoots with Basie at the Reno Club after the death of Bennie Moten and the collapse of the Blue Devils.

By 1936, Kansas City was so thick with musicians that professional jazz hound, record producer, critic, and promoter John Hammond flipped his Vanderbilt wig when he went to Pendergast's town after hearing Basie broadcasting from the Reno. The booklet for the 1980 exhibit *Goin' to Kansas City* recounts what Hammond wrote in *DownBeat* in September of 1936 and what effect was soon had by the national attention brought to the swing capital:

In the article, headlined "Kansas City: A Hotbed for Fine Swing Musicians/Andy Kirk & Count Basie's Elegant Music Spoils City for Out-of-Town Name Bands," Hammond raved about the city and its musicians: "Descriptions of the place as the hotbed of American music are in every way justified, for there is no town in America, New Orleans perhaps excepted, that has produced so much excellent music—Negro, of course." Under the prodding of Hammond and others, record companies and booking agents got busy. Over the next few years, the Count Basie Orchestra, Andy Kirk's Clouds of Joy, Pete Johnson, Joe Turner, Hot Lips Page, Buster Smith, Harlan Leonard's Rockets, the Jay McShann Orchestra, Charlie Christian, and other Kansas City and Mid-American musicians recorded, toured, and established national, even international, reputations. They altered the sound of jazz not only collectively, by demonstrating the propulsive qualities of riff-based swing, but also individually, by blowing in the solo styles they had developed in years of playing dance halls and jam sessions.

Jay McShann arrived in Kansas City in the mid-1930s and was soon a part of the local groove. He started with a small group and put together a big band in 1939, which included Charlie Parker, just returned from a trip to New York and ready to refine a style destined to provide the central impetus for the bebop movement of the mid-1940s. It was in that band, which was heavily influenced by Basie's, that the substance of the Kansas City style reached its last peak in that period, for only Basie would continue to develop what he had helped organize conceptually and technically, leading extremely fine bands almost nonstop until his death.

When the McShann Orchestra arrived for a Savoy Ballroom battle of the bands in New York in early 1942, it defeated Lucky Millinder's men and got quite a reputation in a short period of time. It had a hit recording in "Confessin' the Blues" and an extremely influential one in "Hootie Blues," which contained an improvisation by Charlie Parker that began his impact. When the band worked the Apollo, it did saxophone and rhythm section work with the tap-dancing giant Baby Laurence.

One of the great partnerships of jazz was that of Andy Kirk and Mary Lou Williams, who did most of the writing for the Clouds of Joy, originals and arrangements of pieces written by others. Of perhaps special interest to some is the fact that her "Walkin' and Swingin'" is from 1936 and contains the basic material for "Rhythm-a-Ning," which Thelonious Monk recorded more than twenty years later. In all of the Kansas City music, one will notice the percussive snap of the riffs and the fluidity of the phrasing, emblematic of what Mary Lou Williams quite aptly termed a "heavenly city." Of course, Williams must have meant musically. But the rolling of the good times being what they are, with so many variations, who can say anything better than the fact that the swing of Kansas City did provide a perfect example of Broch's dictum, "The civilization of an epoch is its myth in action"? In Kansas City, those who sought to travel to heaven every night booked passage on the momentum of the local myth remade in rhythm, and the world has since been all the better for it.

THE STREET

1944

Unpublished, undated: archival evidence suggests this is a complete chapter from a planned second volume of S.C.'s Charlie Parker biography. The first volume, Kansas City Lightning, *ends in 1939.*

A T 72 WEST 52ND STREET, the Three Deuces was the first club off Sixth Avenue when you entered the block. It sat right next to Nedick's, and if you got off the subway at 50th and Sixth Avenue on a summer evening, you could hear notes faintly floating from the room as you came up the station's steps: the club's doors were left open in the heat. Like most of the music rooms clustered and facing each other in the half block off Sixth Avenue, the Deuces was long and narrow, occupying the first floor of a weathered brownstone, part of the liberated zone between aristocratic Fifth Avenue and the rushing white blare of Broadway one block away. Its clientele, like that of all the clubs, was integrated; the social life circulating from one place to another from nine o'clock at night to four o'clock in the morning was thick and various. Rich patrons of "21" found they could slum by walking a few hundred feet instead of taking a cab to Harlem, while the hard and fast fans were awed by offerings ranging from New Orleans jazz to the new music of Gillespie and Parker, with pianists, violinists, drummers, saxophonists, bassists, and brass players moving from room to room on their breaks, sometimes listening, sometimes taking to another bandstand to musically battle for half an hour before returning to their own jobs. In the Three Deuces, as in the Spotlight and in the Onyx, the ladies' toilet was right next to the kitchen, and peepholes had been drilled so that when an especially attractive woman went to the bathroom, sometimes an entire band on break would rush to the kitchen and fight for viewing space. So, like a transvestite who looks best in the least light, 52nd Street was transformed with the disappearance of the sun.

That half block was also Frank Costello's domain, and flashy, sullen men in dark cars would roll into 52nd Street just after the closing of the clubs to loom imperiously over the cash registers as the night's earnings were tallied. Some nights they would leave with cash, others they would take either literal or mental notes, have a drink or two, or give a small private party with their women friends. On those occasions, the band at work would stay over, doors would be locked, and the kitchen staff would prepare better food amid the *foop* of champagne corks rocketing toward the ceiling. Tips would be huge, gangsters throwing bills at the band, pushing them into the musician's breast pockets, dropping them into the bells of saxophones, sticking them to sweating foreheads. If a gangster took a liking to a musician, that musician had it made—work was guaranteed, and the staff would give him a wide berth.

Bird understood this kind of scene, as becoming a pet of the mob had been imperative in Kansas City, where one night a couple of goons had been stomped to death behind the Reno Club for insulting the favorite Negro bootblack of some Italian and Irish puppeteers who kept the good times jumping. Bird was able to stay clear of them, however, because New York wasn't wholly controlled by gangsters. And though he had done everything from calling square dances at the country and western club in

K.C. to befuddling dancers with the new music of Billy Eckstine's band, now was the time to think only of his and Dizzy's groove—no singers, no band uniforms, no one-nighters. At the same time, the boroughs of greater New York perpetually fascinated him, from the Bronx to Brooklyn. There were so many different kinds of people, such a wealth of shops, of restaurants, movies, stores, and high-rises. But especially appealing to him was the mingling of races and classes that took place on 52nd Street, making it a circumscribed vision of democracy after dark.

During the day, that half block of clubs that became known as *The Street* was only a row of bland four-story brownstones, their awnings frayed and faded, their worn marquees sporting the names of current attractions. In Harlem, at ten o'clock, Bird would arise hungover and check his pockets for the money to get fixed up—the bag of heroin that would iron out all anxieties and envelop him in a bubble of sensuousness and absolute concentration. If he was broke, he would find someone to loan him a few dollars, make his way to a "high station" where the dope fiends took off, shoot up in a gallery, a basement, on a roof—sometimes tearing or staining his clothes in the process—then stop off to visit a girlfriend and cadge a couple of bucks for food, before returning home to 146th Street for his saxophone. Then he'd catch the train for 52nd Street. He was never late for rehearsals at one o'clock.

Those afternoons were almost conspiratorial in their delight. Bird thrived on finding novel and tricky ways to work out the music; collaring strange notes into tunes and arrangements was like taking crayons to the familiar images in coloring books and figuring out how to make seemingly bizarre combinations of hues palatable *and* logical. Any piece of music they chose to arrange or to lift chords from for their own distortions was put through a variety of paces, Charlie playfully trying to trip Dizzy up or the trumpeter excitedly pushing Al Haig from the keyboard to lay some harmonies on the saxophonist through which Bird would have to immediately fend his way, by ear, usually unerringly. If Dizzy did catch him or throw him, Bird's will and ability to digest Dizzy's voicings was such that he would never get caught *that* way again. The tempos were also a challenge, faster than anyone had ever played— so much so that Stan Levey was often left in the lurch, humbled, as was Al Haig, by the boldness and virtuosity of these musicians. Curley Russell caught on faster with his bass. And though Bird rarely had much to say, Dizzy was always ready with a suggestion, literally shaping the rhythm section, illustrating at the piano or urging Levey to play what seemed arbitrary rhythms to outsiders but were in fact a new way of accompanying—almost as if the drummer took the place of the shouting brass and labile reeds of the big band.

In the past six months, Dizzy had become increasingly confident, repulsing other trumpet players with his thin, gray tone but washing them away with both the harmonic daring and the new fingerings that allowed him to get over the horn more adroitly than anyone ever had. Yet he was often awed at the ideas Bird would force him to address on those afternoons. Then there was that area Dizzy knew he could never challenge Bird on: the blues. Yard played them with no more effort than a man dropping some ham hocks in a pot of greens. Just as Bird could converse brilliantly with the most learned of their community and later be seen passing a bottle back and forth with a wino, he made those kinds of sweeps in his blues—from flitting, high-minded harmonic wizardry to the deathless sorrow and sensuality of the most low-down cries and funky grunts. Yard had it all. Together they would kick ass up and down The Street.

Because the frontier quality of the music made the band so enthusiastic, rehearsals might last until six or seven, and night would have fallen when they began packing up. Danny Mulqueen, the bartender, would be coming on, as would the waitresses, checking their stations and preparing for the arrival of customers. The endless night Bird often spoke of with Dizzy, the night he had read of in Baudelaire and had first known in Kansas City, was bringing with its dimness the response of neon, an expectation of homemade or high-flown finery, and with it the willingness to let loose troubles by pursuing joy. Soon that little half block would be filled with music—twelve bands at least, sometimes fourteen, as every club had two groups spelling each other. Musicians, record producers, recording engineers, and lawyers elbowed through the crowds, traveling from club to club until they ended up on Sixth Avenue at the White Rose Bar, a room cordial to Negro men but hostile to the integrated couples that were starting to proliferate in the little half block. If servicemen from the South were in that bar or on The Street, that half block of interracial romance could provoke them to violence.

For that reason almost all musicians were armed: a few with pistols, the rest with knives. Dizzy and Pettiford had been attacked by sailors on Sixth Avenue because a light-skinned Negro woman in their company was mistaken for white; Dizzy's carpet knife and trumpet saved them from a terrible beating. And though the threat was always taken seriously, regulars on 52nd Street didn't curtail their activities, making jokes about the white servicemen who would drunkenly shout, "We're fighting overseas and you niggers are here taking our women." The musicians also took pleasure in the availability of white women—sometimes from the South or from midwestern towns, as frequently local and Jewish, or now and again, either enthralled European Negrophiles or upper-class Protestant white women who had missed the Harlem Renaissance. Sexual adventures were had, with the most ready, in horse-drawn cabs turning through Central Park during a break; the returning Don Juan, eager to tell his buddies about it, found himself taunted into the dressing room where he'd show off the lipstick on his drawers and privates.

"I didn't have time for breakfast in bed, so I gave her a sausage sandwich. Where you monkeys think I got this, huh?"

"You probably put the lipstick on and sucked it yourself, you faggot."

In that environment, because almost all the bands were Black, Charlie Parker saw Negro men express a power over others that was rare in the America of the war years. Here they had white musicians fawning over them, imitating their every gesture and every bit of slang, white women unabashedly staring as these men played or stood at a bar or contemplated the marquee at another club. Jazz writers interviewed them; disc jockeys tried to get them on the air. Even though the area was extremely small, it provided Bird with a relief from the paranoia about white people that had developed in his experiences in traveling bands, and, for the first time in his life, he began to realize that his musical importance stretched beyond ethnicity and made people of various races feel variously better or threatened, uplifted or assaulted.

Often, while waiting for the gig to come up at the Three Deuces, Bird and Dizzy would devise musical assaults they called "ambushes." Armed with their instruments, they would sneak into a club while another player was up there blowing his brains out and sweating with his eyes closed, pull their horns from beneath their coats as they came through the door, then begin blowing, marching up to the stage, startling and thrilling the audience, roughing up the featured musician with new melodic lines and dissonant harmonies, propelled by the rhythmic fluidity that bristled quirky and bitchy accents into the beat. It was a dramatic, carefully conceived plot to spread intimidation along The Street and to create even more excitement for their upcoming job.

When the engagement began, the Three Deuces was filled every night, the satiric and percussive style of Errol Garner producing a mood of buoyant pleasure that extended to curiosity, bewilderment, and hostility when Dizzy and Bird took the stage. Some musicians tried their damnedest to make out what they were doing, smiling as certain passages came clear to them; others, resenting the unfamiliar, angrily muttered criticisms of everything from Bird's soiled and wrinkled attire to what they described as "noise" and "exercises" that didn't "swing." Their opinions were echoed by reviewers, but nothing daunted the audience—even those who scratched their heads usually came back. Howard Hughes was frequently there, sitting alone in a dark blue suit and string tie surrounded by show people, socialites, college students, and classical musicians who had heard about the rumble on The Street caused by the daredevil arrogance of a new virtuosity. As Dizzy and Bird became the controversial main topic of musical discussion, the two of them became so close in their musical thinking that on one memorable evening, when a customer requested "Melancholy Baby," Bird and Dizzy improvised the same first line after stating the theme—note for note, rhythm for rhythm, inspiring chortled approval from the audience and their fellow musicians as they lovingly glanced at each other in mutual surprise.

Popularity and steady work still brought with it the kinds of insulting demands Black musicians had long known how to handle. A drunken white man shouted, "Hey, boys, why don't you boys play 'Shine'?" Bird immediately peeled off the notes of a street chant, "You're the horse's ass," followed by a blues lick that translated, "You dirty motherfucker"—then smiled around his mouthpiece as the notes sang through his horn an old childhood insult, "Your mama don't wear no drawers!" Dizzy and Curley Russell laughed; then the trumpeter said, "I'm sorry, but we don't know that one."

Cabaret laws, initially written to thwart the hustling of patrons by B-girls, made it illegal for employees to fraternize with customers at the tables, so the band members went either to the dressing room or onto the sidewalk, where they would listen to other groups or relax at the White Rose Bar. Often, during intermissions, Charlie would get into conversations with patrons, reversing the tables and cheerfully grilling a man or a woman about his or her occupation. He would first ask why something was done; then what its rules were; then how one brought it off when equipment was faulty or situations difficult. In this way, he gradually amassed knowledge of esoteric subjects, and the mystique of his knowing about everything began to develop, for few could figure out how a man so given to the obsession of constantly playing music and exploring almost every sensual delight had time to become so well-versed.

WHEN THE ENGAGEMENT ended, the band had a few weeks off and Max Roach returned to New York.

"Yard!"

"Yeah."

"Max is back in town."

"What?"

"When we go back in the Deuces, he says he can make it with us."

"All right!"

"We'll start rehearsing with him next week."

One afternoon late the following week, they had been waiting almost an hour and a half when Dizzy turned around on the bandstand as he heard the front door open and close. It was Roach, late and swaggering, sure that nothing could start until he got there: With Kenny Clarke being in the army, Roach was indisputably the new style's king of the hill.

"Hey, Yard, he's here."

"Hey, Max," said Charlie Parker, sitting behind the drums, his saxophone held by its strap and resting on his stomach.

"Yeah, Bird."

"Can you do this?" Parker asked, smiling. Then, with his right foot, Bird played constant series of quarter notes on the bass drum—bomp, bomp, bomp, bomp; on the sock cymbal, his other foot started a Charleston beat—chick-chick, chick-chick; his left hand drummed a shuffle on the snare as he held the stick with a professional grip—a-tootie-toot, a-tootie-toot; the basic bebop beat was played on the ride cymbal with the stick in his right hand—ting-tinka-ting, ting-tinka-ting.

Roach listened to the four rhythms, independent but simultaneously executed. Then, as Parker got up, he went to the drums and attempted to play what he'd just heard. He couldn't. His arrogance melted right through the bandstand as the message came to him: Only the man who can play everything can afford to be late.

Yet because of his increasing appetite for heroin, Parker's appearances at the club for evening performances soon became, unlike his commitment to afternoon rehearsals, unpredictable. The job started at nine and lasted to half past three. If Bird was there by eleven consistently, he was doing well. If he had too much dope, he might nod off and miss cues; too much liquor, and his lines would be filled with illogical hesitations. He couldn't keep up with the tempo, the control of his attack would go, and he would fall back into an amateurish sound far in his past, when he couldn't articulate and his tone was soppy. But when he was right, which was still more often than not, the band, now enlarged through the savage and singular breakups of rhythm provided by Roach, rolled joyously and sometimes vindictively across the language of jazz, remaking it all in their own images.

As things got worse, Dizzy began to feel the pressure of having to endure Sammy Kaye's anger.

"Dizzy, it's almost time for the band to play. Where's Charlie?"

"I don't know."

"You're being paid for a quintet, you know."

"Right."

"Well, where is he?"

"I said I don't know."

"He was just here and you don't know where he is."

"We'll start without him."

"Dizzy, I don't understand this man. Here the two of you are on the verge of a great career and we never know if the man will get to work on time. Does he know this is a business and that these people are here to hear the both of you?"

"We'll start without him."

Dizzy wondered what Yard was trying to do. If you loaned him money, you never got it back. If he said he'd be someplace, he might get there, he might not. You didn't even know whether, when he did get there, he would have his horn. Then you had to figure ways to con him out of spending his whole salary long before payday, as Bird would draw the money for the entire run if you let him. None of that, bad as it was, would be so bad if he could be counted on to play at the top of his form when he arrived. But Bird was becoming so incoherent at times it was frightening. How could a man with that much talent do that to himself? "Dizzy, my good man," Bird would answer, "perhaps I'm attaining this level of notoriety in order to show others what they *shouldn't* do!" Then he'd turn on his heel and disappear, possibly to return so drunk Dizzy would have to leave him in the hands of Gene Ramey, his old friend from Kansas City, who was playing bass across the street with Ben Webster at the Onyx: "Gene, your baby is over in the Deuces. They want to close the club and he's passed out in the dressing room."

Ramey would always see Parker home, first getting a carton of coffee before taking him to the subway, then forcing him to drink it and, if necessary, pouring it over his head when he wouldn't swallow. Ramey had been told by a doctor that Bird's nightly consumption of heroin, barbiturates, Benzedrine, and nearly a fifth of 151-proof rum made for a combination that could either burst his heart or cause him never to wake up if he were allowed to remain unconscious too long. But in spite of his condition, on those subway trips to 146th Street, Ramey discovered that Bird had developed what amounted to a sixth sense for detecting the presence of plainclothes police. With his eyes closed and his head bobbing up and down as he swallowed or choked on the hot black coffee, Bird would turn to the bassist and call him by his middle name, "Glasco, Dick Tracy's on the train." "Where?" "That's him over there." And Ramey looked, and he could see that Parker was right. Though they were never stopped, they were often followed until they got to Charlie's apartment, where Ramey remained until the saxophonist was fully conscious. Only then would Ramey leave, hoping his old friend would be in better shape the following night.

One night the club was filled and Dizzy was extremely angry because Bird had not shown up. He'd made a rehearsal earlier that afternoon; they had worked out a great arrangement of "A Night in Tunisia," with interludes, spooky jungle rhythms that played hide and seek with the beat, and a different introduction for each horn to take his solo break, that four bars when the band disappeared and your horn could dance on the air alone. It was eleven o'clock and the band was performing as a quartet, Dizzy having to nearly blow himself into a hernia to provide the expectant audience with an excitement so much more easily achieved with two horns. Sammy Kaye had been on his back all night, and those he saw in The Street during the breaks asked him when Bird was showing. Dizzy chose not to answer, pretending to be preoccupied or changing the subject. Finally Errol Garner finished his set to loud applause, and Kaye was announcing that the Dizzy Gillespie band would shortly provide more music.

"Any sign of Yard?" Max Roach asked as they left the dressing room for the bandstand.

"No." They mounted the low bandstand. Al Haig seated himself at the piano that stood on the floor. Dizzy immediately kicked off a fast tempo and went into an original that was based on the chords of "I Got Rhythm." As he finished a solo that not only sailed through the tempo but popped angry high notes into the listeners' faces, Bird was seen making his way through the crowd that filled the aisle between the bar and the wall. Disheveled and sweating, his saxophone case under his arm, Bird bent forward, walking with the solid but careful tread that periodic pain in his flat feet forced him to adopt. Avoiding the faces of the customers, he got to the bandstand, placed his horn by the drums, and disappeared into the bathroom just to the left of Al Haig. The band continued and finished the performance; Dizzy acknowledged the applause. They went into another tune. No Parker. They played a slow ballad with the tempo dragged out, Gillespie nursing each note in a long improvisation. Still no Parker. Furious, Gillespie quietly stepped off stage and went through the bathroom's swinging doors while the song continued. He returned quickly, his face expressionless, fingering the valves on his trumpet.

Max Roach looked up. "What's with Bird?"

"The motherfucker is in there with a needle in his goddam arm," Gillespie hissed. He was standing next to an open mike, so his statement went straight into the room. Spoons clattered; an atmosphere of shocked embarrassment reshaped the mood of the club. Then, suddenly, the bathroom door banged open and Parker stood there, his face drenched in sweat, his eyes cold on Dizzy, the unbuttoned cuff of his left shirt sleeve sticking out from beneath his rumpled pin-striped suit.

"Why you do that to me, man? Dizzy, why you do that?" Parker asked. He stepped up onto the bandstand.

Gillespie was sick with embarrassment and shame. "I didn't know the mike was open."

Parker continued to stare at Gillespie, then turned to take out his saxophone and prepared to play. He had nothing more to say.

"Tunisia," Dizzy said softly, and the bass and drums began the Afro-Cuban rhythm. As was usually the case when he was high on heroin, Bird's sound had a shrill coloring; his eyes, though dreamy, were half-closed and cynical, cold. Then, when they got to the introduction for his saxophone break, Parker stood there, motionless; he had closed his eyes, he was in a nod. Quickly, Gillespie took the break. When he finished, he motioned Haig to play, using his trumpet to set the stage for the saxophone break when the pianist beckoned him in. Still Parker stood there, seemingly asleep as Gillespie nervously rendered his introduction, screaming the last few notes like a desperate whistle. Then the band dropped out and suddenly the saxophone blazed. Dizzy screamed in approval. Yard leaned forward, twisting the tune, fighting the rhythms—playing against the beat, with it, between it. His rage took him to altissimo extremes of the alto, notes from that register came like darts, then he swooped all the way down, his horn honking and grunting, then suddenly moved to smooth melodic lines, sensual and ethereal in their translucency. At one moment he seemed to be sobbing, at another cursing—himself, the world, his condition—only to resolve it all into a tenderness full of bereavement and mystery, before bowing out with a flippant, staccato muttering of "you dirty mother-fucker." The bandstand seemed to float, the audience went wild. Charlie Parker refused to acknowledge Dizzy Gillespie's presence. He would never forgive him that.

LOWDOWN AND LOFTY,
EDDIE "LOCKJAW" DAVIS

Though Eddie "Lockjaw" Davis is now another casualty lost to cancer, we should appreciate the triumph his tenor style represented as much as we grieve his absence. Davis was the product of an era when aesthetic discipline was often engendered by contempt. In the jam sessions that could become boot camps, those who didn't know what they were doing before waiting in line to play were served hot trouble with a cold topping of insult. Lockjaw loved to recall how, as a kid growing up in Harlem who thought he knew something about the saxophone, the old guys used to ridicule his upstart ass back home to practice. The young Lockjaw took them seriously, intent on earning one of the commissions accorded professional improvisers—those guys who knew all the tunes in all the keys and could say something mightily distinctive through them.

He got that commission at Minton's, one of the clubs where so much bebop revolution once moved through the air before it moved south to 52nd Street. With the smoke clearing but the scent of battle ever present, Lockjaw led the house band and ruled the rhythm of the jam session. There he received the respect shown an officer recognized for his outpost skill at handling the fascinating-to-combative local population. Mounting the bandstand, holding his saxophone in one hand by the bell, Lockjaw brooked no bullshit and manhandled much arrogance through his horn.

"Guys used to tell me, 'Jaws, I'm coming up to Minton's and tear your ass up tonight.' Ain't nobody left with nothing yet!" I doubt they did. Jimmy Lyons once witnessed a young saxophonist strutting up to the bandstand gleaming with self-esteem: "Lockjaw asked the kid if he knew 'Lover.' The kid nodded and you could see he was thinking he was going to get Lockjaw. So Lockjaw leans back, snapping his fingers for a really burning tempo, and says real fast, 'Okay: 'Lover' in D. You got it!'" Lyons bursts into laughter: "The kid almost broke his fingers trying to find those notes. Then Lockjaw was just fluttering through those changes, just fluttering. Man, you didn't mess with cats like Lockjaw."

One of the reasons Eddie Davis was not to be messed with is that when he learned, he learned his own way, developing a style that is still mysterious.

Davis was ever reminiscent of the giants who traversed a Cumberland Gap through formless emotion into the open but disciplined vision of civilization that informs all art forms. Ask anyone who worked with him what he was playing, and you will usually spark a smile in recollection of an unplumbed wonder, a way of moving through harmony that was original to the point of perplexity. Mysterious.

Oh, he was an original who knew how to tell a whopper through the rousing torque textures of his vibrato, of his inflections, and of his phrasing. Sir Lockjaw knew all the gutbucket tricks. There was the near hiss that barely misted itself into recognizable pitch; the howling wobbles down in the grotto of the horn; the skill of muttering moods at you in scratchy whispers or snow-leopard pelts of timbre; then the angular italicizing of the shriek that snaked out of the upper register. His Honor Lockjaw could also shape a ballad with such sumptuous control that the horn became the morning star of Venus, crooning radiant love calls and lulling the listener against a dream partner who might become a grotesque tar-baby parody in the last measures—yowling to shock the sentimental!

Lockjaw the Lowdown and Lofty knew to a "T" the loops that loped inside the blues—such as the soft-pedal slippers of the loafer who'd rather ski than lift his feet; the rotary teeth of the hustlers so smoothly tailing the nicks and blood smells of gullibility in chumps; the sour gruel of self-pity and rage when the spurned lover mulls over the detail of betrayal, sipping or guzzling an elixir sure to make the hangover triangle throb even more painfully the next day. He was also given to rendering the blues to be with you, the blues to let you know how goddam good I feel; the blues to celebrate the sartorial magnificence of this combination I'm wearing—this cloth, this baby-butt soft leather, this suede, this cut, these colors; the blues to smack my greasy lips over the wonder of this food; the blues to keep my dance-ready boody from flying off my body, or rolling off, or slowly sliding away; the blues to be alive with eyes bucked by the ever-rolling beauty or squinted to catch the image way over there, where inevitable breathing life lights on yet another surface, changing into the camouflaged invisible but remaining its solid, pulsating self—if you happen to be one of the gang who knows how to look.

Up until his death at sixty-five, Lockjaw carried that talent and expertise quite gracefully and was never reluctant to express his admiration for mentors Coleman Hawkins, Chu Berry, Ben Webster, and Don Byas. I remember hearing him more than a decade ago in Los Angeles's Parisian Room, where he was traveling through as a hired gunfighter, backed up by the posse of a local rhythm section. His job was to slap the cuffs on the moment and bring the music in alive. Ben Webster hadn't been dead very long, and Jaws decided to remind the listeners of what they were never going to hear again. He brought off an aesthetic séance, discussing the wonder of Webster's style with the older master himself, making observations across the grave in his own voice and listening as the departed maestro replied through Davis's fingers, mouth, and lungs. Webster's name was never mentioned at the microphone, but Davis smiled when I asked him about the tribute. Leaning his head to the side as he held his regular drink of scotch and milk, he said "I loved Ben, you know."

Given all the fine work on his own, as part of Norman Granz's jam session package, and with Basie, Johnny Griffin, Shirley Scott, and Harry "Sweets" Edison, perhaps his lack of critical recognition was connected to the disregard Lockjaw had for those who tried to push him around. He knew what he could do and wasn't one for smooching boody cakes. Once a famous critic came up to Minton's:

> He asked me to clear the bandstand so this piano player could play by himself. I told him I had all these guys lined up with their horns and they weren't going to be told by me to get down so this other musician could give a concert. So he says, "His name is George Shearing," I says, "I don't give a goddam what his name is. Either he comes up here and plays in turn like everyone else or he can forget it." After that, whenever there was a write-up of a night at Minton's, my name wasn't mentioned. These guys can be very petty.

Lockjaw Davis had invincible integrity and was capable of playing perfectly in any situation. There was no discouraging his distinctive tone and attack, his disdain for imitation, his hammerhead humor and sophisticated wit, his lyric gift for a refined mimesis of intimate frailty, and his butt-kicking, catch-me-if-you-can inclinations to line, harmony, swing, and color. If one listens to no more than his phrasing of the melody lines on *Jaws* (OJC-218)—not to mention his often startling ideas when his imagination is completely unleashed on the moment—the presence of a master fully rounded becomes obvious. And for perfect public performances hear "I'll Remember April," "Woodyn' You," "In Walked Bud," "Land of Dreams," and "Robbins Nest" on *Eddie "Lockjaw" Davis & Johnny Griffin Live at Minton's* (Prestige P24099). I can see him now, leaning into his saxophone, embouchure as unorthodox as his homemade style. He was a man of intelligence, sensitivity, and unforced majesty. We are all lucky that he ever existed.

December 1986

1000 NIGHTS AT
THE VILLAGE VANGUARD

Every Monday night at the Village Vanguard for the past twenty years, Mel Lewis has been swinging the ensemble he now calls the Jazz Orchestra. It was formerly known as the Thad Jones/Mel Lewis Orchestra, and much of its distinctiveness came from the pen of Jones, long respected for his writing and his trumpet playing. But in 1978 Jones packed up and left for Europe, dropping the band in the drummer's lap. Since then, Lewis has held it together, commissioning new material, beating the bushes for European tours and recordings. A loquacious spirit confident sometimes to the verge of abrasiveness, he has maintained the morale of his orchestra and has kept an edge on the performances that make it one of the best big bands to evolve since the innovations of Dizzy Gillespie, Tadd Dameron, and Gil Fuller.

In an art where white musicians are often disparaged for their rhythmic shortcomings, Lewis's authority is undeniable. He understands what to do and when to do it. There are no tempos that give him trouble, and on a night that might be listless, Lewis will sit there hardly moving and push that band into the feeling of dance that underlies all swing. His beat is rich with variety, and the tuning of his drums gives a heavy texture to the ensemble, playing off a dark, humming cymbal sound that stops just short of irritating brightness. Lewis's sense of timbre equals the sweep of textures in the arrangements, all punched or patted by the vocal whomp of his bass drum. The drummer who swings the band is a wonder of precision and passion. His story is a fascinating tale of the world in which the light folks and the dark folks met.

On a spring Friday, May 10, 1929, Melvin Sokoloff was given the bum's rush from the womb.

I was born in the Jewish ghetto of Buffalo, New York, and then we moved farther down to a section that was basically Black. Jefferson Street going down to Williams was the swing area where Jimmie Lunceford, Stuff Smith, Cab Calloway, and everybody was playing. Then when I was four or five we moved into a small Italian area next to it filled with people from northern Italy. They were still old style. In the backyard, they were growing grapes.

The biggest ethnic breakdown was Poles. In Buffalo it was different from what people usually think about Poles in stereotypic ways—hating all the groups I've mentioned. Even though they were steelworkers, the Poles in Buffalo were great connoisseurs of the arts. They loved music and things like that. So they became good fans. Everybody who played—the Blacks, the Jews, and the Italians—had an audience. Maybe things were so good because it was a poor town, a town of not rich people—middle class, a little upper middle class, and lower, mostly lower. We had a family feeling. Everybody was different and everybody respected everybody else.

Lewis's father, Sam Sokoloff, was a self-taught musician who played violin and saxophone before taking up the drums. Sam Sokoloff had come to America from Russia and grew up on Williams Street in the same building as Harold Arlen, not far from Buffalo clubs such as the Moonglow and Montgomery's Little Harlem. Sokoloff and another violin player worked in a band with Arlen, who was writing songs and playing piano. One day Arlen said to Sokoloff, "One of us is going to have to play drums." Sokoloff took one drum lesson, bought himself a set for $15, and soon made a name for himself with his impeccable time. Sokoloff was a show drummer, a wedding drummer, and a dance drummer. His great pride was in his ability to accompany acts, to give them what they wanted. When Bill Robinson worked the Palace Theatre or McVan's, he always used Lewis's father.

Years later in New York, Bill Robinson told me how much he enjoyed my father's playing. Bill Robinson didn't wear metal taps, he had these leather ones and he loved to be thirty feet out there from the band dancing softly. So you had to play as softly as possible, and my father could do that. My dad had a nice light touch and he had a side cymbal on his big brass drum. It made a light skit, skit, skit, skit under the dancers. Later, when I was a kid subbing for my father, I learned how important it was. I was hot stuff, I *thought* I was playing *modern*. That was the old stuff. So I took that little cymbal off and the chorus girls would scream at me, "Put it back on!" The dance captain told me, she said, "Listen, *sonny boy*, I hate to holler at you, but we count off of that cymbal when we're dancing." Out there, jumping around and turning all over the place, they could hear that little sound. Something that soft. You always learn how powerful the drums are in various small, subtle ways and you learn a million things about rhythm watching dancers. A drummer who doesn't understand dancers is in trouble. I bet that's why you don't have any great blind drummers like you have pianists like Art Tatum. They don't see those moves you can put in your rhythms.

Lewis started playing the drums when he was two, banging around on anything he could find because his father never had the instrument set up at home. Sokoloff took his son with him to Jewish weddings and sat him in a chair next to the drums, where he watched what his father did. "Sit still, don't be running all over the place. Here is a cookie. Be quiet. Drink some punch." When his father got up for breaks, Mel would get behind the drums and play. By five, he could play a set of drums. From old drum parts, coat hangers, and wires, he built his own set, hanging his cymbals in the way Chick Webb's were positioned in photographs. A prodigy, by six Lewis was playing in the school orchestra, beginning on bass drum, moving over to snare, and eventually making up his own parts to fit the repertoire of the 84-piece ensemble. There wasn't much chance to practice at home, however. "I could get in three or four minutes before the pounding on the ceiling started. I would rush to the house and shout, 'Is anybody home?' and if nobody answered I would immediately start pounding away. The best I ever got was fifteen or twenty minutes before they were back beating the walls for me to stop."

Though Lewis couldn't read, he held down the drum chair in his grammar school until he was eight and the music teacher switched him over to baritone horn so that she could train someone else to take his place when he graduated. His father tried to get him to play saxophone, but he didn't like it because it was silver and a gold one was what he wanted. Anyway, drums were his fascination. Lewis's love for music was encouraged by his mother, who would wake him up if he went to bed early enough so that he could hear the broadcasts of the big bands.

If I didn't goof around and was in bed and asleep by eight, my mother would wake me up real soft so she wouldn't stir the other children, and I would lay on the floor with a blanket, listening to the radio until 1:30 in the morning, with a five-minute break at the beginning of the hour for the news. In those hours, I could hear four bands. Every night of the week. On Saturdays, you could pick up bands from Detroit, Chicago, St. Louis, Philadelphia, all over the place. You could hear so much music.

By thirteen, Lewis was a professional. The war was on and the local bands needed musicians for all of the dances and fund-raisers. Although Lewis wanted to get into the nightclub world, he worked mostly as a dance drummer who could fill in for his father or handle a job on his own. In a short time, he had his own car and barely made appearances at school because he had been up most of the night, earning money that helped the family and gave him some independence his fellow teenagers didn't have.

When I was sixteen I started getting on the scene with the Black musicians. I got in the union when I was sixteen and was playing dances in the church halls all over the town that had stages and big wooden floors that gave you a good sound. At sixteen, you could go in the clubs but you couldn't drink. When I was big enough, I was there. I would play a gig and then hang out at the Ford Hotel in the restaurant until it was time for the breakfast dance where Bird would be playing. These were Saturday night breakfast dances, which were really Sunday morning because they started at about 4:00 a.m. So here you have Charlie Parker in there and the place is packed with more than three hundred people, it's summer and the windows are open because there's no air-conditioning, and over on the other side of the street Catholics are going to six o'clock mass with all this bebop jazz blasting out of the windows across from them. It was wonderful.

Lewis then was working with white bands and mixed bands. He was the number one substitute in Buffalo and got a chance to perform with many of the Black jump bands, six- to eight-piece units that set up over the bars in clubs with little dance floors. He frequented rooms at the Anchor Bar, Montgomery's Little Harlem, the Club Moonglow where dancers and comedians such as Teddy Hale, Baby Laurence, and Pigmeat Markham were presented. Through his father, Lewis gained entry to the circle of traveling musicians who respected Sam Sokoloff and had heard of his son.

At McVan's, my father worked the dance set between the Black bands. I saw Art Tatum there, Nat Cole, Coleman Hawkins, Cozy Cole. That was when I got to play with Oscar Pettiford, who just came out and picked up his bass while I was there filling in for my father. Art Tatum did the same thing. I got to play with Tatum a lot, just the two of us. He would say, "Where are you? Come on. I enjoyed it." By this time I'm beginning to figure I've got something because nobody can be that nice. If I'm not playing something, they would say, you know musicians—"Somebody get this kid out of here!" My confidence was growing, but I was still listening because there was so much to learn.

Though Lewis would gain a reputation for his ability to swing a big band in a bebop style, his first influences were from the so-called swing era, and they gave him his sense of grace and color. Though he was impressed initially by Gene Krupa, then Moe Purtill with Glenn Miller, his most important early models were Sonny Greer, Jo Jones, and Dave

Tough. He loved Greer for his fills and his colors. Lewis now realizes that some of his first recordings reflect Greer's impact on his own fills.

> He was a swinger, a master of fills, and a great, great colorist who added so much to Ellington's band that we really didn't realize it until he left. Nobody ever added more tasteful things to a band than Sonny Greer. Jo Jones was smooth. Everything had polish and a flow to it. He could make the smallest thing dynamic, like one rim shot. In all other bands, the drummer usually sounded like he was by himself, but with Basie, there was a rhythm section, a *unit*. I found a similarity between the smoothness of Jo Jones and Dave Tough, who got a great sound and used a Chinese cymbal to ride on. Big Sid Catlett was more of a bounce. He and Jo Jones played softer than anybody else. I learned that the power of the drums was in this smooth glide of rhythm; it *wasn't* the volume. It goes back to what I learned when the dancers were screaming at me.

The bebop style was brought home to Lewis by Max Roach.

> When I heard that, I said to myself, "Now this is the way I want to play." Later I heard Shelly Manne and other guys. Then I heard Roy Haynes, who was the most modern I had ever heard. That was his downfall. He was so far ahead of everybody, playing what led to Elvin Jones and Tony Williams, that I think it hurt him for a while. Roy could play so complex, people didn't know what he was doing. I think they were afraid of him.

In 1948, Mel Lewis came to New York with the Lenny Lewis band, a racially mixed outfit that had a style much like that of the early Billy Eckstine band, part Basie, part bebop. Because it was integrated, the band could only work in the North and was cut off from the lucrative southern circuit. Count Basie hired Mel, then had to let him go before any work came up because the band was getting ready to travel south. Within a week or two, Mel got into Boyd Raeburn's wild band.

Lewis loved working in Raeburn's band. The music was very hard but the musicianship was high.

In those days, everybody wanted to play bebop and make it swing. Here you have this integrated unit playing this difficult music, avant-garde music, and we are on the colored theater circuit. That was our trip. We went out into Pigmeat Markham land, on a show with Pigmeat, the Ink Spots, the Step Brothers. A few dances, mostly theaters, one-day theaters, three-day theaters, the whole week. The tour ended with the Apollo in New York, but we played the Howard in Boston, the Royal in Baltimore, the Earl in Philly. We played places like Erie and John-stown, Pennsylvania, where we had a scene over accommodations. The Black musicians knew. They weren't surprised, but the white musicians were really up in arms because we didn't know in our little northern area there were still such places. It was a good lesson even though it was a drag. You had to find out what was going on. So I learned that it wasn't only in the South, it was wherever you had people like that.

After Raeburn, Lewis went with Alvino Rey for about six months, spent a little time back in Buffalo, became bored, chose a day to return to Manhattan, took the Empire Express, and had another drum chair by four o'clock that afternoon. "Ray Anthony was auditioning for that gig, and twenty-five guys had been there all morning. I walked in at the end and wiped them all out and took the gig."

In 1949, with Ray Anthony, the drummer got a new professional name. The bandleader had trouble pronouncing Sokoloff.

Ray found out that my brother's name was Lewis so he put them together. He had his manager call Gretsch, which was about to put me in an ad, and told them I had changed my name to Lewis. We were working the road when I saw the magazine and I was as embarrassed as hell. I called my folks and apologized to them for it. They had seen it, "Mel *Lewis*," and they said they thought it might be a good idea. Then I told them "there might be a lot of Mel Lewises, but there was only one Mel Sokoloff. They said if I ever amounted to anything, I would find out. But the funny thing is that I've met only two or three Mel Lewises in my entire career, none of them in music. But I have met a lot of people with my *real* name.

Lewis and Anthony didn't see eye to eye on the music, but there were no overwhelming problems. When the drummer left, he was immediately scooped up by Tex Beneke, who was leading the Glenn Miller band. The old Miller fans and the people who financed the ensemble weren't happy with the bebop that was rearing its head. "They didn't realize that Glenn himself," says Lewis, "would have changed had he been around. Everybody was modernizing their music, starting with the drums—Duke, Count Basie, you name 'em. It was our time and it wasn't going to be stopped."

None of those jobs got Lewis the attention he felt his talent deserved. He was sitting in around New York with just about everybody who was playing something interesting, and everyone told him they liked his style, but Lewis was overlooked when important drum chairs became available. He was feeling some frustration until he got to Stan Kenton's orchestra.

When I joined Stan, I started getting my credits. The style of drumming that was inside me came all the way out. The band started swinging, and I was getting the recognition for it because the Kenton band had never swung prior to that. Suddenly, the big-shot critics who had always hated Kenton started loving him. Bill Holman was the arranger and I was the drummer.

Lewis moved to Los Angeles in 1954, after three years with Kenton. He performed with many small units and did some jazz studio work, feeling that he didn't get into commercial studio work because he wasn't a brown-noser.

I didn't know how to lick boots or lick anything else for that matter, so I was the wrong man for Hollywood. At the time, I wasn't aware of that. But I saw what was happening shortly afterwards. They could shove it if I had to go through anything other than showing up and doing a first-class job, which isn't enough for people who like submission.

In Los Angeles, Lewis shared bandstands with Gerald Wilson, got many calls for small groups, and was often used when musicians from the East came to California and needed to put together a band. In 1960, he joined Gerry Mulligan, who would fly him out from California, even for two nights. When not with Mulligan, Lewis subbed for Gus Johnson with Ella Fitzgerald. In 1962, after traveling east with Peggy Lee, Lewis was hired to go to Russia with Benny Goodman. He started hankering for the New York scene when he returned to Los Angeles and was soon on the way to Manhattan.

When I moved back to New York in 1963 and worked Harlem with Ben Webster for the entire summer, it had changed from when I used to walk the streets by myself in the late 1940s, wearing my bebop tie, my dark suit, and carrying my sticks. Now it was junkie time. Once a guy approached me in the wrong way and he got the crap beaten out of him in two seconds. I didn't know it, but Ben had people looking out for me wherever I went. Ben had them looking out for him, too. "They're watching me too because this is not the same people who used to live up here." Junkies he meant, not the regular people. They were always great.

The same year, Thad Jones left Basie and joined Gerry Mulligan. Just as Jones began writing something for Mulligan, the saxophonist announced that he was breaking up the band. Lewis looked at Jones and suggested that they put together their own band. They were finally ready on February 10, 1966, for their first job at the Vanguard.

We bought some brand-new cardboard music stands and spent all the time trying to figure out how we could get all the musicians on the bandstand. We went to get a bite to eat and when we came back, we couldn't get in. There was a line around the corner. We had to bang on the back door to get in. Then we had only nine charts, so we had to twist them around to finish the night. Max Gordon was smiling, and we were off the ground.

For the first two years, the regular personnel were Snooky Young, Bill Berry, Jimmy Nottingham, and Richard Williams, trumpets; Joe Farrell, Jerry Dodgion, Jerome Richardson, Eddie Daniels, and Pepper Adams, reeds; Cliff Heather, Bob Brookmeyer, Garnett Brown, and Jimmy Knepper, trombones; Roland Hanna, piano; Sam Herman, guitar; Richard Davis, bass; Thad Jones, conductor and trumpet; and Lewis. Red Keller, who worked the door, remembers the band well: "It was celebrity night every Monday, with movie stars, comedians, socialites, whatever. And I have never heard or known of a band that had the kind of affection these guys had for each other. Nor have I ever known musicians so anxious to play the music. They were working the studios all the time, and they couldn't *wait* to get here to play Thad's music."

"We got very hot," Lewis remembers.

We went through Germany, Holland, Switzerland, on a battle of the bands tour. Every place we played, we won. It didn't matter which bands they put up against us, we tore the pants off of them. We did an ill-fated tour of Japan in 1968 where there were no gigs and no money and the promoter had the greatest stories ever told day after day. But we survived the two-week ordeal and made some good music in the process. We did sixteen-week tours of Europe, sixteen weeks, can you imagine? But we could never get anything in this country."

In 1972, we went to Russia. When I first went over there in 1962, you could see the police-state routine. We couldn't go anyplace on our own. When Thad and I went over with the guys, people looked better, they were smiling more. They could come to our room and see us this time, which they couldn't do before. The food is terrible over there, but it was less terrible the second time. Greasy boiled chicken or roast chicken, and you can see the feathers are still in the skin. Scallions, potatoes and they have blue lumps in them. They don't know how to cook eggs either. But the baked goods are delicious. I could see the same things in the Russian Jews over there that you see in New York today—the way they talk and walk and how they gesture.

When we were there the first time, musicians played jazz, but they couldn't say jazz, they called it radio music. The government was against it, but they didn't even know what it was when they heard it. Everything had to be okayed by the government through the ministry of culture. When I met this cat Alex Batashev, who was the president of the jazz club in Russia, the government gave him hell. But I saw

him in Poland in 1976, and he said the officials started opening up
and giving them some musical assistance with places to play and what
have you. Maybe that had something to do with my telling the big-
wigs over there how good their musicians were and what they weren't
really benefiting from as much as they could.

In 1978, when Thad Jones left and Lewis had to take the helm, the
drummer made a decision that he thinks was central to the orchestra's
development,

> I decided that I should let each section leader run his musicians
> because I didn't play their instruments. Earl Gardner runs the trum-
> pets, John Mosca and Earl McIntyre handle the trombones, Dick
> Oatts takes care of the reeds. Now we can play parts ten different
> ways without anybody saying anything, and make it work. I think this
> is the best and the most consistent band we've ever had. The first band
> was great without a doubt, but it didn't have the consistency this one
> does. A lot of times the guys would have such a good time between
> shows that they might not be able to play as well by the end of the
> night as they did at the start. Oh, it could rise to the occasion. If we
> had to play opposite Duke in Central Park or something like that,
> they could give you everything you wanted to hear and *better*. Under
> pressure, that was the greatest big band out there at that time. Still, it
> wasn't consistent. This band is another story.

I must have heard the band a hundred times by now myself, and
Lewis may be right. Mel Lewis and the Jazz Orchestra play with the
urgency of musicians committed more to music than to money. The years
have drained it of the stars it once had, but the players who are there
every Monday give the music its necessary human animation. Other than

Lewis, the musicians now are Earl Gardner, Glen Drewes, John Marshall, and Jim Powell, trumpets; John Mosca and Ed Neumeister, bass trombones; Doug Purviance and Earl McIntyre, trombones; Stephanie Fauber, French horn; Dick Oatts, alto, soprano, flute; Ted Nash, alto, soprano, clarinet, flute; Joe Lovano, tenor, clarinet, and flute; Ralph Lalama, tenor, clarinet, flute; Gary Smulyan, baritone and bass clarinet; Kenny Werner, piano; and Dennis Irwin, bass.

Last week, as they celebrated their twentieth anniversary with a full week at the Vanguard, the players gave some of the best big-band performances one could ask for. Playing from a book that spanned the writings of Thad Jones, Bob Brookmeyer, Bill Holman, Bob Mintzer, and Earl McIntyre, the Jazz Orchestra showed its stuff with such precision and passion that even those who might have dismissed it as no more than a largely white band lucky enough to have a great swinger at the drums would have had to back off, listen, and have a good time. Oh, there are times when the band has that transparent weightlessness that disconnects so many white bands from idiomatic sonority. Though they always play the hell out of Holman's "Just Friends" arrangement, last week it was delivered with a swing and fervid lyricism laced with humor that bowled everybody over. Renee Manning, the girl singer, was especially good, rocking the house as always and drowned out by the impetuous trumpets on occasion as always. Of the horns, Lalama, Lovano, and Smulyan rose to the drummer's swing with the most authority. But a big band is about a big sound, and the character that comes from Mel Lewis and the Jazz Orchestra is large of heart and rich with dedication. Max Gordon said to Mel many years ago, "We'll keep it going until it tapers off." They are still there, and they will be there.

March 1986

REMEMBERING BUDDY RICH

BEING WHITE AND ONE OF THE BEST and a jazz musician usually carries with it certain privileges and certain problems. The white press will often magnify your idiomatic authority, if only to justify its own right to say which Black musicians sound good and which don't. The Euro-American public, which often listens to music with its eyes and tends to prefer what looks most like itself, will love your work for reasons that have little to do with any appreciation of the quality of your art. Especially when the attention leads to great financial success, understandably sensitive Black musicians will either deny your skills or carp at shortcomings they might overlook in one of their ethnic own. The charge of "politics" might be raised if you are the only white member of a Black band, meaning that the leader hired you in a jazz version of the worst kind of affirmative action—to placate social forces regardless of how well the job is done. So what you want to do, which is play, will turn into something so mucked up by sociology, envy, misbegotten racial pride, and so on that you're all but forced to cultivate an unchanging focus on what attracted you to the music in the first place—a feeling for jazz.

I'm sure Buddy Rich knew all of this, but I doubt that he ever allowed it to get in his way. He began as a boy wonder, appearing on Broadway by the age of four, and his Napoleonic stature never limited the size of his skill, a skill that instigated in him the grating and ingratiating arrogance of a man who knew in great detail his position in the world, that he was one of the best who ever did it. I'm also sure that Rich privately agreed with those who described him as some sort of miraculous freak whose gift from the impenetrable gene pool allowed him to do things on the drums that few would have imagined possible had they not heard them executed, initially by him and him only.

Rich may have been the fastest and most precise snare-drum player jazz has produced; many consider him the most imposingly swift ever to sit behind the traps. "You may not have liked his jazz playing," said Ray Brown, "which is your business. But you better not go one-on-one with that sonofabitch because that would definitely be your ass." There was a pugnacious pout on his face as he whipped out the ride-cymbal beat, and his grimaces were always intimations of a self-assurance that could lean over into cruelty. As he filled holes in arrangements, turned his head to the side and roared over his instrument, or turned his sticks into beams of light shining from his hands, it was obvious that this was a far from humble man. Then there were his solos, complemented by an Olympian sneer as the snare-drum beats became faster and faster, as he moved across the entire instrument—every cymbal and drum—in one beat. He surely had a physical genius for the instrument.

Easily the best-known jazz drummer after Gene Krupa, Buddy Rich was neither an innovator nor part of any movement that influenced the direction of the art. But like Art Tatum, he presaged the kind of instrumental control that would become so basic to jazz after Charlie Parker,

Dizzy Gillespie, Bud Powell, Ray Brown, and Max Roach. Though dismissed by some as a tasteless technician who couldn't make music if God gave him permission, he always valued blues and a swinging groove above all. When I asked him to describe his most memorable musical experience, he cited the time in Los Angeles more than forty years ago when he subbed for two weeks with Count Basie. I asked him what they played. "Blues, blues, and more blues," he smiled. "Sitting behind that band was heaven for me."

But what I remember most about him as a drummer was what Philly Joe Jones said in one of his nightly discourses on the art of jazz after the doors were closed at the Tin Palace:

> Look, I worked with the man. I heard him every night. He helped me out when I was scuffling and never threw it up in my face or in anybody else's either. I needed work and he gave it to me. I traveled with him. When he was singing and dancing, I was playing. When he was playing, I was listening. I don't care what anybody says, when you listen to that man play you will hear some things that you can't believe are coming out of the instrument. It doesn't matter if you think his style isn't what you want to hear, either. Some people think it's corny. A lot of people think it's corny. But I'm talking about playing the drums. If you love the drums you have to love some of the unbelievable things he does. And if you don't love the drums you don't really love jazz.

When he died of a heart attack on April 2, 1987—the prodigious instrumentalist who had never taken a lesson and never practiced, who made it clear to one and all that the only thing he needed in the world was his drums, who was never dictated to once he reached maturity and never said anything he couldn't back up, who loved most the Count Basie groove and was fascinated by flamenco dancers, who was a practical joker and loyal friend—he left a legacy of precision and velocity, of will and courage. Most of all, he left a feeling for jazz that was even greater than his humbling virtuosity.

April 1987

FUSIONISM

WAYNE SHORTER / DEXTER GORDON

JAZZ HAS BEEN BEDEVILED by two kinds of fusion for sixty years on one hand and twenty on the other. Since the 1920s, various musicians have attempted to merge jazz with symphonic conventions, and since the late 1960s, a number of jazz players have experimented with (more often sold out to) pop idioms. Recently I heard two musicians elevate the possibilities of these areas. Wayne Shorter led a band at the Beacon Theatre on May 2 and transformed fusion just as surely as Louis Armstrong uncaged the birds that existed behind the bars of Tin Pan Alley sentimentality; and Dexter Gordon was backed up by the New York Philharmonic on June 4–6 for a performance made momentous by an emotional empathy, so often lacking in these attempts at synthesis.*

Shorter's performance was a reckoning. In about an hour, two decades of fusion were redefined as a loud preamble to Shorter's powers of compo-

---

* Both performances occurred in 1987.

sition and improvisation. One heard the beats and the electronic timbres that identify pop, rock, and funk replace the standard song structures that previous jazz musicians had used as bridges to the mass audience. Yet there was no reductive submission to the primitive expression of the urban jungle, no "going native" by embracing the albeit real but circumscribed adolescent concerns that have swallowed up giants such as Miles Davis; it was an event in which Shorter's architectural invention erected structures made invincible by his integrity. Nothing was too long, and no rhythm, texture, voicing, or thematic reference existed only as "interesting." No: Shorter did not stoop to pander.

Shorter's compositional gifts have greatly influenced the designs of his improvisations, which are equally full of luminous and mysterious contrasts, counterpoint, harmonic snakiness, and impassioned lyricism offset by great wit, if not high comedy. With dramatic precision, he orders harmony and rhythm, using intervallic surprise and unpredictable changes of register for the illusion of accents. As has been possible since Charlie Parker, he plays the saxophone like a keyboard, as though independently weaving right- and left-hand materials. But Shorter uses the technique in a completely compositional way, not placing his ideas "on top" of his group. Every aspect of the composition—line, voicing, harmonic register—is whirled through the holes in the band as vines are through a trellis.

Atlantis and *Phantom Navigator*, the two recordings he has made since leaving the Weather Report crypt after almost fifteen years, say nothing about Shorter's improvisation in person. On stage he moves with sureness from tenor to soprano and back in a homemade concerto. The electric keyboards of Jim Beard ("the utility man," Shorter calls him), the electric bass of Carl James, the trap drums of Terri Lyne Carrington, and the percussion of Marilyn Mazur respond to the saxophones, but the improvisational glory is nearly all Shorter's, as it once was Armstrong's.

Unlike those who have only tapped the slick, exotic surfaces of electronics and "world music," Shorter brings the force of an adult sensibility to this usually greasy kid stuff. His is an epic sensibility resulting from a sweep of musical and nonmusical influences. "I'll never forget seeing Stravinsky conduct when I was eight years old," Shorter said, "or sitting up with my brother singing the themes from Frankenstein and Wolfman movies, practicing Chopin arpeggios, building the world with clay on the round kitchen table, and stuff like saying to my mother, 'I can't finish this pork chop, because I'm on the way to bebop *rehearsal*.'"

Though many of the things I liked when I was very young were from Caucasian sources, they didn't keep me out of the through traffic of Charlie Parker, Monk, and Bud Powell I heard first over WNEW. I didn't take any exits. But I also liked Lennie Tristano, Warne Marsh, and Lee Konitz because they were consciously trying something else. Dexter Gordon, of course, Sonny Rollins, and John Coltrane. You have to learn the music of the masters in order to discover yourself. Charlie Parker put the music under an X-ray so that he could see right into the blood of the harmony, and the blood of the harmony is akin to the blood of living in some way. Notes are always attached to human experiences, and what you know will get you where you have to go if you aren't afraid to subject yourself to the responsibility of learning to listen clearly enough to *hear*. I can almost hear every part in a whole orchestra now. It took me a very long time to get where I am now, and I think everything is getting ready to *move*.

It most surely is because Shorter is now playing with an authority that puts him at the forefront of a music that was once easily dismissed and, except for his work and the better moments of Ornette Coleman's Prime Time, is still largely insignificant in any aesthetic sense. But what makes

Shorter's band really happen beyond his own playing is Carrington, whose background in jazz makes her statements of the rhythms take on the groove of swing. Of her Shorter says, "Somehow she puts a swinging nudge on the beats and gives them what the physicists call *vectors*." With Carrington and the backlog of knowledge gained on the bandstands of Horace Silver, Art Blakey, and Miles Davis, Shorter is now looming, capable of becoming the musical force that his talent has always suggested.

As exciting as Shorter's elevation of fusion was Dexter Gordon's playing with the New York Philharmonic after a four-year absence from public performance. Daniel Windhan of the philharmonic asked Gordon last February if he would like to have a work written for him and the orchestra. While vacationing in Mexico, Gordon discussed the project and agreed upon David Baker as composer. Gordon also asked for pianist Tommy Flanagan and bassist Richard Davis, who was later replaced by Ron Carter when Davis had an accident. Upon returning to New York in May, Gordon began rehearsing with the orchestra and his two fellow jazzmen.

The performance itself, which was part of three evenings celebrating the concert music of George Gershwin and Duke Ellington, had intriguing precedents. Because Gordon formed his style during the 1940s, when Parker and Lester Young were the dominant reed influences, it is important to note that Parker had dreamed of studying composition and orchestration in Paris so that he could write concerti for his alto saxophone. "One of the last times I interviewed Bird up in Boston," recalls Nat Hentoff, "he brought Bartók's Second Piano Concerto and played it over the air. He then said that he wanted to do the same thing but in *his* style. Bird felt that he needed a bigger situation to play in and saw himself one day having the wherewithal to work with an orchestra. But he wasn't talking about writing European music. No, he wanted it to sound like him and to extend, what he had already done. Had he lived to do that, no one can imagine what kind of impact it might have had."

The closest Parker ever got to that was performing mediocre to good arrangements of popular songs with a string ensemble, a fact that Lester Young was envious of because he never got the financial backing to float his tone over the fiddle. Parker would surely have been proud of what Gordon brought to the occasion, though he might have been disappointed by the first evening's performance. Under the baton of James DePreist, the philharmonic mutilated the music, which Baker entitled *Ellingtones*. Gordon was still seeking the appropriate sound to get through the mass of the orchestra on that first evening, making references to Ben Webster, sometimes barbing his tone with a combative vibrato, sometimes whooshing his way through subtones. Even though his characteristic timbre filled Avery Fisher Hall, he often sounded tentative.

I returned Saturday night and was awed by the difference. But upon hearing a bootleg tape of this same performance, I realized that the strength of the orchestra itself and Gordon were what had come together, not Baker's composition. *Ellingtones* never rises to the level of authority inherent in the ensemble or soloist. The opening owed much to Bartók's *Miraculous Mandarin*, then references to "Caravan," "Drop Me Off in Harlem," and "Minnehaha" coursed through the orchestra as Gordon's saxophone was backed up by strings. His projection consistently parted the orchestra, taking its own musical space. A swinging section took off with the tenor rising over the philharmonic on the pulse of Carter and Flanagan for visceral excitement, Gordon's every note bruising into or sailing above the meter.

Baker's writing then made a large reference to Coltrane's "Central Park West." It had an iridescent texture that set the way for "All Too Soon" where Gordon laid with or moved in contrast to the timbres of the orchestra. The "Central Park West" material was briefly reprised. "It Don't Mean a Thing" rolled up into the air, and the three jazzmen laid down more and more powerful beats as their swing set fire to the backdrop, inspiring both the conductor and the orchestra, which very nearly swung. Gordon then provided the evening's pinnacle with an extended cadenza in which he quoted "In a Sentimental Mood," "Cotton Tail," and "Sophisticated Lady," sauntering his lines through the hall with sanguine but idealistic lyricism. A last compression of motives from the philharmonic and it was over. There was a standing ovation and applause for Gordon from the orchestra itself. Rejuvenated, the saxophonist had brought off an imposing moment in American music.

Gordon said in retrospect:

I don't want to dwell too much on it, but I consider it the highlight of my career thus far, primarily because it had never been done and because I had come up playing with Lionel Hampton, with Bird in Billy Eckstine's band, and worked on 52nd Street in the 1940s, when we thought of the New York Philharmonic as something apart from what we were doing. It never crossed my mind that I would ever be playing with a whole orchestra behind me in a concerto for saxophone. When we first rehearsed, the musicians were nice but just professional. As things progressed, more warmth began to show and the feeling became rapturous. Afterwards, the first cellist came over to me and said that he had never heard a sound like that come out of a saxophone. He didn't know anything like that existed. And then there was the response of the audience and the orchestra. I felt that I had done something that spoke of the level of quality that had always impressed me when I was inspired by the work of Lester Young, Charlie Parker, and all of the musicians who are part of me. They are responsible for me being what I am as a musician, and I am responsible to them.

July 1987

BLACK LIKE HUCK

T HE IDEA WAS FOR RICHARD FORD and me to retrace the voyage of Huck and Jim down the Mississippi, traveling in an open boat on the big liquid serpent that has been such a magical, monstrous force in the biography of our nation. We were to begin near Hannibal, Missouri, Mark Twain's hometown, and make our way down to Cairo, Illinois—Huck and Jim's destination. But we didn't get nearly that far. One November day was it.

The journey was meant as an opportunity to meditate on race relations since the publication of *Huckleberry Finn* in 1884. On the surface, the idea was contrived and might have been insulting, except that I welcomed the chance to see some more of America. It had also occurred to me that, given how much has shifted, we could not be sure that Huck today would be white and Jim would be Black; that some boy with, say, Ennis Cosby's background might not be looking out for an older, less privileged white guy who was on the run, maybe had some serious trouble with the law.

The night I arrived in Missouri, our captain, Larry Orick, a sturdy man in his fifties with a gray mustache and a love of the blues, told me he was not much impressed by Mark Twain as a riverman and didn't consider him too knowledgeable about the ways of the Mississippi. Good: the whittling had already begun. I knew I would be doing some of my own before it was all over.

Hannibal, where we set out, is now a tourist town devoted to Mark Twain. The names and images of his characters are everywhere—on menus, statues, buildings, and streets. With its packaged Americana ("America's Hometown") and its overwhelming whiteness, Hannibal is the kind of place for which I have both great affection and absolute disgust.

I say affection because the brutality in our history has always been redeemed by the peacemakers, the idealists, and the martyrs who—through bravery or humor or both—inevitably climb over the fences that intrude upon our shared human connections. I can't help loving all of that.

I say disgust because, at the same time, I have this melancholy resentment about how long it took the Negro to be recognized as one of the chief architects of Americana.

This ambivalence extends to my attitude about Twain. Slavery twisted up old Mr. Twain's world, which is why he wrote *Huckleberry Finn* twenty years after the end of the Civil War. He was still trying to resolve something. Twain knew that Negroes and whites would either achieve freedom together or share mutual diminishment. He knew that it was the duty of whites with moral courage to ensure that bigots and opportunists not be allowed to sustain the immoralities of bias that petrify our nation. For Twain, Jim was at least as good as any of the white people in the novel.

Even so, Twain was never able to fully imagine sophisticated, educated Negroes of the sort represented by Frederick Douglass, men and women whose very existence remains one of the grand achievements of this nation. In this, Twain is like all those modern American writers for whom Negroes beyond the familiar stereotypes—be it the dependent Jim or the dangerous Tupac Shakur—are still too hot to handle. Such provincial writers might as well be in cahoots with Pa Finn, Huck's brutal father, who rages against a well-dressed mulatto from Ohio, a man with "a cool way" whom he heard was "a p'fessor in a college, and could talk all kinds of languages, and knowed everything."

Fortunately, in our time, the best of television has gone far beyond our fiction and our theater when it comes to providing a wide range of Black people: homeboys and master surgeons, hoochies and sharp female lawyers, gangbangers and diplomats, illiterates and technocrats and every workaday type in between. There was no such range in Twain's time, when minstrelsy was king and the standard Negro never met a stolen chicken that he didn't like.

Now there is a new minstrelsy, but of a peculiarly customized sort. This steamed into my mind when we were getting ready to shove off. In the store at the dock, I bought a T-shirt. It had some licorice-black cartoon Negroes in pickaninny hairdos dancing and looking just like the characters in the illustration of "Jim's Coat of Arms" in the original edition of *Huckleberry Finn*. The slogan on the front of the T-shirt read, "We Be Jammin'."

The young white woman who sold it to me said rather proudly that, "as a party animal," she had worn one all last summer. Everybody loved them, she said. Everybody. Could sell a ton of them. The image of a party full of white people wearing those T-shirts and dancing to rock and rap brought me to attention.

Negroes would have been outraged by such an image when I was coming up in the 1950s but, of course, they hadn't yet embraced what I call "pickaninny chic." As things stand now, no previously denigrating image of Afro-Americans is out of bounds. Every last one of them has been snatched up by Negro college professors, rappers, and middle-class Black kids trying to find something "authentic"—an antidote to being absorbed, a token of vitality.

This impulse is very different from the gutbucket consciousness of remaining in touch with the spit, grit, and mother wit of the sidewalk. What we have here is a psychological crisis in the face of imminent or expanding personal privilege. The further that insecure Negroes get away from poverty and ignorance, the more they fear selling out and becoming "neo-whites." So they wear dreadlocks or discuss rappers as though they have something profound to say or, most pathetic of all, feel it necessary to imitate a "street culture" they've seen on television.

With my symbol of contemporary minstrelsy bought and paid for, I was soon on the water with three white guys, not one of whom came from a similar place but each of whom was recognizable. Ford was the southern writer; Orick, the riverman; and Mitch Epstein, the Jewish beanpole from New York, who took photographs and nearly set himself afire on the boat but later came through like a champ when trouble hit the fuel line and gas had to be hand pumped to keep us moving.

We laughed at the same things, were equally impressed by the goodness or the badness of our luck, and felt, at least early in the day when the boat was running smoothly, the sense of connection to every person who had ever been out in the clear air and the wide-open light of the Mississippi.

Out here with these three men I was much freer than Jim or Huck had ever been. In my life and in the life of the nation, so much has fallen away. Forty years ago, when I was a teenager joining civil rights picket lines, the appearance of Black and white people together was a social statement. When we went anywhere together in the Black or white communities of Los Angeles, there were stares. Back then, Negroes were far more exotic and so had little investment in maintaining an exotic identity. Today there are Black mayors, astronauts, models—and Oprah Winfrey.

So I felt none of the old feeling of making a statement by being on the same boat with those guys. It was not us against the world, looking out for a better day when a person would finally be a person. No, this was as natural as water running down a hill.

This camaraderie, this sense that we now consciously share a much broader vision of Americana, became ever clearer as we spoke of books, films, families, the landscape. When the boat's fuel line went haywire, I thought of all the times Americans had been brought together by problems. I thought, too, of how much of our story plays itself out in the moments when will, muscle, spirit, and experience are called on to take the place of machines that fall down on the job. An improvisational inclination underlies our national tale. Individually or collectively, we invent a way.

On our boat, we did. When there was trouble, we pumped and bailed and fiddled with the engine until, with the sky growing dark, we saw beyond us, glowing in gold lights, the bridge at Alton, Illinois, the town where Miles Davis was born. We were safe. The boat ride was over.

In St. Louis the next evening, I went to a blues club with Larry Orick and found myself surrounded by white people who loved the blues, no matter who played them. The presence of the Negro was in the air, but now as part of a national aesthetic that just about anybody felt free to adopt. While few Negroes now support the blues or grow up playing them, the blues are out there, waiting. They waited for Huck and Jim, just as they wait for all of us. That is one sound of America, one of the many we now share.

June 1999

A BIRD IN THE WORLD

Charlie Parker was blessed with the eternal quality of existing forever.

—ORNETTE COLEMAN

Charlie Parker was the highest level of modern music of that period and continues to be that today. Everybody—technically, harmonically, rhythmically, and melodically—is affected by Charlie Parker. Once you heard him, it was like a stamp in your mind. He came up in a time when most people understood basic music. People had pianos and they knew the tunes. So when they heard him, it wasn't foreign to them but it was revolutionary.

—ANTOINE RONEY

CHARLES PARKER JR. WAS BORN August 29, 1920, in Kansas City, Kansas. For those who care, he was in a cluster of Virgos important to him, only a few days away from his mother, a half Choctaw Indian from Oklahoma, and from two of his most important musical influences, Lester Young and Buster Smith. Some said he didn't live life, he swallowed it whole. Perhaps it swallowed him. On March 12, 1955, he was dead at the age of thirty-four in New York at the Stanhope Hotel, in the apartment of a Jewish baroness who had driven ambulances in North Africa during World War II and whose family had bankrolled Wellington against Napoleon at Waterloo. At least, that's how Thelonious Monk described her family. Maybe he had seen the movie *The House of Rothschild*. Parker's corpse looked more than fifty years old. Laid out, he appeared odd to his third wife, Doris, and to Dizzy Gillespie, because his fingers were flat. He was so much a part of his saxophone when alive that, as photographs prove, his fingers were always curved as they had to be to finger that horn.

When he was no more than another midwestern Negro kid growing into early manhood in Kansas City, no one could have predicted the impact that he would have on the language of jazz because genius, being what it is, plays no favorites and has no special hangouts. It arrives— *wham*—is developed or not, and moves on, looking for another container in which to play its endless variations. As it turned out, however, Parker was one of a number of geniuses who walked the earth and who inhabited his world. Genius, by the way, comes in all sizes. His was one of the larger ones.

Charlie Parker's father worked the trains and wore shoes shined to such characteristic brightness that the saxophonist's first wife knew his dad's line of work the first time she, then a teenager, saw him. On those trips, choo-chooing from one part of the country to the other, the older Parker learned a lot from overhearing subjects tossed around between customers or traveling artists or among his own coworkers. His musician son always described him as a very sophisticated man with a number of talents. On his own time, when he came off the rails, Parker's father was an alcoholic and what Duke Ellington called "a night creature," a man who loved to party in the streets, which he seemed to do most of the time. Addie, the mother of Charles Jr., was loyal, but her husband burned that loyalty to the ground and blew away the ashes. Mrs. Parker was very straight, wore her hair in a cat-and-mouse style, never smoked, and never drank. She was a simple woman given to a combination of private hoodoo superstition and public Christian worship. When she had had enough of her husband's drunken ways, Addie Parker moved from Kansas City, Kansas, and made herself and her son a new home at 1516 Olive Street in Kansas City, Missouri, soon to become a boomtown for nightlife—music, gambling, liquor, dancing, and girls. Corruption and gangsters helped things along. Some think of those criminals as patrons of the arts, which they were—by accident. They kept a party going that seemed as if it would never stop. There were clubs upon clubs upon clubs. At the Reno Club, where the teenage Charlie Parker would go to listen to Lester Young, the musicians hung out behind the club where prostitutes sat on benches, waiting to be called for by the bar customers. It was a world upside down. When the musicians were going home, regular people were getting up to go to work. As the musicians rose and began preparing to go to their jobs, working people were starting to go home. Given the corruption, Tom Pendergast worked with the crooks, and the cops were in cahoots as well. It was a town in which one could easily be misled, especially because the corruption meant that Kansas City, Missouri, didn't suffer the same devastation of nightlife that hit the rest of the country during the Great Depression of the early 1930s. Those grafters, those hustlers, those whores, those gangsters, those audiences ready to be put in a swoon by the beauty of the night and the music, those dancers ready to let the meaning of life be compressed in turns and steps, those musicians prepared to play shows, to give order to the present through their improvisations, to create a new dialect of pulsation that would be called "Kansas City Swing." And all of them together, along with all the gold dust, blood, and smut of the corruption, created an overall vitality that inspired Mary Lou Williams to describe that town as a "heavenly city."

The little Parker boy was sent to Catholic school for his earliest education by his mother, who spoiled him and reared the boy as though he

was a prince who did not have to do things the way others did. First: no
work. He was given an allowance instead of earning his money the way
other boys did. Second: duded up. He wore the latest clothes, such as
knickers and tailor-made suits. Third: whatever food he liked. Fourth:
quick forgiveness for any shortcoming. If a spoiled child would have happened to have a special smell about him, Charles Parker Jr. could have
been whiffed five blocks away. This may account for something, as most
Negro innovators in jazz have been spoiled children. They are told they
are right about almost anything. They are sheltered from many kinds of
trouble. They are given the impression that they are superior to the run of
the mill. That certitude separates them from others and can make them
somewhat accustomed to being out of line with the crowd or not always
liked because of their narcissistic ways. That spoiling might be a form of
elite training. So there may well be a connection between the way his
mother treated him and the feeling of special privilege that sent him
down his artistic path and gave him the grit when the time came to stand
against dislike and deliver. Lacking the inborn talent, of course, all this
speculation is irrelevant.

On April 10, 1934, a family moved in and rented the upstairs part of
Addie Parker's house. Birdy Ruffin, the mother of the family, had recently
separated from her husband; she brought her daughters and her son with
her. The second daughter, Rebecca, looked down the stairs at Charles
Parker Jr., who was standing there with his mother. Almost fourteen and
wearing his knickers, he was fascinated by these new people moving in.
As lazy as they made them, this mama's boy was not about to supply
help in bringing anything up the stairs, but he was there, the same age
as Rebecca, and exuding such a stunning combination of loneliness and
charm that she fell in love the moment her eye lay upon him and knew
that she was in trouble.

Birdy Ruffin didn't like the boy, who had sadistic tendencies and would sometimes play far too rough with her daughters, pinching them, twisting their arms, shoving snow in their faces or down into their clothes. He did nothing other than eat, sleep, and play. There was no evident discipline. He lived by whim. When she looked out of her window upstairs and saw him on his knees shooting marbles, Birdy called him nothing more than an "alley rat." But there was also a magnetic quality about him. His melancholic distance was countered by his quickness of mind, his ability to joke, the way he fit in with the Ruffin kids, even entertaining them with renditions of boogie-woogie tunes on his mother's piano. There was also something elegant, even poetic, about this young man with a reddish tone under his skin, this boy who was a dreamer and could talk softly about things so idealistic they would seem naive to an adult but could easily dazzle the second daughter of a woman named Birdy.

Charlie and Rebecca were soon into an adolescent romance. They went to the same school and thought about each other more than anything else in the universe. He was her dream and she was his. Rebecca stood at the fence watching him as he became interested in music, moving along in the marching band from instrument to instrument until he found that saxophone. When she worked at the library after school, Charlie would come in, check out a book, usually about something far out and idealistic, and sit on the steps reading until she was finished, then walk her home. One time they went down a forbidden street, where there were all of those clubs, and Charlie stood looking in the window, taken by the near-empty interiors that would fill up later, when the smooth lightning of Kansas City jazz struck its groove and burned away the boredom, the blues, and the need for the affirmation of a swinging beat. Soon, Charlie stopped going to school and remained home practicing the saxophone. His mother let him do whatever he wanted. Birdy Ruffin found that disgusting.

One afternoon Rebecca's younger sister walked in on Rebecca and Charlie. According to the sister they were having sex, although Rebecca claimed it was nothing that heavy. Shortly afterward, there was a terrible row and Rebecca, in tears, was shouting that she didn't care what anyone said, she was in love with Charlie. Addie Parker took the position that they were just kids in love and should not be punished. Birdy Ruffin was hearing none of that and chose to move out.

They still saw each other. On the quiet, secret-like. Rebecca's older sister, Octavia, was central to the game. She took Rebecca with her when she went out, and their mother never suspected that they met Charlie at the movies on Saturdays or went to hear him on Sundays when he was playing with the Deans of Swing and already had a following, though none of the musicians could understand how that lightweight saxophone player drew so many admiring girls to hear him blow. Odd. Women. Music.

It was June 19, 1936, the night of the first Joe Louis fight with Max Schmeling. People listening to the fight over the radio were on the steps of the library or could be seen on porch after porch throughout the whole twelve rounds. Louis was not doing well. Charles Parker Jr. had other things on his mind. He proposed to Rebecca, saying that her mother would do both of them in if she found out that they were still seeing each other without her knowledge. A few days before they were to marry, Rebecca packed her bags, announced that she was leaving to become Charlie's wife, and was told by Birdy Ruffin that she would need her mother before her mother would need her.

When Rebecca arrived at the Parker home, Addie told Charlie that his fiancée had to get her wedding dress together and that she should stay across the street with a friend of the Parkers until it was time to get married. On Saturday morning, July 25, 1936, Addie Parker gave Rebecca a white Bible, put her in a white hat, yellow blouse, and white skirt, told her son to wear his brown suit, and took them by trolley to the justice of the peace. When it came time for Charlie to place a ring on his near-wife's finger, Addie Parker took off her two wedding rings and gave them to Rebecca to slip on. They returned home to a small reception. Charlie's father, uncle, and half-brother were there. The groom stuck the end of a napkin in his collar and was soon walking around the parlor constantly eating ice cream and cake, pausing only to wash them down with punch. Everybody was in good spirits, the family and the few female friends that Addie had invited. That night Rebecca and Charlie moved upstairs.

Charlie was all the way into being a musician now, and when he was not practicing his horn he was out in the streets either jamming or looking for a job. He had been thrown off a few bandstands for not knowing what he was doing when he sat in, once unaware that the chords of "Up a Lazy River" and the bridge of "Honeysuckle Rose"—which were the only chord sequences he knew—didn't fit all tunes. The musicians laughed at him and he went home crushed. He didn't stay crushed. He decided that he was going to be a good musician and pushed aside his lazy tendencies when it came to music. Now Charlie was always learning. It got so that just about any time somebody was passing that Parker house the sound of a saxophone was heard coming into the street. Whenever there was a musician willing to share some information or help him with something that kept him in the minor leagues, Charlie was there, ready to take instruction and put in the time at home until he had mastered whatever it was that he was studying.

Parker got a good job in the Ozarks, where, whenever they stayed overnight, he listened with the other musicians to Roy Eldridge broadcasting from Chicago. That was inspiring. Charlie and one of the other musicians would transcribe solos Eldridge took on his recordings and discuss as well as practice them. Then, during the Thanksgiving weekend of 1936, Parker was hurt in an automobile accident while traveling to that gig in the Ozarks. One of the musicians was killed, and Charlie returned home with his ribs taped. The young man remained in the house for a while, recovering from the collision and smoking marijuana upstairs in the room he shared with Rebecca. He kept a big bag of that stuff under his pillow. By the summer of 1937 when he was still a determined but lightweight saxophonist, Charlie became a drug addict, shooting up not heroin but morphine.

In January of 1938, the saxophonist became a father, naming his son Francis Leon Parker, for Francis Scott Key and Leon "Chu" Berry, the great tenor saxophonist who played with Cab Calloway. By the winter, he was ready to go, having rapidly separated himself from those who were laughed off bandstands for arrogant incompetence. It had taken only about three years. Because of constant practice and genius in the area of muscle memory, everything came to him very quickly: his mouth, his throat, his lungs, his fingers, and his diaphragm soon remembered what they were to do when executing certain musical passages. But the drugs also had him, and he stole everything in the house that could be sold quickly. He would disappear for days, return home worn out, his clothes stained with the swill and dirt of fast living, go to bed and sleep for two or three days. Sometimes he looked as though he had lost his mind. On other occasions, when he descended the stairs high and aloof, Charlie Parker looked as though he had been put in charge of the entire world. He was gone then.

During that period in Kansas City, Parker had listened to Lester Young jamming and broke into a cold sweat one night when he realized what the tall, yellow tenor man was innovating right in front of everybody. A different sound, a different rhythm, a different conception of organizing his ideas. Young's originality overwhelmed the young alto saxophonist. When "Lady Be Good" came out, recorded by a small group extracted from Count Basie's band, Parker learned Young's solo note for note and fired it out at some jam sessions. He also absorbed the alto style of Buster Smith, who became his employer and mentor. That Smith style was full of blues, and there was a unique tendency to double-timing that Ralph Ellison thought Smith might have picked up from following the dancers on the floor of Slaughter's Hall in Oklahoma City, when the older saxophonist was in the Blue Devils, a local band that included Lester Young. Having grown up in Oklahoma City, Ellison remembered a dance called either the Two-in-One or the One-in-Two, which contained moments when the dancers would double the tempo and collectively sweep from one end of the floor to the other. That could be important, since we know Lester Young once observed that he loved to play dances because watching the movement on the floor gave him ideas. So there is the possibility that some of those Parker rhythms might have their roots in the Oklahoma City patterns those Negro dancers created as they turned the wooden floor into music paper and wrote their double-timing story in scuff marks.

During the day, Charlie practiced with Smith, loving fast songs like "Dinah." He had kept his problems in check while working in the older man's band—though Smith did comment that the boy needed to get more sleep so he wouldn't almost drift into dreamland. Parker, now in a voracious mood for knowledge, deeply missed the older man when he up and headed for Manhattan, where the best of the Kansas City musicians—Lester Young, Count Basie, and Hot Lips Page—had already gone.

Either in late 1938 or early 1939, having exhausted every venue in Kansas City, Parker hopped a train. He too was bound for the Big Apple but stopped off first in Chicago, where he shocked the locals with his abilities, stole a horn loaned to him, and traveled on to New York. He arrived with a nickel and a nail in his pocket, went to Harlem and stood looking up at the sign outside of the Savoy Ballroom, "the home of happy feet," the citadel in which the dance bands of the era had battles of music. He dreamed of someday playing there. That was the big time. His clothes were filthy, and he had worn his shoes for so long that his feet and legs were swollen. Who knows what he had lived through on those train rides and in those hobo jungles, where rape and beating were not uncommon? Perhaps nothing, perhaps everything.

In Harlem, his improvising was met with silence from audiences at jam sessions or sometimes they would clap loudly as though they were thrilled because he had stopped. Occasionally, he wondered out loud whether he should just imitate Benny Carter or Johnny Hodges or Rudy Williams, whom he called "Red Rudy" and who was the alto player in the super-swinging Savoy Sultans. At one point it was clear that he was bound to his own path. That was when he told his guitarist buddy, Biddy Fleet, that he had decided not to go to an audition for Duke Ellington's band. It was probably only a subbing job, but Parker had chosen to stay where he was and continued to go through more and more intricate harmony with Fleet, who was known, and disliked, for his "fancy chords." The musical motion in Parker's mind got smoother. As mature work bears out, Parker wanted to bring together melody, harmony, and rhythm on equal levels of complexity, all three soaked in highly sophisticated as well as gutbucket blues material and thrust into the air by that swing, that heroic motion through the time, that phrasing that was still new to the planet and that had swelled up from the soul of the Negro, contaminating all who were ready for it, and providing the music of the modern world with another way to shake its stuff.

By the time he returned to Kansas City, in May of 1940, Parker could play the lacquer off a horn. He had come home for the funeral of his father, who had been cut down in some kind of a nightlife squabble with a prostitute. Instead of trying New York again, he went back to living at his mother's place and began working around Kansas City. This was not the same Charlie Parker who had left town fifteen months ago. Before he had hopped that train, Parker was not unpopular. Jay McShann remembered seeing people following Parker around in the Kansas City night to see where he was going to play. They loved him there; he had left a hometown hero. He was even stronger by now, and so he was soon in McShann's band, which was the hottest unit left in town. Parker was not an addict when he returned home and had not been one in New York, but he came to live on a hook again, through the efforts of a local drummer buddy and a Black nurse nicknamed "Little Mama," who worked in the local hospital and boosted enough dope to keep a little bit of a business going. At the time, few musicians used heavy drugs, only drank and smoked some marijuana, or a lot of it, depending on the individual appetite.

When Parker joined the McShann band, his talent started talking a whole lot of stuff through his horn. He was seeking a fresh kind of fluidity. His rhythms were moving into areas that had not been heard before. He could play the blues with ever more depth, calling into the bell of his horn all of the loneliness and ambivalence in the world and all of the erotic ecstasy, turmoil, disappointment, and frustration. McShann says that he had "a crying soul," which is to say that Charlie Parker could truly cry the blues. He knew well the tragedy at the center of life, which is decay and death, and he was far from unaware of how hard it was to keep from being pulled down into the beds of appetites that were hills of intoxicating fishhooks, each sharp, curved piece of metal held in place by a wire so that when it went into the flesh, one had to experience the wound of a tear in order to get away. There was also an idealism to his music, high thoughts delivered in notes—visions of gallantry and compassion, of love and mercy, of truth and justice. Yes, he could walk a listener through the cries of hell while looking up and thinking about heaven. He was not free of the joy of life either, which meant that he could get unbounded exultation through the bell of his horn as well. In every way, the complexity of his life and his world were brought to that alto saxophone, were served up without the convention of vibrato, and had that quality of playing jacks or hopscotching in the shadows of the skyscrapers and the airplanes. Parker understood the children's games on the sidewalk and felt deeply the architecture, the hope, the exploration, and the destruction of his moment. For all that aviation symbolized about the rise of human aspirations, the bomber plane was an innovation of his era, as was the passenger plane. He knew the contradictions, which were made deeper by the conditions that arrived with dark skin, even with a reddish tone. The score didn't get by him. He knew what was going on. And like all great poets, he could summon an era into a line of melody.

Traveling with McShann meant moving through the Midwest and playing and playing and playing, usually staying in the homes of Black people because there were no open accommodations or because the towns might not have had hotels and motels. Inconsiderate almost to perfection, Charlie would come downstairs early when breakfast was served and eat up everything if the other band members didn't get there in time. He would borrow money and never pay it back. But he would also fix the cars, having picked up mechanical skills somewhere in his experience, and was not unwilling to put his shoulder to the car or the band truck when it got stuck in a hole and had to be pushed out. He would work on the mouthpieces of the other saxophone players, keep everyone laughing with his gift for mimicry, and spark the band night after night. Even though his ways ran everyone up the wall, Parker's unexpected generosity, his charm, and the endless musical creativity he brought to the bandstand put the guys in awe of him. He was special. Very.

When the McShann gang traveled east to Harlem for a battle of the bands with Lucky Millinder in early 1942, they were the underdogs. Millinder had mailed them a note saying that he was going to "send you hicks back to the sticks." They walked on Millinder's head with that Kansas City swing. It was too smooth and it was too hot, too plainly shining and too surprising. The Kansas City groove came from the rhythm section and the heat from the band as a whole, a bunch of country knotheads, if you asked Lucky Millinder, but they were still putting goo-gobs of swing in the air, soaking everybody in it. Surprise came from that alto player, the "hot man," the secret weapon, Charlie Parker, who blew down the Millinder house with every feature.

Musicians were quickly talking about him, but hardly anyone who hadn't been down to the Savoy knew what he sounded like. Who is this guy? You heard him? No, but I heard about him. Then the McShann band had to do an afternoon radio broadcast. Parker was late, but when they saw him moving toward the bandstand with his saxophone case, McShann kicked off an express train tempo for "Cherokee," a tune Parker had been working on for a few years. He dived into that harmonic barbed wire and cut himself free with every note and every phrase. Standing still as a statue with sweat puddling at his feet, Parker so excited the guy from the radio crew that he kept signaling McShann to keep going, don't stop, let him go, let him go.

Charlie Barnet's band was working in Newark, New Jersey, sixteen miles away at the Adams Theatre. While they were on their break, bassist Chubby Jackson decided to see if that new band playing opposite Lucky Millinder was showing anything special on the Savoy broadcast. As soon as he turned the radio on, a sound that was almost brutal in its disavowal of a vibrato shot out of the speaker, notes as thick as buckshot slapped the chords this way and that, rambling quicker and with more different kinds of rhythms than they had ever heard from a saxophone. Everybody stopped talking, messing around, fiddling with instruments. Who the hell is this? Oklahoma trumpeter Howard McGhee was there, and he chuckled as he remembered that every musician standing there with his mouth open knew where he was going that night. McGhee was right. That evening the Savoy was filled with dancers—and musicians such as Dizzy Gillespie and Thelonious Monk. It was clear that someone with something else to say had come to town and cut himself a seat in the Big Apple with his saxophone.

Parker and Gillespie became close buddies very quickly, because the trumpeter had been looking for something and Parker had it. Gillespie, Thelonious Monk, and Kenny Clarke, geniuses all, had put together most of another way to play. Monk and Gillespie worked out the chord progressions, Clarke invented a new drum style, and Gillespie would teach the bass players how to walk the notes that would inspire instead of impede. They had all of the bricks but they lacked the mortar of phrasing. Charlie Parker was the mortar that held the bricks in place. His sense of melodic line and his "sanctified phrasing," as Gillespie called it, set a movement afire. "When we heard him, we knew the music had to go his way," Gillespie has recalled.

These recordings* capture a genius in the blooming, as in the 1944 "Red Cross"; and sometimes in the storm, as with the catastrophic Los Angeles session in 1946 when Parker recorded "Lover Man" while undergoing a nervous breakdown brought on by bad heroin ("Mexican mud"), alcohol, and pills. Some of the sessions are well prepared and rehearsed, others are off the cuff, little riffs Parker threw together in order to make a record date and get his royalty advances. Overall, on good or bad horns, with smoothness or with stridency, his playing has that grand consistency that the tallest giants always bring to their work. Most important is the audible truth that he was a great melodist and that he could play anything, inject an original perspective into any mood. No one could play with more coherence and freedom at high speed than he. He was unexceeded in his generation when it came to blues at any tempo. The rhythmic audacity of his work is still scandalously pleasurable. What he could do on a ballad will remove the breath from a listener almost phrase by phrase. He had learned so much about living and about playing in so little time. And when there had been nothing to learn that could help him

---

* *Charlie Parker: The Complete Savoy & Dial Master Takes.*

achieve his ends, he invented his own methods, which is what we expect of the genius.

In 1944, when he was with Billy Eckstine's band, Charlie Parker brought Rebecca to St. Louis, where he was working. After she had heard them and Charlie had taken her back to his hotel room, he told the woman that he had run ragged with his troubles and his obsessions that he wanted her to let him go because he knew then that he could become a great musician. He begged her. He had to go. Like the great bluesmen, he had to take his sense of wonder and woe on up the road. He did go. And he was right. He became great. The proof is right here.

2002

MILES DAVIS, ROMANTIC HERO

Written on the occasion of Davis's posthumous induction by Herbie Hancock into the Rock & Roll Hall of Fame, S.C. resists previous arguments regarding crossover jazz and the electronic Miles to provide a selective and nuanced consideration of Davis's legacy as a cultural icon and the rituals of masculinity.

FOR THE INNOCENT LISTENER who hasn't been convinced by the noisy claims and special pleading for the artistic significance of jazz improvisation, Miles Davis's *My Funny Valentine* is one of the most persuasive arguments. With this recording, Davis was never to be captured playing again with such virtuosic command of varied emotional detail. It is hard to imagine another rhythm section improvising with more adventurous looseness and equal sensitivity to each moment of the music, and it is equally difficult to imagine another young tenor saxophonist, unaware of the tempo and rhythmic freedom that was going to rise about him, responding with more ease, formal beauty, and eloquence than what we hear from George Coleman on selection after selection. It was, as they say in the business, "One of those nights."

What made the recording so special when it came out—and makes it even more special in our decadent and pornographic moment—is the depth of its romantic feeling. There is an intimacy and a great tenderness to the music, both wounded and reverential. In 1964, this engagement in romantic expression was still relatively new because male Negro singers had only been recording romantic songs for about twenty-five years, having been forced to leave the province to Caucasians because of the sexual limits of racism. But instrumentalists had no such limitations imposed upon them. Jazzmen had used the Tin Pan Alley love song as a common form of American expression, and the most inspired of them bent the melodies until special sounds came out. The champions in the business of instrumental romance were almost always saxophone players, and the "boudoir saxophone" was a stable force in American music. A player was expected to lean his tone against a song and make it sigh with an erotic fire.

The command of the poetic emotion made Miles Davis the greatest player of romantic songs to emerge since World War II and the innovations of Charlie Parker. By the mid-1950s, he had come into his first period of maturity and developed a style in which his lyricism was so revealing that it brought unexpected pleasure to his listeners. Davis's improvisation testified to his willingness to share the facts of very introspective feelings. And none of what he did seemed easy. As *My Funny Valentine* shows, great difficulty was audible in every musical gesture: The notes had points on them; they were slurred and bent suggestively or painfully; a tone could disappear into a sigh or begin as a pitchless whisper and tellingly work its way up into a note. This delicacy could ascend through sudden moans to yelps or descend to dark growls devoid of vibrato that were nearly embarrassing in their exposure.

Listening to that side of Davis's talent is like a form of eavesdropping. The trumpet sounds are neither crass nor vulgar but are, even so, more than a bit reminiscent of the communicative noises made by lovers at close quarters. We hear clearly why Davis came to prominence in a time when the cold and removed masculinity defined by the night world of criminals and hustlers had a big influence on the Negro sense of male power, especially in the clubs where musicians plied their trade. In that night-world context, Davis's expressive inclinations made him a symbol of tender and complex courage. Consequently, his musical presence was adored by women and envied by men.

Davis became a matinee idol in the mid-1950s when dark-skinned men were beginning to break through the barriers that kept them from being seen in romantic roles or thought of as superb interpreters of love songs. Davis shared this moment with Sidney Poitier and Nat Cole, but his persona included something that neither of theirs did. Following Charlie Parker, in whose band he did some of his earliest work, Davis was moody. He gave the impression that he was not even interested in being known, especially by white folks. The trumpeter was not given to any aspect of the minstrel tradition that has dogged the Negro artist for more than a hundred years and has most recently restated itself in the jigaboo antics of rap videos.

It was not that Davis did not smile as much as the fact that Davis, like Parker, did not consider smiling part of his job. The glowering Black trumpeter was there, in those little murky clubs from one end of the country to the other, leading a band and making beautiful music in circumstances that were about as opposed to artistic statement as one could imagine. Drinks were sold, people talked, drugs were pushed, prostitutes circulated, and the cash registers rang. At their worst, those circumstances could be as wild as any in the Old West, which is why some of the joints were referred to as "buckets of blood."

Miles Davis, however, tamed those savage surroundings and made it clear that if he didn't feel respected or comfortable he would leave, and the paying customers could have it out with the club owners. But if he stayed and felt like playing, his music did not hold back on the lyric quality. That element gave a charismatic frailness to his ballad interpretations. It was a sound that rarely arrived full-blown in American popular art, though it was strongly alluded to by actors such as Leslie Howard, who was often cast as a dreamer just a bit too soft for the world. There was an atmosphere of inevitable doom surrounding such characters, most of whom might be called "gallant fools." Through such types a basic idea was sustained in popular art: Romance was itself a form of heroic engagement, and falling in love with an idea, a cause, or a person was an act of bravery.

By bringing that to his music, Miles Davis remade the expectations of the audience. As we hear throughout *My Funny Valentine*, the trumpeter taught his listeners that a whisper could be as powerful as a shout. A gallant fool, yes, but free of the maudlin Jell-O that usually came with the white American idea of the poetic soul. Davis was just as free, it seemed, of the pool-hall and street-corner braggadocio of the Negro hustling world. Little, dark, touchy, even evil, Miles Davis walked onto his bandstand and made public visions of tenderness that were, finally, absolute rejections of everything silly about the version of masculinity that might hobble men in either the white or the Black world. That was his power and that is what makes *My Funny Valentine* so uniquely touching.

March 2006

BLUES FOR KRAZY KAT

M ANY OF US WERE INTRODUCED to George Herriman's ethnicity when Ishmael Reed dedicated his 1972 novel *Mumbo Jumbo* to
him. Herriman's *Krazy Kat* had long held its position as one of the few
American cartoons that had been appreciated by intellectuals, beginning
with Gilbert Seldes in 1925. Some time after Reed had dedicated his
novel to Herriman, I had a conversation with Ralph Ellison in which he
expressed amazement at the fact Herriman was, as he said, "a Negro."
Because Ellison was a first-class cultural detective and possessed of the
most penetrating mind of any American intellectual, we can assume that
this was not general knowledge and had not even appeared in the mum-
bled underground of claims and half truths that all ethnic minorities seem
to have in common; "proof" of someone hiding out among the majority or
"proof" that the identity of a member of the group has been "suppressed"
in order to maintain the majority's false image of superiority.

This does not seem to have been the case of George Herriman. He was born in New Orleans in 1880 and was almost assuredly a product of the Creole culture that produced Jelly Roll Morton, who once admonished a fellow light-skinned musician not to call himself a Negro because "a Negro is dumber than two dead police dogs buried in somebody's backyard." Herriman might not have had sentiments as strong as Morton's, but we do know that he did not parade his ethnic roots and was what James Weldon Johnson would have called an "ex-colored man." In other words, he did not advertise his African blood but even took the precaution of never removing his hat, in or out of doors, because he had telltale Black kinks of the sort that would have raised more than a few questions. Or answered them all.

What is most interesting about Herriman, however, is that he had been bitten by the mysterious bug of innovation and created a comic strip that broke all of the rules in order to make a world both unsteady and surreal. In *Still I Rise: A Cartoon History of African Americans*, Charles Johnson wrote of this place of action: "Located in the dreamlike world of Coconino County, which recalls the artist's fondness for Monument Valley in the desert of southeastern Utah, Herriman's characters performed against a constantly transmogrifying background—in the space of two panels, their external world fluidly changed from surrealistic mesas and cactuses to forest scenery and seascapes, ever blurring the border between appearance and reality." In terms of its overall position in American art, this world is interesting beyond the realm of the cartoon because John Ford, perhaps our nation's greatest filmmaker, found the landscape magnetic and a perfect backdrop for his tragic tales of the winning of the West. That the Creole whom many consider the greatest of all domestic cartoonists and the Irish American maestro of our cinema would be inspired by the same actual place is far beyond minor. Perhaps both men realized that the desert is especially American because it is in the far end of the West, which is the United States, and has none of the associations that bring North Africa to mind, the territory once called "the Orient" and that we now know as the Middle East. The desert in America is the harsh landscape that always reminds us of some the most brutal conflicts fought in this country.

Because *Krazy Kat* was born in 1913 and published until Herriman's death in 1944, we can say that it is a product of the same age in which Mack Sennett emerged and made slapstick a fundamental part of American comedy. The crash, the collision, the pratfall, the explosion are all essential elements of a comic sense in which tension is released by violence that is anarchic and dismantling but harmless. The democratic tool of the slapstick comedy is the pie. When thrown in the face it becomes an equalizing force that crosses classes and makes the upper-class person look as ridiculous as the lower-class person or the cop or the bureaucrat or the day laborer. Its violent use is in the interest of the absurd, not the cruel or harmful. No one is ever wounded, crippled, or killed by a pie in the face. But one's pride can take a beating or one's pretension can be deflated, if not one's belief that he or she is above the travails of those with less money. The pie is an airborne antidote to all of that illusion. In a sense, it is as democratic as death, which plays by no rules other than its own. You can hide in the closet or under the bed or down in the basement, but when you emerge, that pie, flying on the "wings of scorn," as Wallace Shawn has written, will be on its way. You will not escape.

Krazy Kat is in love with a mouse; the mouse, Ignatz, always expresses its contempt for the feline with a brick to the cat's head; Offissa Pupp, both a dog and a cop, loves the cat and is happy to put the violent rodent in jail. Of course, everything "natural" is messed up: The cat loves the mouse and the dog loves the cat, only the rodent is free of unexpected feeling. Once Herriman establishes the surprising as the normal, the reader experiences his dreamworld anticipation of the surreal, which, as some have pointed out, precedes the French movement by at least a decade. In reality, cats love to torture mice in a process that includes battering them about until they cannot move, then toying with them a bit more before biting off their heads. Savage confrontations between cats and dogs can conclude with the eyes of the dogs scratched out or the cats coming out on the short end, torn apart and dead. Reality is discarded in the interest of comedy, and the violent wound is replaced by the humiliating act that is misinterpreted and, therefore, deprived of its power.

The American quality of Herriman's comedy is always on top because it is the result of a world that was consistently built on contradictions and counterpoint, the very old and the newly industrial, the stationary and the innovative, the totally planned out and the improvised. The United States was a land where a man born in 1880 knew of the aboriginal languages and customs of those who fell before a civilization that was making itself in motion. In Herriman's hometown, his parents must have become accustomed to the Old World of Europe meeting the timeless ways of Louisiana; the tuneful parades and festivals; the Catholic symbols and saints absorbed by voodoo; the oral history of what had been left of Africa—and of slavery!—in the Negro community; the gloom of a funeral ending with the arrogant affirmation of "Didn't He Ramble?" But because his father hightailed it out of the Crescent City as the laws of segregation began to increase with a fury that limited the lives of even those who could claim a good portion of white blood, Herriman probably heard all he needed to hear about the culture of New Orleans from his parents. This cannot be discounted. As we all know, nothing is more important than the memories of tales told until the child begins to remember them as though he or she was there, felt the weather, ate the food, did the dances, played the games, inhaled the smells, and heard clearly the distinctions of the sounds that attended events either human or those rising from the world of nature.

From all that surrounded him and all that he had heard and everything that he could imagine and realize on the flat pages that held his cartoon inventions, George Herriman grew into his own and took his idiom with him (*Krazy Kat*'s influential progeny includes variously important talents such as Walt Disney, Charles Schulz, and Saul Steinberg). A few years before he was twenty years old, the comic strip was born in America and had been a stable expectation when *Krazy Kat* appeared in 1913 and was immediately a favorite of newspaper publisher William Randolph Hearst. Hearst's fictional cinematic model, Charles Foster Kane, was not given the good taste to back such a work of popular art even against the sage decisions of his editors. There again the Herriman story and the story of his amazing cartoon break with convention. Instead of the ruthless magnate submitting to the popular taste for the common and the easily understood, Hearst chose to underwrite what was surely the most far out and imaginative art to appear in that form of popular expression. This is an example of a powerful man becoming a patron of the arts that has little if any parallel in America.

But it is improbable that Hearst thought of *Krazy Kat* as art in the way that its intellectual fans did. He probably had that feeling for American life that made obvious to him something that might not have been obvious to many: This was something new and funny and expressed angular thoughts and sentiments that had no precedent. But those ideas and feelings were as purely American as the elements that were creating a new urban civilization from the ground up, or, with the subway, from the underground up. In that sense, George Herriman not only arrived at the right time but also was met by a discerning force that would guarantee his having a place to work until his death. Such sympathetic treatment in the world of commerce now seems even more of a miracle than it must have appeared then.

So when we move our eyes into the small, mutating universe of George Herriman, we benefit from an imagination that brought together the results of this nation's broad diversity, its many contradictions, and its determination to make fun of pain, disrespect, and humiliation. In private, the clown might weep "the buckets," as the Irish say. But when he comes before the public his job is to make the audience laugh, not by forgetting but by remembering just how frail and absurd are the tunings of existence. That is his brave job, and George Herriman never failed to report for duty.

2005

NOIR AMERICANA

F ILM NOIR EVOLVED from the American crime thrillers that rose to
pulp prominence between 1920 and 1940. Hollywood took those
tales and put the focus on cynics, fall guys, sluts, heists, and murders most
foul. The huge screens in movie theaters provided lurid masks for the
resentments that pulse within Americana. Our hatred of the upper class
and of goody-two-shoes morality got plenty of play. So did our repulsive puritanical troubles with sexual attraction, our reluctant but ultimate
belief in the righteousness of force, and our tendency to answer life's pervasive horrors with conspiracy theories.

Noir's popularity was inevitable. How could American audiences
resist the combative stance of an unimpressed hero whose ethos could
be reduced to: "Is that so?" How could they fail to be lured by all of the
actresses cast as Venus flytraps? Everything in film noir takes place at the
bottom, in the sewers of sensibility. It holds that the force of the world is
not only indifferent to, but obviously bigger than, the individual, which

is why personal satisfaction, whether illegal or immoral, is the solution to the obligatory ride through an unavoidably brittle universe.

A black-and-white phenomenon, film noir is thought to have achieved its greatest heights between 1945 and 1950, though the apparent moment of final brilliance arrived in 1958's *Touch of Evil*, directed with the heightened imagination of genius by Orson Welles. As a genre, film noir appeared as an antidote to the Hollywood conventions of pristine character and fulfilled romance because its creators sensed that "rah rah" was no longer the best prescription for the blues. Possessed of a shrewd aesthetic that was both meretricious and rebellious, film noir generously utilized sex *and* violence, firmly rooting itself in American culture.

A number of its most influential directors were European Jews such as Fritz Lang, Otto Preminger, and Billy Wilder, all of whom had escaped the Nazis. The enthusiastic support of the Third Reich by the German people had convinced such artists that conformity always *had* to be questioned, ridiculed, and perhaps resisted. Another assumption was that corruption hid behind images of a gilded civilization, high-class refinement, uplift, and thorough social improvement. So, in one sense, Adolf Hitler was a major player in forming the sensibility of film noir. That Austrian boy whom Chaplin accused of having made off with his mustache had done it again but, as usual, not in the way the paper-hanger intended.

One gets the essentials of the style and all of the information necessary to recognize the "school" that the French saw long before Americans did by viewing Barbara Stanwyck, Claire Trevor, Jane Greer, and Peggy Cummins, each but separately the brilliant stars of: *Double Indemnity*; *Murder, My Sweet*; *Out of the Past*; and *Gun Crazy*. They are the essential film noir amalgamations of Eve, Salome, and Carmen: there to bring men down through the pulsating syncopations of their glistening orifices. After but one night with any of them, men were not only willing to bay at the moon of homicide but snap at it with a determination that pushes a full circle of murder into the air.

Double Indemnity is the first film in which Billy Wilder's impeccable talent as a director and a screenwriter came forward in full force. It is also considered the first pure film noir. Though Stanwyck and Fred MacMurray have been rightfully praised as the murderous lovers, they are nearly overmatched by the imperishable skill of Edward G. Robinson. Robinson's extended speeches are delivered like dark, probing arias—they are full of wit, syncopation, and an intuitive recognition of the sinister that we learn is essential to being a great insurance detective. There is no better performance in all of film noir.

Claire Trevor, an adroit master of subtle vocal modulations, blooms downward in *Murder, My Sweet*, like a flower overladen with a working girl's perfume. The actress appears lyrically jaded, but it is easy to see how she helped define the femme fatale in an era when only allusion was available. Opposite the spectacularly ominous Lawrence Tierney in *Born to Kill*, Trevor projects a sexual longing that is realistic but never overstated, compelling in its desperate but bungling confusion. Her performance gives a viewer the impression of eavesdropping on a soul excruciatingly barbed with tender and dangerous contradictions.

The noir conventions are reversed in John Huston's *The Asphalt Jungle*, as the women are summarily brought to despair by the criminal follies of their men in this matchless heist film. Its epic sense of class and ethnicity is both a noir turn on *e pluribus unum* and a cinematic homage to what Melville gave us in his famous whaling story. Every directorial choice and word of dialogue seems perfect, and the sheer humanity of its characters is often heartbreaking. There is a profoundly visceral quality to the grit and the details of being and feeling that are overshadowed by the sense of how we are all so simply made the victims of "blind accident." One of the shrewdest elements of the plot is how easily the lower-class Jewish bookie is overly impressed and chumped off by the corrupt upper-class WASP lawyer, a secretly bankrupt dreamer who leads almost everyone in on the heist to a thoroughly painful defeat.

Robert Ryan, a singularly great talent, stars in *The Set-Up*, which may provide the most accomplished rendition of the carnivorous world that once surrounded a fixed fight. As the vicious bout takes place in real time, director Robert Wise uses deft cross-cutting to vary the pulse of the film and give it telling qualities of nuanced pacing and counterpoint. Ryan also portrays the Jew-hating murderer in *Crossfire*. With his exceptionally expressive eyes, rubbery face, oily tenor voice, and gangly athleticism, the actor brought out the mix of childishness, resentment, self-loathing, paranoia, and self-aggrandizement that so often underlies the rage of those who answer the world's problems with a plastic bigotry that fits all sizes within the targeted group.

Robert Mitchum, whose low-slung eyelids, sauntering walk, bodyguard's bulk, and voice that expressed disdain or attraction or menace with equal authority and shading brought a fresh personal extension to what we now consider "cool." As the wonderfully paced confrontation with the crime boss in *The Racket* shows, Mitchum was one of the few actors whose masculinity could meet Ryan's sweltering complexity nose to nose. In *Out of the Past*, when his fall guy tells the elegant gangster played by Kirk Douglas not to foolishly trade blows with him, we believe Mitchum. His power seemed limitless but, like Ryan, so did his vulnerability. That was why he was an imposing romantic lead: Mitchum possessed an understated pound of delicacy for every pound of muscle.

One of the most characteristic elements of film noir is its avoidance of racist stereotypes. This is very different from the attitudes expressed in its pulp and detective-story sources. In a particularly brilliant reading of Raymond Chandler written for a 1995 issue of the *New York Review of Books*, Joyce Carol Oates revealed to readers the phrases that fall casually and frequently from Philip Marlowe's lips: "nigger," "shine," "fag," "queen," "Jewess," "Mex," "greaseback," "wetback," "Jap." In this Caucasian-macho landscape, "a pansy has no iron in his bones, whatever he looks like." Marlowe's wisecracks are sometimes indistinguishable from ethnic slurs: "[You're] cute as a Filipino on Saturday night." A minor character in *The High Window* is "a big burly Jew with a Hitler mustache and pop eyes."

Conversely, the Black actors of film noir are quite rarely expected to work their way through the greasy caricatures that have reemerged in the contemporary minstrelsy now so common in rap videos and ethnic Black comedy. In 1944's *Out of the Past*, the Black bit players seem to be people with individual dreams and individual lives, not human whoopee cushions ever ready to shriek and guffaw while being humiliated. That is another casual American victory that we can add to the celebration of the finest things in film noir.

2007

THE ELECTRIC COMPANY

HOW TECHNOLOGY REVIVED ELLINGTON'S CAREER

1. PERHAPS THE GREATEST

Through our remarkable technology we witness the fundamental dilemma of our age, which is the use of machines that bespeak the genius of the species for the trivialization of the profound. We have thus become accustomed to a blizzard of fluff delivered by ingenious high-tech means. An aspect of this fluff is music polluted by its attachment to the cheap, demeaning imagery of videos or losing gravity while largely used as a background score for the activities of a distracted public. People are uncomfortable in silence because it can breed needless contemplation and may engender a floating into the deeper world of the self. In our moment of deracinated intimacy, too many of us have settled for a blob of back-beats and recording-studio tricks that do not swallow but melt away the great force of music in a perpetual submission to contrived novelty.

For all of the shortcomings imposed upon a Washington, D.C., Negro born in 1899, much more was possible for the young Duke Ellington than there would have been had he arrived in our time. To tell it as it actually was, the varieties of bigotry were where they should have been because heroes need huge obstacles to teach them what they must know in order to achieve the victories demanded of them. Ellington succeeded both in adapting to the new technology and in learning how to make recording equipment into his tool rather than a dehumanizing gimmick or even a technological special effect to which he and his artistic purposes could become secondary. The technology submitted to him, not he to it.

Considered from all sides, Ellington was not only the most impressive genius produced by jazz but perhaps the greatest of all twentieth century artists, because he redefined and refined his idiom in a world far more complex and extreme, ranging from the violent to the sublime, than the worlds inhabited by such aesthetic peers as James Joyce, Pablo Picasso, and Igor Stravinsky. (In his memoir *Music Is My Mistress*, Ellington described being summoned more than a few times by the New York City police, taken to the morgue, and asked if he knew a murdered man last seen dancing to the jungle band at the Cotton Club. That he always denied knowing the corpse, even if he did, tells us that he knew a loose lip could sink your own ship.) Ellington produced a body of work so large that it still intimidates our most serious music scholars, and it looms even more imposingly because he best understood that his was an age in which the performing arts would be remade by technology. In *Picasso*, Gertrude Stein says that people do not ever really change; what changes is the way in which they see themselves. This applies perfectly to Ellington. As the summoning power of electrical enhancements and preservations of given moments evolved, Ellington deftly used them, with an authority that increased as he came to understand exactly where he was and what specific things made his time different from those of artists who had come before him and before the technology that was too massively influential to ignore.

Always a contemplative and secretive man, this musician had to learn on the wing because there were no predecessors who could provide models or give him advice. His sacrifices within the enveloping glamour of show business were many, but he knew himself to be very fortunate. Jazz was an art that expressed a level of human clarity across the color line that was not shown in our literature until William Faulkner's *Go Down, Moses* appeared in 1942. The world transformed into music by Duke Ellington was more varied in faces, places, classes, and religions than that of our literary giant. This band-leading composer toured the nation and learned much more about it than any of our writers have thus far shown us.

By his death in 1974, Ellington had performed for everyone from murderous thugs to the cultivated whipped cream of European royalty and American high society. Such people were quite different from our tasteless contemporary jiffy mush—the merely wealthy whom America's gold-rush culture of chance and open opportunity always produces. Ellington's career took the skyrocket route to national recognition through radio broadcasts from the segregated, gangster-owned Cotton Club in Harlem that first employed him in 1927.

The result was that Ellington became a figure comparable to Fred Astaire in the 1930s—a symbol of verve, elegance, and a thorough sophistication expressive of a virtuosity that was capable of transcending all of the shallowness and fluff by which it might be surrounded. The one big difference between the musician and the dancer was that the blues sensibility kept Ellington in the range of boudoir stink, heartbreak, muck, longing, and desperation shared by everyone—the Negroes of all classes with whom he lived and fraternized, whom he presented in an epic musical frame and never fled identification with; the criminals he parodied in his arrangement of Hoagy Carmichael's "March of the Hoodlums"; the society types whose woes he learned of at close range on any of the inevitable occasions when they imposed their private hurts on a handsome and surprisingly sophisticated man who might be considered an expert on the low-down nature of human fate because he was, after all, a Negro, and Negroes were thought to know such things. He absorbed in detail the facts that link all human beings, no matter how unlike one another their manners, professions, and family lines might lead one to believe. Blues, trouble, aspirations, romantic longing, and appetite spared neither genius nor fool and no one in between.

The band worked at the Cotton Club for about five years, performing arrangements of popular songs and original music that the leader composed for dancers, comedians, magicians, and whoever else did their Uptown acts for alabaster night-people seeking a laugh, a moment of awe, and the extra bounty of an unexpected thrill. Ellington's career was also furthered by the technology of cinema and the innovation of added sound. He starred in and wrote the scores for small films and provided featured segments for a few full-length films: 1934's *Belle of the Nineties*, starring Mae West; and Otto Preminger's *Anatomy of a Murder*, released twenty-five years later. For that 1959 film, the Ellington organization produced a score containing some of its very finest music.

When we look at those early films or the forerunners of music videos that were once called "soundies," the wonder is that Ellington never submitted to the coonish stereotypes of the time, even in 1930's *Check and Double Check*, a blackface Amos 'n' Andy comedy. The bandleader first appears briefly, immaculately dressed and taking care of business, then is shown at a private house party, where he and his men give a superb rendition of jazz free from any grating descents into minstrelsy. While they display the canned excitement most performers feign in order to convince their audiences that something out of the ordinary is taking place, trumpeter Freddie Jenkins has a wah-wah muted trumpet solo that radiates heated control paced by effortless purity. Through his every movement the joy, the command, the wit, and the grace of the music itself take on a visceral presence. That composite of aesthetic magic in which the improvised self-definition of the individual musician and the composed context create a whole greater than either or both is the victory of jazz, and we see Ellington at an early point already pursuing what he would throughout his life, brooking few distractions of any kind.

Duke Ellington was a tall, good-looking man possessed of a style that we usually call charming, but few good-looking and charming men have come close to achieving what he brought off in each succeeding decade of his long career. Not particularly well educated—a high school dropout, in fact—he knew how to listen and how to assess. In the process, Ellington learned to speak as clearly to those born in gutbuckets and barrels of butcher knives as to those who had, from birth, sucked the soft, soothing metal of silver spoons.

In an era when audiences, Black or white, had a preferential feeling for the base and the superficial, Ellington brought off a decidedly avant-garde series of compositions that startled classical composers as much as they excited the dancers who came to the tobacco barns, the college proms held in gymnasiums, and the dance halls high and low that he and his musicians played across the country. His listeners grew to love being charmed by the dreamy lyricism of his music, being pleasurably startled by the willful dissonance in his harmonies and driven to the loose beauty of the dance floor, where they could shake a tail feather in the eye of a syncopated brass-and-reed hurricane while being transported to places so special that they had neither names nor addresses. This was the result of the phenomenon of rhythm and tune eventually known as Ellingtonia.

Ellingtonia was an organic musical mass that continued to grow throughout the 1930s, overwhelming obstacles large and small in aesthetic, racial, and social contexts. But Ellington's career dipped after World War II as the era of big dance bands ended and large ensembles went into decline, disbanding for the most part. To the joy of club-owning employers, the small groups popularized by men such as Charlie Parker came into vogue and were much less expensive. Smaller was thought of as better for jazz, for rhythm and blues, and for the bastard child of American dance music, rock and roll, which did not become an audio teenage toy until the mid-1950s.

All the while, Ellingtonia was made ever new by the imagination of the bandleader and his musicians and their uses of the technical influences arriving from others. By personalizing things that were in the air, Ellington revitalized famous audience favorites of his own. He did this with new elements of harmony, tempo, countermelodies, and improvisation from players whose relationships to a given composition could be shifted from the background to a solo feature or vice versa. This improvisation allowed Ellington to continually revisit his own works in the way that a jazzman can always return to give the past a vibrant but only relative importance while proving that the present is *always* potentially vital. In jazz, improvised playing is measured by aesthetic command under the pressure of what Martin Luther King Jr. called "the fierce urgency of now."

Ellington was able to find a new feeling or a new sensibility for the very same reason Picasso said of painting that if one ever actually ceased to feel fresh things about a familiar subject, there would not be so many paintings of it. The 1950 *Masterpieces by Ellington* and the 1951 *Ellington Uptown*, his first two long-playing recordings on forty-minute canvases, show his creation of new three-minute numbers, his expansion of other well-known ones, and his commitment to such longer compositions as "The Tattooed Bride," from the 1950 recording, and "Harlem," from the following year. In each of the long pieces, the delicate sumptuousness of romance and the turbulence of life are not opposed but are organic parts of the composer's vision of simultaneity.

With three-minute pieces and what became the kinds of suites that he wrote until his death, Ellington could either hold or fold but was considered a dead duck in the business by the mid-1950s. At that point, a dance band could survive only by playing many one-night appearances and very few extended engagements of a week or more. This meant constant traveling for the Ellington crew in accommodations that had fallen to the uncomfortable band bus, far below the private Pullman railroad cars on which they had traveled through the South during the 1930s and early 1940s to avoid the irritations and insults of segregation. Gone were the days. The band's elite status had left along with all the other bands that were then no more than nostalgic memories.

All of the good intentions, the stripped-down traveling accommodations, the exhausting schedules, and the illusion that everything was as fine as good May wine had melted into a huge stone that Ellington had to push up the unavoidable show-business hill that rose before him every single day. He was not a man given to vacations, nor were his responses to the demands that seemed about to overcome him particularly effective when he arrived at Newport on July 7, 1956.

2. THE WEEKEND THAT CHANGED IT ALL

According to Wynton Marsalis, Duke Ellington was the leader of what just may have been the greatest orchestra in all of Western musical history, with the possible exception of the Chicago Symphony. Although one expects great skill from symphony players, one almost never hears a symphony orchestra in which each section of strings, brass, and woodwinds contains not only virtuoso players but more than one outstanding soloist, a player whose command includes a personal tone, technique, and rhythmic flow as well as a distinctive melodic and harmonic conception. This was true of the Ellington Orchestra from the mid-1930s onward, and the organization was at a particular plateau of mature and regenerated authority the night that it took to the bandstand of the Newport Jazz Festival, after having been made to wait as though the musicians were, as the bandleader angrily said, "the animal act."

In a racist period when second class was thought good enough for Negroes, the idea that Black jazz musicians should be presented well, paid on equal terms with the white musicians, and provided with parallel accommodations made jazz the aesthetic agent of a democratic optimism that had proven its truth through the musicians and the music itself. Although they did not have to, Black and white musicians had made good jazz together and could handle each other the way that human beings do when the nature of their individual sensibilities creates the codes of conduct and the rules of engagement. For musicians, the law of the land, the imperative to which they have to submit, is that talent dictates unpredictably. A journeyman or a genius can come from anywhere.

We should not forget that this was the dark modern age of American life when liberals, wealthy or not, were urban variations on abolitionists. In many instances and contexts, these twentieth century abolitionists were essential to what became alternatives to racism in American society during the hundred years after the Civil War. Those were the years when the redneck South did some stubbornly fancy footwork and won in social policy what it had lost on the battlefield. Southern bigots had established a way to keep Black people as much under their heels as possible, a fact that seemed mythic or at most metaphoric until the harsh and voluminous details were brought forth by Douglas A. Blackmon in his 2008 *Slavery by Another Name*. That book should provide a severely detailed caning for all southern apologists who argue that the good old South has been terribly misunderstood.

The southern combination of the genteel and the crude had formed a pretentious and despicable style of handling race relations. That style might demand aristocratic entitlement or replace the mask of refinement with paranoid and murderous violence if some Negro accidentally or intentionally posed a threat to what was called "the Southern way of life." Given the many nooks and crannies in which racism was to be found, it could be argued that the southern vision of racial hierarchy had so influenced the North that it was close to being the true nature of the nation. This could be shockingly illustrated in the most savage terms by race riots, public murders, and newspaper editorials that were themselves nationwide race riots in journalism after the heavyweight boxing championship victory of Jack Johnson in 1910. As Ralph Ellison's 1952 novel *Invisible Man* posited, the epic frame of Black American life was always a story of partial containment.

What makes John Fass Morton's *Backstory in Blue* so impressive is the way he handles the tensions and releases of that blue containment tale while bringing human complexity to the fore. We feel the flesh-and-blood qualities of the characters who made the story intimate, secret, public, intricate, casual, and even slightly mysterious. Morton makes up for his occasional slips into the ordinary prose of mere reportage with a sense of how to balance the book's pacing through detail that does not mute feeling but becomes a narrative partner.

While sometimes seeming irrelevant until its importance is later revealed, each detail gives nuance and great variety to a story that is fairly simple. A musical genius whose career was a metaphor for how far his art could go beyond its humble and limited origins was in popular decline when contracted to play a newly established jazz festival at Newport, Rhode Island, where high-society types had recently brought together enough of the forces needed to hold the blues of bigotry and social prejudice at bay. Columbia Records, having won the competition against RCA to first produce a long-playing record, or album, managed to get a crew there to document the performance. The new technology would allow Ellington to think in terms of much more time than was allowed in the three-minute records that had built the great mass of his reputation during the past thirty years. The most formidable composer of his idiom, the bandleader had written a three-part suite to celebrate the occasion and to uplift the audience. It was a plateau in a career that had begun to buck racial and aesthetic limitations with the support of the bandleader's Jewish manager, Irving Mills, who had fought all of Ellington's battles with him from the late 1920s to the late 1930s.

When the band went on at Newport, for all that it had been and had meant to American music for so long, the initial response of the audience was indifferent if not bored. Then, as in a film, after failing to thrill the audience with piece after piece, the bandleader decides not to go down without a hard-swinging fight and calls an extended blues work that he wrote nineteen years before, one that nearly created a riot in 1938 when performed at the very first jazz festival on Randall's Island in New York. This time, however, a featured solo was the ace in the hole. It was presented by Paul Gonsalves, the tenor saxophonist who was from Rhode Island's Cape Verdean community but had been with Ellington for six years and had, just a few years earlier, very nearly ignited a Birdland audience to chaotic behavior with his red-hot playing of the same piece. That night in Newport, not very far from his home, Gonsalves again did his duty, lighting the smoking lamp with the golden brass blow torch of his saxophone. The music, the audience, and the night synthesized into a miracle of expression, acceptance, and transcendence. The players owned the evening.

Backstory in Blue makes us aware of more than the comeback tale loved by the media and the public, by circling close to, away from, and back to that performance. Morton significantly gives a brief history of Ellington's career and the development of the recording business. We meet every member of the band and understand why each was hired. Morton shows that although Ellington was in the worst economic period of his career and was being advised by jazz magazines to retire, his band had actually been regenerated by new members and by the return of Johnny Hodges, a supreme and irreplaceable soloist who had defected a few years earlier. At his lowest point, Ellington was leading what may have been his best band. This was made evident over the nearly fifteen years of touring and an incomparable number of masterful recordings that contained an uncontested range of material and original works, large and small. This mass of Ellingtonia was publicly documented or privately stockpiled by Ellington himself until the band, which had been slowly losing its great personnel, lost Hodges to death in 1970 and went into its final downward spiral over the next four years.

Morton is not just filling up space with drool by scrutinizing each musician in the band. His technique gives the reader a sense of the complex internal tensions and releases of Ellington's leadership and, even more important, his dynamic psychological relationship to the quality of the band in performance. The leader ultimately knew that he had to spark his men into charging a hill of potential indifference. If he wanted heat or sweetness or anything in between, it was *his* responsibility to bring it first from the piano and keep it going once all that could be made romantic or molten began to bubble up to the top. In the wonderfully insightful documentary *A Duke Named Ellington*, veteran tenor saxophonist Ben Webster says, "I still don't understand how he does it"—the saxophonist snaps his fingers—"he turns that band on like you turn that faucet on, and the band *plays*. But Duke . . . he's an easy-going man. He never said anything. Never seen Duke lose his temper, but"—squinting his eyes exactly as expected of one whose nickname was The Brute—"he's got a way to let you know *let's take care of business*. You dig?"

Morton brings unforced irony to the highest point of his tale by observing early on that the technicians there to capture the last performance of the night were using magnetic tape developed in Germany during the Third Reich. This is an important detail shrewdly placed because the writer does not say what it means, allowing the reader to figure out how technological advance can quickly become universal, no matter its origins. The Reich could not have imagined that eleven years after it had lost the war at least partially to a country quite schizoid about race, the conquering nation from across the Atlantic Ocean would reveal its epic resources once again but this time through German innovations. Every aspect of ethnic confusion and superstition would, for an imperishable moment, be resolved by a music that the Nazis hated especially because of its assumed ability to bring out the savage even in Aryans. That music would be performed at white heat by a band of Negroes led by one of the geniuses of American feeling who was not unaccustomed to soothing or thrilling or coaxing his audiences until they were *ready* to be driven wild.

Morton structures his tale around the realization that our society has been wired much longer than many assume and that there has never been a stronger influence than that wiring on racial containment as well as on the motion beyond containment that we call "social progress." Wiring established itself in the earlier communication grids of electronic access that began to emerge with film, crystal sets, telephones, and radio. Perhaps most important, electronics united many human kinds, backgrounds, and elements—the musicians, the businesspeople, the corporations, the promoters, the technicians, the audience, the politicians, and the media itself. Recordings were fundamental to a modern musician's career. More than commercial artifacts only, they could define a personal aesthetic by making public an artistic story as accidental but perceivable as an urban skyline. Each release was an aesthetic truth that took in the talent, the convention, and the innovation, if one was being made. As Stevie

Wonder described them, recordings were talking books. They spoke to audiences in ways that helped define the modernity of our lives and how we see ourselves.

John Fass Morton reveals many things that others have missed, and his book could inspire those in our firmly segregated literary world where almost all of our fiction fails to bring artistry and the sort of sweep expected in the best nineteenth century European novels and short stories. Page by page this book makes its way to great importance by showing that one should not be spooked by the range and complications of humanity that appear across the classes, the races, the religions, the professions, and the causes that usually drive great public events in our nation. In all, *Backstory in Blue* gives us a startlingly pure rendition of the private, public, domestic, and international significance of the American community in what may be an era that will more perfectly realize the deeper meanings of why the new president of the United States proudly calls himself a mutt.

2009

I'VE GOT A RIGHT TO TAP MY FEET INSIDE OF THE MACHINE

An age of such delicate balance and splendor that the only word
I can use to describe it is myth.

—SUN RA

IN AMERICAN POPULAR CULTURE, Fred Astaire replaced the romantic knight's suit of armor with a tuxedo and his helmet with a top hat.
His sword was pared all the way down to a couple of kidney-shaped taps
that were nailed onto the heels of those shoes transformed into leather
apparel capable of assisting in the casting of spells. The dancer was then
prepared to turn the beating of the smitten, meditative, jaunty, or fanciful
heart into a percussive symphony. This combination of drumming and
dancing was so enlivened by the rhythms of jazz swing that Astaire in
motion became a lean melting pot of Americana out of which bubbled the
miscegenated aesthetic that is one of the most wholly successful expressions of American grace, power, and frailty.

It is also true that Astaire achieved his aesthetic position through
the technology of film that had only a few years before been elevated to
include sound, which was not only important to the further development
of cinematic narrative but also especially significant to the musical com-

edy in which the dancer did his most telling work with Ginger Rogers before World War II. Andrew Sarris makes the point that sound was particularly effective for the gangster movie because the audience then heard the unique sound of the machine guns. Though dancers can be effective in silent film, any whose artistry includes the signature drumming of tap must be heard to be appreciated or understood.

Now that the compact disc is a talking book that offers moving images, our technology has brought film viewing into the same realm as reading because it can be private and also repeated in the way a reader's eyes repetitiously travel over a personally loved passage. It is ultimately an extension of the player piano that can guarantee sameness as often as one wants. In the newly bottled wines of old films, certain performers do not suffer from being seen over and over; they become even stronger because nothing depletes the indelible and mysterious inspiration that turns them into invincible elements of light. Fred Astaire is one of those.

He was also one of a kind, as we all should know, and his work has inspired a number of books and many thousands of words. However, Joseph Epstein's *Fred Astaire* will probably never be exceeded as a certain kind of thing. It is proof of how hard a time Americana can give intellectuals who want to show that they appreciate it but, actually knowing better than to be completely made one of the contemptible mass, they have to disparage it to show off their academic credentials. That is what makes Epstein's book a minor fascination and a contradicting character study of the writer.

It is a combination of the boorish, the pretentious, and a special degree of resentment so startling and so powerful that Epstein cannot hold back the impulse to condescend to the dancer while building a pedestal for him and expressing an awe at Astaire's gifts that is probably quite sincere. But it is the sort of corkscrewing appreciation we find common to the racist or the anti-Semite who can't stop loving Black people and Jews on an aesthetic or purely intellectual level but can't stop hating them on a human one, where they might have committed the unpardonable sin of being so ordinary that they give no clues to what would explain their talent, which places them closer to light than to any form of human life that we can logically comprehend.

Epstein suffers from that spiritual and intellectual affliction by virtue of the fact that he cannot fully accept the magic of Astaire's art along with the fact that the dancer, like many artists and performers, might actually be as ordinary as he preferred to present himself. People with great talent and the even rarer ability to bend great talent to their will owe us nothing other than what they choose to give us and, the world being what it is, we had better be grateful that they give us anything at all. Of course, gratitude is something out of step with the dominating narcissism and sentimentality of our moment, which fuse into a force of particularized resentment. Notably, such people as Epstein can neither resist the attention given to others nor resist getting as close as possible to those who deserve it.

What happens in artifacts like this book is as embarrassing as it is odd. The groveler in the mysterious temple of public appreciation begins to slowly crawl forward all the way from back in the great distance until he is close to the image of the person who inspires the groveling and, with a loud hawking, then begins spitting at the mummified but somehow timelessly vital subject made incapable of defense by death. This is not idle madness. The groveler seems to have a plan, one in which he knows what to do with this icon. He intends to bring it down to a place from which the groveler can, once again, lift it up, polish it off, and assert that its greatness is beyond our understanding. We are told that, for all of his shortcomings, the man was not merely mortal like the rest of us; he was godly. The groveler then wipes his mouth with his sleeve and continues to make his case.

The slightness of Epstein's book is important to make mention of because it is not only a study in pretension from which we can get a laugh and sometimes simultaneously shudder, but it has value because it, like much intellectual work aimed at this context, fails to address what has become a significant loss in our popular culture. It is a loss made especially obvious by Astaire's career at its height during the Great Depression, but that very career needs to be seen within the context of those whose accomplishments are veritably equal.

While flailing about and taking the longest way from the barn to the house and back, usually because he never lets pass an opportunity to sneer at Astaire's family, his looks, his hairpieces, his friends, and even his casual attitude about art itself, Epstein fails to address one of the greatest achievements of American popular art during the technological innovations of the 1920s and the 1930s. During those years, doggedly vernacular popular art brought high-mindedness to the masses. This arrived through an expression of romantic feeling that was ultimately a way of worshipping the vitality of life through aesthetic means given to lyricism. The unsurpassed tender and revelatory ending of Charlie Chaplin's *City Lights*, Louis Armstrong's impossibly heartbreaking but transcendent improvisation on "Tight Like This" or "I Got a Right to Sing the Blues," and Astaire's more than fabulous and purely affirmative solo features on "I Won't Dance" or "Bojangles of Harlem" give their victories to us with both barrels. We witness and experience perfect examples of what American lyricism offered to the world.

SUCH CREATORS AND their works were absolutely American and universal at the very same time. *City Lights* was arguably the final silent masterpiece; Armstrong had created a concerto format for improvising soloist and large ensemble, or big band, that became an idiomatic formal structure

initially focused on Tin Pan Alley popular songs but that Duke Ellington appropriated for compositions that were as idiomatic as Armstrong's
purely unique trumpet style; and Astaire, in the interest of his own aesthetic individuality, had removed the technological tricks that made the
dancer no more than a moving part in a geometric creation by the directors and editors of film.

Though they are not addressed, Epstein might have done something
important had he made mention of the importance of those artistic and
formal victories. I say that because we are currently overloaded with more
vulgar, shallow, and degrading input than has ever been available. Let me
expand upon an earlier point. Our technology is capable of everything
from oppression to misleading to inspiring and even informing. Against
all technological odds, Astaire, Chaplin, and Armstrong remain invinci-
bly in place as a result of the very same technology. Our machinery makes
it possible for all phenomena other than the actual power of performance
in person to take on the kind of intimate experience once reserved in the
world of reading.

Those who do not care to go to movie theaters or would be irritated if
they could not repeat sections of recorded musical performances as immediately or as often as they want can now experience mobile art the way
stationary art such as reading, sculpture, or painting used to be exclusively
experienced by the mobility of the eyes possessed by the reader or the
viewer. All over our planet, Chaplin, Armstrong, and Astaire continue
to offer the same levels of concentrated humanity that they did through
aesthetic action at the moments when their talents rose to inarguable fruition. In fact, in a time as confused and decadent as this one, they might
even offer more.

Those who might have expected actual thoughts about Fred Astaire
or the era in which he became rightfully famous will almost surely be dis-

appointed if they assumed that perhaps Epstein would provide something especially insightful about the great dancer because the almost limitlessly expressive hoofer provides so many entries for examination. Epstein is far better at describing what Astaire wore than he is at giving us any penetrating details about his art or his performances or what he added to the world that had never existed in a prior era, no matter how much human beings had danced from before there was recorded time.

Epstein spends most of his space looking down on everyone close to the dancer and makes sure to save some darts for the man himself. This takes up a good deal of room in an already brief narrative. He does, however, make it clear that Gene Kelly, while viewed as something of a professional proletariat leading man, director, and a dancer with more obvious muscularity, actually came from an upbringing and a life that had been stable and middle class. Those beginnings were far more comfortable than the show-business school of constant travel and hard knocks from which Astaire earned a few doctorates.

Epstein is not shy about offering us pedestrian readings of what those from the bottom aspire to be, which is finally what makes them so repulsive: their pretensions oil the slide on which they descend into snobbery. It never occurs to Epstein that Astaire might have been looking for a world that matched what he could do as a dancer. After all, Astaire had achieved an almost peerless version of nobility through the same rigors of preparation that went into making the aristocrats with whom he hung out in Europe or in America whenever he could find them or whenever they sought him.

Once this man had perfected his dance routines, he made sure that they not only fulfilled the roles of functional numbers but, even if he only sensed it, made sure that the dancing also transcended the absurd context and created a poetic rendition of romantic elegance. The dancing was then about the pervasive splendor of the feeling for another person and more "real" than the idea that sexual aspirations and conclusions preclude all other male and female activities.

Epstein spends far too much time telling us that Astaire was not handsome and that his hands were "too big" and that he did not have an ample physique and could only lift partners if they were very light. Is this something that we do not know or that should startle us? His ordinary looks were part of his appeal and made him even more a model of modern heroism in a world where violence beyond a slap never takes place. One man said to have had erotic success with a plain-looking but wonderful singer was so startled when he saw her lying there next to him in the morning that he exclaimed, "Wake up and start singing something!"

Astaire's grace and clarion to subtle emotion were the transformative ingredients. While dancing, he realized the deepest meanings of charm, one of the few subjects that Epstein gets right. Charm made all of the corny jokes, the insipid plots, and his failure to be a great singer not only secondary but trivial. While insipid Epstein gets that, he misses this: What makes a hero, especially a romantic one, are not his limitations but his powers. Astaire's were that he could dance and in doing so summon the forces of what we know about human life and what it desires to say about itself or what it would prefer to be. Anatole Broyard once wrote of the coaxing that was part of seduction after World War II and how men would try to bring speech as close to opera singing as possible. They did this in order to best present their sensibilities to the women who could accept or reject them. What Astaire did was make us understand why women sometimes choose certain men, primarily because the feeling that they have for these women illuminates all of their virtues. That is the magic that Epstein seeks to understand but has trouble addressing.

Everyone I know is aware of the fact that musicals are corny and absurd, the recognition of which leads Epstein to say that, ". . . the absurd theater started well before the advent of Samuel Beckett . . . and the rest of the dark playwrights—absurdity to the highest power really began in the musical comedy movies of the 1930s and the '40s." A cute observation but no more. In truth, things almost always have to be made palatable so that men, who are less comfortable with romantic emotion than women, can sit there comfortably and enjoy its expression. American men seem far more at ease with public displays of sexual attraction and have announced it in everything from the old wolf whistles to the demeaning pronounce-ments of hip-hop.

At war with that resistance to romance, the blues and Tin Pan Alley did something about the male problem. They gave men the stark or intended poetry of romantic feeling in terms that sought to clarify the presence of joy or longing felt simply because a certain person was alive in the world. Those working in either idiom knew or sensed that romantic feeling can be compressed into the response a musician said of another, "I just feel happy when I see him." Few do not know how and why that form of happiness can also have its excruciating sides. Those moonless nights of feeling are reduced to high-minded longing in the musical. The musical comedy is a form that very rarely explores tragedy simply because it is not intended to make room for any wagon carrying the tragic heart. So when the musical comedy is successful, the audience has to make do with hap-piness so much more deeply felt on those exceedingly rare occasions when delivered by an artist the caliber of Fred Astaire.

Astaire's power, to be exact, is defined by the immovable limitations of the musical comedy's conventions themselves. Astaire becomes the irresistible force dancing through the heart of the immovable object. His work makes clear the reason that musicals are so trying on most of us. Within them the masculinity of the protagonist is far more often than not too weak to do what Fred Astaire could, which was make gestures and responses to life that might have been declared effeminate become open and available to grace, which has always had a shining quality of primal importance because it is implanted in us during infancy or the earlier periods of parenting. It is then that we learn the limitations of overt force. The comedian Dick Gregory recently said on a panel that he learned the power of softness when he watched the gentle way that his wife handled their children.

Astaire had feet and a body so highly educated that could meet and overcome all resistance so thoroughly he became a symbol of Americana in romantic form. Audiences saw tap shoes become polished versions of drum sticks, floors remade into the faces of drums, and couples so extend and consume each other that a new interpretation of romance was made real by the aesthetic authority of their responses to the melodies, lyrics, and rhythms of songs. If Fred Astaire ever thought about it, might he not have concluded at some point along the way that aristocracy is more a matter of breeding than of blood and that his own universally recognized aristocratic breeding took place in the world of show business, where sweat and steel wool brought a provocative sheen to the most formidable talents?

That is too direct and perhaps too obvious for Epstein. He often comes close to realizing what is going on but is usually flummoxed by a self-involved competition that takes him down. It does not allow the man to feel awe in the way Malraux articulated recognition of what it might all be about: The experience of great art can be the secular parallel to prayer. Any time that Epstein approaches his own version of that realization, he is compelled to tell us that we all feel clumsy after seeing Astaire dance, as if a viewer cannot appreciate him free of personal comparison or competition. We also must read that the writer, too, is short and has big ears and has his own idea which of the dancer's partners was most beautiful and so on. He even ventures so far as to take the position that someone as perfect as Astaire could be in the action of his art might just be an unfeeling technician who is so impressive that he gets to us through the uninvolved mastery he exhibits. Who cares or should care?

Epstein uses Schopenhauer to explain why he does not think that Astaire was a genius. The grim philosopher said that genius hit a mark that others could not even see while talent was merely given to greater accuracy when shooting at visible targets. If we are going to go there, just which artists hit the target Charlie Chaplin did at the conclusion of *City Lights* or that Armstrong did in his performance of "I Got a Right to Sing the Blues" or that Fred Astaire cut through the center of when he remade the musical comedy in order to technologically open up a space big enough for his unprecedented and still unequaled individuality in vernacular American dance?

Previously unpublished, 2013

THE COLOSSUS

SONNY ROLLINS ON THE BANDSTAND

Not long ago, the jazz drummer Victor Lewis was hanging out at the Village Vanguard and declared that he had finally decided what he wanted to be when he became an old man: Sonny Rollins. Lewis had recently performed with Rollins in Antibes. "Do you know that man stood up there and gave a three-and-a-half-hour concert and did most of the playing?" Lewis said. "He wasn't coasting or floating, either. He was deep in it, playing his ass off. That's surreal. Seventy-three years old, out in the hot sun, blowing a saxophone for that long—who can believe that?"

Rollins works at extremes. He is either astounding or barely all right. He hates clichés and signature phrases—"licks"—and refuses to play them. Consequently, for him there are no highly polished professional performances. When he's on, which is seven or eight times out of ten, Rollins—known as "the saxophone colossus"—seems immense, summoning the entire history of jazz, capable of blowing a hole through a wall. On his off nights, though, he can seem no more than another guy with a saxophone and a band, creeping through a gig. Those who hear him on such nights come away convinced that the Sonny Rollins of legend is long gone.

I've heard Rollins play many times during the past several years, and I've seen many versions of him. In an amphitheater in Washington, D.C., a few summers ago, he was in good form, teasing the audience by embellishing familiar songs with new, invented melodies and fast themes. For an encore, he played "I'll Be Seeing You," a ballad turned swinger, and sent the notes soaring out over the crowd. Later, at the New Jersey Performing Arts Center, in Newark, he pulled out a song that very few in the audience would know, "Let's Start the New Year Right," which was played by Louis Armstrong, one of Rollins's musical heroes. ("He found the Rosetta stone. He could translate everything," Rollins has said of Armstrong. "He could find the good in the worst material.") Rollins's calypso "Global Warming" was shrieking and rhythmic; the low notes hit with a thud. He played his horn almost to the point of hyperventilating. On the song "Why Was I Born?" he came up with a distinct motive for each eight-bar section—a remarkable expression of the power of his idiom. Rollins was heard over the hill that night.

But when Rollins is faced with a young crowd he often resorts to banal calypso tunes, playing one after another. This was the case at the House of Blues in New Orleans one night a few years ago, when I went to hear him with a writer and pianist friend. My friend was so disgusted that he vowed never to take another chance on seeing Rollins live. "Sonny gets insecure in front of young people and doesn't have the confidence to depend on his swing," a musician who used to play regularly with Rollins told me. "He knows the kids can hear that calypso beat, and he gives it to them."

Since 1980, Rollins has made more than a dozen records in the studio, but unlike many of his fellow titans on the tenor saxophone—

Coleman Hawkins, Lester Young, John Coltrane—he has realized his talent almost exclusively on the bandstand. His finest recordings in the past twenty-five years have been live ones, legal and bootlegged. Running through a repertoire of Tin Pan Alley songs, jazz standards, originals, and festive calypsos—something old, something new—Rollins seems to have an endless catalogue on which to draw. If jazz improvisation is a kind of democratic expression, then Rollins may well be our greatest purveyor of utopian feeling.

For more than thirty years, Rollins has lived in a modest two-story house in Germantown, New York, a couple of hours north of Manhattan. (He kept an apartment in Tribeca, near the World Trade Center, but gave it up after September 11. Television audiences saw Rollins board the evacuation bus wearing a surgical mask and carrying his saxophone.) The Germantown property includes a large converted stable that is used as a garage. There is a swimming pool in the back and, beyond it, a small house where Rollins writes and practices music for many hours a day. In the studio, there are pictures of Rollins on bandstands around the world; a Japanese ceramic version of him wearing Oriental robes and blowing a horn; stacks of music; an electric keyboard; and various trophies and mementos.

Rollins lives alone; Lucille, his wife of nearly forty years, died in November 2004. (They had no children.) The bucolic simplicity of the place and the soft tones in which Rollins tends to express himself are at odds with the muscularity of his music. "I like the quiet, and I prefer being left alone," Rollins said when I went to visit him last spring. "Up here, I can choose contact with the world when I want it. That kind of freedom is a blessing, and I don't take it lightly."

Unlike Armstrong or Dizzy Gillespie, Rollins has no talent for stage-craft or show. He doesn't tell jokes onstage; he barely even smiles. He conveys his sense of humor subtly, through his music, quoting Billy Strayhorn's "Rain Check" when caught performing in a drizzle or walking through an irritated audience and playing "Will You Still Be Mine?" when arriving late. And yet he has a gift for unexpected display. He shaved his head in the 1960s, when a hairless dome was cause for comment, and changed his style constantly, alternating beautiful suits with ethnic robes, T-shirts, floppy purple hats, and tennis shoes. In the 1980s, he dyed his hair and beard shoe-polish black. Nowadays, he has come to himself: He wears a silver-white beard and mustache, and the effect is handsome and majestic.

The youngest child of hardworking Caribbean parents, Rollins was born in Harlem on September 7, 1930. His parents were from the Virgin Islands. His father, a U.S. Navy man, was often away at sea. He had an older brother, Valdemar, and an older sister named Gloria. Rollins's given name was Walter Theodore, but, he told me, "they started to call me Sonny because I was the baby, the youngest."

When Rollins was a boy, Harlem suffered—as parts of it still do— from terrible poverty. Yet there was an intellectual and artistic renaissance. Ralph Ellison described Harlem in the 1930s as "an outpost of American optimism" and "our own homegrown version of Paris." Rollins recalls the period as a happy time. "I remember us kids playing in the lobbies of the old theatres," he said. "I remember all that wonderful music that came out of Abyssinian Baptist Church and Mother Zion. There was a great feeling then. It was a very warm thing." In 1939, the Rollins family moved to 371 Edgecomb Avenue, between 150th and 155th Streets. This was Sugar Hill, an elite neighborhood. There, Rollins often saw three very striking men: W. E. B. Du Bois; Thurgood Marshall; and Walter White, the executive secretary of the NAACP, a Negro whose light skin allowed him to go on daring undercover missions among violent southern white racists.

But it was Coleman Hawkins, the father of the jazz tenor saxophone, who most impressed him. Around the time the family moved to Sugar Hill, Hawkins's version of "Body and Soul" was on jukeboxes across the country. "When I was a kid, even though I didn't really know what it was, you could hear Coleman playing that song all over Harlem," Rollins said. "It was coming out of all these windows like it was sort of a theme song." To the consternation of his family, who were conservative and practical-minded, he fell in love with the saxophone and decided to become a musician. Only his mother supported his ambition, and it was she who bought him his first horn, an alto saxophone, when he was nine.

Living on Sugar Hill gave Rollins a chance to get close to the musicians he revered. "I used to see all of these great musicians," Rollins said.

> There was Coleman Hawkins and his Cadillac and those wonderful suits he wore. Just standing on the corner, I could see Duke Ellington, Andy Kirk, Don Redman, Benny Carter, Sid Catlett, Jimmy Crawford, Charlie Shavers, Al Hall, Denzil Best, and all of these kinds of men. Those guys commanded respect in the way they carried themselves. You knew something was very true when you saw Coleman Hawkins or any of those people. They were not pretending. When they went up on the bandstand, they proved that they were just what you thought they were. You weren't dreaming. It was all real. You couldn't be more inspired.

Though the dictates of show business meant that Negro musicians had to tolerate minstrelsy and all the other commonplace denigrations, most jazz musicians of the era formed an avant-garde of suave, well-spoken men in lovely suits and ties, with their shoes shining and their pomaded hair glittering under the lights, artists ranging in color from bone and beige to brown and black. Their very sophistication was a form of rebellion: These musicians made a liar of every bigot who sought to limit what Black people could and could not do, could and could not feel.

Having switched to tenor saxophone in the early 1940s, Rollins then led a band with some other young men from Sugar Hill: the alto saxophonist Jackie McLean, the drummer Art Taylor, and the pianist Kenny Drew. They played "cocktail sips" in the early evening for working people and the numbers runners who moved through the crowd. "Those gigs could be something else, man," Rollins said. "Those weren't always peaceful people out to have a good time. They could get ugly. At the dances particularly, it could get very rough. You had to be vigilant every second, because fights could break out and you would have to protect yourself and your horn." What he observed in those situations—the frailty of peace and calm, as well as the ballroom ambience of slow, close dancing and whispered courtship—has never left his ballad playing.

Rollins intently studied the tenor players: Ben Webster, of Kansas City; Don Byas, of Muskogee, Oklahoma; and Lester Young, of Woodville, Mississippi, and New Orleans. "That was the best ear training," he told me.

Natural musicians have to be able to do that, to cop stuff quickly by ear. That's what I am, an intuitive player. I didn't go to school to learn what I do. I spent a lot of time just practicing my horn. So I think I was playing a lot of stuff before I knew what it was. I was in the middle of that golden period of popular songs and movie music, and I retained all of that stuff. I know most of those songs, and most of the lyrics. The story begins with the melody; you keep the story going by using the melody the way you hear it as something to improvise on. In reality, it should all be connected—the melody, the chords, the rhythm. It should all turn out to be one complete thing.

Rollins also spent a lot of time at the Apollo Theater in Harlem.

> You could get it all at the Apollo, man, all of it. If you wanted to
> hear Frank Sinatra, you had to go downtown, but everything else—
> I'm talking about giants like Billy Eckstine, Billie Holiday, and
> Sarah Vaughan—was at the Apollo. There would be two movies,
> maybe a Western and a jungle movie or a comedy and a detective or
> gangster picture. There would be comedians, jugglers, dancers, and
> Duke Ellington, Count Basie, and every kind of band. You would
> have experienced all of these styles and emotions by the end of the
> shows.

Even then, Rollins's playing was imbued with a vast array of musical
Americana.

Rollins didn't become aware of the alto saxophonist Charlie "Bird"
Parker until he bought a recording in the mid-1940s that featured
Don Byas playing "How High the Moon" on one side and Parker sailing through "Ko Ko" on the other. Soon, he was hearing Parker at the
Apollo, too. Parker was considered the most important musician in the
emerging school of bebop, which demanded a new level of velocity technique, melody, and harmony, and a mastery of slippery triplet rhythms.
He also brought with him the troubles of heroin. Just as musicians a
generation earlier had smoked reefers when they found out that Louis
Armstrong liked the stuff, so, now, did the members of the bebop movement follow Parker's self-destructive path. The result was disastrous,
with many musicians dying young. Rollins said that he and his musical
buddies from Sugar Hill foolishly thought that taking heroin "would
make us play better."

By the end of the 1940s, Rollins had an addiction he couldn't shake.
"Sonny was a real junkie," one musician recalls. "He was a bandit, and he

even looked like one. His hair was gassed up and looked real greasy. He burned just about everybody he came in contact with. That heroin had him so desperate that if he got his hands on your instrument it would end up in the pawn shop." Rollins became, as he himself put it, "persona non grata among my family." He went on:

> It made me mad then, but I can understand, because I did a lot of bad things. Always stealing, always lying, always trying to get the money for those drugs. I was lost out there, like all of us were, and the only person who would forgive me and still believe in me was my mother. She never turned her back on me. I was her baby son, no matter what.

For much of 1951, Rollins was in prison for attempted robbery. "When I was out there on Rikers Island, imprisoned among those criminals, I was disgusted with myself, when I wasn't thinking about the time I was losing not practicing my horn," he told me.

But even as Rollins struggled, he began to emerge as an artist. Jackie McLean told me:

> I remember when Sonny came back from Rikers Island and he was standing in the door listening to one of the gigs I was holding down for him while he was gone. He asked if he could play my horn, the alto, and I handed it over. People missed that Sonny Rollins on *alto*. Sonny got up there and played 'There Will Never Be Another You.' He spat out so much music—so *much* music—that when he finished I didn't want to *touch* that horn. It was on *fire*.

In December of 1951, Rollins made a surprisingly mature recording, "Time on My Hands." His tone is big and sensual, as delicate as it is forceful. Already, at twenty-one, he had the ability to express as much tenderness as strength, melding the romantic ease of Lester Young, the robust power of Coleman Hawkins, and the lyricism of Charlie Parker. In pacing, tone, feeling, and melodic development, "Time on My Hands" is Rollins's first great piece. Loren Schoenberg, a jazz musician and scholar, says of the performance:

> Compared to the other young saxophone players recording during that period—Stan Getz, Wardell Gray, Sonny Stitt, Zoot Sims, Gene Ammons—Rollins is accessing everything that had happened to the tenor saxophone. He was not just approaching the surface of the sound and the technique but the emotional depth and breadth. What is most shocking about it is that all of these other men were several years older. But Rollins sounds more mature than any of them sounded at that time.

Out of Rollins's attentiveness to his musical forebears had come a heightened sensitivity to melody, harmony, rhythm, and timbre, the shading that gives a note its emotional texture. "Those kinds of hearing are exactly the elements that make jazz so great," Gunther Schuller, the conductor and composer, says.

> In the arena of art, they make the idea of schizophrenia—or multiphrenia, perhaps—not a problem but a profoundly positive thing. One is splitting up the brain to achieve all of these tasks in the interest of creative order, not any kind of fumbling disarray.
>
> These are the things that are beyond even most concert musicians, because, unlike Sonny Rollins and Ben Webster and those kinds of musicians, the classical musician—no matter how great—is, on the one hand, reading music or playing it from memory. On the other, he is too closely connected to what he was told about how to play by

his most influential teachers. This makes it veritably impossible for him even to encounter, much less master, that kind of personal hearing knowledge from within his own being. Sonny Rollins discovered those things for himself, as all jazz musicians must, and what he has done with those discoveries makes him one of the greatest musicians of any serious music, no matter what name we give it, and no matter what the era or century in which it was made.

In the mid-1950s, after recording classic numbers with a variety of musicians, including Miles Davis, Thelonious Monk, and the members of The Modern Jazz Quartet, Rollins checked into a rehab program in Lexington, Kentucky, where he kicked his heroin habit. From there, he went to Chicago, where he began playing with the trumpeter Clifford Brown and the drummer Max Roach. Rollins had a special affection for Brown. "Clifford was pure," he said. "He didn't do any of the things the others of us got messed up in. He was a witty guy, very quick. He could play a strong game of chess." Brown's music reflected his acuity. "His command of his horn was intimidating," Rollins said.

> He had an angelic sound. Other musicians were free to ask him technical questions and he would tell them. He didn't try to mislead you and stunt your growth like some of the competitive guys out there. Being around him lifted me up completely. Near the end, we got that unified sound you almost never hear—there was no saxophone, there was no trumpet.

In Chicago, Rollins met Lucille Pearson at one of his performances. Lucille was white, and when, in 1971, she took over Rollins's business affairs, he noticed that she got more respect than he ever did.

In 1956, Brown died, at the age of twenty-five, in an automobile accident on the Pennsylvania Turnpike. He and the band's pianist, Richie Powell, who also died, were on their way to Chicago for a gig. Roach and Rollins were waiting for them there in a hotel when they got the news. "When I told Sonny what had happened, he just turned around and went back to his room," Roach said. "You could hear that tenor saxophone playing all night."

Shortly thereafter, Rollins and Lucille moved back to New York, and he recorded *Saxophone Colossus*. One of the great small-group recordings, it showcased Rollins's improvisational powers. In 1957, he made the equally extraordinary *Way Out West*, his first recording using only bass and drums. On the album cover, Rollins wears the high-camp garb of a gunslinger: a ten-gallon hat and a holster. The following year, he recorded his most adventurous composition, "Freedom Suite," a twenty-minute trio piece for tenor, bass, and drums, and revealed his skill as an arranger, giving the piece four distinct themes. Part of its excitement stems from the interplay between Rollins and Roach, which clearly anticipates the avant-garde elasticity of the 1960s.

Rollins, an activist before "protest music" became common fare in jazz, wrote a manifesto to accompany the album: "America is deeply rooted in Negro culture: its colloquialisms, its humor, its music. How ironic that the Negro, who more than any other people can claim America's culture as his own, is being persecuted and repressed; that the Negro, who has exemplified the humanities in his very existence, is being rewarded with inhumanity." It is hard to find the precise political meaning of the music itself, but it is clearly less playful than his earlier recordings. Gone are the witty quotations from other tunes and the unexpected shifts of color that Rollins had so often inserted into his playing. The music has a stoic quality, a heroic certitude, and a grand lyricism without being stiff or cold or pretentious. It is a timeless achievement.

Just when Rollins was becoming one of the leading figures in jazz, a new force emerged, in the form of John Coltrane, a tenor player from Philadelphia by way of North Carolina. Coltrane, who also struggled with drugs, was then in the process of leaving the Miles Davis Quintet. After playing with Monk at New York's Five Spot in 1957, Coltrane began to ascend very quickly, startling the jazz world with his innovative harmonic schemes and the complex originality of his phrasing. Before long, people were saying that Rollins had been left behind; he felt the slight profoundly.

"Sonny never found a way to discover how great he really was, and he never recovered from the disapproval of the jazz community when Coltrane was coming up," Branford Marsalis told me. "It's a shame that he never understood that they didn't have the capacity to understand how great he was."

In 1959, Rollins decided to stop performing for a few years, and Lucille helped support him with a secretarial job in the physics department at New York University. Rollins often practiced his horn on the Williamsburg Bridge, pushing himself to play loud enough to compete with the industrial noise of the city. Though he was working earnestly on his music, it was hard to avoid the impression that he had been eclipsed by Coltrane. "You know what happened to Sonny Rollins?" went a joke that circulated in the jazz world at the time. "A 'Trane ran over him."

Even now, Rollins resents that suggestion. "I left the scene to work on some things because I was getting all of this press and I was near the top in the polls, but I wasn't satisfying myself and I didn't feel like I was satisfying the public," he said. "I wanted to work on my horn, I wanted to study more harmony, I wanted to better myself, and I wanted to get out of the environment of all that smoke and alcohol and drugs. In order to avoid disturbing anyone, I went up on the Williamsburg Bridge and practiced."

"What he was playing at the time was so powerful you couldn't believe it," Freddie Hubbard, the great trumpeter, told me.

Other saxophone players were scared of him. He was feared. I played
with him and I played with Coltrane, and Sonny was definitely the
strongest. He could play so fast you couldn't pat your foot, and then
he could double that. Plus, he could keep that big sound going at that
tempo, which is impossible. And when he was going at those notes
like a tornado, or something like that, each one was right. He wasn't
hotfooting along and missing any of those damn chords.

The difference between him and Coltrane was that Coltrane
worked his harmony out very scientifically. He studied Nicolas
Slonimsky's *Thesaurus of Scales and Melodic Patterns*. Sonny was different. Spontaneous. There was no fear in him—not of the saxophone,
not of the music. He was like Bird, because he wasn't thinking about
practicing intervals and scales and all that stuff, like Coltrane. All
he needed was a song and he could hear the freedom of the music
through his own personality.

Though Rollins and Coltrane were considered rivals by the music
community, they admired each other. Hubbard said:

Oh, man, Coltrane loved Sonny. And Sonny loved Coltrane. They
didn't talk too much about each other, but whatever they said was
always complimentary. But, when I would practice with one of them
and then go practice with the other one, they both wanted to know
what the other was doing. Both of them were fired up about music,
too, because they had both been drug addicts and were trying to make
up for the time they lost out in the streets chasing that heroin.

Rollins and Coltrane also had an intellectual kinship, which was
based on shared spiritual concerns. Rollins recalled:

During the time that I was on the bridge, Coltrane and I were both reading a lot of books about spiritual things—Buddhism, Sufism, and I was into Rosicrucianism. And we talked about music reflecting those disciplines. We were optimistic about things. Coltrane and I would talk about changing the world through music. We thought we might get so good that our music would influence everything around us. I think he stuck to that path, but sometimes I became disconsolate about whether music could change the world. I thought about all the music that Louis Armstrong, Billie Holiday, and Art Tatum and all these people played, and how it hadn't had any effect. But now I know that you can uplift people with your music. They can feel bad, and, if you play something, they might feel better. I have to satisfy myself with that kind of contribution.

When Rollins returned to the stage in late 1961, fronting a band that featured the guitarist Jim Hall, the jazz scene had fractured. Some critics and musicians felt that they were in the midst of a new bebop revolution; others felt that jazz, rather than expanding, was being overthrown in favor of self-indulgence and chaos. Ornette Coleman, a composer and alto saxophonist from Fort Worth, Texas, was considered the most outrageous jazz innovator. Coleman played "free jazz," which used neither chords nor set tempos. His music, with its floating melodies, idiosyncratic phrasing, and echoes of the blues, was exalted as being primitively profound; it was also dismissed as inept. Then, there was Coltrane's furnace-blast modality. He stacked scales and used few chords, and his music was driven by the dense triplet complexities of the drummer Elvin Jones. Coltrane performed forty-minute solos and sometimes so exhausted himself that he fell to his knees on the bandstand, still playing.

In contrast to Coleman and Coltrane, Rollins—who now kept his hair close-cropped and wore tailored suits and tuxedos—was seen as a standard bearer of convention, and perhaps as the only one who could save jazz. He was hardly comfortable in this role. "I didn't feel like I was there to save anything—I was just ready to play," Rollins said. *The Bridge*, his first recording after returning to professional life, documents a luminous moment when he used superior arrangements, including tempo and metric modulations, saxophone and guitar riffs, and group phrasing that resembled conversation. He hadn't lost his sense of adventure, but it seemed impossible for him to fake the shrieks and screams that characterized the tumultuous avant-garde. He obviously still believed in the many powers of the musical notes, which put him at odds with someone like the late Albert Ayler, a screeching saxophonist who influenced Coltrane. "It's not about notes anymore," Ayler once said. "It's about feelings."

But then Rollins began playing standard songs and his own originals from the 1950s in the style of Ornette Coleman. "I figured if that kind of playing was valid, you could do it on any kind of material, just like every other style," he said. "You didn't need special material. If the conception was valid, the playing should be special enough." Rollins hired two of Coleman's former sidemen, the trumpeter Don Cherry and the drummer Billy Higgins. The music that resulted—the RCA Victor recordings (particularly *Our Man in Jazz*), a series of European bootlegs, and an especially stunning appearance on Italian television—seemed even more daring than what either Coltrane or Coleman was up to at the time. The music, which was based on split-second shifts in direction, mutated rapidly, sometimes turning a song into a suite, as with "Oleo." Rollins told a European interviewer at the time, "I think I sound like Ornette now." But the band was short-lived. Cherry and Higgins, both of whom were drug addicts, tended to arrive at gigs high. Rollins, who was trying to stay clean, fired them and hired the pianist Paul Bley, who had brought Coleman's approach to the keyboard.

Rollins, meanwhile, was becoming more and more eccentric. Still known as a sharp dresser, in 1963 he started wearing a Mohawk. "The Mohawk, to me, signified a form of social rebellion, and it was a nod to the Native American," he said. "I was listening to some Native American music and reading some Native American cultural stuff, and I felt very close to the aboriginal feeling. It made me feel more powerful." Most people thought that the Mohawk made Rollins look both ridiculous and dangerous. A sizable man to begin with, he took up bodybuilding and yoga, grew a thick black mustache, and came to resemble an ominous bouncer. There was a new strangeness to his stage persona as well. At the Five Spot in 1964, when he wasn't playing to the walls or walking among the tables as he performed, he might come onstage in a cowboy hat and a Lone Ranger mask, with cap pistols strapped on. "Maybe my memories of shows at the Apollo had gotten the best of me," Rollins said sheepishly.

While recording for RCA Victor, Rollins produced a number of successful pieces and masterly performances that influenced younger players, such as Pharoah Sanders and Archie Shepp. To some, this creative ingenuity seemed forced. One person who was involved with the RCA recordings has said:

> It was almost a tragic period for him. Sonny was really at sea. He didn't know what to do, which way to go. Sonny was absolutely confused by the press, the music community, and everything else. He seemed afraid of being considered old-fashioned. I think the attention that Coltrane was getting and the many who were starting to imitate him made Sonny feel left out, not at the center of things. It was very sad, this tremendous talent turning in circles as he lost more and more confidence. He could do anything he wanted; it was just that he didn't know what to do.

Rollins now admits:

> I don't think that Coltrane was thinking about competing with me
> or had any bad feeling toward me, but I did start to resent him at
> one point and I feel very embarrassed by that now. When I was up
> on the bridge and he used to come by my place and see me, we were
> together. In fact, if I was uptight for money I could get a loan from
> him, or from Monk, and know that it would never end up in the
> gossip of the jazz world about how bad off Sonny was. They were
> real friends. But when I came down from the bridge, I think I let his
> success and the attention that he was receiving get to me. It should
> never be like that. Never.

By the summer of 1965, Rollins had recovered from his insecurities
enough to make the excellent *On Impulse!* Ray Bryant, who played piano
on the album, says that the title was perfect, because Rollins just came
into the studio and began playing. "He might say a title and be gone!"
Every track is strong. Rollins handles his instrument with the authority
that James Joyce attributed to the superior artist, who works with the ease
of a god paring his nails. Early in 1966, he recorded the score for the film
Alfie, another triumph. The trumpeter Nicholas Payton says of *Alfie*:

> Except for Monk, I don't know if anybody else could play with that
> architecture, except that Sonny was doing it all his own way, which
> made it an innovation. The title track is actually like a movie being
> made right in front of you, from start to end, with major characters
> and minor characters functioning inside a serious plot that takes them
> here and there, some disappearing and popping up later in a dramatic
> way. Harmonically, he knew how to play a phrase that never resolves,

that hints at something that is never played, but he won't finish the phrase. He creates more and more suspense by playing a series of these phrases, then he'll drop that bomb that brings it all together, that resolves everything. Boom. If you could do something like that and not be noticed, I can understand why some people say Sonny was acting crazy during that period.

Like Louis Armstrong, who always claimed to be nostalgic for the way things were before he became famous, Rollins didn't particularly enjoy the responsibilities of leadership or notoriety.

Well, I'll tell you, I never really liked being a bandleader, because if things didn't sound good all the disappointment fell on me. At the same time, I couldn't be the real Sonny unless I was leading the band. So it was a riddle that I couldn't solve, and I don't think that I solved it for a long time. Now, even though I still don't really like it, they have my name up there and I have to show up and call the tunes and lead the musicians I've hired to play with me.

In 1969, Rollins retreated again and did not return to the studio or the bandstand until 1971.

I was looking for something spiritual, something that would make sense out of the mess I felt that I was in. I hated music at the time, because there didn't seem to be enough love between the musicians, not the kind I grew up with. I was sick of the whole thing. The clubs, the traveling—everything meant nothing to me at that time. I went to India and had no idea whether I would ever play the saxophone professionally again.

By the time Rollins reappeared, things had begun to change once more. Imitating Miles Davis, certain major jazz musicians, such as Freddie Hubbard, Herbie Hancock, and Wayne Shorter, began to embrace rock, or submit to it, or sell out entirely. To the annoyance of many of his fans, Rollins began using electric bass and electric keyboards, while abruptly transforming himself into a rhythm-and-blues player. His recordings were dismal, and he seemed incapable of making a good one. To this day, he hasn't recorded anything that approaches *Saxophone Colossus*, *Way Out West*, *Freedom Suite*, *The Bridge*, *On Impulse!*, or *Alfie*. The late Joe Henderson, whose style was firmly based in the Rollins mode of the early 1960s, made recordings in the 1980s and 1990s that were so much better than his mentor's that uninformed listeners might rank him above Rollins. The formidable jazz drummer Al Foster, who worked with both of them, told me, "Joe always sounded great, but when I was going back and forth between his band and Sonny's I realized that Joe, who could outplay almost everybody, wasn't even close to Sonny. There was no contest. Joe was a master; Sonny is *the* master. But you have to hear him in person to know that."

Until recently, it appeared that Rollins was destined to become a legend whose best work in the last phase of his career would probably go undocumented. Thankfully, this is not to be. Not long ago, I went to Portland, Maine, to see Carl Smith, a collector in his sixties who already has more than three hundred bootleg performances of Rollins—seemingly every session, radio broadcast, nightclub appearance, and concert recorded from 1949 to the present. He is trying to persuade Rollins's label, Milestone Records, to put out the best of them, at no profit to himself. He wants the world to enjoy what he has enjoyed, and he believes that those recordings, properly selected and edited, would not only create a major shift in Rollins's stature but also rejuvenate jazz by showing what a great living improviser can truly do.* I agree.

Sitting in Smith's neat apartment—it has a harbor view—and listening to performance after performance, I came to realize that Rollins is like all truly great players: No matter how well you think they can play, they always exceed your expectations. Smith said that during the bewildering period of the mid-1970s, Rollins "never matched the classics of the fifties." He went on, "The records show that. He seemed to have lost it. Then, in performance at least, he rediscovered himself around 1978. He stood up again and began to build back up to a kind of ecstatic playing that achieved miraculous heights in the eighties and has sustained itself to this very day."

Over and over, decade after decade, from the late 1970s through the 1980s and the 1990s, there he is, Sonny Rollins, the saxophone colossus, playing somewhere in the world, some afternoon or some eight o'clock somewhere, pursuing the combination of emotion, memory, thought, and aesthetic design with a command that allows him to achieve spontaneous grandiloquence. With its brass body, its pearl-button keys, its mouthpiece, and its cane reed, that horn becomes the vessel for the epic of Rollins's talent and the undimmed power and lore of his jazz ancestors.

Rollins told me:

> We never really know too much, not really. We need to be humble about that. But we do get to know certain things, and we have to do the best with them. Right now, I know what I got from Coleman Hawkins, from Ben Webster, from Dexter Gordon, from Don Byas, from Charlie Parker, and all the other guys who gave their lives to

---

* The album *Without a Song: The 9/11 Concert*, recorded at a performance in Boston on September 15, 2001, was released in August 2005.

this music. I know that without a doubt. From childhood, I've known this. All the way from back then, when it was coming out of the windows, when it was on the stage at the Apollo, when it was on the new records coming out. So now, after all these years, it's pretty clear to me, finally. All I want to do is stand up for them, and for the music, and for what they inspired in me. I'm going to play as long as I can. I want to do that as long as I can pick up that horn and represent this music with honor. That's all it's about, as far as I can see. I don't know anything else, but I know that.

May 2005

A BARONESS OF
BLUES AND SWING

NICA'S DREAM IS DAVID KASTIN's small but often good biography of a European aristocrat who made a new life for herself in America after World War II. Kathleen Annie Pannonica Rothschild de Koenigswarter was a supremely well-to-do British Rothschild at birth in 1913 but became a baroness by marriage and was known as such in the unexpected context she chose for herself, the nightlife world of New York jazz. Her childhood had the sort of suffocating luxury focused on manners, restraint, and impenetrable privacy that was as common to the most privileged aristocracy as it was bloodless, dehumanizing, and repulsive to the most sensitive among them. Her tendency was to do battle with those constraints and seek any opportunity to become a runaway.

In the process, she was awarded prizes for her artistic talent, studied in Paris and Germany, learned to fly a plane without maps, then married another wealthy Jew, Jules de Koenigswarter. Her future husband initially met her at an airport and was astonished by the casual bravery shown at the controls of the plane she had just landed. He was also a flier and soon became a war hero after he left their chosen home in Normandy and joined the Free French Forces. Together with their children, the Koenigswarters went back to England on one of the last boats preceding the German invasion.

Many of her relatives were not so lucky. A few died horribly as part of the "final solution" made manifest in the knee-deep human ash emptied on the ground of the woods surrounding concentration camps. Others survived and returned home permanently despondent. Never one satisfied to sit around, especially while the world was on fire, "Nica" went to Africa, broadcast war commentary on French radio, then became an ambulance driver for the Free French Forces in North Africa, reuniting with her husband. The week that Hitler committed suicide, she had come back to France and worked again in war medicine, separating the corpses from the wounded. That is more than enough for a Kate Winslet film, but far from Nica's whole story.

After 1945, she and Jules moved to Mexico in order to fulfill a diplomatic assignment, but Nica found herself compulsively attracted to New York for longer and longer periods, which finally destroyed their marriage. Upon hearing recorded selections from Duke Ellington's mammoth attempt to tell the Black American story in his 1943 *Black, Brown, and Beige,* she discovered the beauty of jazz and those who made it. Given what experience had taught her about the ever-vulnerable frailty of life and the attendant illusion of safety, she found in blues, jazz, and the pulsation of swing something understood only by special people: In order for true joy to achieve itself, it must contain the very states and moods being transcended—all the pain, all the hopelessness. In New York City, far above the dead metaphors and the frivolous distractions that the spiritually wounded members of her class too often mistook for fun, the woman found herself suddenly alive all the way up to the top, discovered her truest relatives in sensibility, and found what would be her lifelong mission: to help those in the jazz world as much as she could.

Nica had developed a high profile in the jazz community beginning in the 1950s but was not an element of public attention until Walter Winchell and other professional lunkheads muddied the air with nasty innuendos. The stage whispers of neon sandpaper came forward so fast because a charming and charismatic friend, Charlie Parker, had died in her Fifth Avenue Hotel Stanhope suite, across the street from the Metropolitan Museum of Art, in 1955. By 1963, she rose again from the hot and misty world of jazz when *Time* magazine put Thelonious Monk on the cover and she was photographed looking at him exactly like the enthralled patron of his that she had been for the previous ten years—and would remain until his death in 1982, five years before her own.

Kastin's book informs us about Nica's early life but focuses on her associations with Monk and many other jazz musicians to whom she appeared as a fairy godmother from a world that they did not know or understand. What they clearly understood was how free of bias Nica was and how supportive she could be in providing a place where they could play their music, relax, get high, and live life as close to normal, in her company, as a Black person could during her three decades as a patron. That she saw these people as human beings made her unique, though there were other white people, many of them Jewish, who could see the humanity of jazz musicians, good or bad, mysterious or profoundly clear. These people, accurately enough, were not decoyed by ethnic stereotypes or the inarticulate crust of slang and purported hip behavior considered a collectively cool dismissal of the puritanical manners of the time.

Usually seen out in the company of Monk, Nica became familiar through her expensive cars, her fur coats, her flask of Chivas Regal, her shoulder-length black hair, and her long cigarette holders. In the various hotel suites from which she was eventually evicted, the inspiration for many jazz songs arose in the all-night jam sessions that could go on from three o'clock in the morning until about nine o'clock, when all that was left were the musicians who had fallen asleep and the memories of those invisible notes that had appeared and disappeared as soon as they were played. Given all of that—which is not much information on which to build a biography—Kastin bases the bulk of his story on the relationship that Nica had with Monk but gives too much attention to those in the art, literary, and film worlds who mistook jazz for something innately primitive or given to an anarchy that it did not have and would never truly develop as anything other than a side pocket of the art. Kastin does do a good job of telling where that relationship took both Monk and Nica as he emerged from beneath the sole of show business. The pianist-composer-bandleader became, for a very brief period, a jazz star, until his various mental problems turned him nearly catatonic for the last decade of his life.

Nica never abandoned Monk and chose to take a drug-possession rap for him in Delaware during the fall of 1958. The arrest and the charge were as much about her being white and his being Black as it was about the very small amount of marijuana found in the trunk of her Rolls Royce. It could have led to her being deported, but neither Monk nor his wife, Nellie, with whom Nica was very, very close, ever knew about that. As she always did, Kathleen Annie Pannonica Rothschild de Koenigswarter stood her ground, asked for no favors, took life as it came, fought as best she could, and said no more than she thought necessary. She was terrified of losing her new home in a new country and only confided her inner trepidation in a letter to very close friend, Mary Lou Williams, the jazz pianist who had first introduced Nica to Monk in Paris during his first visit in 1954. The almost inseparable pair were never lovers, but their friendship had the kind of pathos, heroic but unsentimental optimism, and essential nobility that attracted her to jazz. Her story is as unlikely as the music itself and contains the full measure of hard blues that all true jazz musicians, beyond school or style, dedicate themselves to blowing away in a magical starburst of swing.

July 2011

A SONG FOR LADY DAY

Billie Holiday was, and still remains, the greatest single musical
influence on me. Lady Day is unquestionably the most important
influence on American popular singing in the last twenty years.

—FRANK SINATRA, 1958

L IFE IS ULTIMATELY MYSTERIOUS and indifferent about whom it
gives much and from whom it expects a measure equal to its gifts.
Those gifts are passed out with the same careless precision as handfuls of
chicken feed hurled into a high wind.

Billie Holiday was obviously given much more than most, and her
talent revealed itself through her intensity, her phrasing, and her control
of nuance more so than the conventional strengths of big sound, great
range, and stunning projection. Her voice was small, and her range was
equally small. Standing next to most singers, she would never get you to
put your money on her, unless you knew in advance that her emotional
force and her ability to summon pathos, joy, and melancholy with naked
precision would demolish almost anyone intent on making a contest out
of a hazardous moment on the bandstand with her.

There's the story of one performance with super virtuoso Sarah
Vaughan. Vaughan was so profoundly endowed with a superior instrument

that she sometimes could not avoid strutting her stuff to the point of obnoxiousness. But the ax fell. When Vaughan called up "I Cried for You," Holiday whispered, "You done screwed up now, bitch. That's my song."

That sounds like a person who had discovered what she had and bet
her life on it. In the face of virtuoso moves, Holiday was so far ahead on
human feeling as to be invincible. She had learned her craft from Louis
Armstrong and Bessie Smith, desiring Armstrong's sense of time and his
brilliant choice of notes as well as Smith's big sound. She did better with
Armstrong than she did with Smith, whom Langston Hughes said one
could hear out on the street when she was singing in a theater before
microphones had been developed to the point that Armstrong, Holiday,
and Sinatra could make the most of them.

Neither Armstrong nor Holiday nor Sinatra was a belter or would
have been much in the world of opera where size, projection, and nuance
were taken to levels far beyond what one expected in popular music. Each
of them brought popular music to heights of varied expression, emotional
complexity, and even psychological revelation that were far beyond what
had been intended by most popular composers or made functionally limited in their strident pluck by Broadway types like Ethel Merman, who
was capable of shivering the timbers.

Holiday was so special because she imbued her performances with a
tenderness so charismatic that her example and her unbending musical
presence forced instrumentalists to do their best at making up melodies
or coming as close to crooners as whatever talent they had made possible. One could not be completely satisfied with a brass or reed instrument unless it took on qualities close to a voice elevated by artistry of
the sort that only jazz could bring to its material. This was done by combining the highest level of improvisation with the skill to fit a context
and the absolutely essential ability to express oneself best by meeting
the demands of the ensemble, adjusting breath by breath to where one is

and to what is going on, as well as recognizing what to do with reality in motion.

She first appeared on record in the mid-1930s and had become a big influence on fellow singers by the end of the decade. The inarguably great Ella Fitzgerald has never failed to call Holiday the greatest jazz singer of all time. Abbey Lincoln, the only singer since Holiday who has a parallel level of feeling, of vulnerability and pathos so far from self-pity, says the same thing. Miles Davis's sense of rhythm and tendency to float over the beat was deeply influenced by Holiday, as was the growing confidence he brought to lyrical recognition of the interwoven mystery of melancholy, frailty, and unbounded but unsentimental joy.

That unsentimental joy has often been misunderstood as some sort of Negro foolishness too far removed from the world of the substantial to be taken seriously. But mindless and empty-headed frivolousness is not the issue at all. Thorough acknowledgment of life's tragic facts is what makes the art of Armstrong, of Holiday, and of many other major jazz musicians so compelling. It is much like singing a fervently happy song in the morgue not because we don't know what awaits us, but because joy is a protest against all that would take us down. So the will to live becomes more than desperation and ascends to a combatively affirmative morale. No minor accomplishment, this may be the most impressive thing that American Negroes have offered the world at large. There can be no doubt that Billie Holiday knew how to bring it.

For those interested in an eloquent and perfectly clear assessment, the very best writing about Holiday's artistry is contained in *The Jazz Tradition* by Martin Williams. Then there are some recordings that make it understandable what inspired all of the talk. *The Essential Billie Holiday*, a 1956 performance at Carnegie Hall, documents her craft at a penthouse point of perfection in which ballads, blues, and extremely hard but floating swing are as good as anything she ever recorded. *Songs for Distingué*

Lovers from 1957, just two years before her death, finds the incomparable Lady Day at the height of her talent and possessed of a mature wisdom that one does not hear in her early work, no matter how good it might be.

Then there is her personal favorite, *Lady in Satin*, done with strings about 17 months before she died.

There are those who enjoy pitying Billie Holiday for the hard life that she led due to drugs, alcohol, and the rough men who were incapable of breaking her spirit.

But we should not be decoyed by those unpleasant truths to the extent that we miss what the great Betty Carter observed about the great Billie Holiday. "I think she was only free when she was singing. Everything else didn't mean much except that it led up to the moment when she stepped out on that stage and became what we all wanted but only she could give us. She was free then, and everybody knew it. When someone brings that much freedom and makes you believe it, you have to get happy. You can't help it."

July 2009

PART THREE

In Defense
of Taboos

The blues are about all of us standing before the mysterious, seductively patterned, and destructive surf of existence. Playing the blues is one indelibly American way of seizing fists full of that ocean, a means of acknowledging the smooth, protean wetness and the cutting salt of the way it is. Yes, the blues are a sense of life. They are how we sometimes grow up enough to get ourselves straight—or at least straight until we bend down again before our shortcomings. That is why the feeling of the blues never leaves. In the best of times, the blues ride our minds mounted on a very light saddle, hardly pressing, but surely there. They also always know how to bear down on you.

Becoming an adult beyond the numbers on your birth certificate has been an especially hard job since the end of World War II, but listening to and understanding the unsentimental meaning of the blues will help you get there. You'll come away knowing one thing: No matter what it's like right now, there'll always be a blues for tomorrow.

—STANLEY CROUCH, *INTERVIEW* MAGAZINE

The title of this part, like "Outlaws and Gladiators" earlier, comes directly from Crouch. The implicit defense is that taboos serve to remind us civilization is fundamentally at war with xenophobia. Both titles were books that either he or his publisher had announced but either became subsumed into other collections or remained uncollected until now.

Here are some of the choice pickings of S.C.'s big bad film book. Crouch holding forth on cinema was something to behold, reserving his greatest affection for noir and Western genres, John Ford's, above all (no relation to S.C.'s grandmother Matilda Ford . . . read on for her blistering public defense of Butterfly McQueen). To the end, Crouch was still addicted to the Turner Classic Movies channel. Watching television with him could turn into a full-blown seminar. In film literature he found bits of philosophy that jibed with his own and seemed always at hand: "Hangin' is any man's business that's around," from the mouth of Henry Fonda in *The Ox-Bow Incident*. In print, his critiques of directors (Spike Lee, Quentin Tarantino, Steve McQueen v. Gordon Parks) could be barbed with complexity, the compliments double-edged. Crouch could deliver the cream pie, "airborne antidote to all of that illusion." He wouldn't give anyone a pass for past work. This is not the way Hollywood entertainment or popular media runs things. Those he praised loudest and earliest in their careers often came in for the harshest excoriation, perhaps because they had set the standard so high themselves. There is also what S.C. wrote of Fred Astaire, "What a genius sees when experiencing someone else working within his idiom is usually not only what is going on but what is *implied*." He doesn't neglect to put in a good word for Anna Magnani, that Roman queen with a swing in her backyard.

Controversial to the end, here are large critical essays on W. E. B. Du Bois, a demystification, and on Harold Cruse, an assessment of his legacy. In the end is our beginning, and this collection returns with one last poem that seems to presage the still dangerous lion in winter; and the grand finale, his epistolary eulogy, a work of last farewell.

VOLUPTUARY

WHEN I WAS A YOUNG MAN, some forty years ago, certain of us preferred our women big, with plenty of sensual wobble. Take Anna Magnani, the Italian actress who was nobody's ingénue. Magnani was the spiritual symbol of the female in a full blast of vitality. She was fleshy, had bags under her eyes, was far from a kid, and was possessed of a molten sensuality that would humble anyone looking to dismiss her humanity or her evident knowledge of how sweet it could be close-up and purely personal.

For all the stuff imposed on us by Hollywood and the world of the fashion model, an expanding vision of female beauty is once again finding a place for the voluptuous. There is an ever greater appreciation of the lush bottom, the backside wave, the "history"—meaning a woman with much behind her. This is one of the best things that could happen to our unfortunately immature society, which focuses on everything adolescent, giving deep blues to anyone who is neither as slim as a teenager nor close to a Hollywood ideal. Finally, our culture is catching up with a diversity of taste and a varied sense of physical pride.

Believe it or not, there have always been women who were, like Magnani, sure of themselves and what they had and what that possession could do to somebody who was ready for it. And, let me make it clear right now, more were ready for it than you might think. Some men knew just what was meant when a woman was proud of every ounce of her flesh and sent forth a beam of confidence that signaled she had plenty of intimate charms. Such women used to say when teased about their weight, "Nobody loves a bone but a dog."

But it takes the Empress of the Blues to get to the substance of the matter. If women in our time are to grow up—and bring men along with them—they will embrace the attitude of Bessie Smith, a full-figured spout of enormous emotion, from absolute joy to abject loneliness. With the confidence of a woman who has been loved and who has given love and who knows what it all means, she sang in one of her blues numbers: "I'm a big fat mama / Got the meat shakin' on my bones / And every time I shake some skinny gal loses her home."

You better watch that wobble. It can set the world on fire.

August 2003

HAROLD CRUSE

Originally two essays, here combined: the first published as the introduction to The Crisis of the Negro Intellectual *(New York Review Books, 2005), and the second as the foreword to* The Essential Harold Cruse, *edited by Jelani Cobb (St. Martin's Griffin, 2002).*

THE BLUES TOOK THE FORM OF CRISIS

In this book—at times brilliant, sometimes shrill, but seldom unimportant—we are in the presence of a man freeing himself from the abstractions that have attempted to shape him into an abstraction: a man who wants not only to know who he is but who is acting to extend that knowledge existentially, and who insists on establishing his own field of vision. It is, in part, a book about the crises of the intellectual community whatever its shading.

—ARTHUR TOBIER, *COMMONWEAL*, 1968

The Crisis of the Negro Intellectual is a book that stood alone when it was published almost forty years ago in 1967. The civil rights movement had been growing for more than ten years. In 1954, *Brown v. Board of Education* came down from the Supreme Court and school segregation was deemed illegal. It was one hundred and one years after the Emancipation Proclamation and ninety-nine years after the Civil War concluded with the defeat of the Confederate Army, ending the plantation system that was the foundation of chattel slavery. *Brown v. Board of Education* seemed a declaration of war against all of the racist elements that had been put into policy since the War Between the States had ended. Much had happened during that long sweep of American history, and the recent Supreme Court decision, arriving near the middle of the twentieth century, found the Negro still doing battle with one form of racism or another, North or South. It was again a time of war, without a doubt, and it was again being fought in the South, but it was a new kind of conflict. It was nonviolent and drew upon the charisma of men such as Martin Luther King Jr. and the peerless bravery of the Negroes and whites who put their bodies in the way of a terrorist regime, one given to fire bombing, beating, lynching, and any other form of coercion considered necessary to keep the Negro in his rightful place.

The Negroes of the civil rights movement had waged boycotts and called for massive civil disobedience, the filling of jails, and the bringing of normal order to a halt. Their struggle dominated the national news and became an issue of international discussion as barriers were broken down and new laws were passed to ensure the liberation of the Negro from a set of circumstances forming a clear contradiction to the idea of the "land of the free and the home of the brave." Those were turbulent years and, as the questions became more complex, things changed in the North as people began to wonder what form the movement would take as it moved out of the South. The problems that needed to be addressed were seen as calling for something other than integrationist reform. A feeling of ambivalence emerged, especially among the student population. It seemed that something needed to be done beyond what was happening under the nonviolent leadership of the movement. The entire system itself was being reassessed, and it resulted in an unprecedented mood.

Such a mood meant that *The Crisis of the Negro Intellectual* was an immediate success. Throughout the late 1960s and the early 1970s, one could see the signal bright-red cover almost everywhere that young people were gathered. There it was, again and again, under the arms of Negro college students at rallies and the various gatherings occasioned by the intellectual fogginess that was characteristic of the era. The confusion of the period was not merely their problem. It was a confusion that took over the Western world as ideas about revolutionary change began to dominate theories conceived to address issues raging or violently resolving themselves in the Third World as colonialism fell. Some were convinced that Marxist ideas seemed to have better answers than those that could rise from the capitalist democracies, which were defined as impotent and doomed. During that time, those ideas spread throughout the university system and from there into the circles of young people in American society. The rejection of middle-class convention would soon be nationally felt in the vagabond ethos, drug use, and sexual freedom of the hippie movement, all of which were part of the rise of rock-and-roll youth culture. The members of that generation would eventually witness extremists embrace the violent anarchy of terrorist groups such as the Weathermen.

All of this meant the ethnic conflict at the center of the situation American Negroes found themselves in was one of uniquely high pressure. The very specific realities of ethnic conflict meant that rejecting good manners, hygiene, sexual restraint, and all admonitions against wild living and drug use would not lift the Negro out of second-class citizenship. These young Black people were not opposed to action or to commitment. They found themselves not wanting to be bystanders; they did not intend to involve themselves in futile efforts; this generation of Black youth felt a great hunger for some kind of direction that would ensure the full liberation of the Negro. There was a need for a grand strategy and there seemed to be none.

Born shortly before or sometime not long after the end of World War II, these were not the children of segregation who, whether born in the North or the South, went to Negro colleges and planned to become successful in the professions of medicine, law, and education or in the military. This new generation attended integrated colleges around the nation and was influenced by the turbulent currents of the time. For better or for worse they were intellectuals of some kind, meaning they were open to theories that went beyond the conventions under which they had been reared.

Of necessity, every generation of Negroes within the United States had questioned the legalized racism that was a glaring contradiction to the nation's goals and claims, but the young Black people of the mid-1960s were hit with a head-spinning set of ideas that went far beyond mere criticism of the country; not only were capitalism and liberal democracy rejected, but also Christianity was dismissed as unscientific superstition or a tool used by the white folks to control Negroes. It seemed that every day there was some group or some would-be messiah arguing or preaching that Black people had been kept in the darkness for hundreds of years, so much so that they neither knew their African roots nor were capable of seeing the clear facts of their struggle within the appropriate context, be it domestic or international. Within this context, *The Crisis of the Negro Intellectual* veritably flew off the shelves of bookstores because it spoke to the burgeoning Black movements in the late 1960s that would have described themselves as either "nationalist" or "revolutionary."

Until that publication Harold Cruse had been no more than a minor figure who had achieved neither success as a dramatist nor influence as a

thinker. His position had been one of ambition and intellectual engagement that expressed itself in unproduced plays and articles in left-wing
publications that had no impressive readership. With *The Crisis of the
Negro Intellectual*, Cruse was heard loudly and clearly, and his ideas took a
major position in the discourse of the time because those thoughts fiercely
examined integrationist reform. They also clarified the shortcomings and
illusions of both Negro American Black nationalism and the revolutionary pretensions of those intent on, somehow, overthrowing the system.
The book brought forward a good deal of controversy because the thinking was so localized and so independent from the fast and loose applica-
tions of third-world Marxist thought to American circumstances. Cruse
recognized that, with few exceptions, there had always been a deep confusion in the minds of Negroes who even contemplated the intellectual,
cultural, and economic troubles had by Black people due to racism; he also
knew that myopia was as common to whites as it was to Negroes when
any actual ideas were focused on the questions raised by Afro-American
experience in the United States. As an analyst and a thinker he had the
field almost to himself.

The Crisis of the Negro Intellectual seemed to assume that there was a
substantial intellectual tradition among American Negroes. That was neither true forty years ago nor is it true now. Very little arrived that would
challenge the depth of thought found in the works of men such as Ralph
Waldo Emerson, Edmund Wilson, T. S. Eliot, Gilbert Seldes, Lincoln
Kirstein, Malcolm Cowley, Alfred Kazin, and so on. There has never
been a substantial body of thought on any Afro-American subject that
was formed of deep studies, original theories, probing cultural examination, complex religious assessment, and schools of philosophical concern
that raised questions about essences as opposed to superstitions, hearsay,
and propaganda. There have been attempts here and there, usually caught
up in Negro politics or Negro art movements based more in exotica than

the kinds of challenges to convention that jazz brought to the table of Western music. No serious gathering of ideas, as full of yea as of nay, has appeared that was so well conceived and so eloquently expressed that it would add something of value to either American thinking or the larger and more formidable fact of life we call Western thought.

The Crisis of the Negro Intellectual was believed to be such a book at the time that it appeared but was not at all. As the remarkable Black scholar Mia Bay says:

> The book was more about what Cruse thought was right or wrong about the positions that Black people on the left were taking during those years. It was narrowly focused, not comprehensive, and its value to us is in how well it delivers the urgency of his concerns. I think of it as an intellectual memoir that amounts to an autobiography of the politics, cultural thoughts, and aesthetic ideas of Harold Cruse.

Bay is, of course, correct, but that does not reduce the importance of the book or its substance. We are fortunate as readers that Harold Cruse was a man of such wide interests and sensibility, because no one else of his generation produced a book so sweeping and so well argued when focused on particular concerns. Cruse still stands alone. Most of the loudmouths and loons who dominated the ethnic lost genera- tion of the late 1960s and early 1970s remain in memory as no more than embarrassments. Whether they considered themselves "revolu- tionaries" or were given to costumes as part of their romantic fanta- sies about Africa, neither extreme did anything of lasting political or cultural importance. Hot air now seems their specialty. Black Panther founder Huey Newton turned out to be less a revolutionary and more a dope fiend, a gang leader, a murderer, and a thug; Stokely Carmichael descended into the world of rabble-rousing after calling for "Black

Power" in 1966 and never regained serious footing; Rap Brown is now
serving a life sentence for the murder of one Black Atlanta police officer
and the wounding of another; though he has abused his artistic talent
with a shifting body of writing polluted by propaganda, the most lasting thing LeRoi Jones has done since 1965 is change his name to Amiri
Baraka; and most of what were then called "cultural nationalists" have
disappeared into the largely unscholarly world of indoctrination known
as Black studies, which is tolerated by colleges and universities across
the nation in the interest of campus order as opposed to academic
respect. (For fear of alienating Black students, Black academics only
whisper about this problem behind closed doors.) So we must understand that *The Crisis of the Negro Intellectual* was a challenge when it
appeared and now remains before us as an explanatory tombstone, a
rather heavy obituary of a confused era in which its would-be race leaders in politics and the arts neither knew nor understood their roots and
how purely American those roots, like themselves, actually were.

Harold Cruse was very different in that respect because he, like Ralph
Ellison and Albert Murray, was completely aware of his own Americanness and had a grasp of the things that had preceded him and that defined
the terms of the life that he was living. Big theories that swept together
enormous populations on different continents were of no interest to him
because Cruse was conscious of how unique the life and the experience
of the Negro in America had become over many generations. The Negro
was not a colonial, like Africans and West Indians; the Negro had not
been a serf who graduated to a lower-class worker, like many Europeans,
nor was the Negro a peasant in the classic meaning because the elasticity
of American society allowed for a unique freedom of movement. The tra-
vail and evolution of the Negro began in American slavery and had been
much more diffuse in the texture of experience than any simplistic definitions would have it.

Perhaps what made Cruse so different from the conventional Negroes of the time is that his book has none of the contempt for black people that was so common to the influential rhetoric of Malcolm X. To be sure, many things ticked Cruse off, but they were seen as part of the overall intellectual imprecision of a nation that was not up to thinking very clearly about the ethnic aspects of its identity. Cruse was not so broad in his strokes that all of the problems in America and Europe could be described as "white"; he was too sophisticated to think all Africans and those possessed of African blood could be considered "Black" and, therefore, somehow closely related in potential, purpose, and ambition. His sense of ethnicity brought observations about ethnic breakdowns of power within "white" society, which far too often was not examined in terms of its Christian and Jewish components but which Cruse did not ignore.

Part of what Cruse thought of as "the crisis" was grounded in coming to terms with the complexity of all that was obscured by the prevalence of broad and basically useless categories. Black nationalist separatism was essentially defeatist and not so much a message of hope as a form of hostile resignation. Revolution was no more than a fantasy because the weapons necessary and the amount of popular national support were neither at hand nor inclined to be supportive of tearing down the government, killing off or defeating the military and law enforcement. In both ethnic "ideologies" the future was never original; it was always based on a Hollywood vision of paradise regained or the "workers' paradise" so clumsily depicted in posters from Communist China, Russia, or Cuba. Both Hollywood and the totalitarian Marxist regimes had the same low level of confidence in the ability of the masses to address complicated materials, which meant that the cartoon or something very close to it was the conventional means of communicating what was considered a revolutionary agenda.

Cruse bought none of it and took all of the ideas on and discussed them as though they were actually born of serious intent. The writer

Playthell Benjamin met Harold Cruse about a year before the book came out. He met him through Max Stanford, who was looking for a more radical alternative to the civil rights movement. Stanford was a student at Central State, a Black college in Ohio, that was not so far from Antioch. He and Benjamin had grown disillusioned with the reformist ideology of the civil rights movement and were involved in their own revolutionary fantasies. They were both aware of Harold Cruse because he had written an essay in the journal *Studies on the Left*, which was called "Revolutionary Nationalism and the Afro-American." The essay really shook up Stanford and Benjamin because it made revolutionary nationalism of the sort they were drifting toward seem insipid and futile. The two went to see him.

"At that time," remembers Benjamin,

Harold Cruse was living at 14th Street and Seventh Avenue in New York City. It was a walk-up and he had the top floor. He had newspapers and magazines stacked up to the ceiling all the way around the apartment. He seemed to be busy reading everything that came out at the time. Some of the magazines were well known and some were obscure journals. At that time, he was working on *Crisis*. I remember him having glasses hanging on his nose. What he was saying was complex and nuanced, so much so that it wasn't clear what he was saying. In reality, his frames of reference were so much larger than ours that he frequently lost us. When asked if he thought it was possible to bring about a revolution in America, Cruse said it was possible if the revolutionaries could figure out how to neutralize CBS, NBC, and ABC. That's how brilliant he was. Nobody at that time was talking about the importance of the mass media, which is now common wisdom, but almost forty years ago Harold Cruse understood how crucial an aspect mass communications were to modern life and to the political thought and mood of a nation as large and complex as the United States.

That is not all that Harold Cruse understood. He had a large vision and a sense of how many, many things made up the reality of American life in ethnic, political, cultural, and aesthetic terms. *The Crisis of the Negro Intellectual* has been called many things over the years but brilliant and provocative are the two most important and lasting descriptions of a work that will have a very long shelf life in our pursuit of a comprehensive American identity.

BLUES FOR BROTHER CRUSE

Even these many years later, the bulk of what Harold Cruse has written remains surprising. That is because it is always surprising to read anyone who thinks about Negro Americans as both part of a particular cultural development and part of the overall question of American identity. Far, far too often there is a segregated vision of Black Americans as though they could have lived in this country—as chattel or not—for close to four hundred years yet function forever outside of the context of the nation. Because of that both uninformed and irresponsible vision, there is little argument, analysis, and deduction about the virtues and the troubles of color within the contexts of the aesthetic, the social, the political, and the economic planes of human life. There is no sense of the varieties and victories and failures of engagement within the mobile and not-so-mobile realities of American life. A set of clichés once dominated and continues to dominate discussion, the only changes amounting to newly shaped bottles for old slop.

Cruse did not have that problem because he was always thinking about something far more complex than what was expected in the discussion of racial matters. His work—while sometimes right and sometimes either wrong or optimistically naive or incomplete—was much more consistently insightful or substantial in its reporting than what could be expected from those who condescendingly considered themselves "radical" or "progressive." I am referring to those who were always willing to resort to a theoretical basis for taking on the problems of American life. This was true even if those theories were not based in the facts of that very life they assumed would change for the better if the ideology to which these "progressives" adhered took over the terms of thought and action. Which, as we know, never happened.

Today, it is easy to talk about so-called Black or so-called white, but one almost never reads any discussion of what Cruse takes on when looking at the matrix of what he calls "white protestants, white Catholics, and white Jews," obviously alluding to the fact that there are Black versions of all three. This is especially profound because it makes it clear that there has never been the kind of monolithic ethnicity based solely on color some would have us believe. This means we have to look at how ethnic backgrounds and Americana at large combine to create certain points of view—with all the possibilities for surprise that human nature makes nearly inevitable.

The reason that almost no one would talk of such a matrix now is not because it has disappeared but because to suggest that Jews, in particular, have any kind of cultural power, especially in the world of the arts, is to run the risk of being accused of anti-Semitism. That is because there are those who remember well the Black Power years when, among its most hysterical advocates, anti-Semitism became an article of racist faith. (LeRoi Jones almost singlehandedly introduced this into Black politics and it is, therefore, quite interesting to read how Cruse assessed him and the saxophonist Archie Shepp, who were both married to white women, living in New York's East Village, and working out what was then a stage animus indicative of the pollution to come.) So any mention of Jews having power and influence now zooms us back to that low point in aspects of our national discourse focused on the dilemmas wrought by color prejudice or misdirected support or cultural envy. Cruse, however, was not promoting bigotry, he was trying to understand how we all contribute to the majesty and the morass of Americana. He was intent on solving or delineating a riddle with assessments based upon actual experience and very close observations of the varied ethnic worlds in which he lived and moved. This thinker was not willing to have a theory handed to him after he came to maturity.

Cruse was also unafraid to call forth opinions and observations from a world far too often veiled by stereotypes or inadequate assessment. Negroes did actually think things and did actually agree and disagree and did actually have allegiance to or hostility toward each other on the basis of what classes they were from and what parts of the country they were from and whether or not they were actually natives or came into this country with all the prejudices that Black colonials could have toward the Black descendants of people who had been central to the making of American culture. In short, no matter how far removed from so-called intellectual consensus what he heard among Black people might have been, Cruse was willing to put it on the table and move from there, giving us much to think about within the parameters of the periods in which he was writing. He raises very serious aesthetic questions when discussing the work, the thought, the politics, and the careers of Gilbert Seldes, Lorraine Hansberry, Josephine Baker, James Baldwin, Nat Cole, and Harry Belafonte, as examples. Those questions move from the arena of art and entertainment to the complex of regions of race, convention, aspirations, individual and group identity, and so on.

If he is talking about Greenwich Village forty years ago, Cruse lets us in on the dynamics that dictated the behavior that was once rebellious and isolated but is now, we can easily see, part of the popular menu in which dissent from certain social conventions has become no more than another commodity pumped out by MTV and BET. At the time, however, Cruse moved into very fresh areas by putting bohemian rebellion within an over-all American frame. He saw—as no American novelists or screenwriters or playwrights then did—that the social and sexual freedoms of Greenwich Village were taken seriously by some and were no more than slumming rights for others. Those who were serious were attracted to a world less racially repressive or intellectually vacant. Some such Negroes were only on the make for the kinds of whites ready to jump into bed and "go native" in the Village bush. Cruse also added to the record the fact that Negroes had been downtown for a few hundred years and, therefore, were not new-comers to that part of Manhattan, which sent up the idea that they were social interlopers. Then, as now, there was no interest on the part of white liberals in the Americanness of Negroes. That Americanness almost inev-itably predates the ancestry of those given the opportunity by skin tone to look down on those with far deeper historical and cultural roots.

We can, therefore, see in this gathering of work that Cruse was on the case long before the 1967 publication of his monumental work, *The Crisis of the Negro Intellectual*. In fact, when we look at his other work, we under-stand how he was able to bring off so important a work as *Crisis*, which dwarfed almost all other books of the period when it came to bringing together politics, art, and social movements related to or inspired by the Afro-American condition. With that book, Cruse did, in his own way, what Ralph Ellison and Albert Murray have become either well known or barely known for arguing. He recognized that the call and response between the Negro and America at large is central to what Negroes became and what this nation became.

But when *The Crisis of the Negro Intellectual* was published, there was no plethora of Black studies programs across the country, there was hardly any recognition of the fact that anything like a Black intellectual even existed. In 1967, however, Ellison published his extraordinary collection of essays, *Shadow and Act*, which took the discussion of the Negro and of America to such heights that Stanley Edgar Hyman deemed him the finest critic of American culture at large. Murray's reputation was years away and still remains small, even though he produced far more material than Ellison did while living—one novel and two books of essays.

Harold Cruse, however, was not necessarily in dialogue with either man. He was announcing that there was a crisis in the world of the Negro intellectual and that its causes were far from simple. At this point, we can understand how poorly understood meanings of culture and cultural life and group independence can create a reductive vision shared by both the layperson and the intellectual. The crisis Cruse was onto thirty-five years ago has spread out into Afro-American culture at large and is currently celebrated as some sort of a liberation from "white middle-class values," meaning that thug scum, whorish behavior, drooling materialism, and all of the dictates of "street knowledge" somehow provide an alternative to restrictive, external values. Cruse understood how all of that is wound up in the American quest for something beyond where someone starts, which is a quintessential issue. He surely recognized how color and career and class and art and economic support and sex and pretension and would-be radical politics all fuse in the arena of identity—lawd, lawd, lawd. That recognition makes this collection,* whatever one's disagreements with particular parts might be, a truly powerful addition to understanding who we are and where we came from and, perhaps, where we are going.

---

* *The Essential Harold Cruse.*

INVENTION ON
THE BLACK WILLIE BLUES

Part one excerpt of a two-part essay, S.C. in a dialogue with Playthell Benjamin on the life, work, and legacy of W. E. B. Du Bois, published in Reconsidering the Souls of Black Folk *(Running Press, 2003).*

An American can read almost anything about the past and feel as if he or she has already been there, especially if the topic is the strife provoked by relationships that are based on race, which are so complex and cross so much territory that they are basic to any accurately epic sense of the history of this nation. These conflicted relationships also reflect a certain body of argued ideas about ancestry, blood, scientifically proven distinction, culture, intellectual capacity, and civilization. With these arguments in place and the events that resulted from them, it should be far easier now to clearly see how the Negro fits into the history of this nation, and how the part of West Africa—from which that ancestral side comes—fits in as well. Yet, that is far from true even now, and when we find ourselves contemplating W. E. B. Du Bois and his life as well as his times, it is obvious that there is a vast tradition that precedes him in the realms of reason and irrationality, the former sometimes so connected to the latter that we must call into question almost everything we have ever thought was stable and everything that we thought had any one answer, any single victim, any one-sided way of looking at things.

We cannot deny that, for a few hundred years, American men in power who were white, and also those who were not powerful but had the cachet of skin privilege, did terrible things to those who were sold into America as slaves or who were free men and women but of African descent. We should also note that some American men and women who were white did far more in opposition to the enslavement of Negroes than anyone in Africa did or even considered doing. Though we can brag about the democratic ideas that came from the Founding Fathers, we can also point at how even men of genius, such as Thomas Jefferson, were mightily flawed when it came to matters of color and bondage. At the same time that we can self-righteously talk of the hypocrisy of white Americans, we must also acknowledge that had the most enlightened of them not been willing to push an abolitionist's agenda for so long—and had thousands upon thousands of others not been willing to lay down their lives to hasten the destruction of the slave system—our history would be very, very different.

So it is all a mixed bag of fact, passion, rhetoric, superstition, junk science, technology, economics, and religious belief that makes the story of the Negro in America so complex. The life and thought of Du Bois are at the center of the best to the worst aspects of that story. It is the tale of an intellectual who championed some of the best and the worst of the ideas proposed to make the world better for Negroes. That bag of troubles formed the kind of mess that Du Bois found himself facing throughout his lifetime and the same kind of mess—part brilliant, part ridiculous—that one finds in his own thinking when it comes to defining the meaning of race, of heritage, and group potential that he tries to order in his *The Souls of Black Folk*. What made Du Bois important, however, was the fact that he had a high level of intelligence joined with a bracing and charismatic arrogance that caused him to assume before he was twenty-five, while he was still a student in Germany, that he would make an impression on the world. Oh, yeah: the young brown-skinned man from Barrington, Massachusetts, had a messianic sense of his fate, which is to say that on some level he assumed his role would be to teach people the profound things that they desperately needed to know if they were ever to save themselves from the narrows of misinformation, superstition, and manipulative lies. The ordinary messiah often has a religious message that rocks the wall and turns the present order into Humpty Dumpty. In the case of Black Willie from New England, the message was political and cultural primarily because the question of color was so twisted up in the nation's politics and in the assumptions underlying the "correct way of living" that abided a racist hierarchy.

As a man who can be called nothing other than an intellectual, Du Bois inherited not so much the "zeitgeist of the age," as Mr. Benjamin puts it, but the ideas that purified a body of thought and were extraordinarily complex because of the intricacy of the human situations out of which they arrived. They were ideas that came forward during the Age of Reason and were refined through great struggle within the United States, where the African slave trade, Afro-American bondage, the Enlightenment, the American Revolution, and the epoch-making Industrial Revolution, that mechanical enforcer of the idea of progress, all these concepts wove themselves together and inspired a new thing, a fresh perspective. That new thing came to define the possibilities of democracy through the demanding means of representative government, public argument, bloody constraints, and political positions that evolved—by way of the checks and balances process inspired by Montaigne—into the specific dictates of policy determined by the rule of law. In terms of social rights, those unprecedented aspects of democratic identity arrived within a context of ongoing reconsideration that led to an innovatively broad reassessment of human equality that eventually moved across the lines of color and sex.

While the completion of the process did not arrive in his lifetime, Du Bois knew that shifts in society, the motion of rights and privileges across lines that finally did come to fruition because of the quality of ongoing reconsideration, were not what the Founding Fathers had in mind when they drew up and ratified the Constitution. That, finally, means nothing of significance in terms of the ideas themselves. After all, because our democracy posits the idea that greatness can arrive from under the very filthiest soles of the society or from the humblest of beginnings, we should not be so sentimentally shocked or disappointed or outraged or grow too, too self-righteous when that rule spins around and we see that those at the top turn out to be low-down and rotten—even given to stinking up their private lives with the fumes of avarice, opportunism, and greed—but remain, however comfortable within their shells of bigotry, capable of producing unprecedented pearls of social vision. That is how it actually was.

That is not all of how it was, however. What has to be said clearly and with no drop in volume is that, just as unintentionally as the Founding Fathers, the bush league kings of West Africa—lovers of umbrellas, rum, and rifles—made their greatest contribution to the world in the past five hundred years by selling other Africans into the Western Hemisphere, especially those who arrived in America. The consequences were huge, and those primitive kings have to be given, with a sense of tragic irony, the same kind of slack as the Founding Fathers, but for very different reasons.

Let us get very clear, as the subjects are individual liberty and democracy, they are issues of such great significance that once in America, Alexis de Tocqueville realized that the democratic form of government the Founding Fathers created to bring order to the United States was relevant to the future of the world at large, not just a former set of British colonies.

The democratic ideals written into the Declaration of Independence and the Constitution were so profoundly important—when taken seriously by the people of the United States—that the South had to be beaten within an inch of its life once enough people realized that a country could not exist half-slave and half-free. As far as those ideals and the questions that they raised went, the kings of West Africa provided no ideas—or ideals—of any democratic importance because there was nothing inside the "pure" African vision of life itself that would have ever led to the end of the slave trade, primarily because tribalism—which is the father of racism, by the way—was in full and bloody swing. That ethnic enmity was so strong that all was possible. But from beneath the tribal dress that identified these bigots, and even when accompanied by majestic and intricate polyrhythms produced with hands attuned to the nuances of drums, no inspiring pearls of social philosophy ascended. None. Absolutely.

Further, the slave trade in Africa met resistance here and there, mounted by such as the Christian King Alfonso I of the Congo and the Angolan Queen Nzinga, Alfonso following the dictates of the Bible, Nzinga aiming to free her country from the rule of the Portuguese. But these examples are not really germane to the point, because, as George Steiner points out in *In Bluebeard's Castle*, our Western culture is one in which the fall of a convention almost always comes from within, not from without. As is more than slightly evident, the African regimes committed to slavery were devoid of the kinds of internal arguments and the movements to abolish slavery—in the interest of other ethnic groups—that had a considerable history, for instance, in a city such as Philadelphia and its surroundings. These were the kinds of arguments that the young Du Bois intended to sustain and to use in order to redress the arrogantly thick, bloody, and sticky residue of racism. His knowledge and his imagination were dedicated to things that were not of any importance within the traditional African context.

This cannot be set aside if we are to address the thinking of a man more than a few consider a major intellectual. While Playthell Benjamin exaggerates its actual value and more than generously celebrates the young Du Bois's 1890 commencement talk on Jefferson Davis—given that it was an argument of the sort that had been made by certain critical Negroes more than forty years earlier—I think my point can be better made by quoting one aspect of his discussion of the tradition of the Strong Man, referring to the Goths and the Visigoths who sacked Rome, "The Teutonic met civilization and crushed it—the Negro met civilization and was crushed by it." Perhaps the Negro in Africa had already been crushed before "meeting" civilization. In Ghana is Salaga, which was a major port of slave sale back in those days when the area was known as the Gold Coast. On the BBC, the major king of Salaga recently said for the record:

> Salaga is in the southern part of the northern region. Salaga was an old slave market. Caravans used to come all the way from northern Nigeria and other places, Burkina Faso, Mali, and so on. Salaga became important for its market in human beings.
>
> The slaves were brought in here. There were places to store them, and most of the time they were actually tied around trees in the market. There were just one or two rooms that can even be seen up to this date. But most of the time they were tied around, big, big trees, guava trees, close to the markets.

The regent went on to say that with hindsight, he and his subjects feel remorse over what their ancestors did. But at the time, it was only normal. Just as in our day, it was a market, and people were buying.

Unlike the majority who showed a lack of concern in Africa by supporting slavery or ignoring its existence, certain religious and successful men in the America of the late seventeenth century as well as the eighteenth and nineteenth centuries—Quakers, Methodists, and Presbyterians early on—made resolutions, organized societies, and worked against the dirty blues wrought by that so "peculiar institution." From such people descended early supporters of Du Bois. These were special people. In the last quarter of the eighteenth century, Quakers expelled from their congregations any who refused to free their slaves. Their official public expression of disagreement with the business of slavery in the environs of the City of Brotherly Love began in 1688 when four German Quakers raised their voices against the trade in Germantown, which was then just outside of Philadelphia.

True: There were surely limitations within the anti-slavery perspective that cannot be denied. They rhyme with the troubles Du Bois had when his career ambitions were not seen as the kind that would do his ethnic group any good. In hard fact, not all were even up to being moral Cub Scouts and Campfire Girls. One strain of the abolitionists who sought to end slavery thought Black people inferior and would, therefore, now have to be considered akin to members of a fervent society for the prevention of cruelty to animals. Even so, the ups and downs of the developing abolition movement in America had no parallels of any sort in Africa; this was a purely Western phenomenon played out in a nation that was defining itself on the run, on the go, in motion, as it settled and fought and slaughtered its way into an ever larger land mass. Yet, however hard that might be to deal with in such self-flagellating times as these, wrap your mind around this: Those sustaining the idea of freeing the slaves were Christians, who are so often addressed exclusively as hypocrites. Without a doubt many were, and some were quite willing to use the Bible to excuse the sale of human beings. There were also those who were not willing and did not choose to hold their silence over the matter either.

At the same time, in order to understand the world that Du Bois inherited, we have to look at the arguments against slavery as another aspect of progression—when it actually progresses—in which an essential aspect of social evolution and democratic ideas rose up against monarchies. While Europeans were concerned with monarchies of religion and class, Negroes in America had first to struggle against monarchies that were based on color, which is what each plantation actually was. This was equally true but far, far less brutal in the ethnic pecking order beyond the plantations in the North. (Though there were cases such as the one of Philadelphia in which Negroes remained at home after the Fourth of July celebration of 1805, when drunken white mobs attacked Black people as if they had not the right to enjoy a national holiday, even though thousands of them had done plenty of what historian Ira Berlin in his illuminating *Many Thousands Gone* calls "the dirty work of war.")

In this northern world of slave and half-free and free Blacks, the fight for recognition of the Negro's humanity should also be comprehended as part of the extraordinary battle against hierarchy, and Du Bois can surely be seen as one who chose to join up. That very battle, in all of its breadth, could quite easily be the most monumental reinterpretation of social and natural rights in the history of the species, especially as it has expanded over the past one hundred fifty years to include not only all colors and nationalities as well as both sexes, but also labor issues and sexual issues such as harassment in the workplace. As a lover of the pastoral, I'm sure that Du Bois would be glad to know that this battle against hierarchy has evolved to embrace lower forms of animal life and even the inanimate environment, primarily because all of its most high-minded aspects can be reduced to something as simple but as fundamental as the Golden Rule of doing unto others as . . . (Though, at its worst, such struggles with hierarchy have brought about a bullshit academic vision of leveling that pretends all things are "culturally determined," meaning that there is no such thing as a fact that is good or bad, high or low, great or insignificant—which is as insipid as the idea of innate superiority based in assumed value.)

The central value of democracy is the rejection of prestige and power that are based on ancestry (a tenet of what Du Bois continued to lay before the United States). So in a profound sense, the struggle of the Negro within the context of the American experiment was the most important post-Enlightenment battle with hierarchy because it took on issues of individual liberty and argued against the clenched fist of superstition that is the idea of race, which was basic to hierarchy in the United States. Yet part of what those Black people had to argue against came from the Enlightenment in its initial form, which we usually think of as a body of ideas rooted in reason and a rejection of the power of the church in favor of science and philosophical deduction. So far so good but not good enough when an unsentimental pupil is cast upon the eighteenth century. Both the science and the nature of the deductions in the area of color were not only off, they were racist to the core and prove out why skepticism should be basic to the democratic mind and sensibility. In the face of so much external agreement by men of letters and respected adherents to what we now call the scientific method, those Negroes proved themselves farseeing marvels in their confrontations with science as it was thought of over the century preceding the birth of "Black Willie." They eloquently rejected the purported reason underlying the science of the time and championed an idea about universal humanity that would later—much, much later—be borne out by brain research, blood plasma, DNA, organ transplants, and all of the other things that can now be proven.

A good deal of what Du Bois's predecessors had to face, when we step all the way down into the snake pit of racism, is located in the assumptions focused upon physiognomy because the Negro, of all of those people whom we do not associate with Europe, looks least like the white man and the white woman. The Negro is darker in skin tone, has thicker lips more often than not, does not possess as wide a range of eye color, and has, in kinky or nappy hair, a quality that is separate from that of the European, the American Indian, the Indians of India, and the Asians who have impressed the West since the expeditions into China that produced the imitative European trend of chinoiserie in the seventeenth century, when things Chinese took on status as both exotic and highly refined. Because Europeans and Americans who arrived after the Renaissance were given to imitating nothing from Black Africa before the start of the twentieth century, they were left with what academics now call "the Black body." Thomas Jefferson, for one, thought Negroes somehow less human because their skin tone did not give in to blushing and, therefore, made their emotions more mysterious and less obvious to the eye. So once that Negro was accepted as a human being, not a lower order, everybody else had a much easier ride. An idea about human equality began its most difficult journey—which is to move beyond physiognomy—and may well be said to have set the stage for the United Nations, which stands as a paean to universal humanity, however jive the nature of politics and alliances sometimes makes the organization seem. Du Bois was a child of that version of the Enlightenment perspective, those ideas, the most important rejection of racism in the history of the modern world, a turning away from the high-toned rhetoric of tribalism that gave the provincial version of the Age of Reason an intellectual stench, which had to be washed away so that the fundamental union of humankind could be apprehended. That is the door through which he enters history. What we now know, in fact, due to Mia Bay's *The White Image in the Black Mind*, is that almost every idea and stance that we associate with Du Bois at the time of *The Souls of Black Folk* had its precedents in the eloquent and brave refutations of racist ideology and the rejection of the "rightness" of the slave system by Negro Americans who had showered down the rebuttals and counteraccusations by 1835.

But in order to put all of these things in the right perspective, we have to take another kind of a look at the decades that preceded Du Bois, understanding that what we will see is that Afro-American history basically breaks down into three parts—slavery from 1619 to 1865, Reconstruction from 1865 to 1877, and the struggle for local and national civil rights that did not finish until 1968, when the civil rights movement ended shortly after half of Martin Luther King Jr.'s face was blown off as he stood on the balcony of the Lorraine Motel in Memphis, Tennessee. Du Bois had died only five years earlier at ninety-five, having finished out his life in Ghana too soon to see how his shared fantasies of Pan-Africanism would confuse and mislead the young American Negroes who then thought themselves radicals and were beginning to pretend that they were Africans "lost" in America.

THE ADMIRAL AND THE DUKE

Ford was always the admiral. He was the admiral on the set . . .
and everybody else was just sort of an enlisted seaman.

—SCOTT EYMAN, *JOHN FORD: THE COMPLETE FILMS*

T HE GREATEST ADMIRAL in the history of American popular art
was John Ford, and he famously worked with one of its two great
dukes—John Wayne (the other, of course, being Edward Kennedy Ellington). Recognizing the greatness of Wayne or Ford is particularly difficult
today because there have been so many chastening disappointments since
the McCarthy era, Watergate, and Vietnam. The abuses of power, these
corruptions and debacles, have resulted in love of America being too often
defined as a dangerous form of superstition. From that perspective, Ford
is looked upon with impatient contempt while Wayne is dismissed as no
more than a steel-balled Red-baiter.

Ford was surely patriotic but not in a simple way; his best work always
contains a celebration of the nation and of its mythologies as well as a
rough-and-tumble listing of its inherent troubles. Ford understood that
America's essential anti-aristocratic attitude was good as long as it brought
forth a vitality that was heroic and possessed of a sacrificial sense of duty.

But he also knew that the common man was not above submitting to the delicious fever of anarchy or becoming a happy member of a lynch mob. Perhaps worst of all, as Ford tells us, is that the sheer weight of a man's pain and loss can transform him in despicable ways.

In *The Searchers* (1956), the admiral used the Duke to tell his most harrowing tragedy in the Homeric world of the Old West. *The Searchers* is about the wages of heartbreak and what they do to Ethan Edwards, the film's conflicted and difficult hero. Edwards is the ultimate loser: Everything—from a woman to a family to a cause—has evaded his grasp, been destroyed or defeated. At the beginning of the movie, he returns to Texas to see his only remaining relatives, and we discover that he has lost his true and secret love, Martha, to his brother, Aaron. He was also on the losing side of the Civil War. Then Martha and Aaron and two of their three children are massacred during a Comanche raid.

When Wayne, as Ethan, comes upon the black smoke and the orange flame of the burning house left by the Comanches, his face is one of absolute terror, panic, and rage. At the top of a hill, Wayne flings out his right arm to free his rifle from the long, colorful buckskin sleeve in which it has been sheathed. The force of that flung arm is one of the most explosive gestures in all of cinema, and also among the most impotent: No one down there is alive, and Ethan knows it. He is, at that moment, like the man in Bruegel's *The Triumph of Death* who so impressed Hemingway because his choice was to draw a sword when faced with the irreversible horror of encroaching doom.

The wonder of the film and Wayne's performance is how well it details the way in which his character's suffering completely transforms him. Ethan devolves from a resourceful cynic who is quite knowledgeable of Indian ways of fighting, hunting, fleeing, and worshiping into an indomitable redneck. Though culturally part Comanche himself, Ethan is willing to murder his own kidnapped niece in order to avenge the slaughtered members of her family. That willingness arrives through the racist bile chilling his soul at the very thought of his niece having slept with an Indian chief as but *one* of his wives.

Masterfully, Ford lets us realize that this is merely a darker version of the resentment Ethan felt toward the sexual relationship between Martha and Aaron. It is also an example of the exceeding achievement of the film: a matchless pictorial sense of narrative in which every action or situation has an apparent and an alternate meaning. *The Searchers* questions a raw bigotry so pervasive that, to our surprise, the salt-of-the-earth blond woman in a white silk dress on her wedding day furiously spits out a murderous sense of self-righteous xenophobia.

In the 1939 *Stagecoach* and the 1946 *My Darling Clementine*, Ford elevated the genre from a child's throwaway 90 minutes in front of a theater screen to a fully adult entertainment. By *Fort Apache* in 1948, Ford turned the conventions of the Western around by refusing to condescend to the humanity of the Indian. Henry Fonda's Lt. Col. Owen Thursday is deeply concerned with the welfare of his daughter (a somewhat monstrous and adolescent Shirley Temple); he feels thrown aside to a meaningless command in the Southwest and is obsessed with personal glory to the point of leading his troop to doom. The commander and his men are massacred primarily because he will not accept the Apaches as shrewd equals at warfare. Caught in class and race prejudice, Thursday is a melancholy and misplaced man made tragically naive by his bigotry.

No director has ever dealt more insightfully with the offhanded, snide, and potentially suicidal aspects of bigotry than Ford. This sets him above almost all other directors because he could understand and make art of the tragedies that attended bigotry, one of the most pernicious forms of superstition. Beyond that, Ford recognizes how community acts as a protection against the inevitable meaninglessness of human life, which is no more than anarchic energy unless put in a story of some sort.

But, as Ford tells us in *The Wings of Eagles* (1957), no amount of horse-play, drinking, flying, commendations, and skill make a man amount to much more than a frail toy buffeted by chance. Superbly inhabited by Wayne, Spig Wead, the seemingly invincible but suddenly crippled airman, has lost his family through neglect and is alone with all of his successes and failures at the end of the film. Wead is another of Ford's impotent heroes who, like Ethan Edwards, has no home other than the memories of what his dreams *might* have meant if any of them had ever come true.

September 2006

SHUT UP, SCARLETT!

A s those interested in our popular culture should know, this is the seventieth anniversary of the release of the 1939 *Gone With the Wind*, which the estimable Molly Haskell so recently praised in her book, *Frankly, My Dear.* Good for Haskell, but I always realize that I have never liked *Gone With the Wind* and have liked it less and less over the years because there is no evidence to support what critic Richard Schickel correctly called "the South's yokel notion that it once supported a new age of chivalry and grace."

Yet I have found that there are unexpected others who do adore the film. One of them included a Black college student of mine named Hubert. On a privileged California campus during the Black studies heyday of pretentious hostility toward white people, Hubert nearly stunned me in the early 1970s by unabashedly loving the film because Clark Gable was "sharp as a *motherfucker.*" Obsessively having seen the film a number of times, Hubert had counted *every one* of Gable's costume changes and could run each of them down. That's actual Americana for you, always stronger than race politics.

My mother also liked *GWTW* because she thought that Gable was "almost as handsome as Duke Ellington." However, grandmother, whose married name was Matilda Ford but was nicknamed Day-Day, did not have a taste for the most famous cinematic lie about supposedly refined rednecks since 1915's *The Birth of a Nation*. As was her patented way, Day-Day made her distaste for the movie shockingly and audibly clear one afternoon among well-to-do white folks.

In 1954, there was a re-release of the first blockbuster, and it was being shown at the fancy Carthay Circle Theatre in West Los Angeles. My mother was very excited about taking her mama, my baby sister, and me out to a movie house much better than the Lincoln Theatre on Central Avenue, which was near our home in what is now known as South Central Los Angeles. That section of town was just the "East Side" then, and the Lincoln, which had already seen its glory days of Negro jazz bands, comedians, jugglers, dancers, and magicians, was run down, as were all of the movie theaters in the working-class Black community. None of them showed first-run movies.

On Saturdays at the Lincoln, popcorn boxes folded flat were thrown into the air during intermission. Kids hooted, screamed, and shouted as one sat back in worn seats with feet sometimes turned on their shoe edges because the floors were sticky from spilled sodas and whatever else made them sticky. There were advertisements that had been shown so many times that they were crackling, hissing images. Among them were 7-Up advertisements in which we could see Negroes living the way middle-class Black people do in television advertisements now. These advertisement Black people were quite exotic to all of us because we knew no one anywhere in Los Angeles who lived as 7-Up told us that they did: families traveling together to spacious parks and playing games we did not know

in very neat casual clothes but never once eating any barbecue, which usually went with Black family outings to the park. Odd. Maybe there was
another state where one could find Negroes like those. We didn't know.

So traveling out to the Carthay Circle Theatre in West Los Angeles
on San Vincente Boulevard was a big deal. Only first-run movies were
shown there, and people dressed up to attend them. The Carthay Circle
had been highly regarded since the Spanish-style film palace had opened
in 1926 but was to be destroyed and replaced by a bland office building
in 1969, nine years after my grandmother died and more than a decade
following the afternoon that Day-Day proved herself much more ready
for Scarlett O'Hara than either Hattie McDaniel or Butterfly McQueen.

My grandmother could not respond in a silent way to things that
she did not like. It was even more difficult if she saw something that
she actually hated and would not have accepted if done to her. That day,
when Vivien Leigh's Scarlett O'Hara slapped Butterfly McQueen's Prissy
for being what Clark Gable's Rhett Butler called "a simple darkie," the
white audience roared with laughter. But Day-Day was appalled. Matilda
Ford immediately silenced the laughing audience when she shouted with
irrepressible anger, "Hit her *back!* You *better* hit that heifer back!" You
couldn't hear a peep in the theater for the rest of the movie.

My maternal grandmother was like that and had *always* been. Her
sensibility was the same as those pioneer women who walked next to the
wagon trains, fought Indians, and settled those towns in the Old West.
Day-Day was a family legend because of feats that lodged in anybody's
mind that either saw or heard about them. Like her husband, Lilborn
Ford, she "treated everybody like they was one color," as one of my grand
uncles described the two of them. Lilborn was known as a "crazy nigger"
because he took no stuff and was ready to die on the spot if anybody got
out of line. He was, however, no more hard-to-handle than his wife, who
stood less than five feet tall, had hands a little large for her petite size, and

the kind of resolute stare that left little doubt as to what she was thinking if on the verge of being riled.

Born the daughter of an African sailor from Madagascar and a Choctaw woman from Mississippi some time around 1890, Day-Day began to acquire her reputation early on. She first got her gossip bars as a defender of herself when she took a mop with a very heavy handle to a Negro bully whom she knocked cold and who used to come through her neighborhood in Jefferson, Texas, with no good on his mind.

She crossed the color line in her refusal to take any stuff when the white judge of Jefferson drove over the hoof of her buggy horse as she and sister Mary were enjoying themselves. The new-fangled metal contraption left their animal wheezing, moaning, and screeching as only a horse does.

The irritated judge said the roads were no longer for horse flesh but for au-to-mobiles. "You little nigger girls need to stay off these roads now," he said. Snatching the buggy whip, Day-Day got out, went to the door of the strange machine, began pulling the door handle, and demanded that the man get out. The judge's wife cooed that Day-Day and her sister were only little girls and he should ignore them. "Little girls, hell," replied my grandmother. "You let that redhead son of a bitch out of this damn thing and we will beat the shit out of him."

The judge did not get out.

When her family moved to Los Angeles in the mid-1930s, Day-Day sometimes worked as a domestic and found it necessary to pour ice water on the security blankets of entitlement some of the white women she worked for tried to wear with customary ease. Matilda Ford was obviously not well made for the servant class. She bought rental property in Los Angeles after her husband died in the early 1940s and also owned a chili joint in Bakersfield, a hot and dry town one hundred ten miles north of L.A. Bakersfield was where rough and country Negroes picked cotton all week but then, full of that cheap wine carried in brown paper bags and called "short dogs," might cut each other with pocket knives all through the weekend.

Day-Day was ready for them. A .45 was worn under her apron, just as I found when spending the night at her house that there was a pistol under each of the pillows on her bed. (You could come up with a handful of harm no matter what side of the bed you slept on.) She also had a pistol in the glove compartment of her mint-green Pontiac, and I saw her pull it on a man and threaten to blow his head off when he came to her car window, calling her everything but a child of God and threatening to put his foot in her ass for slowing down traffic to let a goddam woman cross the street. I had never and have never since seen such a quick reversal of mood and etiquette. It was as if the man had been suddenly and magically turned from a ruffian to a knight luminously intent upon upholding Day-Day's honor.

When not ruffled by drivers or knuckleheads or Scarlett O'Hara, Day-Day was one of the sweetest people you would ever meet. Whenever contemplating the role John Wayne played as the seasoned gunfighter in *The Shootist*, another movie beaming out from the screen, I have sometimes thought of my grandmother when Duke says in a tone of magisterial melancholy, "I won't be wronged. I won't be insulted. I won't be laid a-hand on. I don't do these things to other people, and I require the same from them."

December 2009

BETTE DAVIS

THE GREATEST WHITE BITCH OF ALL

"In my day we didn't talk much about happiness. If it came, we were grateful for it. But we were brought up in the belief that there were other things more important."

"What things?"

"Oh, old fogey fantastic notions such as duty and personal responsibility."

IN THIS OUR LIFE WAS RELEASED in 1942 and provided a blistering rejoinder to *Gone With the Wind*, one of the most deluded fantasies ever left on film. Though apparently no more than a 1940s melodrama about upper-class corruption in which a spoiled heifer meets her violent end because the audience was thought to want it that way, the hot and bothered tale is far more. It is much like a pie to the mask of the cinematic masquerade balls in which white southerners were depicted wearing the false faces of endless down-home charm and grace to the exclusion of deadly common characteristics.

Starring Bette Davis, perhaps the greatest white bitch of them all, under the direction of John Huston, surely one of our finest directors, *In This Our Life* provides recognition of how southern bigotry functioned just before World War II. It also clarifies how its casual presence in the daily lives of southern whites had become so natural that ill intent seemed absent. At least to those who were not required to think about it.

Working from a script made remarkable by its focus on race as a way to intensify its narrative and reveal more of the central character, the part played by Davis asks her to step up in all of her dancer's physicality and special skill at liberating a character's fury. The moody actress understood the task before her and played what could only be called a white bitch (literally) on wheels: Always a reckless driver, the oddly named Stanley Timberlake (Davis) tries to blame a young Black man for a death she caused by speeding through town while tipsy and is angry because she had just failed at tempting her sister's boyfriend into using her ample bosom as a pillow.

The young man is the son of the family servant, played by Hattie McDaniel, who has the rare chance to express actual pathos with the unsentimental intensity that briefly pushes the viewer's heart through a blue meat-grinder of tragic recognition. Her pathos is so intense because she believes, without ever saying it, that her son is doomed because his word might have to stand against a well-to-do white woman's, which was never a winning position. White was *always* right, and Black was always *assumed* to be wrong. That was just how it was, and Hollywood never risked southern box-office revenue by holding the real face of high-falutin' or lower-class rednecks up to a cinematic mirror.

Huston was attracted to the script because of something still quite unusual. The son is a good-natured but far from stereotypical southern colored guy; this Negro kid is bound for college and full of the steam rising from his dreams. Against the odds, which he and his mother know quite well, the young man wants to be a lawyer. In hindsight, one can imagine him as perhaps an eventual member of the team that Charles Hamilton Houston used to grind the NAACP Legal Defense Fund's steel-toed boot up the aft hole of segregation.

Huston's interest in southern racial reality was noticed by Bosley Crowther in his 1942 *New York Times* review. He wrote of the plan to blame the Negro as a "brief but frank allusion to racial discrimination. And it is presented in a realistic manner, uncommon to Hollywood, by the definition of the Negro as an educated and comprehending character."

Educated and comprehending: hmmm. This is still exotic in our new age of minstrelsy where the cruder and stupider the Black man or woman, the more "authentic" the character is supposed to be. In order to actually get up to date, contemporary screenwriters need to see what the little-known actor Ernest Anderson was allowed to express way back in 1942.

Bette Davis uses all of her gifts to show us a portrait of a self-centered white woman whose character reveals a casually racist South, which was just as dangerous as the South with a deeper red tinted in its neck. Simply described, Davis *brings* it.

The star with a tantrum-ridden past fully, and perhaps even recklessly, inhabits this wild woman who gives everyone the blues. Davis makes repulsively radiant what would be a compelling vitality were it not completely perverted by the privileged woman's unrelenting narcissism. She is an infantilized monster swaying nervously over a gluteus minimus, often using her frog eyes like high beams.

This creature is legendary among Black servants, especially Black women. Not exactly plain but never quite pretty, full to the brim with epic feelings of entitlement, lazy, manipulative, charming when necessary, almost whorish but not quite, and ultimately driven by an overheated childishness that cannot acknowledge the limits of life. As my mother and other domestic workers said of such a woman, "Now that is a 'real' white heifer up to the damn gills: deadweight dumb enough to stumble like a bull through a china shop and then have the nerve to curtsy every time she destroys something valuable."

Those characteristics are common to just about anybody who has too

much money to develop good judgment. So we recognize them as universal and notice that such women are depicted the world over, by both men
and women. In short, a bitch is a bitch is a bitch. So is a dangerous asshole
of a man unlimited by race, class, religion, or geography. The most natural
source for the blues is human.

In American film, however, we have rarely seen a hussy with a cast-
iron heart who could stand up to the Scarlett O'Hara woman-child. After
having already given a more essential portrait of a southern belle than
Vivien Leigh in *Gone With the Wind*, Davis brings her 1938 *Jezebel* character up from 1840s New Orleans to the South shortly after the Depression began.

Davis is so effective because she was more of an artist than a star, and
a challenging part took precedence over how she looked in makeup and
costume or whether she was liked. Warner Bros. hated the makeup conceived for Davis, perhaps because it made her look like another woman
and then amounted to a mask through which the actress hurled her
thunderbolts.

James Baldwin loved Davis in this role and so did Harlem, he claimed,
because of the star's willingness to go where the part took her when white
skin privilege was the ultimate trump card. Davis's girl gone wild makes
an observation about the Black mother's denial of the charges against her
son that could easily have been said about the tragically unfair people
actually responsible for the racist horrors of the South: "Whenever they're
in a tight spot they always lie for each other." Sounds like the redneck
rules of order to me.

In This Our Life is ultimately a melodrama that makes many of its
points in the symbolic shorthand that moves too quickly for its fine cast
to build believable motivations. Only Charles Coburn has a part that can
step up to Davis, who seems to swell and simultaneously sink further
into naive self-obsession with each successive scene. A familiar subject

for tales of southern decadence is boldly implied by Coburn as the uncle tottering on the brink of incest. He is as free of moral comprehension as his niece and erotic target, the wide-eyed, fast-tailed hussy in heart-shaped, fire-engine-red lipstick, always on the verge of manic laughter, contempt, or tears.

The film also foresaw the insufferably narcissistic age in which we now live because Stanley Timberlake's favorite word is the first person pronoun—I, me, my, mine—and her sense of life is that she is due her happiness as the supreme expression of privileged existence. Endless entitlement is what this woman interprets as love, from within her family or without. It does not matter who has to die or be imprisoned or which arrogant blood relative will die within six months. They were all born to service her appetite for fun in some way, which is why Bette Davis knew what Stanley was and how well her very presence, even on the silver screen, explained so much about why the stubborn quality of southern bigotry stood in place for so, so long. Letting the privileges of bigotry go would have meant growing up, a condition we Americans—North and South, East and West—have never enjoyed because it gets in the way of our "gusto."

Facing that ruthless childishness is also why Bette Davis became a celebrated goddess in Harlem. She had stepped up into the orbit that Eleanor Roosevelt was making more and more familiar to all concerned, regardless of race, sex, religion, or class. There it is again: The human grandeur of American women is unexcelled anywhere in the world but is probably equaled by women everywhere in the world. Women are like that.

December 2009

THE IMPECCABLE
SIDNEY POITIER

S PECIAL IS AS SPECIAL DOES, and Sidney Poitier is special for very
specific reasons. Few can honestly say that they may have actually
changed something of great importance to the world at large. Poitier can
easily say that, without however much of a blush would show on his indelibly Black skin. The reason is that he has walked the walk, talked the talk,
and beaten clichés and stereotypes as though they had stolen something,
which is what things substantially removed from the facts of life always
do. In the worst years of American racial misunderstanding, clichés and
stereotypes stole the universal human truth showing itself across the lines
of color, but did not stop there. They who swore by those distortions stood
up, daring anyone to challenge their intentional or dangerously naive misreading of things as they truly are.

That misunderstanding led to a set of conventions that defined the
tone and set the practices common to motion pictures. The intertwining of
profit with national race politics was irresistibly influenced by what must be

seen as charismatic, even highly innovative storytelling. D. W. Griffith's 1915 *Birth of a Nation* was a technical masterpiece, the first blockbuster, and a tale made monstrous by the racist bile at the center of its narrative. Griffith's most influential work, it greatly advanced cinematic technique and set the pace for projecting huge, paranoid lies as acceptable versions of the truth in black and white, light and shadow. From that point on, southern audiences choosing not to attend a movie could cost any film company considerable revenue. Consequently, the Dream Machine adhered to the racial limitations of Black stereotypes as though the head office of every studio was run by rednecks. Servile or buffoon darkies were preferred to any other. "Demanded" would better describe the situation. Such lies, such distortions, and such denigration maintained power in Hollywood for more than thirty years, and every departure from what amounted to a despicably nauseating tradition was considered bold and laden with risks.

Moving against those conventions called for a hero, which is not expected in the temple of mediocre but highly polished dreams, supported by a chorus formed of evening jackets, gowns, and red carpets. The worshippers who fall to their knees in that temple almost never use the words *courage* or *integrity* to describe anything tilted toward artistry. Even so, had anyone decided to say that Hollywood is not a place for heroic behavior, that person would be as inaccurate as possible because Hollywood is fundamentally a place for heroes and for heroic behavior. That is because audiences love two things more than anything else: the heroes, romantic or not, and the villains, romantic or not; the former just a bit more than the latter. That is formidable territory in which few write their own parts. Yet right there, in the middle of all of those deals, all of those budgetary concerns, all of that cinematic technology, all those wardrobes, sets, and screenwriters, as well as the actors taking direction from men who had to recognize each film as a whole while making it, right there is where Poitier became a two-dimensional hero up on the screen and helped expand our understanding of human commonality by imposing his will, courage, and integrity in three dimensions. What you saw was what you got.

The roller coaster of successful movie careers begins with minor vehicles, proceeds to growing notice, achieves success, becomes so predictable that the actor and the style represented are rejected, the films begin to make less and less money, and all that can be said has usually been said and most of what could be done was or was not done. Poitier's career is very different because what made him important when he was one of the most popular actors in Hollywood is almost as important today as it was in the 1950s when his career began to ascend. The parts were many and varied but, like all things in the arts, there were central themes to his first films, and they remained in place throughout a long and complex career.

If two films are closely examined, *No Way Out* from 1950 and *Edge of the City* from 1957, one can see how Poitier, from the very beginning, delivered something that few Black actors in Hollywood had been allowed to bring to a role before he arrived on the screen. Many enduring aesthetic choices can be seen in his film debut, *No Way Out*, a Joseph L. Mankiewicz minor masterpiece. It uses the conventions of film noir to explore the tensions and releases from bigotry as successfully as John Ford took advantage of what the Old West made possible in order to examine the meanings and ramifications of irresponsible leadership, genocide, miscegenation, the American character, and so on.

In a script written and directed by Mankiewicz but brought to fruition by Darryl F. Zanuck, Poitier plays a young doctor periodically slapped in the face by race prejudice. America had never seen a cinematic lead character like his Dr. Luther Brooks, who was sophisticated, intelligent, just out of medical school, and in possession of exacting skill. He also had a sense of humor far removed from the updates of minstrel buffoonery that continue today. Right now, Dr. Brooks seems like a contemporary Black American put into a time machine and sent to America sixty years ago.

The kind of deep feeling rendered by Poitier and elaborated upon by all of the Black characters in the film had not been seen since King Vidor's 1929 *Hallelujah!* In the Mankiewicz film, we see what the actor brought and the extensive influence it had on so many following him. First, Poitier broke the color line accepted by whites and Blacks for a leading man. He was as black as a Mississippi evening at the deep point of midnight. His hair was not mucked up by the desire to be straightened and, while making *No Way Out*, it was discovered that he was far too dark to do an intended scene near a coal bin because the camera could not have "seen" him, so the scene was cut from the script and never shot. No matter how handsome the actor looks today, his presence in close-up was new in itself because men of his complexion were not considered attractive in the 1950s. So, along with Miles Davis, Poitier's presence up there on the screen expanded the idea of the male matinee idol.

His persona provided the aesthetic clay out of which the actor molded all of his intelligent characters whose very existence within realistic contexts made it clear just how crude and off the mark racism was in its constricted vision of human variety. Luther Brooks evolves into the doctor engaged to the young liberal white woman in *Guess Who's Coming to Dinner* (1967); the snappy detective of *In the Heat of the Night* (1967); the tall, dark, and handsome love interest in *For Love of Ivy* (1968); the upper-class doctor from *A Patch of Blue* (1965); the prison psychiatrist in *Pressure Point* (1962); the popular teacher of *To Sir, With Love* (1967); and so on. All were depicted as civilized men who had worked their way up to the top of their professions. They had done what needed to be done in order to rise up from where they started. Self-confidence, familial support, and the backbone provided by close friends were basic. They got there faster if they had them; if they did not, they bit the bullet, perhaps broke a few teeth, but still got there. All of them shared a slight veneer of unforced arrogance mixed in with what usually turned out to be a healthy sense of self-deprecation. That may now seem insignificant, but it was not and still is not. Any time a group denies the possibility or the existence of various kinds of achievers in arenas that demand high quality from their participants, the group paints itself into the sticky corner of low expectations. Poitier was well aware of this and chose his roles accordingly. This did not please hysterics and racists, but they should never be on the "to please" list.

What must have been very troubling to racial ideologues was the easeful authority Poitier gives Dr. Brooks and the conventionally wholesome quality of the doctor's family. By now everyone should know that good art does not automatically result from good politics or highmindedness. *No Way Out* does not suffer the limitations of agitprop, and that is why it has a lasting feeling. There is the mysteriousness of their quirks and internal reactions to the life around them that the director and his actors brought to the internal dimensions of the characters so that they continue to surprise us.

Possessed of a superior performer's sense of nuance, Poitier already understands the levels of undertone possible in the reaction shots that any important film actor must master. Therefore, the ethnic backstory appears in the actor's face when he is silently responding to Richard Widmark's unapologetic racist. Strong, subtle, and ambivalent emotion comes out in layers of revulsion, assertiveness, and the awe felt by the young doctor going nose to nose with an irrationality capable of violence or murder but beyond shame or guilt. Manipulative and bitter, essentially childish and full of self-pity, Widmark's character suffers the waves of hysteria that demand his attention and that of everyone else. He stands with Robert Ryan's anti-Semitic murderer in *Crossfire*. The visceral realization of evil remains extremely powerful but never overdone because the artistry has a full force that stops short of the melodramatic.

In 1957, Poitier performed opposite John Cassavetes in *Edge of the City*. Pauline Kael wrote of Poitier's Tommy Tyler portrayal that the actor was "startlingly good," and the tale was proclaimed a milestone by film critics and civil rights organizations for having portrayed an interracial friendship that may have been the first of its kind in American film. What makes it tower over many films made then or since is the unbridled natural grasp of the human quality delivered in spades by Poitier, Cassavetes, Ruby Dee, and Kathleen Maguire. Poitier's Tommy has an almost heartbreaking effect in his absolute freedom from the stereotypic, moving with such vitality through so many more moods than would be expected of a Black character then or now.

He is defensively cocky, humorous, realistically in love with his wife, so playful that he is given to satirical and fully conscious pretensions, a compassionate listener, an almost timidly affectionate father, a fair dancer, a matchmaker, and a man who would rather laugh at or ignore racism than take the chance of being inwardly affected by it. His tragedy is that he does not realize how much resentment his relaxed attitude brings out in the bigoted foreman whom Jack Warden makes so menacing; the man's hatred for Tommy builds until any disagreement or dismissal, however lightly delivered, is interpreted as symbolic ethnic castration, a loss of power and terrain that is finally unacceptable. The shock, terror, and rage that sears Tommy's face when he realizes that his calm has sparked a life-or-death situation in which he could be murdered and lose everything about which he deeply cares is one of the highest of the high points in Poitier's career. The absurdity of the entire moment telescopes the deeper and most universal meaning of true bigotry: its deafness to reason and commitment to paranoid exclusion and destruction.

What Poitier discovered as he went about the making of Tommy into a three-dimensional person allowed him access to the common man that democracy always celebrates and which people the world over always find attractive and inspiring. The common man's mythic openness to life is the centerpiece of the democratic idea: goodness, humor, talent, and empathy are not limited by ethnic packaging, social status, religion, or geography—nor are all of the bad things in life. Tommy made possible what the actor brought to *The Defiant Ones* (1958), *A Raisin in the Sun* (1961), *Lilies of the Field* (1963), and even the 1970s "Uptown" comedies co-starring Bill Cosby.

In Poitier's myriad kinds of reaction shots, one can see the fundamental uses of the eyes, the mouth, and the positions of the head of which almost every outstanding Black actor who has come forward in his wake also employs. It is a veritable compendium for all of the originals who still refer to him in the way that the most original jazz musicians always echo some aspect of Louis Armstrong, the seer of instrumental and vocal blues and swing, usually known as jazz. One can see essences of Tommy Tyler in the work of Denzel Washington, Morgan Freeman, Samuel L. Jackson, Laurence Fishburne, Forest Whitaker, Don Cheadle, and Terrence Howard, for starters; just as what Marlon Brando does in *On the Waterfront* opens the way for Paul Newman, Warren Beatty, Jack Nicholson, Robert De Niro, Al Pacino, and Leonardo DiCaprio. Pay close attention, you will see what I mean in both films.

Inarguable: Special is as special does, and Sidney Poitier deserves that description as much as any other artist in the popular arts of our time. He is a genius of human feeling, and those kinds of people last as long as the species does.

May 2011

TARANTINO ENCHAINED

L EADING FROM BEHIND, sliding downhill, abusing all the talent previously shown in directing, in writing, in coaxing the best from actors—this is a serious charge. Yet that is what Quentin Tarantino has done in *Django Unchained*. The recent Oscar is simply further proof of Hollywood's cult of superficial cool. With *Django*, Tarantino has slipped down behind himself into a shallow and bloodstained hip-hop turn that his own best work has well refuted. Often refuted.

Tarantino wrote and directed the finest Blaxploitation film ever made, 1997's *Jackie Brown*. This film was an inventive and even courageous victory. Choosing not to sucker-punch the Black audience through bad taste or even to exploit it, the director/writer created something revolutionary, a well-made Black action movie set in the criminal world.

We must understand what Blaxploitation was to fully comprehend Tarantino's earlier success before the recent and resounding failure. Blaxploitation was a short-lived, highly superficial but commercially successful genre of the mid-1970s. The trend was well documented in Isaac Julien's sobering and somewhat depressing documentary, *BaadAssss Cinema*. As Julien's documentary shows, the genre was actually something like a may-fly assigned to save Hollywood with large profits. Junk in the trunk, Blax-ploitation introduced to the Dream Machine the salient fact of a Black audience and how easily it could be appealed to, with almost no effort at all. Just put chocolate on top, white down below—kicked, stomped, or shot down, if necessary. Writers, directors, and actors seemed to fall out of the trees. It became lucratively evident that every group has a taste for a Sylvester Stallone—wham, bam, thank you, ma'am. Once the sinking ship was safely afloat, things got back to segregated business as usual.

No genius need apply in order to explain that Blaxploitation began the backward road to pro-pimp, pro-street gangster chants, unmercifully exposed with due diligence in Byron Hurt's almost astounding *Hip Hop: Beyond Beats and Rhymes*. Both documentaries are essential to a viewer who wants to understand how far removed from so-called rebellion *Django Unchained* actually is. Though true art never moves forward or backward, trends do.

IN *JACKIE BROWN*, Tarantino ignored the single-minded and simplistic rules of Blaxploitation, and he made a very important decision. He switched Elmore Leonard's middle-aged but still attractive blond, Jackie Burke, into the embodiment of pop Black femininity, Pam Grier, the buxom queen of bargain-basement Black movies. Then Tarantino went about sending his film in the direction of *The Asphalt Jungle* and *The Killing*, introducing the force of quality and a very rarely expressed subtlety of character develop-ment into the crime tale, especially the Black cartoon version. This was very different from the way that Blaxploitation began and maintained itself. Tarantino's dip into that popularized heart of darkness, however, was not a nostalgic reading of a flimsy trend that appealed to the Black American version of sustained adolescence. Down the tubes went the stale garishness, nudity, violence, and the absurd plots in which these knock-off films focused on sleazy, pretentious cartoon rage, presenting themselves as a version of "militant" politics. There was little blood in the young filmmaker's Blaxploitation script, but lots of well-drawn personalities.

Until *Django Unchained,* none of Tarantino's narratives showed predictable Black versions of hollow men and women, characters that always responded to life with guns, explosives, martial arts, and bloody special effects. The most enduring and easily misused American feeling is the sense that power must always be literally fought in order to make room for authentic vitality. Of course in the adolescent world of male childishness, there was always a rumble in the cinematic jungle; it showed its giant face in James Bond beating down a number of Black criminals, and in the indie world, Nicholas Cage begins *Wild at Heart* by becoming so enraged that he beats the brains out of a Black hit man with a switchblade, staining the stone floor of a movie theater's lobby. Revenge is the teenage mindset. In Blaxploitation, this was given an ethnic spin, usually explosive. Black people—male and female—not only fought the white man, but were victorious every time.

Tarantino turned in another direction and built a cinematic world focused on a human agenda of rich complexity. He was much like Robert Altman, Sam Peckinpah, and Martin Scorsese in that regard, yet he brought a personal originality with blistering, comic, and resoundingly inventive character studies. In *Jackie Brown,* his character faces up to contemporary urban problems far better than loudmouth Black professional protestors such as the New Black Panthers, who profit from complaint and draw their styles from impotent saber rattlers.

ETHNIC INSIGHTS DO not always weather storms, however, particularly if one, Black or not, is too committed to common cloudbursts: They can slowly evolve into an aesthetic version of sleeping sickness. Tarantino surprises us again because his *Django Unchained* is one of the worst versions of Blaxploitation ever seen. It yields to convention in the most impotent ways. From controversy to commercial success, the troubles began with its star, Jamie Foxx, a third-rate actor whose shortcomings seem infinite. What was written for him was an insipid tale that Foxx, predictably cocksure, inhabits woodenly, missing the strike zone of an actual performance. The star, representative of pop culture at its most obvious, uses only about a half-dozen facial expressions, none mysterious or suggesting unmentioned depths. Foxx is given such a contrived and impossible task that he is forced to be a superhero to do even a bit of it. Obsessed by his wife whom he intends to rescue from slavery, Django does what he must do because they have such a touching and impassioned cup of thick home-brewed affection, though the two barely speak to each other on-screen, only dream or stare longingly, equal in dialogue to a pair of black sheep in a pasture.

Slavery, the film implies, was a sharp blade. It cut all the fat from romance, and the lean meat left has only a deliciousness exclusive to Django and his Broomhilda, neither sharing the taste of it with the audience. And that is how it goes, their love running silent and never close to deep. Overlong scenes never bring off a masterpiece of formal creativity equal to the long basement scene of *Inglourious Basterds*, which, by the way, already stands with any compelling extended scene, tightened up with surprise, pace, humor, menace, and suspense. There Tarantino took up Altman's anger at short scenes and swift cuts inspired by television commercials, where so many new directors get their start. Tarantino did not talk about it but he proved the durable aesthetic value of a cinematic section almost twenty minutes long. Things are very different in *Django*.

Foxx's performance reveals him to be an amateur next to the mas-terful Samuel L. Jackson, who brought off a nuanced performance as the hired killer in *Pulp Fiction* and as the illegal gun dealer in *Jackie Brown*, an arms hustler who uses Black nationalist rhetoric on his intended vic-tims, talking of the white man trying to set "Black against Black." Jack-son delivers some of Tarantino's most truly insightful writing. Though Jackson gives an exceptional performance as a house slave in *Django*, a man who is quite intelligent and given to jokingly running everything on the plantation, brutal or not, his character is never matched or counter-pointed. The film has no comparably complicated Black character, good or bad (or somewhere in between, like most people). It appears that more than one Negro character on a large plantation with plenty of slaves is too much for a thin postcard covered with dirty notes.

TARANTINO'S CAREER BEGAN with films that used ethnic diversity in a natural way, and he also made stinging fun of racism. In *Pulp Fiction*, he went to town with the idea that lynching could have hypnotic and confused homoerotic underpinnings, which could explain why these gory rituals so often built up to a peak of savage intensity when castrating the Black man, as if exorcising a sexual demon by removing the testicles. Tarantino had taken the shock of violent racism to a new place in cinema. Examples of his thinking across ethnic lines arrive in casual allusions to Apaches in the basement's parlor game played by the Nazis, which thematically connects to the nickname of Brad Pitt's character, Aldo the Apache. The terrorist American officer intends to brutally horrify troops and Gestapo officers, alluding, through scalping, to the cutting off of Nazi ears in Sam Fuller's *The Big Red One*. Only Tarantino would have the terrifying American officer played by Pitt bring up the Negro as a folk hero by asking whether the next exciting thing done by the German officer who has captured Pitt

will be "Eliza on the ice," a reference to the once well-known character in
the stage version of Uncle Tom's Cabin—perhaps the source of the clichéd
sacrificial dark buddy of the melodramatic white hero who appears in far
too many Hollywood action films.

The characters are conceived and performed with such charm, sophistication, humor, and personal mystery that they are much more frightening than the Halloween monsters of domestic war movies. Tarantino's
Nazis force us to see how enjoyable it is to be part of the chosen Aryan
few. They carry themselves as if blessed by the invincibility of cosmic
mercy—unlike those who are desperate, resourcefully undignified ver-
min; those who must be removed to better the world and keep the floors
clean to a point of slippery glossiness. These elements allow the film, for
all of the willed combinations that move outside of reality or history, to
do something marvelous: ascend to a place right next to historically close
encounters, such as Conspiracy and Downfall. This was due to its human
insight.

Tarantino's gifts as a writer were revealed early in his penetrating
sense of the human labyrinth that transcends good and evil and confuses
too many Americans. He confounded the audience's preference for cartoon obviousness so inventively that it led to an international career of
great commercial success. (Spike Lee has convinced himself this is about
race instead of superior writing ability.) Then there is the younger director's syncopated sense of narrative form in which the unexpected rhythm
of purposefully disordered sequences appears, goes beyond befuddlement,
and helps create worshipful international cults worldwide. That gift for
the unexpected is only blunted if the filmmaker sees both the subject and
its intended audience far, far too simply, deluding himself into believing
that he understands it all much too quickly.

TARANTINO DOES NOT address the shades of gray in the context of his largely parallel southern characters in *Django,* those who benefit from slavery and make the most of the power it delivers. He claims to have itched to make a film set during slavery, needing substantial time and research and to do a great deal of reading on the subject. It came to no avail, not with any of the luminous ideas and images we think we should expect from him. In this film, we are given no sense of the tethered superiority felt by the so-called white trash required to do the most dangerous work. There was a simple reason: Injury and mutilation of slaves cost the masters much more than any terrible accident had by poor whites; the lower rung of a superior species was always available and inexpensive.

Sexual pleasure for the white men is alluded to but never seen; nor do we find slave women who knew how to parley two heads on a pillow until they arrived at some kind of privilege. In Tarantino's oddly simplified and inaccurate world, women are there more as set decoration or props, not living characters. All of the complicated life in the context of slavery has been well documented through personal testimony and astute observation, so ignorance is no excuse. There is too much artistic work from Faulkner, Ellison, and recent writers, not to mention the clearinghouse on the subject of slavery that academics have brought to American campuses of higher education, a pyramid reaching from a large base of mediocre data to a slim peak full of stoic and indispensable information.

Tarantino seems not to be meeting the most famous clichés with a strong sense of touchingly complex and confounding humanity that may have been pushed down but was hardly destroyed. Ralph Ellison and I once agreed that a grand irony of American culture is how something meant to deceive and hide another action can do its assignment but also turn against the obvious in the process. The context blooms with alternate energy, sometimes becoming a moving, even captivating, aesthetic force that cannot be shot down.

Some of the finest spirituals entertained and distracted the slave owners while runaways prepared to steal away from the plantation. John Ford varied this fundamental motif from American culture when the singing Indian woman in *Stagecoach* distracts and deceives the endangered passengers while their horses are stolen. What could be heard during slavery is the lyrical grandeur the Black community spreads through "Deep River," the great spiritual sung in *The Sun Shines Bright.* The recently freed slaves and their Negro preacher bring an unexcelled purity commonly found in the most gifted of the poor, the educated and uneducated, and the unrelenting buffoons known to all ethnic groups.

Ford's continuing dismissal of social prejudice comes forward in this tale about a southern town being held back from self-righteous homicidal anarchy. An older judge stands up to the mob; he is neither infected by the invisible blood poison of bigotry nor willing to sacrifice a young, innocent Black man to yowling townspeople demanding a gurgling death and ready to tear down the jail to see it, though one of them is later discovered as the culprit, the actual rapist and killer of a girl.

Given his pride for being a so-called nerd who learned film by working in a video store and by reading so much criticism, Tarantino's claim of hating Ford for both riding as a Klansman in *The Birth of a Nation* and killing off dehumanized Indians "like zombies" in his westerns sounds like a self-righteous and fraudulent billboard of advertised condescension. It reminds me of William Knowland, who in 1964 ran with Barry Goldwater, attempting to score a debate point as he reminded Hubert Humphrey that Lyndon Johnson had been a voter for segregation in 1948. Humphrey smacked him down with a lightning response: "That's what I like about Lyndon Johnson: he learns."

The self-made bad boy seems not to have made much of Ford's eventual rejection of his own aesthetic shortcomings and his decision to avoid reducing any group (white, red, or Black) to a simplistic reading.

He absorbed the lesson of William Faulkner, who in 1942 threw down
the gauntlet in American fiction with *Go Down, Moses*, introducing an
unmatched and layered complexity to race relations that has yet to be
excelled. All normalized national shortcomings were howled at in Ford's
1948 *Fort Apache*, which lifts the worm-filled can of internal bigotry until
it is seen in Henry Fonda's character, the eastern man transferred to the
Southwest, Lt. Col. Owen Thursday—a supreme embodiment of alienated leadership, melancholy, class prejudice, bravery, defensive belittling,
and outrage at governmental corruption, but an even greater outrage at an
underestimated Indian chief having the nerve to defy him, the military
representative of the United States government, which he will *not* tolerate.
Thursday leads his men to their doom. Cementing the fate of his command, he dismisses all seasoned admonitions and flesh-and-blood advice,
demurring that no "breech clouted savage" had learned the tragic art of
battle "under Alexander the Great, or Bonaparte, at the least." Fonda's
character is a fictionalized Custer, going down foolishly and being celebrated by every schoolboy for his arrogance and glory hunting and for
dying with his boots on.

In *Sergeant Rutledge*, bigoted assumptions compel the father of a murdered and raped girl to fire on a Negro before asking any questions. He
is there, as is her naked body, so he must be guilty. The highly respected
Black cavalryman is pursued, brought to justice, and prosecuted by a man
quite willing to rely on the sort of stereotypes that would have guaranteed
victory in the terms of *The Birth of a Nation*. Things are so logically turned
around by the facts, however, that Rutledge is acquitted at the film's end.
The guilty man confesses on the witness stand, and it has become apparent that a stereotypic conclusion can be fatal, a tragedy.

One of Ford's intentions was to tear the bark off many different kinds
of bigotry, while arguing for the importance of diverse agreement, as he
did through modern situations in *The Last Hurrah*, where he lampooned

Nixon's Checkers speech and warns the audience through the speaker's success about the dangerous combination of the soppy love of pets and the tendency to be impressed by a gadget made attractive through electronic media. This astute level of understanding remains in vehicles up to and including his last western, in 1964, *Cheyenne Autumn*.

THOSE WHO DON'T look and pay too much attention to the tomfoolery of a young braggart might miss Tarantino's debt to the past master. Because Ford also shows a horse dancing at the end of *The Sun Shines Bright*, you might assume that *Django*'s conclusion is part of a muddled allusion to the work of his predecessor—if not an attempt to get away clean with a theft of no consequence. In *Django*, Tarantino attempts to top himself by using the tale of Siegfried and Brunhilde, flipping over Ford's meaning to say what would work perfectly for a contrived hip-hop hero. The townspeople of *The Sun Shines Bright* finish the 1953 film carrying a banner reading, "He saved us from ourselves." Django saves the whites and the faithful slaves from themselves. The rebel angel, downy white feathers replaced by black coiffed naps, marches down the ice-cream-cold popsicle stick, destroys the Valhalla of the big house, and mass murders "all ye faithful" with good old Dy-no-mite. Jimmy Walker would approve.

For a creator who has produced such complex female characters, per-haps the worst sin of *Django* is not its replacing drama with endless blood-letting, and romance with sensation, but the abuse of Kerry Washington's talent. The filmmaker becomes an insider and expert on Black culture in a very stilted way, nearly competing with Spike Lee for the barber-shop crown so perfectly parodied by Eddie Murphy in *Coming to America*. Blackface sensibility makes almost any white man into a minstrel among the sables, imitating the kind of Negro many Black women have been disgusted by because he will sell out to sexism rather than defend his African queens in the only way a real man would. Perhaps naively expecting the compromised bad boy to participate with outstanding originality in what could be seen in Kasi Lemmons's *Eve's Bayou* or Denzel Washington's *The Great Debaters*, we got what we did not at all expect.

The Dream Machine's indifference to female talent remains, with or without an ethnic twist. *Eve's Bayou* introduced Jurnee Smollett in one of the most remarkable beginnings since Elizabeth Taylor in 1944's *National Velvet*. She has since grown up to languish on the same heap with Angela Bassett and all of the Black actresses who are victims of talent-blindness (this is a snowstorm that always manages to freeze the careers of gifted performers, past and present, such as Kim Stanley or Laura Dern). From the stunning *Nothing but a Man* to right now, enough well-written parts for black, brown, beige, and bone-colored women have been produced every so often for one to be startled by the shallowness of all the women in *Django*, Black or white, but definitely the thinly conceived, inarticulate darkie girls.

Our most successful "postmodern" filmmaker was not up to the real revolution possible for Black Americans. Some see the real deal and come on with it: total humanity, equal to all. The real change all over the world is the female demand for equality, not the submission to corn-pone ideology, greasy junk food drowned in ketchup, as if fake blood will make it better for the duped customer. Humanity straight, no chaser, will always do the job. As with fans of the most corroding hip-hop, Tarantino has been taken in. He does not write strong silent types, male and female, and in the case of the prized slave woman, only a weak and silent type. There is another way to look at the problem and to do something revolutionary.

Tarantino is trapped by ideology. Just attempting to fashion a programmatic purpose can bring down the best of us. Low-hanging fruit poisons the person too anxious to pick and polish it. Talking about what he intended in *Django*, Tarantino sounds as doomed as LeRoi Jones did at the bottom of his "hate whitey" period or as Spike Lee when he was referring to himself as "a Black nationalist with a camera." He makes himself into one of the white child extras in Bing Crosby's *The Birth of the Blues*, rising from behind cotton bales and astonishing darkies overcome by his hot clarinet improvising. A perfect update would be the NAACP's Image Awards; or Trick Daddy's video "I'm a Thug," with white kids who are thrilled to be there and to watch this hip-hop slumgullion with gold teeth and braids eat take-out fried chicken at an expensive hotel restaurant in Los Angeles, scandalizing the white folks at every turn. Of course, of course.

These are not far-out ideas at all. While telling Howard Stern about the new film and his successful career, Tarantino pulled the covers off. Last December, the filmmaker described going to a party with Jamie Foxx and getting into a polluted one-night stand with an aggressive, unattractive woman because, of course, he wanted Foxx and his friends to see him as a cool guy who could get down with an unknown woman immediately. Down is what he got.

Quentin Tarantino can run around with or hang out among whomever he wants. A writer gets material or inspiration from everywhere, but it is shocking to hear a major voice in Hollywood say something this delusional: "I've always wanted to explore slavery, but I guess the reason that actually made me put pen to paper was to give Black American males a western hero—give them a cool folkloric hero that could actually be empowering and pay back blood for blood."

The depth of the long, soulful game played by Martin Luther King Jr. and his cohorts succeeded, all the while rejected by a lucrative version of Blaxploitation in the saber-rattling desert of giant faces, but simple minds do not know it. Minstrelsy came back, as James Brown said, talking loud but saying nothing. In short, Mr. Tarantino, you see there is nothing about skin tones and its pleasures or troubles to be learned from The Big Black Human Being in the middle of the room, not from Foxx and his friends. You already proved yourself with *Jackie Brown*. There it is.

2013

THEN AND NOW, I AM A NEGRO

"It has come to my attention that certain people are disturbed by my use of the word 'Negro' rather than the contemporary mouthful 'African American.' I don't care, but some at this paper have urged me to explain myself." So S.C. began a column that had been requested by "certain people" at the New York Daily News, *where he was a biweekly columnist, in part, it is presumed, to stem the tide of reader complaints and appease corporate anxiety over his use of the term. The result was a May 1996 op-ed with the blunt headline: "Why I Choose to Say 'Negro.'" More than a decade later, Crouch was again asked for his explanation, this time to mollify the anxiety of newspaper editors that ran his syndicated column, who had heard from their readers. The term also rubbed across the grain of many in-house style guides. A national headcount seemed the right time.*

As the Census Bureau begins embedding a test in the 2010 census that "will measure the effect of removing the term 'Negro' on reports about a person's racial identity," my preference is not with those who either feel insulted or think *Negro* outdated and derogatory. That actually applies to another N-word.

As a writer, I find the term *African American* unwieldy. I use terms such as *Negro*, *Black*, and am sometimes tempted to use *colored* because that range of skin tones is so undeniably epic. All of them are no more than words, but there is something far from backward about the sound of *Negro* and the magnificent people who used that word to describe themselves. They gave it majesty; they made it luminous. They inspired, organized, and led what amounted to our most recent civil war. They welcomed all comers as they went about removing the teeth from the Grand Dragons of southern racism.

Of course, hip-hop has demeaned millions for the making of millions and used it at every chance. But that's another story.

When Black nationalism was on the rise, a hostility toward white people and the Western world came into vogue among young people who were then usually called Negroes. Few people wanted to be called *Black*, and some were almost ready to fight about it.

It was something of an improvement when *Black* became a term that was no longer considered demeaning. It is, in fact, a rather natural development of what was often said about the Negro race, which, we were told by our parents and others, was like a flower garden because it "included every color from blue-black to lily white."

Vernon Davis, brother of the trumpeter Miles, once told me he felt integration actually began during segregation in what were public schools reserved for those possessing Negro blood but who could be "actual blonds or redheads, with white skin and blue or green eyes."

In 1959, Mike Wallace and what would today be called "the white media" discovered the Nation of Islam. The "Nation" was a Black nationalist cult that had woven together science fiction, ethnic nationalism and a bizarre version of Islam that was always dismissed as a perversion of the religion by Middle Eastern Muslims.

Many Black Americans seemed more gullible or at least loved to hear Malcolm X castigate and threaten the white man while he was the central mouthpiece for the cult. To hear him tell it, the white man was cruising for a bruising and would get his when "the word was given." It was never given, of course.

During the 1960s, when calls for "Black unity" became more harsh, the Rev. Martin Luther King Jr. and all of those who were actually tearing down the cotton curtain of southern segregation were dismissed by Malcolm X and his many imitators as cowards because they used nonviolence instead of violence and were disdained for supposedly repressing the "Black manhood" that was ready to burst out.

America was bettered by the nonviolent and multiracial civil rights movement, not by those who saw anything less than Black-approved self-segregation as a form of selling out. They did not call themselves African Americans, which is a pretentious term conceived by Jesse Jackson and some Black academics.

Those so willing to pretend that they are Africans and not Americans or who claim their Americanness almost as an unavoidable burden are just caught up in yet another meaningless trend that has been swallowed by the country as a whole. Freedom of choice is finally the point, above all else. We are, after all, Americans.

January 2010

12 YEARS A SLAVE

Versions of this piece were published in the New York Daily News *and in syndication on January 27 and February 10, 2014, here combined. Crouch, Jelani Cobb, Khalil Muhammad, and others took part in a panel discussion about the film at the Museum of the Moving Image in Queens. Cobb writes, "the vantage point Crouch brought to that film was consistent with themes in his writing that go all the way back to* Notes of a Hanging Judge."

HOLLYWOOD'S SMUG
SLAVE-TRADE HUSTLE

The national victimhood game has addicted many—and that helps us understand how the Academy of Motion Picture Arts and Sciences nominated the brutal and shallow *12 Years a Slave* for nine awards, effectively declaring it to be, in the eyes of Hollywood, one of the year's important films.

No matter how beautifully painted the shell of a spoiled egg might be, it will smell rough enough when peeled to choke a maggot. Hollywood needed to let out the emotional pus that had welled up under racial wounds inflicted over decades. It needed to declare to itself that there will be no more screens filled with grinning, shuffling, and dancing. No more new minstrelsy—now is the time for the new guilt, interwoven with the gilt of box-office profit. Suffer through the violence, and you shall be purified.

This cheap vision has been seen before. In the 1970s, the short-lived horror show of Blaxploitation was supposed to have liberated Black men and women to be more authentic and less traditionally buffoonish. Well-chronicled in *BaadAssss Cinema*, the documentary takes a serious stand against the genre while showing how many filmmakers and performers took pride in a blighted set of images. What had begun with D. W. Griffith's tainted 1915 masterwork, *The Birth of a Nation*, was stepped away from with fiercely meretricious pride. Here, finally, was a chance to stick it to the man, the satanic force no longer hidden behind the cotton curtain and the white walls of the plantation big house.

Finally seeing advantage in their color, Black Americans were ready for the hip strut. Cheap films, with them moving in garish clothes, spewing corny slang, saved a destitute Hollywood that had fallen on the sword of overly expensive spectacles, with casts of thousands, many costumes, and ancient settings calling for big sets. A gaggle of Black actors was much cheaper and brought in profits big enough to rebuild Hollywood. Too many complaints from civil rights organizations doomed the trend, troubling the waters. The quickly successful second-rate actors who became the shooting stars of Blaxploitation were then ignored and kicked to the curb.

Since then, the cult of the victim has been pushed in the Academy of Motion Picture Arts and Sciences, dressed up in militant theories that do not usually touch the Black community very deeply. While it is no more immune to being duped than any other ethnic group—the Tawana Brawley fraud proved that—Black American culture has always been the result of cosmopolitan blood lines: part African, part European, part so-called Native American, and part Asian. That complexity underlay the civil rights movement, a fully formed example of what has held Black

Americans up and kept them largely free of narcissism, decadence, or foolhardiness.

An inner something I now call "heroic optimism," an all-American but universal quality of great charisma, helped ward off the ever-present sentimentality that can lead not only to overstatement but also chaotic behavior. Facing the bittersweet reality of life allowed Black Americans to fight for their education and discipline themselves along the lines of their dreams.

12 Years a Slave is almost totally devoid of the force that inspired the abolition movement and finally our great Civil War, dripping with gore and inspiration. The film loved so much by Hollywood now has little understanding of slavery, showing slaves so dehumanized by brutality that they seem to be talking livestock.

Carole Boyce Davies, writing in *The Guardian*, recognized the film's strong cinematography, but charged screenwriter John Ridley and director Steve McQueen with removing complex, humanizing parts from the 1853 slave narrative they narrowed to a cruel cartoon. For them, slavery is meat and potatoes, easy to consume.

Any actual complexity would not have achieved what Ridley and McQueen were seeking—a callow melodrama made dramatic by extreme cruelty, bloodletting, and sexual abuse. Above all else, the white actors—especially the astounding Michael Fassbender—are directed in a way that allows them to act circles around the sweating, smoke-black chattel—figures in vast need of the American Society for the Prevention of Cruelty to Animals.

THE ARTIFICIAL AGONY and the purported anguish of victimhood do not deny contemporary or historical wrongs, but they can be effectively summoned in melodramatic terms for career benefits. That may well be why *12*

Years a Slave did so well at the Academy Awards, and such hoopla attended the award of a dark-black woman in pursuit of the Dream Machine's counterfeit golden statue, given in this case for best supporting actress.

It was once a public cliché, perhaps begun by James Baldwin's eloquent but bitter essays about his own unattractiveness, that made so many assume that Black men and women thought themselves repulsive because of their skin tone and the preferences of white standards of beauty that were imposed upon them, and when so much fun had been made of the "darkie" from nineteenth century minstrelsy to about fifty years ago. *12 Years* was supposed to be seen as a corrective to balderdash like that and the astoundingly innovative and insipid *The Birth of a Nation*—half genius, half bigoted craziness. But we saw another version as the Oscars drew near.

So when that small and elegant woman Lupita Nyong'o went to the podium at an event hosted by *Essence* magazine, she became symbolic of a refreshing sacrilege because of her very Blackness. The unforced richness of her soft voice and her unapologetic weeping in appreciation of being recognized and honored with her nomination by the Oscars not only seemed genuine but also was quite touching. She was so effortlessly charming, sincere, and beyond the trivia of self-promoting careerist moves that she deeply moved the many colored women in the audience, few of whom probably ever felt as unattractive as she claimed to be when younger and praying to God—every single day—that she be made lighter in skin tone.

Hollywood believes it can liberate Black people from such an unhealthy "lack of self-esteem." How does this ongoing feeling of being ravaged by "white beauty standards" continue or has it ever been true?

A far firmer grasp of human complexity is needed in this time so dominated by slogans. If she were a writer, Lupita Nyong'o might write herself a part as rich as what she brought to her short speech at the *Essence* event.

HOW TO USE SLAVERY
FOR ART AND PROFIT

Gordon Parks was a fine photographer, the first Black person hired by *Vogue* and *Life* magazines, and the first Black director hired by a major Hollywood studio. Like so many in show business, he is mostly forgotten now. And that is one of the things wrong with all of the talk about *12 Years a Slave*, which purports to be based on a memoir of the same name by Solomon Northup published in 1853, a fairly famous book that the overwhelming majority of those studying domestic slavery have read.

When the film's director, Steve McQueen, told PBS that, although he wanted to make a film about slavery in America for years, he never heard of the book before reading it, that proved one or two things. First: how little McQueen knew about American slavery. It may also have shown a showman's cynicism, almost an Alex Haley lie intended to present or shine up something that chose to be more commercially violent, to sell agitprop shock.

Almost seventy-two years old and at the height of his artistic powers, Parks made *Solomon Northup's Odyssey*, a film aired in 1984 on PBS (now available on streaming services). Compared to McQueen's version, it is a far superior and more humane depiction of slaves. Given his age, Parks had probably heard from grandparents (or those of their generation) much more folklore that could fill the historical blanks and avoid the stereotypes. Under his direction, slaves were much more than talking livestock, traumatized by plantation violence. Parks's slaves are people, where McQueen's are cardboard stock symbols.

There is a tradition of work that comes from some mix of paternalism, contempt, and the lust or desperation for a profitable career that, when artfully presented, finds a receptive audience seeking out the addictive sensation of victimhood or the paternal need to feel somehow ashamed on behalf of those below. It is this gathering of American tendencies that underlies every irresponsible decision.

We first witnessed it with Alex Haley's fraudulent *Roots*, with its made-to-sell backstory about tracing out his own family history and its whole-sale plagiarizing from Harold Courlander's novel *The African*. Haley paid $650,000 for the rip-off—$2 million in today's dollars, though he could well afford it because the book made him a millionaire and a celebrity speaker.

Despite being thoroughly exposed—by Philip Nobile in the *Village Voice* and then in a BBC documentary—for not only plagiarizing but also packaging a fictional story as his own history and for letting his editor do much of the actual writing, people continue to revere *Roots*. The judge in Haley's plagiarism trial flatly told the BBC that "Haley perpetrated hoax," adding that he pressed for a settlement because "Haley was a significant symbol in the Black community." Well, then.

Another self-appointed friend of the Negro, Lisa Drew, one of Haley's editors at Doubleday, defended publishing a non-true book as non-fiction because, "I was terribly afraid that if we called this book fiction, although it had fiction elements in it, the people who are not sympathetic to the viewpoint of the book would use this as an excuse to say . . . this is fiction and it is all made up and it didn't happen that way."

What about the truth?

That is why I am writing this—not to accuse McQueen and the others who made this film of theft or falsehood, like Haley's, but to say they are repeating his sin of putting Hollywood attention ahead of the human story they pretend to tell but sell short. For all those who just want to believe a good story, there remain many more interested in the dangerous hoax of reducing slaves to one-dimensional victims, as Haley and now McQueen have done.

GOOSE-LOOSE BLUES
FOR THE MELTING POT

S.C. didn't put much stock in the term melting pot, *preferring the concept of American culture as a collective gumbo or improvised bouillabaisse, the source of each flavor and ingredient distinctly recognizable in the roux. Published in* Reinventing the Melting Pot: The New Immigrants and What It Means to Be American *(Basic Books, 2004).*

WE WOULD DO OURSELVES a favor by backing away from the rhetorical hostility that attends the issue of assimilation. Assimilation is not the destruction of one's true identity. It is not, as advocates of separatism would teach us, a matter of domination and subordination, nor the conquest of one culture by another. On the contrary, it's about the great intermingling of cultural influences that comprises the American condition: the fresh ideas brought forward in our folklore, our entertainment, our humor, our athletic contests, our workplaces, even our celebrity trials and political scandals. Only the rhetorical violence left over from the 1960s prevents us from understanding what assimilation really means and how it actually happens in America.

This isn't to pretend that we as a nation have shed all bigotry based on skin tone, or sex, or religion, or nationality, or class. But if we still have troubles, and plenty of them, that doesn't mean we haven't advanced

VICTORY IS ASSURED

remarkably when it comes to race and ethnicity (and it doesn't mean we aren't capable of going even further). If we examine things as they actually are, we can see that what it means to be American has never been fixed or static or impervious to outsiders; we are continually creating and re-creating our traditions. In fact, American society is now so demonstrably open to variety, and so successful at gathering in those who would join it, that it is the international model of a free and progressively integrated nation.

WHEN THE CIVIL RIGHTS movement began, its enemy was racism, not white people per se. But as the irrational elements of Black Power congealed, the boldly nonviolent movement began to descend to a politics based in ethnic identity, sexual identity, and sexual preference. The hysteria, sentimentality, bigotry, and fantasies of Black Power extremists were taken up by other (so-called) ethnic minorities, by women, and by homosexuals. And over time, this politics of identity corroded into a politics of hostility, to the point that many Americans confused the real enemy—hateful visions such as racism, sexism, and homophobia—with the white race.

Among the effects of this shift from understanding to misunderstanding was the creation of "alienation studies" programs on campuses from one end of this nation to the other. Purportedly oppressed groups were taught that their only hope was "within their own." This separatism was often joined to a naive internationalism rooted in the paradigm of Marxist liberation. Black Americans were supposed to see themselves as part of a Third World struggle. People of color were supposed to reassert their "true" cultures, which had allegedly been ground to dust under the heels of the whites.

Not surprisingly, in this upside-down world, assimilation was seen as the destruction of true identity. Why should one want to disappear into an unvaried mass when one could be part of something more vital, more "authentic"? Under no circumstances was a Black American to forget that, as Malcolm X had said, "You are not an American, you are a victim of Americanism." One had to get back to one's true roots (which were in Africa), one's true religion (which was Islam), and one's true interests (which could never coincide with the interests of the United States). Variants of these Black Power ideas have been adopted by other ostensibly oppressed groups: Latinos, Asians, women, and homosexuals have each invented versions of the "Oreo" motif (black on the outside, white on the inside), regarding assimilation as a form of "selling out." Authenticity, according to this outlook, has become an absolute—and it is an impossible condition to achieve in a melting pot.

But the separatist alienation-studies crowd couldn't be more wrong about assimilation. For most Americans, identity has never been static. It never could be, especially in an experimental society that has forever had to create its own traditions. Indeed, even against our will, we Americans have a difficult time being provincial. The different groups that make up the nation need and attract and influence each other—even those brainwashed by alienation studies partake of the nation's shifting common culture. The notion that any group could remain separate and untouched is nothing more than a mad joke.

DECADES AGO, THE great Constance Rourke, author of the classics *American Humor* and *The Roots of American Culture*, proposed that there are four mythic figures at the core of American culture: the Indian, the Yankee, the Frontiersman, and the Negro. Director John Ford picked up the idea from her (or at least made use of it) at the conclusion of his 1939 film *Drums Along the Mohawk*, which is set during the Revolutionary War. The Indian, the Yankee, the Frontiersman, and the Negro all watch as an American flag is raised over an upstate New York fort, and they realize that its flapping colors and stars symbolize a human connection, one finalized through the death and tragedy of a war fought to make a new nation. From those four archetypes come our sense of the land, our folklore, our vision of adventure, our humor, our dance, our music, and our acknowledgment—as Ralph Ellison would add—of the importance of improvisation, of learning to absorb and invent on the spot.

Improvisation is essential to understanding these United States. It was especially necessary for a nation always faced with the unknown, forever at a frontier of some sort. The unknown was often the natural environment, as the frontier moved at first gingerly and then brutally west. The unknown frontier could also be the big city, drawing people from the countryside and teaching them breathtaking, illuminating, and destructive lessons. These encounters with the new quite often demanded invention-on-the-spot. Bringing mother wit to emergency situations is surely our national ideal, so much so that in Hollywood films, the villain or the monster is often dispatched by an improvised turn, an unexpected solution, a jerry-built contraption that does the job.

As the nation expanded through immigration and other means, it became equally necessary to improvise the idea of what it means to be American. The result is that cultural improvisation has become second nature as Rourke's four archetypes have been expanded. Mexican, Asian, Irish, Italian, and Eastern European strains have become part of the national identity, affecting our cowboy culture, our cuisine, our dance, our music, our slang, our Broadway shows, our films, our popular music, and our spiritual practices. American identity is never fixed or final; we are always working toward a better and deeper recognition of how to make one out of the many. The diffuse nature of our democracy leaves us with no choice. Consequently, out of this perpetual negotiation comes a collective identity that has to be, finally, as loose as the proverbial goose.

This goose-loose identity also involved some ongoing and usually constructive conflict—the struggle of the most high-minded Americans against the worst elements of our social past. Even when our sense of ourselves was profoundly bigoted—as far back as the three-fifths rule agreed upon by our Founding Fathers, which made Black slaves less human than white men—we always had a sense of a collective American reality. And even bigotry never stopped people from making use of any part of any culture that they found enjoyable or functional. Already in 1930, when psychoanalyst Carl Jung visited the United States, he observed that white Americans walked, talked, and laughed like Negroes, something we would hardly expect if we were to look at the stereotypical ways in which Black people were depicted at the time in American writing, theater, film, cartoons, and advertisements.

This cross-cultural borrowing and influence works the other way as well. As more than a few Negro Americans have found out when they went back to "the motherland," Africans look upon them—unless they are trying to hustle them for money—not as their brothers or sisters but as white people with black skins. In other words, Jung could see how much Black Americans had influenced white Americans, and Africans can see how much white Americans have influenced Black Americans. In the same way, European immigrants to America soon discovered that their kids were influenced by what they picked up while playing in the streets and by what was being sung and laughed about in popular entertainment. This is not the result of any melting pot that destroys distinctions; it is the expression of the mutations of choice and style that occur through our living close to each other.

Again, Ralph Ellison is important to our understanding of this messy, mixed-up way of being. Ellison knew that improvisation is essential to what we make of ourselves as Americans. He recognized that we are constantly integrating the things that we find attractive in others, whether the integration is conscious or unconscious. We all know that the American wears a top hat with an Indian feather sticking out of it, carries a banjo and a harmonica, knows how to summon the voice of the blues by applying a bathroom plunger to the bell of a trumpet or a trombone, will argue about the best Chinese restaurants, eat sushi with you one on one, turn the corner and explain the differences between the dishes on the menu at an Indian restaurant, drink plenty of tequila, get down with the martial arts, sip some vodka, recite favorite passages from the Koran, have some scotch on the rocks, show you the yarmulke worn at a friend's wedding, savor some French and Italian wine made from grapes grown in the Napa Valley, charm a snake, roll some ham and cheese up in a heated flour tortilla, tell what it was like learning to square dance or ballroom or get the pelvic twists of rhythm and blues right or how it felt in one of those sweltering Latin dance halls when the mambo got as hot as gumbo on a high boil. That's how American assimilation works. It's a quintessential part of our national adventure. Our society maintains its essential identity while new layers and nuances give greater vitality to the mix.

PERHAPS THE BEST way to understand where we are now, and what we have made of ourselves as Americans, is to look at the Kennedy era that began in 1960 when a handsome young Irishman became the first of his ethnic group to take the Oval Office. Back then, newspapers, magazines, television, and presidential conventions told us that just about anything of true importance was thought about, argued about, and accomplished by white men. They ran the country, the states, the cities, the towns, the villages, the networks, the stock market, the athletic teams, the entertainment world, the universities—and they were not shy about letting you know it. It was not so much that they were arrogant; they were simply the only ones around. You did not see Black people or any other people who were not white or any women in the highest governmental positions in Washington, D.C., or in individual state or city government. Such people were, of course, human, but they just didn't make the cut. America walked through a blizzard of white men.

Only a lunatic would cling to the idea that the America of today is that same America of 1960. That world is as long gone as the Los Angeles through which saber-toothed tigers once strode and roared. When one turns on the television today, one sees people of every color and both sexes anchoring the local news, giving their analysis of the stock market, international politics, the entertainment industry, and whatever else might be of human concern, whether important or trivial or somewhere between those extremes. Ours is now a far more integrated society, and the aspirations of children from every group are far different now that there are flesh-and-blood human beings upon whom they can base their dreams.

I began to see how deeply things had changed when my daughter, born in 1977, was around six years old, and I asked her what she intended to be when she grew up. She answered that she might be an astronaut, a Supreme Court justice, a police officer, a fireman, a doctor, or maybe a pilot. I was rather startled, to be honest, because, having been born in 1945, I had heard six-year-old girls say "a mother, a teacher, or a nurse." In the early 1950s, no rational young girl—or woman—would have thought she could become a Supreme Court justice. But when I considered what my daughter had said, I realized that the feminists had won the battle for the minds and aspirations of her generation. A Black girl living in Compton, California, had absorbed, through all those vastly different television images, a sense of life and possibility that included imagining women in every significant career. Life seemed an open sky.

More than a decade and a half later, the influences that inspired my daughter to express such a broad range of career options have only intensified. Over and over, throughout the day and night, our advertisements project an integrated America. What's more, they tell us that no group of Americans is defined by the worst among them. Above all, we see that whites, Negroes, Hispanics, and Asians, whether men or women, work in every capacity, from the world of the blue collar all the way up to the business suites. We also see that every group, across all classes, has families—wives, husbands, children—and what sociologist Todd Gitlin has called "common dreams." This is profoundly important, no matter its commercial motivations. In attempting to sell products by making all Americans feel free to spend money, the brain trust of the advertising world takes every opportunity to tell us that, no matter what we look like, we are all human and have as much access to what is good as the next person. Come on in. Feel welcome. Sit down. Pull out your credit card.

Toward that end, our advertising culture is based on the assumption that normal, everyday life is integrated. We are shown that people need not be ill at ease when talking with others superficially different from themselves. Nor should they assume that any kind of human problem is color-bound. In the civil rights era of the mid-1960s, it used to be joked (playing off the stereotype that dark people smelled worse than white people) that Blacks would have made it all the way into American society once a Negro could be shown in a deodorant commercial. That problem has surely gone by the boards in an era when anybody can advertise anything.

Skill, intelligence, and advice cross all racial lines. In one commercial, a white man who promises his kids that he will build a tree house for them finds himself in the lumber store getting perfect advice from a Black man. In another, a Black woman who wants to repaint the inside of her house buys paint from a white woman who tells her that she can't be afraid of yellow, advice she repeats both to her husband and to an Asian woman and a white man who come over to see what she has done. Insurance meant to appeal to older Americans has crosscuts of various ethnic faces. Advertisements for vans show smiling families that may or may not be white. It is not surprising to see an integrated group of women laughing and joking together or extolling the supposed virtues of brands of lipstick and facial powders and lingerie and sanitary napkins. A supervisor and his or her employees can cross the spectrum. And when children are depicted at schools or playing together or Christmas shopping, the gang's all there, providing our young people with early recognition of their common connections.

By the time they are teenagers, most Americans are completely converted to this notion, above all by music television. No matter what we might think of the songs they promote or the obnoxious attitudes they celebrate, in these shows integration is a given. It does not surprise the audience to see an Asian girl compete with a Black one in learning dance routines from a rap group and win! Using the inarticulate language of adolescent self-promotion, the Asian girl assumes she is as much of a fan as the Black girl and has such confidence in her ability to dance that she laughs off the idea that anyone else could learn faster or move with more finesse. An All-American girl of our moment.

Talk shows also convince us of our common humanity—and of everyone's capacity for every human quality, from heroic compassion to unflappable crassness. The popularity of Oprah Winfrey and Montel Williams obviates all color lines as they address human problems of almost every sort. We see Black and white men and women and young people, as well as members of every other ethnic group, discussing their troubles in their romances, in their marriages, with their children, with their addictions, in their careers and elsewhere. We see every kind of emotion expressed by white, Black, red, and yellow people. We see women and men of every hue break down in tears, overwhelmed by their humanity and reiterating what deep feeling can do to all of us.

On those talk shows, we also see a wide range of knuckleheads, male and female, from troubled children to repulsive adults. Jerry Springer has surely proved to those who might have doubted it that neither ethnicity nor religion is automatic protection from ignorance or stupidity or trivial obsessions or abysmally crude thoughts or even more abysmal behavior. In that sense, regardless of his obvious appeal to the very lowest common denominator, he has provided us with a public service.

Nor is democratic recognition of our humanity limited to the worlds of advertising and television. In every team sport we see integration at work. In our streets, we see men and women of every ethnic group employed as public servants. Our armed forces are distinguished by male and female professionals of every hue and religious background. It is no longer odd to see a Black person or a woman at the top of city government. We even saw a Negro, Doug Wilder, elected governor of Robert E. Lee's home state: Virginia, that pearl of the Confederacy. Venus and Serena Williams dominate tennis. Tiger Woods, his father Black and his mother Asian, is the miracle man of a game that once lay under a snowdrift of white men that seemed beyond melting. When someone is reporting on television from Washington, D.C., that person could be of any color or either sex.

This recognition even extends beyond color and class and religion to include those with physical disabilities. We are beginning to understand what Victor Hugo was after with his famous character Quasimodo: to see the nobility beneath a grotesque surface, the spirit of the prince within the frog. Yes, just as we have learned that skin tone and genitalia do not obviate humanity, we have been battling our way toward embracing the humanity of the blind, the lame, the disfigured, the obese, the person who might have to struggle through cerebral palsy to have his or her heart and soul and mind recognized. Here—in our classrooms, in our workplaces, in our popular media—is the melancholic grandeur and compassion of democracy. Here, in slow and accumulating human detail, is how we play out that very demanding American game, working ever harder to see ourselves in others and others in ourselves.

OF COURSE, IF you are in the wrong place at the wrong time, none of this matters—and it can often seem that the American Dream does not apply if you are Black or brown. Racial hatred can seem to run deep, the police and the courts can be grimly disappointing. Take the example of New York City, where race relations could not have been more bitter or raw in recent years. Surely, many say, this makes a mockery of what we as a nation seem to have achieved since the 1960s. Maybe it does, maybe it doesn't. For some of the worst racial conflicts of the past decade turn out to be more complex than we usually think, and even offer some potentially encouraging lessons.

True enough, there was a terrible race riot in New York in 1991, in the mixed Black and Jewish neighborhood of Crown Heights. The motorcade of a powerful Orthodox rabbi drove through a red light and swerved onto the sidewalk, killing a seven-year-old Black child, Gavin Cato. A Black mob gathered, grumbling—even though the city was then governed by a Black mayor—that Jews were running the city and Black life had no value in New York. Soon they were yelling "Get the Jew," and a few hours later a rabbinical student from Australia was fatally stabbed. As he died, Yankel Rosenbaum identified a young Black man, Lemrick Nelson, as his assailant. When Nelson was brought to trial, his Black lawyer implied that the Black police officers testifying for the prosecution were no more than slaves following the orders of their masters. Nelson was ultimately found innocent by a predominantly Black jury.

Six years later, in the summer of 1997, Haitian immigrant Abner Louima was arrested, beaten, taken to a precinct house in Brooklyn, and sodomized with a broken broom handle. He nearly died from the wounds he received in his rectum. From his hospital bed, he charged that the cops who assaulted him had jeered: "It's Giuliani time!" To some, this seemed proof enough that New York policemen using excessive force were acting on racist orders from the white mayor, Rudolph Giuliani.

Nor was the Louima case the end of the story. As Giuliani's mayoralty continued, the cops were often accused of turning New York City into a police state. An aggressive plainclothes division, working in the crime-ridden streets of Harlem and the Bronx, could claim as the official motto of their unit: "We own the night." On February 4, 1999, four white members of that division fired forty-one shots at Amadou Diallo, an unarmed immigrant from Africa, hitting and killing him with nineteen bullets. Surely, it was said, there is something racially rancid at the center of the American Dream. Had Diallo been white, even in a high-crime Bronx neighborhood of the sort in which he lived, he would not have been shot in such a hysterically clumsy, deadly display.

The Diallo case was tried not in New York City but upstate, in Albany. The jury consisted of eight whites and four Blacks. The prosecution demonstrated that Diallo had been shot repeatedly even after going down. The defense countered that the four policemen had been looking for a criminal; when they approached, Diallo didn't answer questions and appeared to have drawn a gun. One of the cops wept on the stand. When the jury foreman, a Black woman, read the verdict, the cops were exonerated of all charges. Black New Yorkers seethed with anger, and the Rev. Al Sharpton, not always known for acting responsibly, admonished them not to besmirch the slaughtered man's memory with the kind of violence that had brought him down. There were no incidents. Yet race relations seemed at a dismal low.

Then, over the next few years, tempers began to cool, and the truth about the city's decade-long racial nightmare began to come out. In Crown Heights, reporters discovered that the racial antipathy behind the riots had been brought in from outside the community by rabble-rousers quite unknown to the Black kids who lived there. In fact, it turned out, the Black and Jewish people in the neighborhood got along rather well. In 1997, Lemrick Nelson was brought to justice again, found guilty, and sentenced to nearly twenty years for violating Yankel Rosenbaum's civil rights. That decision was later overturned on appeal due to the judge's heavy-handed attempt to fight racism with more racism by insisting that the jury be racially balanced. Still, in May 2003, after three trials, Nelson was convicted of violating Rosenbaum's civil rights, though not of causing his death. (His defense was that he had nothing against Jews; he was just drunk, got excited, and went along with the flow of the mob.)

In the Louima case, the sodomizing cop, Justin Volpe, was identified by fellow officers, tried, and sentenced to thirty years in prison. What's more, however monstrous his actions, it turned out that Volpe may not be a racist in any way that we can ascertain: He was never accused of being a bigot by his coworkers, and he even had a Black fiancée. In fact, she was often harassed by Black cops for going out with him—and it's possible that this is what lit a fuse in him. Without forgiving Volpe for the unforgivable, it's worth considering: If the NYPD had offered a program to address such harassment of interracial couples, perhaps Louima would have been spared his assault.

Louima, meanwhile, admitted to having lied when he claimed his assailants yelled, "It's Giuliani time": He said he had been advised to say so to bring attention to his case. When his civil case got to court, he was awarded millions by the city, something that would never have happened in his native Haiti. And in the wake of the Diallo tragedy, the New York Police Academy has instituted an elaborate set of training procedures designed to prevent anything of the sort from happening again.

Those high-profile cases did not all come out perfectly, to say the least. Yet in no case was the truth as stark as it seemed at first. In almost every instance, both Blacks and whites participated in bringing the city back from the brink—and again and again justice transcended race. Our deeply American humanity triumphed over even the most divisive kinds of violence and xenophobic murder.

THESE LESSONS FROM New York's recent history are even more important in the wake of the terrorist attacks of September 11, 2001. Since then, we have learned the deeper reason why the twin towers were called the World Trade Center: The three thousand people who worked and died there were of every color and both sexes, they believed in all of the major religions, and they worked in every capacity from cleaning floors to trading stocks. What we saw on September 11 was integrated America under attack—and our hearts collectively broke as the buildings went down and the clouds of dust spread. Black and white and red and yellow people helped and supported one another. Americans and immigrants on their way to becoming Americans, in their work clothes and their business suits, their police uniforms and their fire department gear—all moved together through the streets and across the Brooklyn Bridge. And at that tragic moment, in their collectivity and their willingness to suffer with and for each other, they symbolized the ability of the species to stand up to disaster as human beings. The one thing that has always been true about the nation became even more true on that unforgettable morning: Our surface differences are far less important than what we have in common and what we will ourselves to be, as men and women and Americans.

THE LIES THAT BLIND

BLACK GIRL / WHITE GIRL

No living American writer is more skilled at showing the human heart in conflict with itself than Joyce Carol Oates. However gifted at plot development and the use of motifs and thematic clues to provide psychological and emotional depth, Oates is, finally, a writer of moral fiction. She often writes about costs and responsibility. In her work there is always a culprit or a set of culprits responsible for those costs, which are forever high. A death or the destruction of a career can result because of a mistake made by someone else. Though profoundly aware that we are often most human in the middle of misunderstanding others, Oates is also telling us that so many of our most haunting tragedies are rooted in wrong judgments. What makes her particularly important to our time is how she brings those technical skills and that overview to the most demanding front line of our era and the epic quality of its errors based in liberal or conservative stereotypes. These received ideas are supposed to explain ethnic behavior, family, history, society, and themselves.

Oates has long avoided the dominant tendency that results in American writers knowing much about their backyards but little about their neighborhoods, cities, or states, and even less about those outside their ethnic groups. That is why *Black Girl / White Girl* is such a marvel and moves the very enterprise of contemporary fiction far beyond the well-worn subject of self-obsession. Oates writes from the frontier of integration, where race is all but tells us so much less than we might assume, imply, or assert. *Black Girl / White Girl* is the third novel in which Oates plays variations on the psychologically complex themes of interwoven class and ethnic conflict. The situation is familiar: During the 1970s, a young female freshman struggles with the deceptive layers of trouble arriving in black and white terms that mystify, disturb, and frustrate her. One is startled by how Oates achieves even greater depths of human understanding than she did in the previous *I'll Take You There* from 2002, both a blue masterwork and an extraordinary advance over the first in this series, 1990's *Because It Is Bitter, and Because It Is My Heart*.

The narrator/main female character makes good and bad decisions in response to surroundings where rational and lunatic modes of address become ritualistic: White and Black people relate to each other while playing all manner of games and wearing all manner of masks. Yet Oates finds human parallels, no matter how far apart her people might be on the social or the color scale. That is the fundamental strength of literary art, and Oates knows, without a doubt, that there is always a human heart beneath the surfaces, and it usually beats frantically or in stunned slow motion.

In making this concealed humanity apparent, the novelist outdoes almost all American writers in her imaginatively ordered structures of revelation. Techniques are borrowed from the detective story; with a virtuosic sense of placement, she provides clues through outbursts in which suppressed thoughts and feelings appear and surprise the teller as much as they do the listener. Her varieties of precision allow for distinct tonal and rhythmic differences if the sudden blurtings take place in public or in private. One can spark anger and embarrassment, the other empathy.

Oates masterfully uses a patient tempo to make everything seemingly clear but not didactic. The middle-aged narrator tells us about herself when she was a white girl living with a Black girl during their freshman year at a liberal arts college founded by Quakers. Though the white girl is so ashamed of her privileges that she hides the fact of being heir to Quaker millions, and though the Black girl has been reared as the spoiled, self-centered daughter of a minister, they are very similar. Both girls feel alienated from their surroundings and equally intimidated by their class-mates, no matter how differently they express their fears or how hard they try to protect themselves.

The white girl pretends to be just another freshman strapped for money, and she brown-noses with a nearly selfless determination much of the time. The Black girl trembles behind a blowfish exterior of con-descending bitchiness that intensifies as her dorm mates—Black and white—lose patience with her and slowly begin to hate the young woman for her apparent sense of superiority, if not a defiantly unquestionable feel-ing of personal perfection.

That they are completely wrong is what so many of the characters in the novel have in common: They misconstrue the motivations of others because every mistake is so much easier to make when marinated in stere-otypes that decisively limit accurate perception. The girls in the dorm do not think that color provides a good enough excuse for studied rudeness and disdain, but they cannot comprehend the fear blocked from sight by the nose of a snooty minister's daughter that rises ever higher in the air as the pressure becomes greater. The white girl accepts every slight from her self-involved roommate, patiently hoping she will be liked at some later date. She eventually deduces that the Black girl got high grades in second-rate public schools that did not provide sufficient sophistication or the skill to do first-rate college work.

When the desperately prideful Black girl realizes how poorly pre-pared public school has left her, the choice is made to retreat into herself, into her Bible, and to consume so much food that her weight balloons until she covers the protective and self-disgusting armor of fat with a hooded overcoat that makes her appear ominous to white storekeepers. Hiding a feeling of defeat, the minister's daughter smugly accepts all of the gushing sympathy that appears when she becomes the target of racist actions and notes.

Oates depicts the interaction between the white shopkeepers and the Black girl with superior insight, and the writer maintains this in showing the clumsiness with which the girls, teachers, and college administrators respond to the stubbornly mysterious presence of assumed racism among them. As one would expect of Oates, the racist actions and the bigoted notes mask a much greater complexity, which rises through the narrative with admirable pacing and a degree of deep concern for the bewildering heartbreak that always, somehow, attends integration.

Oates also peels back the covers on the radical-chic family of her narrator, headed by a wealthy lawyer given to liberal condescension and a mother who has been taken in by the decadence, the psychobabble, and the drugs of the 1960s. Not since Danzy Senna's innovatively compre-hensive *Caucasia* has anyone done an equally powerful analysis of such people and the harsh dangers of the fire with which they played as the high-mindedness of the civil rights movement gave way to a heartlessly romantic sense of "revolutionary" action.

One of the reasons this novel stands so tall is that Oates makes the well-intentioned villains as sympathetic, frail, and naive as everyone else. For all their human qualities, neither the lawyer nor his wife manage to avoid the disgust the narrator has for their irresponsible support of too many dangerous radicals. Oates does not ask the reader to forgive the husband and wife, which would be immoral, but her writing demands that we not fail to recognize their humanity, because dehumanizing them would be an even greater act of immorality. Ignorance of the consequences, the writer tells us in no uncertain terms, is not an excuse but a complicating aspect of our ethnic tragedy.

At the end, the narrator must face the love that she still feels for those she has failed and betrayed. Paced by a terrible campus fire and the fall of a powerful man, the close-ups, flashbacks, foreshadowings, and counterpointing of the narrative become particularly effective in the last one hundred pages. Everything that seemed extraneous before is realized, adding human and thematic resonance.

The grandeur of the achievement cannot be overstated. Few American writers have the necessary spunk and technique to bring a world of more than one ethnic type alive: Even fewer understand the tremulous souls hidden by meaningless class and even more meaningless color. Only those with the biggest hearts have the nerve to enter that bruising frontier of the national life, integration, where nothing is actually what it seems, and no one has a heart bigger, braver, or more full of unsentimental pity than Joyce Carol Oates.

October 2006

JOYCE WEIN'S LIFE AND DEATH, A MODEL FOR ALL OF US

JOYCE ALEXANDER WEIN, wife of jazz impresario George Wein, was laid to rest August 19 in New York at a very unusual funeral. What one comes to expect at a funeral for someone connected to jazz is a lot of self-aggrandizement in which the speakers reveal more about their obsessions than they do about the one considered the dearly departed.

This was so different that it seemed a high point in the culture of our time because the ceremony and the speakers gave vent to their affection for a Black woman who was so far outside the stereotypes that burden the educated, the middle class, and the sophisticated Black people who rise to positions of authority or prominence. They are too often considered inauthentic unless they cannot speak the English language or seem no more sophisticated than a badly cooked pot of chitlins or some low-grade corn bread.

Born in 1928, Joyce Alexander was from the Black middle class of

Boston. When she married her Jewish husband in 1959, he was the one who rose socially and developed layers of taste and understanding from her, which is so often reversed in the conventional tale of the Jewish guy who marries the Black woman and educates her in the finer things of life.

Joyce Alexander had graduated from Girls Latin School at fifteen and from Simmons College as a chemistry major four years later. She loved literature, knew much about painting, and was not a woman who suffered either the limited expectations or the racism of her time in silence. As is traditional at jazz funerals, there was a level of integration that we see too little of when great souls are lost in the worlds of literature, dance, theater, concert music, and film. As one person pointed out, the gathering was integrated in the way that Joyce Wein's personality and intellect were integrated. She was everything that she liked—the joy and variety of jazz, the sweep of literature, the craft of painting, the nuance of cuisine, the discipline common to all people of achievement, the dignity of the species, and the great sense of humor that we Americans all know in our very special way.

Jazz has always celebrated the individual at the same time as it ultimately values group cooperation, and it has been on the front line of integration in the most important ways. In the world of jazz, one gets recognition not for one's color or background but for what one can create alone and in combination with others. Joyce Wein was a founder of the New York Coalition of 100 Black Women and was an influential figure in the world of philanthropy and the arts. She established the Joyce and George Wein Chair in African American Studies at Boston University and the Alexander Family Endowed Scholarship Fund at Simmons College, served on the board of the Studio Museum in Harlem for ten years, and, with her husband, was a known collector of the works of Black American artists. She was not a layabout.

Joyce Alexander Wein represented the best of jazz and the best of American womanhood because she never took a backseat to anyone. She sat in the front and brought as many people to the first row as she could whenever she could. That was her greatness, and that was what she stood for, because she believed much more in fairness than in favors. She was a model for our nation.

August 2005

BY ANY MEANS NECESSARY

HEROES ARE MADE BY LUCK, will, circumstance, and the kind of exaggerations that always follow exceptional actions of some sort. Huey P. Newton founded the Black Panther Party for Self-Defense with Bobby Seale in 1966, the year that Black Power darkened the skies of the civil rights movement. In beret and black leather jacket, Newton presented himself as a man who had no patience for nonviolence and would no longer accept violent action against Black people without retaliating. Echoing Malcolm X, he promised to live by the gun in order to gain the respect that Black people, supposedly, had never shown the courage to demand. "By any means necessary" became the watchword of the Black Panthers, which meant that all was possible in the name of Black revolution. Though he had survived a gunfight with the police, imprisonment, and a number of assassination plots, real or imagined, Newton died in the dark bed that he had made for himself and that only those close to him knew about.

Newton had a cocaine habit that made his personality mercurial and may have provided the impetus to shift his organization into serious crime by the early 1970s. Fawned over by the New Left, the news media, and Hollywood, he was transformed into a messiah expected to fill ever bigger shoes. Newton became so unhinged by megalomania that his increasingly irrational decisions brought about the dissolution of the Black Panther Party, which had given him his moment on the national and international stage.

He was killed in 1989 on the streets of Oakland by a member of the dope-hustling crew called the Black Guerrilla Family, which had, following Newton's lead, associated its criminal activities with radical politics—revolution, if you will. The death of Newton had nothing to do with politics of any sort. The three shots the former symbol of radical politics took to the head were a dealer's expression of intimidation and rage for having been bullied into giving Newton free crack cocaine too many times before.

After his death, Newton was floated along on a pond of crocodile tears by many whom he had disappointed and abused. Attempting to glorify themselves and the years they had wasted in the party, they were quite willing to overlook the considerable blemishes of the man who had come to call himself "the Supreme Servant of the People."

Flores A. Forbes's memoir of his experiences in the Black Panther Party, *Will You Die With Me?*, may startle those who would romanticize this homemade Maoist organization in the same way that T. J. Stiles's biography of Jesse James startled readers when it proved that James was not at all a Robin Hood. In *Jesse James: Last Rebel of the Civil War*, Stiles showed that James was a racist and terrorist always willing to manipulate others through their resentment at losing the Civil War and through the hatred they felt when forced to see Black people move beyond the position of plantation chattel. Newton apparently had the same ability to manipulate his followers—through their understandable hostility toward racism and through their unfortunately romantic fantasies about being revolutionaries in the vanguard of social change so thorough it would bring down the United States government.

Forbes joined the Black Panthers at the end of the 1960s and worked his way up until he functioned as a bodyguard, an enforcer, and a gunman in the inner circle of the party. As the onetime head of the Panthers' "military arm," he has eyewitness things to tell us that have never been made so clear before. In a very low-key, matter-of-fact style that takes attempted murder, gunplay, beatings, extortion, and arrests as normal occurrences, Forbes pulls the covers off Newton with so much authority that the case his book makes against the Black Panther legend will be hard to dismiss. In unparalleled detail, we are given the inside story of a left-wing group of "revolutionaries" whose organization evolved into a lucrative criminal enterprise—the first step of a grand design in which the political structure of Oakland would be taken over. The Chicago of Al Capone may have been a model.

The party was influenced as much by Mario Puzo's novel *The Godfather* as it was by Mao's Little Red Book or Frantz Fanon's *The Wretched of the Earth*. Because they had more trained killers and more guns, the Panthers came to support themselves and purchase real estate with money extorted from Oakland's Black underworld. Early in the 1970s, the organization retreated to Oakland at Newton's command, closing all of its national offices. This was a response to the pressure exerted by local and federal law enforcement; by rival groups such as the Los Angeles Black nationalists who called themselves US; and by those within the Panthers who broke away and started the murderous Black Liberation Army after they had decided that guerrilla war should start immediately, because community Panther efforts such as the free-breakfast program were not revolutionary enough. At the hands of all these forces, many Panthers were killed,

usually by law enforcement, which was understandably intent on destroy-
ing the Black Panthers, either with imprisonment or with hot lead. In
1986, Eldridge Cleaver said to *Reason* magazine: "We would go out and
ambush cops, but if we got caught we would blame it on them and claim
innocence. I did that personally in the case I was involved in."

OF COURSE, GIVEN our bizarrely romantic sense of the Panther years,
we are accustomed to hearing Huey Newton's crew described as heroic
victims who were constantly harassed, imprisoned, and killed by the racist
power structure. *Will You Die With Me?* is a corrective to all that blather. It
is chilling in its unpretentious portrayal of the author as no more than an
ominous automaton who, once he swallowed the ideology as a teenager,
was able to follow orders, no matter how cold and senseless they might
have seemed. He yielded to the many purges without protest and was even
able to silently accept the expulsion from the party of a woman he loved
and had lived with for three years. Forbes was that most dangerous of
people: the true believer who accepts the idea that his job is to do or die,
not ever to ask why.

The book's descriptions of gatherings at Newton's apartment give us
insight into the power he had over his followers: "The menu at these sessions was a steady diet of cocaine, Cognac, and cigarettes. Huey didn't
smoke weed, like most of us, because he said it made him paranoid. Anyway, most of the time he talked about the plan to take over the city of
Oakland and other territories nearby, like the speakeasies and drug dens
in South Berkeley. We would sit around while Huey roamed the house
telling long, intricate stories that always led to a fascinating climax."

In October 1977, after the attempted assassination of a woman who
was expected to testify against Newton in a murder trial, Forbes went on
the run, wounded and reflective. Driving to Chicago with two Panther

buddies, he realized that all three of them could kiss their Black Panther days goodbye. He also concluded that for the past few years their thoughts and beliefs "were personal and narrow-minded. The bigger picture of helping our people had been subordinated. . . . I'm not sure if 'the people' provided our motivation anymore." Forbes wound up surrendering to the police and was eventually sentenced to eight years in prison.

Part of the power of the book is seeing this man slowly shocked free of the iceberg of ideology to which he had submitted and for which he was willing to achieve goals "by any means necessary." Much of its value is that it helps to make up for a decided shortcoming of our national literature, which has never sufficiently examined the radical politics of the 1960s. Doubtless, Flores Forbes does not achieve the kind of depth we would expect from a Ralph Ellison or the Richard Wright of *American Hunger*. Yet what Forbes does with marvelous ease is present a harrowing self-portrait of a man who willingly chilled his own heart, brutalized a number of others, and nearly paid the ultimate price in the process.

September 2006

BLUES FOR NOTE AND PAINT

THERE HAS NEVER BEEN ANYTHING more American than jazz. Jazz music remade every element of Western music in an American way, just as the Declaration of Independence and the Constitution remade the traditions of Western democracy, expanding the idea of freedom to levels it had never known at any prior time. American democracy updated the social order with its checks-and-balances system and its amendment process. These safeguard measures were based in tragic optimism, the idea that abuse of power can create tragic consequences, but if there is a form in place that allows for the righting of wrongs, we can maintain an upbeat vision that is not naive. When things assumed to be right turn out to be wrong, we have to improvise better policies into place. American democracy is an ongoing process that redefines itself through government in order to make up for the shortcomings of government. If the redefinition—as with the attempt at imposing temperance through law during the Prohibition era—doesn't work, we improvise ourselves out of a mess by striking a law from the books.

American democracy is also the governmental form in which the interplay between the individual and the mass takes on a complexity mirrored by the improvising unit of the jazz band. In jazz music, the empathetic imagination of the individual strengthens the ensemble. This happens as the form, which is an outline that is followed but is also played with, is given its dimensions through the collective inventions of the ensemble. In that sense, jazz is a democratic form itself, one in which, as the great jazz critic Martin Williams observed, there is more freedom than ever existed in any previous Western music.

That freedom affected everything that jazz touched. The instruments were played with such redefining conceptions that one could even say that the tools of the music were aesthetically remade. For vocal effects, jazz musicians held rubber plungers in front of the bells of trumpets and trombones, moving them so that the human voice with an American accent marinated in the blues whispered or surged into the air. Reed instruments became vocal as well as string-like and percussive. The string bass, almost always bowed in European concert music, was plucked into an unprecedented kind of heavy-stringed, harmonic percussion. Drums and cymbals were brought together and resulted in an entirely new instrument called the drum set, one that called upon the player's hands and feet. The piano may have been the most resistant, but it, too, submitted to a jazz identity, loping through and trilling the blues and swinging with yet another vista of tuned percussion at the ready. At the will of Thelonious Monk, the piano became something truly new, a harshly lyrical reflection of the steel and concrete form of New York City.

The instruments were changed because they had to express another sensibility, and that sensibility was given its force through the blues, the show tunes, and the original works that formed the basic repertoire of the music. That music was rough at one end and quite refined at the other, arriving from a Negro world of black, brown, beige, and bone-colored people. These were the descendants of slaves and the heirs to bloodlines and layers of culture so profound one can easily understand how jazz rose from those wild to graceful circumstances and was passed on for all to share by the Negro, whom Richard Wright thought of as America's metaphor, the symbol of the best and the most difficult aspects of this nation. Like the people who invented it, jazz came up hard, rising from the blues and out of the gutbuckets where the stickiness and the stink of life as well as its sensual truths and its delicious but slippery textures were evident.

Though it is often resisted and resented, the fact is that the music arrived in New Orleans, that port city where one could hear chants in the streets, blues, funeral marches, parade music, and, in the elegant theaters, the French and Italian opera. A musician coming to maturity in the Crescent City played christenings, weddings, funerals, Mardi Gras, park concerts, and just about anything there was to play, discovering the wide range of human occasions that demanded appropriate rhythms and tunes. Jazz was a development of that amalgamation, an art built upon one talent after another, some trained, some not—which is why the music grew so fast; it was open to anyone who could make musical sense. If the musician could perform with logic, feeling, and command of the idiom, it didn't matter if the voice had a small range or the instrumentalist wasn't effective in more than one register. There was a place for that musician, and that musician, like Billie Holiday, might powerfully influence jazz interpretation. So the music, part quilt and available to any kind of true talent, achieved originality in the same way that all things do; it became more than the parts forming it.

What held those parts together was itself original, an American feeling that arrived around the turn of the twentieth century. They called it the blues. The blues was the tragic and optimistic thread that wove together the various kinds of musical fabrics, from tattered sandpaper underwear to the highest quality silk. It was through blues melody, blues feeling, and blues rhythm that an adult American music arose. In the name of blues, a simple form full of profound feeling came into being, one in which the listener was taken beyond sentimentality into a fluctuating world of deep heartache and lust and frustration and exaltation and rage and remorse and the voluminous memories of tenderness triumphant through the fury against loneliness that is the rhythm of love and romance.

The rhythm of swing, which was brought to an innovative level of phrasing by Louis Armstrong during the middle and late 1920s, gave jazz the rhythmic distinction that matched the melodic originality and the harmonic freshness of blues. With his melodic invention, his swing, and the way in which he was able to push the blues through the harmonies of the Tin Pan Alley tunes that provided a bridge from the world of jazz into the broader society, Armstrong became one of the great creators of the twentieth century. From his range of improvised ideas comes the core of jazz, the roots upon which all the soloists, the rhythm-section players, and the composers built their music, consciously or not. That combination of familiar and unfamiliar themes artistically realized through improvised development provided another flying machine for the human soul.

Just as improvisation is central to jazz, it is improvisation that has long defined so many kinds of visual art as well. Jazz and Western visual art have much more in common than we usually think, and that is why any gallery show featuring jazz works has the potential to highlight that commonality while making us even more aware of how superbly different the silent work of the visual artist is from the aural art of the musician. The essence of those differences arrives through the materials used to create the aesthetic work. When the subjects are painting and music, we are talking about images or sound achieving communication with the eyes or the ears of the audience. It is through those two very different senses that the sensibility of the audience is touched, sometimes on many, many levels. That is why we can think of the unspeaking art of the painter as the art of the visible and the audible but unseeable art of the musician as the art of the invisible.

It is impossible to say which one—music or painting—arrived first. But I mean as an art, not just a pleasurable activity. During the childish years of the species, way back before way back, there were surely people who made noise. They were most probably having fun; expression in precise terms or in poetic abstractions were not at the top of the list of ambitions. There were just as surely people who scratched upon something or, even earlier, stood amused at the fact that they could make impressions with their feet or their hands—or both—in the dirt or in the mud. The evolution into art is something else altogether because the aesthetic proposes that symbols can magnetize worlds of experience and propel them into an audience at the same time. In both visual art and music, that is the problem facing the artist—how well can something summon and how well can it project.

The means through which the vision of the artist is made manifest help determine what is at work, and those means are so often improvisational or are approached with improvisational freedom. There are certain elements that arrive over and over in jazz, and they have their parallels in visual art. In jazz, even in its period of most substantial innovation, the music far more often than not uses 4/4 swing, fast, medium, and slow. Romantic and contemplative ballads are played. The blues is fundamental to the music. And there are uses of Afro-Hispanic rhythms, sometimes called "Latin." In painting, there is the portrait, there is the landscape, there is the still life, there is the religious work, and so on and on. Where jazz and painting really seem related is in the fact that the maker may often take something that is common and, through the improvisations native to bringing forth individuality, restate the very proposition.

Some examples are perhaps necessary. In the world of the painter as in the world of the jazz musician, there is a standard repertoire, a body of themes that have become quite familiar to the audience. The Italian Renaissance is a case in point. The themes were so often biblical and focused on the life of Christ that those themes rendered by the individual artist were dominated by improvisation. The painter got a chance to choose everything once he had decided upon his theme. From the annunciation to the crucifixion, the miracles to the descent from the cross, the lamentations to the ascension, there was an open sky of decisions that constituted improvisation. The painter could decide what time of day it was and, therefore, what position the sun would be in, determining the point of light and the quality of the shadows and the darkness. The painter could decide what was in the foreground and what was in the background. The facial features and the positions of the figures were equally open to improvisation as were the colors of the clothes and the surrounding combination of landscape and human elements of construction (including the texture of the wood of the cross).

So painters have a good deal in common with jazz musicians, regardless of when they arrived after painting had revealed its powers through perspective. From that point on, we were moving toward the kind of work we see in this show,* work that attempts to bring to the canvas, in a silent way, the improvised human song that we hear on jazz bandstands. Jazz musicians, speaking of formal control and substance, have often talked of a first-class improviser as one who "paints a picture." In this show, ample evidence is presented of how improvisation functions in the quiet world

---

* Katonah Museum of Art, catalogue for the exhibit *Jazz and Visual Improvisations*, January 21–April 15, 2001.

of the visual image. We see the human form toyed with, flat rejections of perspective, collages, totally abstract works that attempt to put painting into the abstract arena of feeling and nuance that is the province of the musician. In all, we see many approaches, all of them the expression of freedom, all of them in the spirit of jazz, which is in the spirit of the United States of America.

STEEL CITY SWING

When Crouch told the story of an American, given the space and an indulgent editor, he would begin at the very beginning, bringing all of his knowledge and the experience of prior generations to bear. To tell the story of Pittsburgh Courier *photographer Charles "Teenie" Harris is to tell the story of Pittsburgh, beginning with the Iroquois, the Whiskey Boys, and the French and Indian War, through Carnegie and Frick, their Pinkerton massacre of workers at Homestead, with the Negro League Homestead Grays at the other end of a human chain, all reflected in the chrome and polished steel of a Pontiac sedan with the aspirations of a resplendent Black middle class in the Hill District.*

Pittsburgh . . . is without exception the blackest place which I ever saw. As regards scenery, it is beautifully situated, being just at the juncture of the two rivers, Monongahela and Allegheny. . . . Nothing can be more picturesque than the site. . . . Even the filth and wondrous blackness of the place are picturesque when looked down upon from above.

—ANTHONY TROLLOPE, 1860

It could have been called Three Rivers.

Why?

Moving through those mountains, casual and powerful as they please, the Allegheny and the Monongahela, come together and transform into the Ohio River, don't they?

They do.

I thought so.

T HOSE THREE FLOWING WATERS made what is now Pittsburgh the gateway to the West once upon a pre-America time back when the fur trading and the minerals were competed for by beefeaters and frogs, the British and the French, in the middle of the eighteenth century. Though both groups were imperial interlopers from across the mighty Atlantic, neither was shy about warring for that vastness, that endless land that would someday stretch to the Pacific Ocean.

A lot went with that tale of getting from sea to shining sea. When those who would one day be known as Americans were incapable of making alliances with the people already there or finding some fair way to get more land, they killed and built along the way. They broke and lifted hearts. They also created more freedom than had ever existed as a new nation was framed by its documents. They also found themselves struggling to understand the meaning of that freedom and its attendant sense of dignity. Eventually, the issue of slavery raised the question of how liberty and dignity applied to all born into this world. It became the question that defined the social evolution of the new nation, which had to pull itself loose from the skins of many prejudices. The grand fact of this country is that it did just that, over and over and over. And still is.

Britain and France got their chance to fight before any of that happened. In 1754, young George Washington was on a diplomatic mission to western Pennsylvania while serving as an officer in the Virginia Militia. He and his Indian scouts were to blame for snapping the frail back of the peace by unloading on a French officer* whom they had captured after a violent exchange kicked off between Washington's men and the French and their Indians. One of Washington's scouts—whose red people had been on American soil for more than 10,000 years, having walked into a new world over the Bering Strait—got a little bloody and killed that captive Frenchman. His murder provoked what is now considered the first international war, a conflict that Europeans call the Seven Years' War but we have come to know as the French and Indian War. The British won that one.

During the days of the imperial Iroquois, or the Six Nations (those Indians whose council organization was so sophisticated that we are now told that it influenced the structures laid down in the Constitution), no one in the diminishing 1700s could have imagined the industrial colossus that Pittsburgh would become by the end of the nineteenth century, rising up from the Industrial Revolution like the common man did in the wake of the Revolutionary War, which might have come out rather differently if the French who captured George Washington back in his western Pennsylvania days had hanged him like they started out to instead of changing their minds.

Before that same George Washington—more than six feet tall and riding a white horse at the head of his troops, ordering them to follow his hell-for-leather charges—would lead impetuous rebels to victory over Britain, no one would have imagined a nation such as the United States coming into existence. Nor could they have fantasized that the first challenge to the federal authority of that new nation would come from the town of three rivers. Right: Trouble started in Pittsburgh, when the liquor makers, under the leadership of men ready to rumble, refused to pay the taxes levied on their grog. George Washington, then the first president,

---

* Joseph Coulon de Jumonville.

was not intimidated. He sent troops to smack them into order and let all in the United States understand that federal laws *would* be obeyed.

The people supporting the Whiskey Boys and mourning what they considered the loss of their freedom could not have imagined how culturally resplendent the free Negroes of Pittsburgh would be in the last two or three decades before the Civil War. Nor could any of their contemporaries have imagined how Black abolitionists in Pittsburgh would be so strong and so wily by the middle of the next century that a white man with half a thimble full of sense would avoid bringing his slaves with him into that city of three rivers: As just about everyone knew, he had a very good chance of looking around and finding them gone, spirited away, never to live as his chattel again.

You got it: Those eighteenth century people would surely have been shocked—perhaps senseless in some cases—by what came to take place on their old stomping and battling and meeting and arguing and hunting and cooking and competing grounds. They would not have been prepared for lives lived so differently from what they knew as possible.

Even though they might experience the intensity of the unexpected on a very different level, those with simplistic visions of American life right here, right now will be quite startled if they have to confront the photographs taken by Teenie Harris, who was doing some impressive bobbing and weaving by avoiding the heavy handed yet landing important blows in a special part of the ring of social definition. Known properly as Charles and also nicknamed One Shot, Harris worked for the *Pittsburgh Courier*, a newspaper that carried on the inarguably grand American tradition of liberating the humanity of the Negro from the epithets and the stereotypes backed up by bad science and superstition that had begun as justifications for the chattel enslavement of Black people. This was a job, even at a weekly newspaper, as serious as the guerrilla war against slavery that was fought by those abolitionist ancestors.

The *Pittsburgh Courier* accepted the obligation and the responsibility of scraping off more than a bit of the charisma exuded by the people who may have stood in the shadows of racism at large but whose neighborhood vitality, when laid against that of anyone else, might raise the question of who, exactly, was enjoying the shadow of whom?

Certainly the basketball player–tall Black guy in the evening clothes and top hat doesn't seem to think himself a dark imitation of the caricatured white guy on the town in the advertisement for Hi-Boy Wines.*

That brown beauty on the showroom floor who is so much better designed than the car she is standing next to doesn't appear to be thinking that were she white, life would feel even more fine to her when she is getting exactly what she wants.

We can see as the little white boy stands with the other kids and listens to the Black man play the small piano somewhere out on a Pittsburgh street that he is not assuming that he is among exotics or savages or coons.

The white kids who are present at a Black baptism aren't acting as though they are lost in some kind of urban jungle and might be only a few minutes from a cook pot once the natives notice their presence.

The handsome Black lifeguard and swimming instructor standing in the pool and showing kids, Black and white, how to keep afloat and get from one place to the other exhibits neither subservience nor condescension, just pure professionalism burnished with grace.

Those white guys with the Black girlfriends and the dignified but melancholy white woman sitting next to her Black guy don't seem to feel as though Tarzan and the apes form a good metaphor for their experience.

What each of those Pittsburgh people realizes is what all of us as Americans need to know, which is that our entire story is always about

---

* Throughout this piece, references are made to specific photographs from the book *One Shot Harris: The Photographs of Charles "Teenie" Harris.*

many stories and that we are connected by the history of our nation and by the things that we have either invented or borrowed or refined in order to live lives as close to what we wish as we can.

Notably, what Harris brings off is an astonishing rejoinder to one part of that history, which is the minstrel tradition that has been reborn in rap, with its aggressive coon figures, gold teeth, hoochies, and inarticulate, tasteless, stock figures.

A central creator in minstrelsy the first time around was Stephen Foster, a Pittsburgh man who became the George Gershwin of the middle of the nineteenth century. Foster was popular for his "plantation melodies," his "Ethiopian ballads," his "Negro melodies." His talent was nowhere near the equal of Gershwin's, but Foster also saw that something American could meet in the intersection of Black and white and even tried to get his material up beyond the denigrations so basic to a style that has long been a welcome and unwelcome guest in the history of American art and entertainment. It has been both an innovative way of organizing expression at its best while, at its worst, remaining an old-time way of looking at the world as though it could only be like a glass of black stout liquor, with the white foam always on top.

In a number of ways, one can see that what Gershwin brought off in his *Rhapsody in Blue* has much in common with what Harris achieved in his photographs. *Rhapsody in Blue* is, above all else, a celebration of Harlem, of Negro life and vitality in a big city, of its sweep of grace, of its romance, of its sorrows, of its hope, of its memory of trouble, of its potential to ever enrich the quality of the national culture. The Pittsburgh that Harris's photographs saved from historical disappearance is a Rhapsody in Black and White that proves—as yet another example—just how poorly both Hollywood and Madison Avenue served their nation during the years that he so superbly documented.

Looking at these people as they work and as they play, as they primp and as they pray, as they compete and as they cooperate, as they eat and as they exist in that kind of open-eyed sleep we so perfectly describe as daydreaming, we begin to better understand the contours of the national culture and how strongly it transcended superficial differences. Some of the mystery of our past is pushed aside by these pictures in favor of a range of specifics, and those specifics are as universal as they are particular.

We see all of the things that even the overwhelming majority of our classic films missed by either adhering to those old minstrel conceptions or, now and again, presenting the Negro as no more than a victim of the white folks, there to make neither a moral nor a tragic point but one determined more by the desperate emptiness of propaganda than by any kind of human understanding. That observation is not meant to condescend to people in positions of service, or to say that comedy can survive without some recourse to buffoons, or to ignore the outrages wrought by injustice. The point is that when the Negro was thought of—if at all—that Negro existed in ways quite different from those that we see in this set of images.

The pictures taken by Harris do not narrow life down to but a few cards that can be dealt out of the deck of experience. These photographs argue with the idea that, when honestly rendered, the Negro can only be understood as a victim forever smarting from the wounds of bigotry. This collection provides us with an epic sense of life, which is to say that a civilization and how it worked is laid out before us, from early childhood to four majestic women sitting on a swing in what was once upon a time called "a rest home." Still, as those people captured here in grim circumstances make obvious, Harris did not flee the poverty that made the lives at the bottom so blue in their Black version of wretchedness, but he did not find it appropriate—or true—to solely present Black people in one dire situation after another.

Yet let us not get too carried away. Surely the facts of racism in its historical context are exactly what they are, and we would be far from honest, liars in fact, if we did not acknowledge the part of Afro-American experience laid out in the gruesome horror that so correctly dominates *Without Sanctuary*, that invaluable book that documents in photograph after photograph the lynching bee. The show from which the book comes was raised in 2000 at the New York Historical Society, and it taught the unknowing that a lynching was just as often a joyful mob gathering as it was a social vent through which garroted or charred corpses were pushed into public spaces and recorded for posterity. Any who would know what and who we have been in this country should look closely at those photographs, just as any who would know more than the heart of our national darkness would do well to look closely at the photographs in this collection, which is a series of illumination rounds opening up the darkness of clichés and inviting us to appreciate what we see. It is through the recognition of both the spiritual snake pits and the steeples of our ambitions and achievements that we best understand why this country, for all of its troubles and for all of its coarse, blood-spattered history, is a society unlike any other. Something new was made on this soil, and One Shot Harris, one shot at a time, helps us understand what it was.

That brand new something was made in Pittsburgh through the mass production of things that defined contemporary life going into the nineteenth century. Pittsburgh was where glass, iron, and coal individuated businesses. Those businesses were connected to bottles and to lamps and to seeing through the walls of your home and the walls of shops, to using metal for the sturdiest material, and to warming the dwelling. You could also get to the Mississippi River from that Ohio running out of there and travel all the way down to New Orleans, which put that West Pennsylvania terrain of hills, valleys, and mountains in the middle of trade and travel by water. It was in that future metropolis of even more massive production that the first steamboat was built and there, many years later, that the very first radio and television shows were broadcast, giving it an astonishing relationship to the history of mass communications. Pittsburgh was something.

It became known as Steel City after its readiness for the processing of iron ore into steel made the business success of one very special man enormous. That industry and Harris's pictures of its men who made steel and were made by it are the result of what that enormous fortune created. Those profits drawn from Pittsburgh took the very special guy who was Andrew Carnegie up over the wall of the merely rich into the even less populated arena of what some consider the closely drawn circle of the unconscionably wealthy. Mr. Big Steel gained control of the steel industry in conjunction with Henry Clay Frick, whose beehive coke ovens were essential to the steel-making process. When Carnegie and Frick partnered up, they created the first modern corporation and pioneered the structural gateway to the most thorough version of industrial capitalism that had ever existed. They also helped expand upon the wrecking of the environment by further polluting the waters and the air. Pittsburgh's showering black dust and its factories foaming forth ebony smoke inspired one person to describe it as "hell with the lid off." As with so many things American, there was a deadly imbalance between inarguable progress and destructive means of achievement. My, my, what those shining faucets and all of the other processed metal of gleaming modern life cost the land and the people.

Frick managed the steel wing of empire, and Carnegie didn't break off from him until after Frick put down the workers' strike at Homestead so brutally in 1892—using a hired army of armed and trigger-happy Pinkerton men. As a result of that ruthlessness (which the big boss discussed and stage-managed from a great distance), Carnegie's long-polished reputation as a tycoon in love with the workingman became rusty beyond repair, proving far from stainless. True, Carnegie was a self-made man who had emigrated from Scotland, seen his chances and took them, but his professed support of unionism as well as the unalienable rights of the workingman proved to be bunk. Those steel mill workers, first given short wages and then shot dead, had experienced the worst version of "a Negro moment" and would not forget it.

While it is more than improbable that they were able to make the comparative leap due to their own racism, it is impossible to imagine that they failed to feel the low-down dirty blues falling upon their hearts. The same kind of contradictory dissonance between what the country promised the Negro and what the Negro actually got proved itself democratic. It was stomped down upon those with white faces covered not with burnt cork but the grime that came of toiling in those steel mills. Even so, European immigrants flocked in to work in the steel mills, and because of labor troubles, Black people started migrating from the South into Pittsburgh, often traveling up on the railroad line that came from North Carolina. In Steel City, they could make more money and live far better than they did down home under the boots of rednecks who had lost the Civil War but, not underestimating the national willingness to ignore even violent racism, had surely won the policy war to such an extent that they were able to bar the Constitution from applying to Negroes below the Mason-Dixon line. Come to think of it, this was a heck of an extension of what happened during the Revolutionary War period when one hundred fifty Virginia slaves were brought to Pittsburgh and freed.

It remained true that trouble among the white people worked out well for the Black people. That was already gospel in Pittsburgh during the Civil War when one of the reasons that slavery fell was that those Pittsburgh factories kept stacking up and shipping out the war materials necessary to bloody the Confederacy into surrender. This was again particularly real during World War I. Sixty thousand Pennsylvania men traveling to Europe for the enormous fight that would redefine the modern age in terms of bewildering carnage, and the closing down of immigration, meant that a good number of Black southerners could come north in droves and help keep those steel mills supporting the war effort. Those coal mines, those coke ovens, that iron ore, the workforce of polyglot American energy that never failed to produce as much as was needed, worked in combination to teach the German Kaiser that an imported steel boot would be raised to his backside with ever greater determination until he decided to call his warriors home and promise to make war no more forever. That effort in western Pennsylvania, where Pittsburgh became the gateway to victory, was so profitable that almost any one of the men who owned the factories producing the weapons and the armored vehicles could have been the model, at least in income, for the character of Daddy Warbucks in the comic strip adventures of *Little Orphan Annie*.

What resulted from that Black migration once the Hill District of Pittsburgh became the upper end of the Negro community is another part of why we can be illuminated by a collection of photographs such as these. The light can result from the fact that we are not accustomed to thinking about the period between the mid-1930s and the early 1960s as much more than a prelude to our own time. It can get by us that human beings in every era have always been human beings. The members of our species, no matter their color, have always, in the breadth of their humanity, been beyond the numbers necessary to create the percentages in some sociological tables that purport to tell us far more than they actually do. Those fellow mortals are also more than names and dates on birth records and death certificates. If we are not careful, however, the many thousands gone can be reduced to those very limits. Unless something of imperishable value from the dead world of the past is held onto, the undeclared audience that we all are could get that dead world dead wrong.

For that reason, we might not be aware of the many similarities between our time and those years from the middle of the Depression through the emergence of the Kennedy era, those years when others now gone or now much, much older were there to breathe, think, feel, work, and dream. Sometimes that has to do with how smug we are about how almost everyone nowadays seems so at ease with the technology and the panoply of materials that have such symbolic significance because they form membership cards in the contemporary era.

So our ethnically various society is held together not only by ideas about individual freedom, democratic government, love of the underdog, and recognition of the need to be listened to and respected that drives the outsider. We are also held together by the things that advertisers have recognized we might need in order to live modern lives but that they are bent on convincing us that we must have. That is why those advertisers now construct television ads and posters so as to make it absolutely clear that segregation in the marketplace is long gone. Their point is that you, too, can feel like just another customer and not an interloper when purchasing razors, deodorants, fast foods, long-distance dialing plans, computers, soft drinks, sports or family cars, sanitary napkins, express mail services, and just about anything else.

Perhaps that is the most important aspect of these photographs, which is that they speak of something so far the other side of alienation that all narrow images of these people—or any people—are called to the carpet and forced to grovel. Clichés do not obtain before the breadth of feeling and form that arrives in the urban context of an America that had yet to be sold the idea that there was nothing vital beyond the world of adolescent rebellion. There were common aspirations, no matter how original the ethnic and geographic variations on them might be. That is to say if one was living in a steel town at that time of booming business, one was surely living in a steel town and those steel plants meant the same thing to you that they meant to everyone else once you came to recognize what a particularly valuable product could do for the hometown economy and for the nation.

If you lived in that city, which was essentially like any other modern city, you knew what telephones were, glass windows, automobiles, mass-produced goods of all sorts. You could go dreamy in front of a store window display. You could even say that you were feeling the same as the people who had ore a hundred years earlier, except that there was more to become entranced by. You could get excited when your favorite movie star was coming to town on celluloid. If you were a little girl at a newspaper stand, you might become nearly undone by the joy of looking at a comic book and the feeling of being surrounded by so many other comic books and magazines and papers that might contain things you know nothing of, things upon things that had the chance of becoming personal knowledge forever if you read about them or someone read about them to you and explained what they meant when the stuff got too deep for a kid to comprehend. The newsstand abundance represented the same thing that it always means in a society as bountiful as this one—the very number of choices available lends a certain magic to life.

If you were an impoverished little girl sitting atop some newspapers in the plant where they made them, there was still some kind of magic to being there at the start of something everybody had not necessarily seen, something you could brag about when you came to understand that your experience was largely unique, that you, not they, had been in the plant. If you were two boys experiencing World War II in a playful way, one of you was leaning under the burden of awe while staring at your buddy as he gleefully sat with a metal mixing bowl on his head behind the wheel of a play tank.

If you were a little girl coming down the steps of a store with all kinds of advertisements on the walls and the door, you might not care about

Stanback headache powders or Clabber Girl Four or even realize that the newspaper upside-down in the window behind you had a headline story about Jackie Robinson with his picture on the front page. But you might well have heard about Jackie Robinson and you might have seen him in the flesh or seen him in a Teenie Harris picture, one in which he was looking like a Black knight in a baseball uniform instead of armor, leaning against his bat not his sword. Before Robinson was chosen to slay the grand dragon of segregation in baseball in 1947, there was a Negro National League, and the Pittsburgh Crawfords were champions in 1933, 1935, and 1936. The other Pittsburgh team, the Homestead Grays, won the crown from 1937 to 1945 and in 1948. Apparently, they had some John Henrys who could steel-drive home some runs. Yes, they did, especially the Grays, with Josh Gibson and Buck Leonard, who were the counterparts of Babe Ruth and Lou Gehrig. It is that vision of a broad variety of living that gives these pictures their oomph. Even the compositions are themselves startling at times. We look at the church congregation seeming to impossibly stand straight in front of a church that is also standing straight. But both they and the building are on a mightily inclined hill, the shadows echoing each other, the bricks in the street having jumped from the wall of the church into the street or from the street into the walls of the church; and, as we often witness in this collection, there is that sense of continuity as we look at children among adults. In a number of other photographs, we see people at every stage of life, so that the children, the adolescents, the young men and women, the middle-aged ones, and the older people make us realize that the distance from birth to the last years is always crowded with people filling out the individual facts of that human progression.

We also see the young among the adult in the remarkable picture of the boy on the left staring in the direction of the man on the right, whom he could come to look like years up the way and who, with his hunting buddies, is part of a remarkable combination of geometric variations of the sort only a master painter would conceive, such as the plaid shirts echoing the squares of the bricks or those open squares that are part of the design leading up to the roof of the house, or the three buttons on the coat of the boy echoing those on the coat of the man at the far right.

There is something almost surreal to the patterns of the leopard overcoat and of the suit worn by the woman in contrast to the feather pattern of the doomed turkey she holds and the feather pattern of the equally doomed birds in the window of the store. The woman is the wife of the baritone balladeer, Billy Eckstine, but she is not charming the bird in hand. Her smile seems quite false, and the way she clutches the feet of the turkey prefigures his future.

How about the one with the hunters and the two dead deer on the hood of the car, the barrels of their rifles creating metal lines of power, the geometry of their hats, the variety of their facial expressions, the triumphant pretty girl sitting on the roof of the car with her legs crossed like those of the dead deer on the left but going in the opposite direction, the pyramids and gothic points and chimneys in the background as well as the accidental cross and how the rectangles of the windows on the buildings echo the rectangles of the cards attached to the deer? Death, weapons, machinery, victory, grace, joy, and pride. I don't know that Henri Cartier-Bresson ever caught a moment more revealing of a culture wafting forth its vitality through some people so confidently alive and so far, for the moment, from anything close to alienation.

Those images are corrections, or additions, as was the sense of style and the music that came from Pittsburgh, from what had become a mighty center for entertainment in that Hill District. As one website* devoted to Black migration to the north says of Pittsburgh's most sophisticated Black community:

---

* http://northbysouth.kenyon.edu.

As signs of social status and self-respect, nice shoes and clean clothes
mattered in the Hill District and people tried hard to look their best.
African Americans in Pittsburgh often shopped in Kaufmann's and
Gimbels downtown. . . . Dressed in their most stylish clothes, people
from all over Pittsburgh took buses or streetcars to the Hill. Famous
clubs like the Crawford Grill and the Hurricane Lounge drew the
hottest musicians and the most chic clientele, but many other clubs
flourished as well, like Green Front, Coobus Club, Little Paris, Bam-
boola Club, the Flamingo Hotel, Center Avenue Elks, Perry Bar,
Granada Bar, and the 471 Musicians Club. At the Hill District clubs,
people talked, laughed, and danced steps like "Trucking" until dawn.

Observing the exuberance of the people in these photographs, one can
see why it was also called "Fun City." We can see the waitresses and the
customers and the musicians, civilian or military, at night or during the
day. There they are in clubs, bars, lounges, or on the streets in parades.
Look at them holding their horns and getting ready to do it, jubilant as
musicians on the verge of playing so often are. Don't miss the young men
in their military outfits carrying themselves with the dignity they perhaps
hope will someday evolve to the point that it can project the kind of majesty beaming from the fully grown Black people in varied uniforms who
stretch all the way down the hill.

Steel City people also evolved into some of the most important artists in the history of jazz, men and women whose work set new directions, introduced new techniques, broke down stereotypes, and even
challenged the tradition itself by inventing entirely fresh ways of writing
music and improvising upon it. There was Earl Hines, who invented the
piano response to the innovations of Louis Armstrong, who seems in one
of these pictures to be having the kind of good time with a good-looking
woman that would be expected of a man of his station and his appetite for

the finer human things of life. There was Mary Lou Williams, who not only played piano and was musical director for Andy Kirk's Kansas City band, not only wrote arrangements played by Duke Ellington, but also mentored Thelonious Monk and Bud Powell. Ahmad Jamal, whom we see here as a kid sitting at the piano atop someone's trumpet case, went on to become a major influence on jazz piano, on jazz ensemble playing, jazz material, and on Miles Davis.

Drummers Kenny Clarke and Art Blakey, two of the most important percussion innovators in the history of the art, grew up in the shadows of those steel mills. Billy Eckstine, the first true Afro-American matinee idol, is seen standing with members of his revolutionary big band, two of them geniuses—alto saxophonist Charlie Parker and trumpeter Dizzy Gillespie (though tenor saxophonist Lucky Thompson, a mighty reed master himself, was nobody's fumbling bum). The very great bassist Ray Brown is also from Pittsburgh, and Jeff "Tain" Watts, who is one of the major figures on contemporary jazz drums, hails from that history-rich place where the three rivers meet as well. When you have finished with these photographs, you, too, will somehow have become a child of the Steel City, even though that era is now gone. So gone, too, is the Hill District. Surely every world dies, but every world does not necessarily go to the heaven of memory. Teenie Harris made sure that this one did. We should remain forever proud of that fact and be grateful to him for knowing what had to be done and for rising up from the world of wishing into the very special one where those who choose themselves for the tasks get the invaluably human jobs done.

2002

PIMP'S LAST MACK

DEATH RE QUEST
A FOLK SONG
(for Langston Hughes)

On the way to the bone orchard, the
dirt house of all the gone daddies' bones,
I want to go slump-sided—
on a dago, tilted over just a little.
I want 3 short fat greasy ho's in red on one side
& three creole queens 7 foot tall on the other side
lowering me in the ground from 7 gold chains.
But on the way I want my casket dragged by 13 giant
                          snakes painted riot ruby red

and on top of that gold and silver flip top cigar
I want a 3-headed purple nigguh baby
blowing 11 connected bugles full of burning nappy hair
and smearing the top with his muddy feet
and pissing in the tracks left by my coffin's dragging
and 6 devils' feet behind
I want a crowd of blue-eyed baboons sucking the yellow
                          out of those lines

my casket be leaving on the way to the bone
orchard, dirt house of all the gone daddies' bones.
WAIT!
And in the l a s t of the long road go down
amongst the epitaphs & trees—
wooden ropes holding the grass down—
I want MY grave note to say in gold AND silver:

To dirt, sin, low life
and fast women of river hips
who baptized him nightly
this young man was no stranger.
And when he sat his Black ass down
his butt hole stamped down
   DANGER!

        1972

BLACK AND TAN FANTASY

A LETTER FROM THE BLUES

Completed in the spring of 2016, previously unpublished. In the collection of Wynton Marsalis, who read the piece at a private memorial service for Stanley Crouch at Minton's Playhouse in Harlem on October 26, 2020.

D EAR BORGES:

I am disturbed—quite disturbed—but I can assure you, amigo, that I did not wake up this morning as *la cucaracha*. My enemies can keep the soles of their shoes and their flyswatters to themselves. Someday, perhaps, but not this day. It is not my time to be stomped into oblivion or beaten with a metal screen through which my soul cannot escape. My heart will not fit inside such a meager death. It has been enlarged by the high blood pressure of mad affection. I would say this amounts to the hyper tension of being caught in the endless sway of that never ending symphony of rushing and stamping passion we know as love even if it bobs and weaves away from any name at all.

Still, I have disruptive thoughts. I am surrounded by black and tan fantasies. They do not arrive from the history of terrorism on the grand emerald isle of yesteryear. They arrive from elsewhere. Having their own integrity, they come to me by way of the blues and the death marches some are known to mistake for the first cousins of the very slow dances we, you and I, Borges, once preferred to do with those most special lovers at the indistinct moments before dawn arrived. The women had the clear, glistening masks of perspiration, and their armpits looked as though dark images of celestial spheres had been freshly painted on in an attempt to capture the scent of heaven. Those were times of lonesome farewells, my friend, lonesome farewells. The nights were long and hot, and the moon itself was supine.

No, it is not all good. I seem to be someplace other than where I should be. No. Yes, I am still here, getting older and becoming more frail and accepting the accusations that my intellect has become a bit tipsy. That's it. Now we know the problem. Accusations. I am looked upon as a stuttering pig for my theories. Me, Borges, a "looney tune" as they call what they consider my condition. Such people always have something of no import to say. I cannot take those readings of my condition seriously. How would anyone other than myself know about me? They could be right. Let us be fair. But truth never comes out of the mouths of fools. Hints are the only traffic that truth has with stupidity.

Yes, it must be clear. I know some things, and some of them are startling, Borges. You might not be a betting man, but you can wager on that. I know. I have been around. Some of the things that I know have to do with he who is now reading this. That may surprise someone exactly like you who just happens to be Borges himself. Others have to do with errant imaginings. As all the birds of every era fly past us, the flapping of wings gone and the flutter of wings present remind us that the sky *could* have a living heartbeat. That beat, measured by the pulse, is in pursuit of a miracle, and that miracle might just be something as simple as music, the anthem of the invisible but delivered in a shiny blue cellophane of gutbucket feeling that improvises its own transparent patterns. Keep it simple. It is in doing that, Borges, that the heart must take its bruises.

Let's get to cold cases, shall we? No more beating around the bush: all the leaves have fallen; the branches are cracked; the roots no longer hold their place in the soil; doom is upon us. But that doesn't bother me. Why should it? Those are things about which only the very best jokes can be made, the most imaginative quips, those statements dipped in enough lather to shave the beard off of death, scrape away its disguise with an edge so sharp there is no need for lather.

Let us shovel the feces out of the conversation. Borges, you are surely alive if not well in the way that people mean, which is to say you are not trifling your time away. I know you are filling up your quill with razor-thin arrowheads. Your archery has put the beards of arrow shafts on many rumps here and in the infinite *there*, which is how the past and the future meet: outside the present. It is you who live *there*, whom legend lifts with unavoidable boulders in order to gain the strength for the story. What a workout regimen! Hence, this letter, my old friend.

I SHALL TELL you of these things as accurately as Louis Armstrong played the blues.

I MYSELF AM not sure. In this time there is the fast-growing religion of conspiracy. This American belief system makes unpleasant things into inevitable proof of a detective story that is hidden from the common man. (The common man, by the way, already has a rather long list of unsolved cases with which to wear himself out. The effects are showing. This was just meant as a point of observation.) America is a land of speculators and interpreters. Somewhere beyond the stock market (which some say is not so different from the stock yard) there is the greasy smell of those gathered to plead for spiritual answers. There are many who attend these American camp meetings of great awakening and swear that they know what phony wizards are behind the bells and whistles and bright lights of the big city board we know as this terrible moment.

I dream of hearing a sound louder than anything natural. Yes, Louis Armstrong, the old man whose young face once imitated the round light of the sudden night sky in a Betty Boop cartoon, this son of voodoo and back o'town New Orleans, surely mopped his brow as if preparing it for the inspection given to the deck of a mysterious steamboat coming around the bend. Easy does it; easy as the feeling of shimmer: He was familiar with the demands of this gig in the dream library of babblers and bullshitters. The bandstand beyond the back door was no stranger to his feet. Oh, sure: He knew the meaning of all those books. They like it simple. High-falutin' folks usually do. Give them a circle. It never ends. He was quite aware. The ongoing autopsy of melancholy, the forensic weight of the matter—page upon page upon page—was no more than a primer for the life he had known. The effluvial smell of gunpowder, a stinging cloud, floated through his background. Joy could not wash from his memory the blood of whores. Armstrong had eaten garbage as a boy and he had eaten cuisine as a man and you could *still* bring him a steaming plate of red beans. This one knew who he was . . . there to cure what ails us—he thought of himself in the service of happiness—the good doctor Satchelmouth leaned back his head and closed his eyes (he was sometimes known—also known!—by the fanciful nicknames of Dippermouth, Lil Dip, Dipper, and Papa Dip. In some places, he was called Ursa Minor). This Minor who was always ready to go out mugging and who had grown up in that delta on the Mississippi might well have remembered the frizzy grape-colored clouds or the neon rose sun so hot it made everyone as sticky in summer as a lollypop licked by the public desire for something angelic, pre-primitive, and willing to wear polished policeman's shoes on Sunday morning.

A CRUCIFIX AND a Star of David hanging from his neck, Armstrong nodded in response to the song request of that God so much stronger than myth that He needs no name. Dipper put down his trumpet, stepped to the recording microphone, and transformed it into a reverse stethoscope so that we could hear the dark stormy tempo of his heart, freed from the brass wind beat of his clarion identity. Dark heartbeat. Stripped of all instruments other than the song of himself, Armstrong then moved the notes through his lips. He did not whisper, and he did not tremble. The blue truth of the multitudes was his to tell. He might have felt Napoleonic. He should have. Anyway, Papa Dip was a bold but modest man, which means that those tones were sent winging on his best air of radiant gravel. Such a very special ending was delivered as his eyeglasses glinted in the light of the studio library and the plaid simple shirt he wore proved that he, too, approved of all squares. Everyone heard it: "Do nothing 'til you hear from *me*! And *you* never will." The distances heard that song. As above, so below: North, South, East, and West met on the tango rhythm that begins, first of all, W. C. Handy's "The St. Louis Blues." You know: the way they played it in New Orleans.

That is what the distances knew. The distances had always met in the dark beat slowly marching and muttering under the dirge that called everyone home as the dead were buried aboveground. Entombed, you might say. (Handkerchiefs were used to muffle the snare drums as they spoke of the recently departed, some felled by a shiv in the liver.) You could hear the song forming like a cloud in the distance. "Flee" as it came closer. "Flee as" the point at which it was much nearer. "Flee, as a Bird" it was called. Feeling that shining Armstrong gravel as it showered down, as it fell upon them like a wizard's magical bits of hard, shiny saliva, all of them—the muckety-mucks, the suckers, the mugs, the saints, the central committees of all sins great and small, those who disguised their blessings as kisses, and the deaf who would hear, the blind who would see, and the cold (who had always wished for the pain that would define the heat of life)—*everyone* fell to their knees in darkness.

Each was finally aware of being trapped in flesh that was an acute condition, burdened by the emotional motors of sensibility. They formed a choir babbling in the chill wake of light. One could hear profoundly urgent prayers. They hissed like whispers, just above silence, begging the black and tan air for the mercy of an illuminated ebony that has no color and that has proven, at least since men began to measure time, that silence is the best insurance policy for a secret. Well. Perhaps that is true. Perhaps. At least, we know this: It is not the quiet gold bullion, sitting coldly in the soundless caravan traveling across an infinity of sand dunes, but the smoothly shaped nothingness upon which the wagon train rolls that actually marks, grain by grain, the blue dimensions of our meandering passage, that wildly fleeting moment of demented magic known by the name: life.

VICTORY IS ASSURED

AFTERWORD

READING VARIOUS ARTICLES, SOCIAL POSTS, and obituaries that appeared in the twenty-four hours after Stanley Crouch's passing, I had to laugh out loud at some of them because, as the Bible says, "Death doesn't get the last word" and neither does Stanley. I noticed the sharp opinions of some writers whose work was backgrounded by his mastery, going about the important business of putting him in what they saw as his proper place so that their own opinions and understandings could sit easier (in their minds) as more sensible or superior to his. Funny, because he always said, "When you're dead you can't defend yourself." And he was right.

Stanley and I spoke almost every day for more than thirty-five years. Although many of our conversations ended in argument, speaking with him was one of the most fascinating and richly rewarding experiences of my life. It was impossible to converse with him and not learn something—even if you only learned what you didn't agree with. Stanley, on the other hand, could be incited to new thoughts and ruminations by a strongly argued position and would later acknowledge and even expound on his changed point of view.

He believed in rigorous study and in very direct engagement, preferably in person. It could, on very, very few occasions, end pugilistically. There it is, and there it was. Stanley once called me late at night and announced, "Man, I just wasted two hours listening to another long, boring piece you wrote. Why do you write those long-ass interminable pieces?" I asked him, "What long music do you like?" and went on to give a roll call of great extended compositions. He replied, "None. I don't like ANY of it." We both had to laugh at the absurdity of it all.

Stanley was not for the thin-skinned. Larger than life, he could be over the top in one moment and sweet as pie the next. His way of being right in front of you with a different and often unpopular opinion was absolutely countercultural and out of place in this cultivated era of eye-winks, double and triple meanings, and fanciful and purposeful corruption of language and intention that further discredits our country's media with each passing day.

My relationship with Stanley was rooted in the dozens. I had just turned eighteen when we met for the first time at Mikell's, an Upper West Side jazz club. He started off saying to me, "You can't be that boy from New Orleans they sayin' can play. You sound sad, but that thin raggedy jacket is telling me you don't know anything about this New York winter, so . . . you might be him." I had no idea of who or what he was. I came back to him with, "Man, you got the nerve to talk bad about somebody while you standin' up here looking like a raccoon with them rings around your eyes." We immediately started laughing and hit it off.

Stanley was from the hood, and he had all of the grit and mother wit that came with that pedigree. He was also a homegrown intellectual genius of endless curiosity with abundant ability to make deeply insightful macro AND micro observations. He loved to investigate all kinds of things and was always telling me, "Go see this (Goya) or that (Romare Bearden)," or "Go hear this (Cecil Taylor) or that (Joe Morello)," or "Read this (*Jazz Modernism*) or that (Leon Forrest's *Divine Days*)." Interestingly enough, over time I realized that many of the pieces and ideas he suggested checking out were contrary to his own tastes and philosophical attitudes. He would always say, "Check it all out. Earn your own prejudices, man." That was also my daddy's philosophy, so it was easy to understand where he was coming from.

"Crouch" (I called him by his last name, and he called me by mine) held a PhD in connecting and assimilating an unimaginable diversity of information across time, space, culture, and conception. Years ago, upon viewing a televised Olympic equestrian event, he started talking about training horses, which led him to remember the introduction of Iberian horses to the New World, then on to the Spanish Inquisition, right into the intrinsic value of gold, which inspired a rumination on sixteenth century European battle tactics, leading to an exposition on the Incas' mythological beliefs and their relationship to Christianity, which caused him to speculate on the Catholic Church's expunging of its own mysticism that actually had a fundamental connection with the Incas' mythology (even though Incan beliefs failed them in confronting Pizarro), but after all, the church had also failed important central elements of its basic purpose by employing fetishes and pagan rituals that became a cheap form of popular entertainment but drew such large, enthusiastic crowds that the religion eventually gave up on enlightenment and eventually had to settle on enlisting guilt and shame to control people, but on further examination, not all shame was bad because the absence of remorse leads to runaway criminality, and that's what was going on in Pendergast's Kansas City when Charlie Parker was a kid, you see, when an empowered group of elites fails to police itself, they unleash an unrepentant decadence (like when Pizarro and the Conquistadors started greedily killing each other over who got what of the undreamt-of spoils they had successfully plundered), and that corruption was at the root of the church keeping priests from getting married so they couldn't own land, and that the hypocrisy of a religion accruing wealth in the name of a Savior who took a vow of poverty was coming home to roost on them now, and that, actually, Charlie Parker's mother was maybe having an affair with a married preacher and this broke young Bird's heart and spoiled his relationship to religion but didn't affect his talent because spirituality is so much deeper than religiosity, and that the Incas could not overcome traditional tribal hatreds to amass a sufficiently large army and could not adjust their conventional battle tactics to defeat the superior technology of the Conquistadors, and how internecine fighting and jealousy against Dr. King is what caused the civil rights movement leadership to disintegrate, and that's why people my age (who were children at the time of the movement) needed to develop a personal understanding of what derailed the movement, because you will end up defining your experiences with the enemy's narrative—like the South lost on the battlefield but won the political fight and reversed the gains of the Civil War, returning Black people to peonage for the next hundred years, and then they infected popular culture with nostalgic propaganda pieces like *Birth of a Nation* (which you need to look at again)—and that culture is even more hotly contested because it determines WHO people will be, and did I know any military bugle calls that were played in the Civil War, and do I understand the relationship of the trumpet and drums to war and how difficult it must have been to play a bugle in a battle, and then a rumination about Buffalo Soldiers and the Rough Riders and how your behind feels on a saddle after too many long hours, and do I know any Mexican trumpet players? To which I responded, "Yes, Rafael Méndez. He was one of the greatest ever and as a kid played for Pancho Villa." To which HE laughs and says, "You see? That's why you can't play, you've never played under the life-or-death heat of battle." And I had to laugh because all of that was literally said in three minutes immediately after looking at the kind of equestrian event that he said he never watches.

Well . . . that type of extended solo was natural to HIM, but to witness it over and over again, with subject after subject, was unforgettable. Stanley was also the first one to say, "Let's go visit so-and-so in the hospital," or "Make sure you call so-and-so who lost someone," or "Send some flowers to Miss so-and-so," and, repeatedly, he showed up for someone in our community who was having a tough time. But we don't have to put sugary icing on him as he takes the long journey down the short road; he wouldn't have wanted that. Unlike you and me, he was not perfect—not by a long shot—but he was always present . . . and always in pursuit of deeper and more enduring human meaning. I hope, if he is still pursuing it, that he finds it.

Stanley Crouch was a writer and a poet of uncommon depth and feeling. Don't listen to what is said about what he was saying. Read him if you want to know him. When I was a kid, he used to tell me, "Learn stuff for yourself. Don't take other people's opinions because you might end up slapping yourself . . . and won't even know that's what you're doing."

Crouch once played a tape of his drumming for me when I was eighteen and asked what I thought. I didn't know it was him and said, "It's sad. I mean . . . it's creative, but my man can't really play." After a while, he said, "That was me playing." I replied, "It's even sadder than I thought then," and we both really laughed. Hard. That was more than forty years ago.

Wynton Marsalis
September 18, 2020
New York City

ACKNOWLEDGMENTS

This book belongs to Stanley Crouch, the whole of which is essentially an acknowledgment of his importance as a writer, a literary artist, mentor and friend, and who therefore made it possible to engage his legacy. The most profound gratitude goes to him.

When Bob Weil at Liveright proposed this volume, I knew straightaway the work should be done, even what the title should be, but was at first hesitant to take on the collection myself. My main concern was whether I was clairvoyant enough to summon Crouch. There may be nothing supernatural to the editorial trade, but Bob is a visionary editor and publisher of preternatural gifts, and by his invocation the oracle of Stanley Crouch showed himself, in thought, in word, and in his *blues for tomorrow*, slowly at first, then in a deluge that came through the bloodstreams of everyone acknowledged here.

My false starts and dead ends were initially as labyrinthine as one of Crouch's compound metaphors—Borges's living labyrinth of literature. It was my good fortune that Gary Giddins and Robert Christgau have deep institutional memories from their *Village Voice* years, at the time when Stanley was at the height of his powers there, and that writers, scholars, and archivists of Crouchiana—Paul Devlin; Kinohi Nishikawa; Mark Stryker, over in Detroit; and Vincent Pelote at the Institute of Jazz Studies at Rutgers University Libraries—had their own clippings files, which they opened and shared with estimable esprit de corps.

At key stages this volume was enriched through dialogue, insights, critique, and work past and present from Deb Aaronson, Martine Bisagni, Alina Bloomgarden, Joseph Chaney, Jelani Cobb, Jeff Hamilton, Sally Helgesen, Garrett Hongo, Greil Marcus, Wynton Marsalis, Calvert Morgan, Dan Morgenstern, Chris Richcreek, Loren Schoenberg, and Greg Thomas.

A very special and heartfelt thanks goes to Gloria (Nia) Nixon-Crouch and her many blessings.

The New York Public Library is the closest thing I have to a home institution, and I am particularly indebted to the librarians whose work is crucial to providing access to materials, time, and space for my research. Melanie Locay and the Center for Research in the Humanities has been something of a guardian in this respect, with a desk and resources for me in the Frederick Lewis Allen Memorial Room for recovering journalists.

If not for access to Crouch's papers provided by the Schomburg Center for Research in Black Culture in Harlem, an institution of The New York Public Library, this volume would not have been as comprehensive or even possible in its present form. I had the privilege to be the first to access Stanley's papers and am particularly indebted to Cheryl Beredo, Bridgett Pride, and to Lauren Stark who catalogued the archive with astonishing speed and alacrity at the height of the current pandemic. Coming very near the original deadline for the manuscript, I scrambled to read everything contained in the 70 boxes of Stanley's papers.

Salut et merci to Georges Borchardt and his protégé, the always resourceful Cora Markowitz, for being champions of Stanley's genius and smoothing the way to getting these writings into the hands of readers.

And to everyone at Liveright and W. W. Norton for uncommon acumen, especially assistant editor Haley Bracken for her invaluable work, and to copyeditor Christopher Curioli, project editor Don Rifkin, and to Sarah-may Wilkinson for her swinging jacket design.

Mind and mettle enough would not exist without the benevolence of several saints in the peripatetic monk's life who have opened their homes and their hearts. For the love and magnificence of Gibson Birdie, Jennifer Cooper, Raechell Smith, John Winterman, and Jiyun Jennifer Yoo.

Vobis.

PREVIOUSLY UNPUBLISHED ESSAYS

"Look Out Moan We Standing Round"; "An Epic American Hero: Buddy Bolden"; "Los Angeles: Jazz"; "Invention of the Self: John Coltrane"; "The Street: 1944"; "I've Got a Right to Tap My Feet Inside of the Machine"; "Black and Tan Fantasy."

PREVIOUSLY PUBLISHED ESSAYS

The following have been previously published, many under different titles: *Barnes and Noble Review*: "A Baroness of Blues and Swing" • *Callaloo*: "The 'Scene' of Larry Neal" • *Daily Beast*: "*Shut Up, Scarlett!*" • *New York Daily News*: "12 Years a Slave," "Joyce Wein's Life and Death, a Model for All of Us," "Then and Now, I Am a Negro" • *Dissent*: "An Opera Based on Malcolm X" • *Film Comment*: "The Impeccable Sidney Poitier" • *Harper's Magazine*: "The Electric Company" • *Los Angeles Times Book Review*: "The Lies That Blind: *Black Girl / White Girl*" • *O, Magazine*: "Voluptuary" • *Oxford American*: "Tarantino Enchained," "Way Down Yonder in New Orleans" • *Players*: "Diminuendo and Crescendo in Dues" • *Slate*: "Miles Davis: Romantic Hero," "Noir Americana," "The Admiral and the Duke" • *New Yorker*: "The Colossus" • *New York Times*: "By Any Means Necessary," "Cecil Taylor's Pianistic Fireworks," "Jazz Lofts: A Walk Through the Wild Sounds" • *New York Times Magazine*: "Black Like Huck" • *The Root*: "A Song for Lady Day," "Bette Davis: The Greatest White Bitch of All" • *Soho Weekly News*: "Thinking Big: Max Roach and Cecil Taylor" • *Village Voice*: "1000 Nights at the Village Vanguard," "Comrade, Comrade, Where You Been?" "Ellington the Player," "Fighters," "Fusionism," "Great Escapes," "Laughin' Louis Armstrong," "Marvin Gaye's Interconnections," "Lowdown and Lofty, Eddie 'Lockjaw'

Davis," "Remembering Buddy Rich," "The King of Constant Repudiation," "Saint Monk," "Uptown Again" • *Yardbird Reader V*: "Big Star Calling" • "After the Rain" originally published in *We Speak as Liberators: Young Black Poets*, New York, Dodd, Mead, 1970; later in S.C.'s book of poetry *Ain't No Ambulances for No Nigguhs Tonight*, New York, Richard W. Baron, 1972 • "A Bird in the World" appeared as the liner notes for the recording *Charlie Parker: The Complete Savoy & Dial Master Takes*, Savoy Jazz, 2007 • "Blues for Krazy Kat" appeared in *Masters of American Comics*, co-published by the Hammer Museum, Los Angeles, and The Museum of Contemporary Art, Los Angeles, and Yale University Press, 2005 • "Blues for Note and Paint" appeared in the Katonah Museum of Art catalogue for the exhibit *Jazz and Visual Improvisations*, January 21–April 15, 2001 • "Goose-Loose Blues for the Melting Pot" appeared in *Reinventing the Melting Pot: The New Immigrants and What It Means to Be American*, New York, Basic Books, 2004 • "Harold Cruse" originally appeared as two essays: "The Blues Took the Form of Crisis" as the introduction to *The Crisis of the Negro Intellectual*, New York, New York Review Books, 2005; and "Blues for Brother Cruse" as the foreword to *The Essential Harold Cruse*, edited by William Jelani Cobb, New York, St. Martin's Griffin, 2002 • "Invention on the Black Willie Blues" appeared in *Reconsidering the Souls of Black Folk*, Philadelphia, Running Press, 2003 • "Kansas City Swing and Shout" appeared as the program note for a program of the same title, presented at Lincoln Center on Thursday, August 8, 1991 • "Pimp's Last Mack: Death RE quest," originally published in *Black Spirits: A Festival of New Black Poets in America*, New York, Random House, 1972. Later appeared in *Black Scholar*, vol. 6, no. 9, Arts & Literature (June 1975), where the dedication to Langston Hughes was added • "Premature Autopsies" was written as a sermon for *The Majesty of the Blues*, Wynton Marsalis, Columbia Records, 1989 • "Steel City Swing" was published as the introduction to *One Shot Harris: The Photographs of*

Charles "Teenie" Harris, New York, Harry N. Abrams, 2002 • "The Incomplete Turn of Larry Neal" was published as the introduction to *Visions of a Liberated Future; Black Arts Movement Writings by Larry Neal*, New York, Thunder's Mouth Press, 1989 • "When Watts Burned" appeared in *The Sixties: The Decade Remembered Now by the People Who Lived It Then*, edited by Lynda Rosen Obst, New York, Random House/Rolling Stone Press, 1977.

INDEX

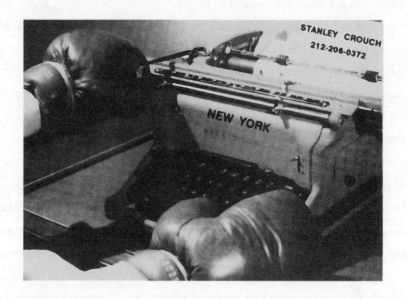

ABOUT THE AUTHOR

STANLEY CROUCH (1945–2020) was the author of eight critically acclaimed books including five collections of essays, the first two of which were nominated for National Book Critics Circle Awards: *Notes of a Hanging Judge* (1990); *The All-American Skin Game, or, The Decoy of Race* (1995); *Always in Pursuit* (1998); a book of essays on identity, *The Artificial White Man* (2004); and *Considering Genius: Writings on Jazz* (2006). He also authored the novel *Don't the Moon Look Lonesome* (2000); the book *One Shot Harris: The Photographs of Charles "Teenie" Harris* (2002); and, with Playthell Benjamin, co-wrote *Reconsidering the Souls of Black Folk: Thoughts on the Groundbreaking Classic Work of W.E.B. DuBois* (2003). He also wrote the acclaimed biography *Kansas City Lightning: The Rise and Times of Charlie Parker* (2013). In 1987, Crouch co-founded and then served as artistic consultant for jazz programming at Lincoln Center, and was a founder of the Jazz Department, known as Jazz at Lincoln Center, playing an integral role in the institution's repertoire and often writing notes and essays for concert programs. He was a biweekly columnist for the *New York Daily News* from 1995 to 2014, writing about culture, politics, and race, and authored hundreds of magazine articles, essays, album liner notes, and reviews on jazz that have influenced the music and championed it for the general public. He was the recipient of a Guggenheim Fellowship, a Whiting Award, a MacArthur Foundation grant, the Jean Stein Award from the American Academy of Arts and Letters, and the Windham-Campbell Prize; he was president of the Louis Armstrong Educational Foundation, an organization created by Armstrong himself; and for his work as a jazz historian and critic, the National Endowment for the Arts named him a Jazz Master in 2019.

ABOUT THE EDITOR
AND THE CONTRIBUTORS

GLENN MOTT edited Crouch's "American Perspectives" columns for more than a decade after bringing him on as a syndicated columnist at Hearst; the columns ran from 2004 to 2016. He has been the recipient of a Davis Fellowship for Peace and was a Fulbright Scholar at Tsinghua University in Beijing. Mott is the author of *Eclogues in a Mustard Seed Garden*, published in 2021, and of *Analects on a Chinese Screen*, published in 2007. Born and raised in Missouri, he has for many years worked between cities in Greater China and New York as a Brooklyn-based editor, journalist, and poet.

JELANI COBB is the dean of the Columbia Journalism School. He has contributed to the *New Yorker* since 2012 and became a staff writer in 2015. He is the recipient of the 2015 Sidney Hillman Award for Opinion and Analysis writing and writes frequently about race, politics, history, and culture. He is also a recipient of fellowships from the Fulbright and Ford Foundations. Cobb is the author of *The Substance of Hope: Barack Obama and the Paradox of Progress* and of *To the Break of Dawn: A Freestyle on the*

Hip Hop Aesthetic. His collection *The Devil and Dave Chappelle and Other Essays* was published in 2007. He is editor of *The Essential Harold Cruse: A Reader.* Born and raised in Queens, New York, he is a graduate of Howard University and of Rutgers University, receiving at the latter his doctorate in American history.

WYNTON MARSALIS is an internationally acclaimed musician, composer, and bandleader, an educator, and an advocate of American culture. Born in New Orleans, Louisiana, Wynton first started playing the trumpet in Danny Barker's Fairview Baptist Church band at eight years old, beginning formal training at age twelve. As a young teenager fresh out of high school, Wynton moved to New York City in 1979. There, his career quickly launched when he traded The Juilliard School for Art Blakey's band, The Jazz Messengers. Marsalis is the winner of nine GRAMMY Awards, and his oratorio *Blood on the Fields* was the first jazz composition to win the Pulitzer Prize for Music. He is the only musician to win a GRAMMY Award in two categories, jazz and classical, during the same year (in both 1983 and 1984). Wynton is deeply passionate about making jazz music accessible to all, having made strides in jazz music education on numerous fronts, including children's books and albums, performance of educational concerts, open sound checks, and development of numerous education programs. He is the founding Artistic and Managing Director of Jazz at Lincoln Center and the founding Director of Jazz Studies at The Juilliard School. Marsalis's core beliefs and foundation for living are based on the principles of jazz. He promotes individual creativity (improvisation), collective cooperation (swing), gratitude and good manners (sophistication), and facing adversity with persistent optimism (the blues).